THE STIGMA OF SUBSTANCE USE DISORDERS

Stigma and discrimination of people with substance use disorders (SUD) contribute massively to the harm done by their condition: stigma has negative effects on service engagement, life opportunities, and personal shame, both for those who struggle with substance abuse and their families. Overcoming the stigma of substance use disorders is essential to aid recovery in those with SUD. This book provides an in-depth understanding of the stigma of SUD and proposes ways to overcome it in different settings, from the criminal justice system to health care. Combining a multitude of viewpoints within a consistent theoretical framework, this book both summarizes the latest evidence and gives hands-on advice and future directions on how to combat the stigma of SUD. People with lived experience of SUD, advocates, family members, policy makers, providers, and researchers in the field of addiction stigma will greatly benefit from reading this book.

GEORG SCHOMERUS is a full professor of psychiatry at Leipzig University. He has authored more than 200 peer-reviewed papers, including on his award-winning pioneering research on the stigma of substance use disorders.

PATRICK W. CORRIGAN is Distinguished Professor of Psychology at the Illinois Institute of Technology and principal investigator of the National Consortium on Stigma and Empowerment. He has written more than 450 peer-reviewed articles and is editor of Stigma and Health.

THE STIGMA OF SUBSTANCE USE DISORDERS

EDITED BY

GEORG SCHOMERUS
University of Leipzig

PATRICK W. CORRIGAN
Illinois Institute of Technology

CAMBRIDGE
UNIVERSITY PRESS

University Printing House, Cambridge CB2 8BS, United Kingdom

One Liberty Plaza, 20th Floor, New York, NY 10006, USA

477 Williamstown Road, Port Melbourne, VIC 3207, Australia

314–321, 3rd Floor, Plot 3, Splendor Forum, Jasola District Centre, New Delhi – 110025, India

103 Penang Road, #05–06/07, Visioncrest Commercial, Singapore 238467

Cambridge University Press is part of the University of Cambridge.

It furthers the University's mission by disseminating knowledge in the pursuit of education, learning, and research at the highest international levels of excellence.

www.cambridge.org
Information on this title: www.cambridge.org/9781108838016
DOI: 10.1017/9781108936972

© Cambridge University Press 2022

This publication is in copyright. Subject to statutory exception and to the provisions of relevant collective licensing agreements, no reproduction of any part may take place without the written permission of Cambridge University Press.

First published 2022

A catalogue record for this publication is available from the British Library.

Library of Congress Cataloging-in-Publication Data
NAMES: Schomerus, Georg, 1973– editor. | Corrigan, Patrick W., editor.
TITLE: The stigma of substance use disorders / edited by Georg Schomerus, Patrick W. Corrigan.
DESCRIPTION: Cambridge ; New York, NY : Cambridge University Press, 2022. | Includes bibliographical references and index.
IDENTIFIERS: LCCN 2021063073 (print) | LCCN 2021063074 (ebook) | ISBN 9781108838016 (hardcover) | ISBN 9781108947664 (paperback) | ISBN 9781108936972 (epub)
SUBJECTS: LCSH: Substance abuse–Social aspects. | Addicts–Social conditions. | Stigma (Social psychology) | BISAC: PSYCHOLOGY / Clinical Psychology
CLASSIFICATION: LCC HV4998 .S74 2022 (print) | LCC HV4998 (ebook) | DDC 362.29–dc23/eng/20220308
LC record available at https://lccn.loc.gov/2021063073
LC ebook record available at https://lccn.loc.gov/2021063074

ISBN 978-1-108-83801-6 Hardback
ISBN 978-1-108-94766-4 Paperback

Cambridge University Press has no responsibility for the persistence or accuracy of URLs for external or third-party internet websites referred to in this publication and does not guarantee that any content on such websites is, or will remain, accurate or appropriate.

Contents

List of Figures		*page* vii
List of Tables		viii
List of Contributors		ix
1	Understanding the Stigma of Substance Use Disorders *Georg Schomerus and Patrick W. Corrigan*	1
2	My Experience with the Stigma of Substance Use *Sonya Ballentine*	15
3	Substance Use Stigma and Policy *Emma E. McGinty and Sarah A. White*	23
4	Experiences of Stigma and Criminal In/Justice among People Who Use Substances *Jamie Livingston, Matthew Bonn, Peter Brown, Steven Deveau, and Anne-Marie Houston*	46
5	Substance Use Disorders, Stigma, and Ethics *Laura Williamson*	68
6	Intersectional Stigma in Substance Use Disorders *Daniel Dittrich and Georg Schomerus*	88
7	International Perspectives on Stigma toward People with Substance Use Disorders *Jakob Manthey, Vivek Benegal, Carolin Kilian, Jayant Mahadevan, Juliana Mejía-Trujillo, Neo Morojele, Pratima Murthy, Maria Neufeld, Augusto Pérez-Gómez, and Jürgen Rehm*	107
8	Using Community-Based Participatory Research to Address the Stigma of Substance Use Disorder *Lindsay Sheehan, Aaron Graham, and Chris White*	144

9	Three Competing Agendas of Addressing Stigma of Substance Use Disorder *Carla D. Kundert and Patrick W. Corrigan*	163
10	The Benefits of Disclosure *Sai Snigdha Talluri and Patrick W. Corrigan*	180
11	The Role of Peers in SUD Stigma Change: A Personal Perspective *David McCartney*	193
12	The Role of Media Reporting for Substance Use Stigma *Eva Baumann, Philip Horsfield, Anna Freytag, and Georg Schomerus*	213
13	Reducing Substance Use Stigma in Health Care *Sven Speerforck and Georg Schomerus*	232
14	Final Considerations and Future Directions for Erasing the Stigma of Substance Use Disorders *Patrick W. Corrigan and Georg Schomerus*	252
Index		265

Figures

1	Stigma as a dysfunctional strategy to control substance use	*page* 4
2	A dynamic model of responsibility in SUD	9
3	Prevalence of alcohol use disorders in 2019, globally	108
4	Prevalence of illegal substance use disorders in 2019, globally	109

Tables

1	CBPR principles and application to case study	page 148
2	Examples of stakeholder involvement at each stage of research	152
3	Recommendations to reduce potentially stigmatizing language surrounding substance use	166
4	The costs and benefits of disclosing for Jane Smith	183
5	Five strategies people might use to disclose their experiences	185
6	Overview of selected media guidelines on mental health/SUD	220
7	Recommendations for changes in clinical practice to change substance use stigma	236

Contributors

SONYA BALLENTINE, Illinois Institute of Technology

EVA BAUMANN, Hannover University of Music, Drama, and Media

VIVEK BENEGAL, Centre for Addiction Medicine, Department of Psychiatry, National Institute of Mental Health and Neurosciences, Bangalore, India

MATTHEW BONN, 7th Step Society of Nova Scotia and Canadian Association of People Who Use Drugs

PETER BROWN, 7th Step Society of Nova Scotia and Direction 180

PATRICK W. CORRIGAN, Illinois Institute of Technology

STEVEN DEVEAU, 7th Step Society of Nova Scotia

DANIEL DITTRICH, University of Leipzig

ANNA FREYTAG, Hannover University of Music, Drama, and Media

AARON GRAHAM, Illinois Institute of Technology

PHILIP HORSFIELD, University of Greifswald

ANNE-MARIE HOUSTON, 7th Step Society of Nova Scotia and Canadian Association of People Who Use Drugs

CAROLIN KILIAN, Technische Universität Dresden

CARLA D. KUNDERT, Illinois Institute of Technology

JAMIE LIVINGSTON, 7th Step Society of Nova Scotia and Saint Mary's University

JAYANT MAHADEVAN, Centre for Addiction Medicine, Department of Psychiatry, National Institute of Mental Health and Neurosciences, Bangalore, India

JAKOB MANTHEY, Center for Interdisciplinary Addiction Research, University Medical Center Hamburg-Eppendorf; Technische Universität Dresden; University of Leipzig

JULIANA MEJÍA-TRUJILLO, Nuevos Rumbos, Bogota, Colombia

DAVID MCCARTNEY, Lothians & Edinburgh Abstinence Programme

EMMA E. MCGINTY, Johns Hopkins Bloomberg School of Public Health

NEO MOROJELE, University of Johannesburg; South African Medical Research Council; University of Cape Town; University of the Witwatersrand

PRATIMA MURTHY, Centre for Addiction Medicine, Department of Psychiatry, National Institute of Mental Health and Neurosciences, Bangalore, India

MARIA NEUFELD, WHO European Office for the Prevention and Control of Noncommunicable Diseases

AUGUSTO PÉREZ-GÓMEZ, Nuevos Rumbos, Bogota, Colombia

JÜRGEN REHM, Institute for Mental Health Policy Research & Campbell Family Mental Health Research Institute, Centre for Addiction and Mental Health, Canada; University of Toronto; I. M. Sechenov First Moscow State Medical University

GEORG SCHOMERUS, University of Leipzig

LINDSAY SHEEHAN, Illinois Institute of Technology

SVEN SPEERFORCK, University of Leipzig

SAI SNIGDHA TALLURI, Illinois Institute of Technology

CHRIS WHITE, Scottish Mental Health Foundation

SARAH A. WHITE, Johns Hopkins Bloomberg School of Public Health

LAURA WILLIAMSON, Augusta University

CHAPTER I

Understanding the Stigma of Substance Use Disorders

Georg Schomerus and Patrick W. Corrigan

A Social Function of Stigma

Substance use disorders (SUD) are among the most stigmatized mental health conditions (Schomerus, Lucht, et al., 2011b). A recent systematic review confirmed that the desire for social distance is particularly strong toward people with SUD, and support for structural discrimination is particularly high when compared to other mental disorders like depression or schizophrenia (Kilian, Manthey, Carr, et al., 2021). People with SUD are more likely to be held responsible for their illness and are more often considered to have a bad character or suffer from moral weakness (Kilian, Manthey, Carr, et al., 2021). Negative stereotypes toward people with alcohol use disorder are remarkably stable and have not improved over the last decades (Schomerus et al., 2014). Emotional reactions even seem to deteriorate: a time trend study of attitudes in Germany found the proportion of respondents reacting angrily toward someone with alcohol use disorder increasing from 15% in 1990 to 24% in 2011, while remaining stable at below 10% for schizophrenia and depression (Angermeyer et al., 2013).

Having an SUD provokes severe and adverse reactions from the social environment. Stigma is a severe additional burden for someone developing an SUD, and it is fundamentally unjust. In this introductory chapter, we will give a conceptual overview as to how the different facets of SUD stigma, public stigma, self-stigma, and structural stigma lead to criminalization, social exclusion, marginalization, inferior health care, and diminished life chances in people with SUD. But before we look at the harm stigma is doing, we will consider the specific social function of SUD stigma. Why are people with SUD stigmatized, and why is the stigma of SUD in many ways different from that of other mental disorders? This might appear as a detour; some theoretical musing detracting from the severe consequences that stigma has on the lives of those with SUD and their families. The stigma of SUD needs to be erased, but we believe that understanding the causes of

SUD stigma is a prerequisite to successful strategies to combat it, particularly in a highly contested area like substance use.

How Should Substances Be Used?

To begin with, using substances is a controversial issue, and while understanding the stigma of SUD is certainly necessary to improve our dealing with substance use, establishing a consensus on what constitutes acceptable, healthy substance use is clearly beyond the scope of this book. Agreement on what constitutes acceptable substance use is constantly changing. From a medical perspective, the assessments of risks associated with substance use change. The considerable risk for cancer at various sites that is attributable to alcohol, for example, has only recently come into focus (Rehm & Shield, 2021). From a legal perspective, changing legislature with regard to taxing, advertising, or legalizing substances like nicotine, alcohol, or cannabis mirrors the constantly shifting public consensus on how we should or should not use substances for recreational purposes, and how substance use should be controlled. Moreover, there are considerable international differences on what constitutes acceptable substance use, and also subcultural differences within countries. Individual choices and preferences stand against perceived and real harm for those who use substances, their close ones, and the community. The balance between individual benefits of substance use and harm to others varies greatly. For example, while smoking cannabis can be seen as an individual choice with individual risks and benefits, it also may affect other people, for example when someone has caregiver responsibility for a child, or is driving a car (Hasin, 2018; World Health Organization, 2016). Cigarette smoking entails the risks of passive smoking (Khoramdad et al., 2020), many substances and particularly alcohol are linked to violent and dangerous behavior (Foran & O'Leary, 2008), and links between childhood abuse and neglect, and parental substance use, are well established (Walsh et al., 2003). Add the varying levels of severity of substance dependence, and balancing the preferences, health, and well-being of people who use substances with those of their social environment is becoming a truly complex and challenging task.

Stigma as a Means to Regulate Substance Use?

The stigma of substance use is right at the center of this challenge. Several aspects of substance use stigma are culturally sanctioned, like the criminalization of substance use, or the perpetuation of negative stereotypes about people using substances in some messages about prevention. Substance use stigma is often stigma on purpose (Corrigan et al., 2017). Phelan et al. (2008) have highlighted that stigma has a social function, and for addiction stigma, they posit that it has the inherent purpose of "keeping people in," to enforce social norms and to demarcate the boundaries of socially acceptable behavior. Other stigmata work differently: Phelan and coworkers observe that racism, for example, is rooted in exploitation or "keeping people down," while the stigma of AIDS or leprosy, as communicable diseases, can be seen as a means of "keeping people away" to avoid contraction. In the case of substance use stigma, they argue that this type of stigma may be an attempt "to make the deviant conform and rejoin the in-group" or "to clarify to other group members the boundaries of acceptable behavior ... and the consequences of nonconformity" (p. 362). Discriminating against people with SUD disorders could thus be seen as a way of signaling to them and to anybody else strong disapproval of their behavior.

This social function aligns with the central position of blame in SUD stigma (Schomerus, Lucht, et al., 2011). Blame confers an expectation that people need to change their behavior. It is also mirrored in the fact that stigma toward people with alcohol use disorders differs according to national drinking cultures. Data from the European Values Survey show that stigma toward heavy drinkers is higher in countries with higher per capita alcohol consumption, a higher prevalence of heavy episodic drinking, and higher consumption of spirits (Kummetat et al., 2022). This is consistent with the role of stigma as a societal reaction to problematic drinking: the bigger the drinking problem on a country level, the more harsh is the reaction of people toward an individual with an SUD in that country. At the same time, the high stigma levels in countries with high alcohol consumption also indicate that stigma does not solve the problem of high alcohol use – if stigma were a successful strategy to control substance use, high stigma levels would have been expected to correlate with low per capita alcohol intake, but the opposite is true.

Stigma Is an Impediment to Helping People Engage in Services for SUD

The stigma of SUD is at the center of how society reacts to substance use – and, as the chapters of this book will show from several perspectives, stigma does little to solve any of the problems associated with substance

	Public stigma	Self stigma	Structural stigma
Enacted stigma	Individual discrimination	Loss of self-efficacy, loss of self-worth, shame	Criminalization of substance use, discrimination in healthcare
Anticipated stigma Label avoidance	Secrecy, avoidance of help, delayed help-seeking, social withdrawal	Denial of problem, misattribution of symptoms, delayed problem-recognition	Non-disclosure in healthcare settings

Goal: keep people in, demarcate boundaries of acceptable behaviour

Consequences: More harm, delayed help-seeking, inferior treatment, criminalization, social exclusion and marginalization

Figure 1   Stigma as a dysfunctional strategy to control substance use

use; on the contrary, it is a driver for additional harm and an impediment to recovery. Figure 1 gives an overview on how the stigma of SUD operates. Fueled by a goal to signal that certain behaviors are unwanted, it takes public stigma, self-stigma, and structural stigma, enacted and anticipated, to do harm to people with SUD and to their families (Earnshaw et al., 2019).

Public Stigma

Models describe stigma as a social cognitive process starting with *labeling* someone and thus creating an outgroup linked to this label (Link & Phelan, 2001). The abundance of derogatory terms for people who use substances, or have an SUD, seems to mirror a desire to put a sharp line between "us" and "those" who cross a boundary of socially acceptable behavior. Describing someone as a "drug addict," for example, has been shown to be associated with more stigma than describing them as "someone with opioid use disorder" (Goodyear et al., 2018). According to Link and Phelan (2001), labels trigger the stigma process by evoking negative stereotypes, leading to prejudice and negative emotional reactions, separation of "us" versus "them," and finally resulting in status loss and discrimination (Corrigan et al., 2017; Link et al., 2004). As a societal phenomenon, stigma affects individuals with SUD at several levels. *Public stigma* describes the attitudes endorsed by the general population leading to individual discrimination of someone with SUD. Discrimination experiences are frequent for people labeled as having an

SUD, corresponding to the particularly high levels of negative attitudes associated with them (Kilian, Manthey, Carr, et al., 2021). In a study conducted in New York in the early 2000s, three out of four people who used drugs reported being rejected by their family, two out of three by their friends, and one out of four reported being denied medical care (Ahern et al., 2007). Stigma has imminent health consequences. In a qualitative study, people who injected drugs recounted how stigmatizing attitudes of healthcare providers posed a barrier in adhering to a methadone treatment regime or purchasing syringes (Paquette et al., 2018), thus interfering with vital harm-reduction measures. But the consequences of public stigma do not stop with open discrimination. There is evidence from several areas of stigma research that perceived public stigma impairs the mental and physical well-being of those stigmatized (Schmitt et al., 2014). Public attitudes form an external cultural reality that determines how we experience an SUD (Link et al., 2011). *Anticipating public stigma* leads to secrecy, avoidance of contacts in times of crisis, and even avoidance of professional help. About 70% of respondents who used drugs stated that they avoided other people because they thought they might look down on them (Ahern et al., 2007). By hiding and withdrawing socially, overt discriminating behavior by others is indeed avoided. The effects of secrecy, social withdrawal, and avoidance of help all result from stigma. *Label avoidance* is also a consequence of anticipated stigma (Corrigan et al., 2014): not talking about substance use problems, trying to hide for as long as possible, and, ultimately, not seeking professional or informal help. These are all strategies to avoid being labeled as having an SUD and to escape stigma. Anticipating stigma from one's family and from the healthcare system is particularly consequential, since these are major sources of help (Smith et al., 2016). Unfortunately, families are also victims of stigma: although evoking less negative reactions than people who use substances, family members are still held responsible for their relatives' substance use problems compared to other mental disorders, and are viewed as more likely to be contaminated by the disorder and are more likely to be socially avoided (Corrigan et al., 2006).

Self-Stigma

Another consequence of public stigma is *self-stigma*. According to Corrigan's progressive model of self-stigma (Corrigan et al., 2011), being aware of negative public attitudes entails, to some degree, agreement with these attitudes, since we are all part of our cultural environment and share prevalent stereotypes about certain groups. If someone develops an SUD, this agreement with negative stereotypes about other people with SUD provokes an inner conflict: to what extent do these stereotypes apply to me? If I agree that people with SUD are weak and unreliable, am I also weak and unreliable now that I have a substance use problem? Studies among people with alcohol use disorder consistently show that stronger awareness of prevalent negative stereotypes is associated with agreement, which in turn is associated with applying these stereotypes to oneself (Schomerus, Corrigan, et al., 2011; Stolzenburg et al., 2018). Self-applying stereotypes is then correlated with harm, for example with reduced self-esteem. The progressive model of self-stigma has been shown to be predictive of drink-refusal self-efficacy, even when controlling for current depressive symptoms, severity of dependence, and duration of the problem (Schomerus, Corrigan, et al., 2011). Label avoidance can also be a strategy to avoid self-stigma: a study among untreated persons with depression showed that the more people endorsed stigmatizing attitudes and were thus more prone to self-stigma, the less likely they were to attribute their own current symptoms to mental illness and feel a need to seek help (Stolzenburg et al., 2017). Conceivably, many people with substance use problems avoid self-stigma and shame by delaying problem recognition, denying that there is a concern or reframing compulsory substance use as continuous free choice. Anticipated self-stigma might thus be a particularly severe barrier to early help-seeking and recovery (Figure 1). A lot of the harm stigma is doing occurs within the individual, invisible from the outside, and seemingly unrelated to any imminent discriminatory behavior. But nevertheless, the internal harm caused by stigma is a mirror of societal attitudes and behaviors that are experienced, anticipated, and finally internalized by people with SUD (Smith et al., 2016).

Structural Stigma

Stigma extends beyond the individual level. Structural stigma is inherent in laws, regulations, and guidelines that work to the disadvantage of people with SUD, even if the people following the rules have no intention to stigmatize. Criminalizing substance use is an example of structural stigma – the "war on drugs" has produced countless victims and still influences policing practices, for example, by increasing police brutality, particularly against young black men (Cooper, 2015). A qualitative study among injecting drug users revealed how police crackdowns impaired their capacity to engage in harm reduction (Cooper et al., 2005). Structural stigma leads to inferior access to health care for people with SUD in general (Livingston, 2020), and to psychiatric help in particular. Frequently, sustained abstinence is a precondition to entering certain services like psychotherapy, resulting in services excluding people with one problem too many. The separation of health services for people with SUD from services for people with mental illness that has developed over decades in many countries also results in barriers for people with SUD to receive adequate mental health care. A commissioned review in Australia stated that "differing institutional cultures, aetiological concepts, philosophical underpinnings, educational requirements, administrative arrangements, and screening and treatment approaches" as well as "issues pertaining to the lack of consistent definitions and conceptual frameworks for comorbidity ... lack of communication, collaboration, and linkages between the sectors" all contribute to inferior care for people with dual diagnoses, that is, a substance use plus another mental disorder (Canaway & Merkes, 2010). The separation of services is a prime example of structural discrimination, particularly of people with co-occurring disorders. Again, label avoidance and reluctance to disclose a substance use problem are likely and harmful strategies to avoid structural discrimination in healthcare settings (Figure 1).

Structural stigma is of course related to population attitudes. With regard to healthcare spending preferences among the general population, alcohol use disorder has consistently been assigned the lowest priority. A series of surveys in 2001, 2011, and 2020 in Germany monitored spending preferences of the public for nine common disorders. Spending for cancer treatment was consistently most popular, spending for depression care became more and more popular over time, while spending for the treatment of alcohol use disorder consistently enjoyed by far the lowest priority (Schomerus et al., 2021).

Where Do We Need to Go?

The Need for Concept Change: Labeling and a Continuum of Substance Use–Related Problems

The weight of labels seems particularly significant for SUD. We explore labeling and label avoidance as an example of how changing the words (and the underlying concepts) related to SUD could help eliminate its stigma. Admitting to the SUD label has long been seen as central to acknowledging the severity of the problem, and initiating the process of recovery, while avoiding the label has been viewed as "denial" and an impediment to accepting help or perceiving necessity for change (Howard et al., 2002). Some self-help approaches, like the 12-step program by Alcoholics Anonymous, and frequently professional treatment settings as well, expect people to submit under an illness label before any recovery process can start. At the same time, Link's modified labeling theory describes how assignment of a label changes the experience of someone with mental illness, increases withdrawal and secrecy, decreases social support, and results in worse mental and physical health outcomes (Link et al., 1989). This theory has been applied and empirically tested to people with SUD (Glass et al., 2013). Avoiding the label of an SUD thus seems like a healthy response, given the threat of public stigma, self-stigma, and structural stigma. But label avoidance is also a serious impediment to early problem recognition, and early help-seeking (Figure 1). So, there is a labeling dilemma and, probably, changing the significance of SUD labels could show a way out.

In an opinion piece in 2013, Jürgen Rehm and colleagues argued that rather than adhering to a yes or no diagnosis of "addiction," a continuum of mild, moderate, and heavy substance use would be sufficient (Rehm et al., 2013). SUD are dimensional conditions with no natural threshold (Hasin et al., 2013), and the DSM-5 accordingly grades severity with the number of criteria met from 2 to 11, categorized into mild, moderate, and severe SUD. This is quite a break from the traditional binary views of addiction.

Continuum views of substance use problems seem to have the potential to lower the stigma of SUD. Population studies show that people who have a continuum view of alcohol use disorder express more pro-social emotions for someone with alcohol use disorder, experience less fear (Schomerus et al., 2013), and have less desire for social distance (Schomerus et al., 2013; Subramaniam et al., 2017), a finding that is in line with various studies about other mental disorders like depression or schizophrenia (Peter et al., 2021). An intervention study among people with harmful drinking (but no addiction experience) found that providing them with a continuum model of alcohol problems made them <u>more</u> likely to recognize their drinking problem, compared to respondents receiving a binary, categorical intervention (Morris et al., 2020). Hence, there is preliminary evidence that a continuum model of SUD could reduce stigma and facilitate early problem recognition and help-seeking. Ultimately, label avoidance could become less necessary by reducing the labels' weight, stressing the dimensionality of substance use problems and promulgating a continuum model.

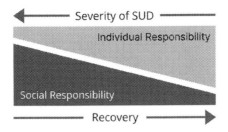

Figure 2 A dynamic model of responsibility in SUD

Responsibility

Another conceptual issue that drives stigma, and hence also offers a way to reduce it, is responsibility. Perceptions of responsibility, or blame, are central to the stigma of SUD. There is a perceived contradiction between an illness model of SUD, which implies low personal responsibility, and a behavioral model, where responsibility is central. While it is evident that severe SUD impairs someone's ability to take responsibility, for example while being intoxicated or in times of severe compulsive substance use, it is also clear that recovery without taking responsibility is difficult to imagine. A broader and dynamic conceptualization of responsibility may resolve this apparent contradiction. First, the focus on the individual needs to be replaced by a focus on individuals within their social context. There is a responsibility of the social environment for substance use, in terms of availability of and access to substances, but also in terms of provision of help, both within the healthcare system and on a personal level. This "social responsibility" (Williamson, 2012) has a dynamic relation to the individual responsibility of someone with an SUD. In a simplified model, both individual and social responsibility can be viewed as being in a dynamic balance, which changes according to the severity of the substance use problem. The more severe a substance use problem, the more responsibility has to be taken by the social environment, by providing help, for example. Recovery would then be a process of regaining individual responsibility (Figure 2). This model could counter the dynamics of blame in SUD stigma, pointing to our social responsibility particularly for people with severe SUD, but would also highlight the necessary growth of individual responsibility during recovery. It also aligns with ongoing biological research on regaining control over drug intake (Heinz et al., 2020).

Protest, Contact, and Education

However, conceptual changes to SUDs will not suffice to effectively erase the stigma of SUD. Eliminating the stigma of SUD will likely involve the three core strategies against public stigma: protest, education, and contact (Corrigan & Penn, 1999), but against the backdrop of the specific social function of SUD stigma, they are particularly challenging. Starting with protest, or social activism, it would be necessary to highlight the injustices of stigma and chastise stigma offenders, for example by protesting unequal access to health care for people with SUD. To enable protest, the widespread blame and shame surrounding SUD and the resulting self-stigma need to be overcome. We need empowerment and broad alliances to make protest feasible. The chapters of this book make a strong case against the fundamental injustice of SUD stigma, including voices of people with lived experience who are leading the way to protest stigma and discrimination. The same holds true for contact, the personal meeting of members of the general population with members of the stigmatized group. Contact is an indispensable cornerstone of any antistigma initiative. It has long been established that contact is among the most important parts of antistigma interventions, and the principles of strategic stigma change established by Corrigan (2011) describe how contact is best employed: targeted, local, credible, and continuous (Corrigan, 2011). For example, a contact-based targeted intervention for police officers to reduce alcohol stigma is probably most effective if the person with lived experience is a police officer, or someone with previous contact with the police from a shared cultural background (local and cultural proximity), who is in recovery from alcohol use disorder (credibility). The intervention should be part of a long-term antistigma strategy (continuity). Contact involves disclosure of people with lived experience, which may be particularly challenging with a condition as severely stigmatized as SUD. Hence, we need to create an environment making disclosure easier. We are proud that this book has offered some room for voicing the lived experiences of some of the authors.

Education, finally, challenges inaccurate stereotypes about SUD, replacing them with factual information. For example, the stereotype that people with SUD are weak-willed can be countered by the fact that behavioral change is similarly challenging for people with other behavior-related conditions, like type 2 diabetes (Sellman, 2010). Education has to relate directly to the social function of SUD stigma. First, we have to show that stigma does not solve the problem of SUD, but adds to its harm. Second, acknowledging that stigma is there for a reason also means that we have to show there are better ways to deal with SUD, without stigma. The chapters of this book will provide both an abundance of examples and mechanisms as to how stigma operates against people with SUD and perspectives on how to address SUD without stigma. In fact, a stigma-free handling of SUD opens up a multitude of ways for better dealing with SUD, within and outside healthcare settings. Addressing the stigma of SUD will help to create a culture of hope, empowerment, and compassion, as well as high-quality, stigma-free care for people with SUD.

References

Ahern, J., Stuber, J., & Galea, S. (2007). Stigma, discrimination and the health of illicit drug users. *Drug and Alcohol Dependence, 88*(2–3), 188–196. https://doi.org/10.1016/j.drugalcdep.2006.10.014

Angermeyer, M. C., Matschinger, H., & Schomerus, G. (2013). Attitudes towards psychiatric treatment and people with mental illness: Changes over two decades. *The British Journal of Psychiatry, 203*(2), 146–151. https://doi.org/10.1192/bjp.bp.112.122978

Canaway, R., & Merkes, M. (2010). Barriers to comorbidity service delivery: The complexities of dual diagnosis and the need to agree on terminology and conceptual frameworks. *Australian Health Review, 34*(3), 262–268. https://doi.org/10.1071/AH08723

Cooper, H. L. (2015). War on drugs policing and police brutality. *Substance Use & Misuse, 50*(8–9), 1188–1194. https://doi.org/10.3109/10826084.2015.1007669

Cooper, H., Moore, L., Gruskin, S., & Krieger, N. (2005). The impact of a police drug crackdown on drug injectors' ability to practice harm reduction: A qualitative study. *Social Science & Medicine, 61*(3), 673–684. https://doi.org/10.1016/j.socscimed.2004.12.030

Corrigan, P. W. (2011). Best practices: Strategic stigma change (SSC): Five principles for social marketing campaigns to reduce stigma. *Psychiatric Services, 62*(8), 824–826. https://doi.org/10.1176/ps.62.8.pss6208_0824

Corrigan, P. W., Druss, B. G., & Perlick, D. A. (2014). The impact of mental illness stigma on seeking and participating in mental health care. *Psychological Science in the Public Interest, 15*(2), 37–70. https://doi.org/10.1177/1529100614531398

Corrigan, P. W., & Penn, D. L. (1999). Lessons from social psychology on discrediting psychiatric stigma. *American Psychologist, 54*(9), 765–776. https://doi.org/10.1037//0003-066x.54.9.765

Corrigan, P. W., Rafacz, J., & Rüsch, N. (2011). Examining a progressive model of self-stigma and its impact on people with serious mental illness. *Psychiatry Research, 189*(3), 339–343. https://doi.org/10.1016/j.psychres.2011.05.024

Corrigan, P. W., Schomerus, G., Shuman, V., et al. (2017). Developing a research agenda for understanding the stigma of addictions Part I: Lessons from the mental health stigma literature. *The American Journal on Addictions, 26*(1), 59–66. https://doi.org/10.1111/ajad.12458

Corrigan, P. W., Watson, A. C., & Miller, F. E. (2006). Blame, shame, and contamination: The impact of mental illness and drug dependence stigma on family members. *Journal of Family Psychology*, *20*(2), 239–246. https://doi.org/10.1037/0893-3200.20.2.239

Earnshaw, V. A., Bogart, L. M., Menino, D. D., et al. (2019). Disclosure, stigma, and social support among young people receiving treatment for substance use disorders and their caregivers: A qualitative analysis. *International Journal of Mental Health and Addiction*, *17*(6), 1535–1549. https://doi.org/10.1007/s11469-018-9930-8

Foran, H. M., & O'Leary, K. D. (2008). Alcohol and intimate partner violence: A meta-analytic review. *Clinical Psychology Review*, *28*(7), 1222–1234. https://doi.org/10.1016/j.cpr.2008.05.001

Glass, J. E., Mowbray, O. P., Link, B. G., Kristjansson, S. D., & Bucholz, K. K. (2013). Alcohol stigma and persistence of alcohol and other psychiatric disorders: A modified labeling theory approach. *Drug and Alcohol Dependence*, *133*(2), 685–692. https://doi.org/10.1016/j.drugalcdep.2013.08.016

Goodyear, K., Haass-Koffler, C. L., & Chavanne, D. (2018). Opioid use and stigma: The role of gender, language and precipitating events. *Drug and Alcohol Dependence*, *185*, 339–346. https://doi.org/10.1016/j.drugalcdep.2017.12.037

Hasin, D. S. (2018). US epidemiology of cannabis use and associated problems. *Neuropsychopharmacology*, *43*(1), 195–212. https://doi.org/10.1038/npp.2017.198

Hasin, D. S., O'Brien, C. P., Auriacombe, M., et al. (2013). DSM-5 criteria for substance use disorders: Recommendations and rationale. *American Journal of Psychiatry*, *170*(8), 834–851. https://doi.org/10.1176/appi.ajp.2013.12060782

Heinz, A., Kiefer, F., Smolka, M. N., et al. (2020). Addiction Research Consortium: Losing and regaining control over drug intake (ReCoDe): From trajectories to mechanisms and interventions. *Addiction Biology*, *25*(2), e12866. https://doi.org/10.1111/adb.12866

Howard, M., McMillen, C., Nower, L., Elze, D., Edmond, T., & Bricout, J. (2002). Denial in addiction: Toward an integrated stage and process model – qualitative findings. *Journal of Psychoactive Drugs*, *34*(4), 371–382. https://doi.org/10.1080/02791072.2002.10399978

Khoramdad, M., Vahedian-azimi, A., Karimi, L., Rahimi-Bashar, F., Amini, H., & Sahebkar, A. (2020). Association between passive smoking and cardiovascular disease: A systematic review and meta-analysis. *IUBMB Life*, *72*(4), 677–686. https://doi.org/10.1002/iub.2207

Kilian, C., Manthey, J., Carr, S., et al. (2021). Stigmatization of people with alcohol use disorders: An updated systematic review of population studies. *Alcoholism: Clinical and Experimental Research*, *45*(5), 899–911. https://doi.org/10.1111/acer.14598

Kummetat, J. L., Leonhard, A., Manthey, J., Speerforck, S., & Schomerus, G. (2022). Understanding the association of public alcohol stigma and alcohol consumption within Europe. [Manuscript submitted].

Link, B. G., Angermeyer, M. C., Phelan, J. C., et al. (2011). Public attitudes towards people with mental illness. In G. Thornicroft, G. Szmukler, K. T. Mueser, & R. E. Drake (Eds.), *Oxford textbook of community mental health* (pp. 253–259). Oxford University Press. https://doi.org/10.1093/med/9780199565498.003.0137

Link, B. G., Cullen, F. T., Struening, E., Shrout, P. E., & Dohrenwend, B. P. (1989). A modified labeling theory approach to mental disorders: An empirical assessment. *American Sociological Review, 54*(3), 400–423. https://doi.org/10.2307/2095613

Link, B. G., & Phelan, J. C. (2001). Conceptualizing stigma. *Annual Review of Sociology, 27*(1), 363–385. https://doi.org/10.1146/annurev.soc.27.1.363

Link, B. G., Yang, L. H., Phelan, J. C., & Collins, P. Y. (2004). Measuring mental illness stigma. *Schizophrenia Bulletin, 30*(3), 511–541. https://doi.org/10.1093/oxfordjournals.schbul.a007098

Livingston, J. D. (2020). *Structural stigma in health-care contexts for people with mental health and substance use issues: A literature review*. Mental Health Commission of Canada.

Morris, J., Albery, I. P., Heather, N., & Moss, A. C. (2020). Continuum beliefs are associated with higher problem recognition than binary beliefs among harmful drinkers without addiction experience. *Addictive Behaviors, 105*, 106292. https://doi.org/10.1016/j.addbeh.2020.106292

Paquette, C. E., Syvertsen, J. L., & Pollini, R. A. (2018). Stigma at every turn: Health services experiences among people who inject drugs. *International Journal of Drug Policy, 57*, 104–110. https://doi.org/10.1016/j.drugpo.2018.04.004

Peter, L. J., Schindler, S., Sander, C., et al. (2021). Continuum beliefs and mental illness stigma: A systematic review and meta-analysis of correlation and intervention studies. *Psychological Medicine, 51*(5), 716–726. https://doi.org/10.1017/S0033291721000854

Phelan, J. C., Link, B. G., & Dovidio, J. F. (2008). Stigma and prejudice: One animal or two? *Social Science & Medicine, 67*(3), 358–367. https://10.1016/j.socscimed.2008.03.022

Rehm, J., Marmet, S., Anderson, P., et al. (2013). Defining substance use disorders: Do we really need more than heavy use? *Alcohol and Alcoholism, 48*(6), 633–640. https://doi.org/10.1093/alcalc/agt127

Rehm, J., & Shield, K. D. (2021). Alcohol use and cancer in the European Union. *European Addiction Research, 27*(1), 1–8. https://doi.org/10.1159/000507017

Schmitt, M. T., Branscombe, N. R., Postmes, T., & Garcia, A. (2014). The consequences of perceived discrimination for psychological well-being: A meta-analytic review. *Psychological Bulletin, 140*(4), 921–948. https://doi.org/10.1037/a0035754

Schomerus, G., Baumann, E., Sander, C., Speerforck, S., & Angermeyer, M. C. (2021). Some good news for psychiatry: Resource allocation preferences of the public during the COVID-19 pandemic. *World Psychiatry, 20*(2), 301–302. https://doi.org/10.1002/wps.20875

Schomerus, G., Corrigan, P. W., Klauer, T., Kuwert, P., Freyberger, H. J., & Lucht, M. (2011). Self-stigma in alcohol dependence: Consequences for drinking-refusal self-efficacy. *Drug and Alcohol Dependence, 114*(1), 12–17. https://doi.org/10.1016/j.drugalcdep.2010.08.013

Schomerus, G., Lucht, M., Holzinger, A., Matschinger, H., Carta, M. G., & Angermeyer, M. C. (2011). The stigma of alcohol dependence compared with other mental disorders: A review of population studies. *Alcohol and Alcoholism, 46*(2), 105–112. https://doi.org/10.1093/alcalc/agq089

Schomerus, G., Matschinger, H., & Angermeyer, M. C. (2013). Continuum beliefs and stigmatizing attitudes towards persons with schizophrenia, depression and alcohol dependence. *Psychiatry Research, 209*(3), 665–669. https://doi.org/10.1016/j.psychres.2013.02.006

(2014). Attitudes towards alcohol dependence and affected individuals: Persistence of negative stereotypes and illness beliefs between 1990 and 2011. *European Addiction Research, 20*(6), 293–299. https://doi.org/10.1159/000362407

Sellman, D. (2010). The 10 most important things known about addiction. *Addiction, 105*(1), 6–13. https://doi.org/10.1111/j.1360-0443.2009.02673.x

Smith, L. R., Earnshaw, V. A., Copenhaver, M. M., & Cunningham, C. O. (2016). Substance use stigma: Reliability and validity of a theory-based scale for substance-using populations. *Drug and Alcohol Dependence, 162*, 34–43. https://doi.org/10.1016/j.drugalcdep.2016.02.019

Stolzenburg, S., Freitag, S., Evans-Lacko, S., Muehlan, H., Schmidt, S., & Schomerus, G. (2017). The stigma of mental illness as a barrier to self labeling as having a mental illness. *The Journal of Nervous and Mental Disease, 205*(12), 903–909. https://doi.org/10.1097/NMD.0000000000000756

Stolzenburg, S., Tessmer, C., Corrigan, P. W., et al. (2018). Childhood trauma and self-stigma of alcohol dependence: Applying the progressive model of self-stigma. *Stigma and Health, 3*(4), 417–423. https://doi.org/10.1037/sah0000112

Subramaniam, M., Abdin, E., Picco, L., et al. (2017). Continuum beliefs and stigmatising beliefs about mental illness: Results from an Asian community survey. *BMJ Open, 7*(4), e014993. https://doi.org/10.1136/bmjopen-2016-014993

Walsh, C., MacMillan, H. L., & Jamieson, E. (2003). The relationship between parental substance abuse and child maltreatment: Findings from the Ontario Health Supplement. *Child Abuse & Neglect, 27*(12), 1409–1425. https://doi.org/10.1016/j.chiabu.2003.07.002

Williamson, L. (2012). Destigmatizing alcohol dependence: The requirement for an ethical (not only medical) remedy. *American Journal of Public Health, 102*(5), e5–e8. https://doi.org/10.2105/AJPH.2011.300629

World Health Organization. (2016). *The health and social effects of nonmedical cannabis use*. World Health Organization. www.who.int/substance_abuse/publications/msbcannabis.pdf

CHAPTER 2

My Experience with the Stigma of Substance Use

Sonya Ballentine

I write this chapter as a person with many lived experiences with stigma that have impacted my journey with substance use disorders including substance use disorder itself, but also serious mental illness, homelessness, incarceration, and African American ethnicity. Stigma is defined as a stain and/or blemish of disgrace associated with a specific situation or circumstance. All these lived experiences gave rise to my picture of self-stigma. Growing up, stigma was not a word or ideology that many in my immediate circle used. However, I do believe that shame and guilt were pretty much everyday occurrences for myself and many of my peers. I grew up a tall skinny black girl on the South side of Chicago. I went to a Catholic school, played team sports, and excelled academically. My family was middle class so all of my childhood needs were met in abundance. I was raised by a single mother who had always been a straight A student. The idea of using any form of mind- or mood-altering substance was never an option. However, my family drank what I believed to be "top shelf liquor," what was then and still is today an acceptable way to socialize. This was all very confusing to my young mind, leading to a much distorted relationship with alcohol and the people who drank it.

In my culture, we use shortened words and thoughts when communicating a point or explaining a person that uses substances. Some of the more palatable terms were functional, recreational, and social. Stigmatizing terms have become dope fiend, addict, crackhead, pothead, drunk, and junkie. These terms are still used in many circles and conversations.

At age 13, I took my first drink and that day I decided I would never drink again. I now understood why alcoholics and people who drank to excess were stigmatized as losers. I was angry not only at the effects of alcohol but also at the decision I had made to experiment. In reflection, I believe that this was my first experience with self-stigma. "How could you not be a loser after allowing something like alcohol to take over your life?" It was poison and no one in their right mind would drink or even be around people who drank.

I was introduced to marijuana by my basketball coach. I was completely naïve about what was going on around me and right under my nose. Why would he offer a 12-year-old a joint? But from what I was told about "potheads", they were dreamers and not doers. And even though day-dreaming was a part of youthful imagination, I was a doer.

I was 15 when my friend and I helped ourselves to her older brother's marijuana stash. Self-stigmatizing thoughts immediately rushed into my mind about how stupid I was being. I was filled with self-doubt, regret, and self-pity. Among my friends, smoking weed was thoroughly acceptable; after all it was a plant and GOD made plants so it cannot be that bad, so I was told. They talked about how people who smoked weed sat back and came up with all types of genius. The best philosophical minds and ideas were formulated from people high on weed. Now I know that this too is a form of stigmatization.

I wanted to reach out to my mother but I was full of fear. I knew she loved me but zero tolerance existed for a "pothead" and to her I would be headed nowhere fast. Once she learned of my experiment with marijuana I was a bum and my life would be a waste of time. I was often banished to my father's house. I was separated from my friends and left to live in squalor.

Marijuana is known as the "gateway" drug. I watched videos about how people start with weed and then shoot heroin. I thought this was a bit extreme and many people I know today smoke a little weed and do not become hardened criminals. That is the thing about stigma; people are able to base some or all of their personal views alongside public beliefs and prejudice then state it as a fact.

I had never seen a black person in a commercial about inhalants so it must be a white people drug. PCP and other hallucinogenic substances were being used by older black men back from the Vietnam War; that is why they are so crazy. Pills were for white women who stayed home with the children. Cocaine was for rich white people and crack was for poor black people. And people who injected any substance at all were at the lowest end of them all. I was offered to inject various forms of substances but said no. What did stigma do in that instance? Did it save me from decades of pain and degradation? Or did it feed a stigmatizing and irrational view that somehow I'm not as bad as them because I'm not shooting a spike into my arm? All of these statements are not only false, but are forms of stigma that have guided American legislation, societal rules, and moral arguments. This is worsened by self-stigma: "What is wrong with me?" "Am I wasting my life away?" "Was I on a fast train headed nowhere and not realizing it?" Self-stigma was constantly filling me with doubt especially during this experimental time in my life. The peers in my life who I was able to disclose with guided and helped me to set in place guardrails that kept me from going too far. Some substances I never tried again and the people who used those substances fell out of my life.

On the other hand, people talked about, waited for, and afterward bragged about drug use. Here is when I began to experience what providers and researchers call substance use disorder. In my circle, it was called addiction, plain and simple. And no matter how you worded it, it was understood that addiction was ugly. There was no dressing it up. What combination of words can we as a society use to dress up racism or slavery? Racism and all that comes with it is ugly and no matter how far we go back in history or how forward thinking we become, racism will always be ugly. This I also believe to be true for substance use. In American society you can be denied employment, housing, and financial assistance if you are linked to substances. These are the same things denied to many black Americans throughout history.

The stigma of substance use became an ongoing challenge that I either had to get ahead of, or was miserably losing to, in many areas of my life. I had to take drug tests for employment. I could not have any drug convictions to move into housing. My social life had become contingent on whether or not others accepted or even understood my drug history.

And to add insult to injury the process of treatment also had stigmatizing views interwoven into the process. I was told in the beginning that I needed at least 90 days, maybe more. Treatment was this weird combination of boot camp, jail, and elementary school. We spent most days with the staff talking to us like children, yelling at us, and being punished for simple mistakes. I could not wait to leave. I was graduating from college and nothing was going to interfere with that goal. I was given an outpatient referral, a list of meetings I could attend in Atlanta, and some tips on how to treat the cravings with honey and orange juice. I was then told that they would be there when I returned. Returned?! There existed this presumption of failure. I was told that many people do not recover the first time but the staff hoped I would prove them wrong. I felt the sincerity but also the skepticism. I wanted nothing more than to prove them wrong. I returned to Atlanta and relapsed maybe two weeks later. Fine, they were right, but I was still going to graduate from college.

I graduated from college in August of 1992 and was on time and able to walk in my place in the procession. I had been using substances all night and into the morning. My family was in town and my boyfriend at the time was concerned for my well-being. I showed up for them as best as I could physically but emotionally I was a mess. Self-stigmatizing thoughts had me filled with shame and guilt, remorse and regret. I believed that I was living a lie inside of some fantasy world. But how could I ever explain that to anyone and moreover who and how would I ask for help this time? I decided to wait and hoped for the best. Maybe my version of harm reduction would work this time; after all I was beginning a new position at the Federal Reserve Bank of Atlanta and the references I received were outstanding. I felt I had something to work toward and better yet there was no drug screening to complete. So, for now I was good to go in my new life of corporate America. Still, the fear of random testing was always hovering like dark clouds waiting to rain on my parade. I had heard conversations of others in various departments failing the test and losing their jobs. I have always questioned why in some positions the individual is offered treatment and in others substance use is grounds for termination.

My next attempt to seek treatment was in 1993. I went to the Fulton County Detox facility. I sat across from a counselor who did my assessment and once we completed the necessary question and answer session he told me that I was not bad enough yet to be given a spot in detox. Again self-stigma rushed in to question all areas of that conversation. What had I said? How bad do you have to be to be allowed into substance use treatment? I left that interaction full of sadness and confusion and did not seek treatment again for another 5 years. On February 14, 1998 I went back to the same facility. The person who did my assessment 5 years earlier was no longer there and with 5 years more experience of pain and life consequences I was sure to convince this person that I now deserved a bed. During that 5-year period, I had been informed and misinformed about treatment. Some providers told me that he was right and that I really was not that bad. "Well, how bad does a person have to be?" To this day no one has been able to answer that question for me. I did not know it then but I had been a victim of this person's stigmatizing views of how bad a person should be or look to warrant treatment and help. The good news is this time I got in.

Detox at that time was 7 days of vitamins, dopamine, and intensive group therapy. I walked the halls all night from insomnia and received multiple consequences from falling asleep in group. I knew that my sleep cycle, body cycle, and thinking patterns were off-centered and I was determined to right my ship. Most of the group therapy was about how skewed our thinking and behavior had become. Many people were singled out for their wrong intentions. It was stated often that everyone was not there for the same reason, to get clean. Some were there because they had nowhere else to go because they were homeless. Some were there because they were mandated by the court system. Some were in fear for their life because they owed their drug dealers. During many groups, the facilitator would tell us to look at the person next to us and make a decision about whether it would be you or them that made it because one of you would relapse. Facilitators often used scare tactics to get people to conform. It was often stated that this would be the last opportunity for most of us because the state was cutting funding. We will not be able to return so we better get it this time. Those of us going home after detox should have a workable plan to not get high again. Stigmatizing language is a common tool used by facilitators in inpatient treatment settings. I now wonder how anyone gets clean and stays clean after such a traumatizing experience.

Next came visitors from the 12-step groups who shared their stories. This was my first introduction to the effectiveness of self-disclosure. I had never heard anyone speak so candidly about topics that were embarrassing, humiliating, and painful. Ultimately, they talked about the reality of life now and how they were achieving newfound goals and aspirations. 12-step speakers gave us hope for the future. We could relate to them as individuals and as members of a larger movement.

Self-stigmatizing thoughts always made me feel alone; the 12-step speakers shared we were not alone. I would often leave those meetings better and looked forward to hearing the speakers share their experiences with substance use and recovery.

We were allowed to thank them for sharing with us after the meeting and get phone numbers to call them later but we could not ask questions during the meeting. There was no question and answer session after the storytelling portion. It wasn't until I was introduced to service work, conferences, conventions, and panel discussions that I could ask unanswered questions. When I finally got the opportunity to share my story with women in treatment centers, I encouraged them to ask questions because I believe in the power of bi-directional learning in a more conversational setting.

I stayed at that detox center for 14 days while they sought additional treatment for me. I thought this was treatment! No, I was in detox, a very different phase. They sent me to St. Jude Recovery Center; I had no say in the choice. I later found out why I was sent there. First, I was not taking psychiatric medications and St. Jude's did not accept people who were being treated for mental illness. I knew that I was having mental health challenges at the time but I made a choice not to disclose this to them because I would not be admitted. Second, it was a 1-year program and the counselors decided that a minimum of 1 year was needed for me to experience success. Third, St. Jude's was for the worst of the worst of substance users; they said more than 90% successfully transitioned into independent living upon completion of the program. Lastly, you would not be accepted if you used heroin. I completed intake at St. Jude's after a weeklong process. They divided the week into what they thought to be bite-sized pieces that seemed to go on forever. Even though you must be taking no mental health medications to be admitted into the program, we all visited a psychiatrist within 2 weeks to receive financial aid. It was all very confusing because we were told on a regular basis how crazy we were and how distorted our thinking had become by using substances. The first 60 days were brutal. We attended nonstop groups from 8 am to 5 pm then had to attend a minimum of 5 outside 12-step meetings once we completed that first 60 days. After 45 days you were required to attend job readiness and were given 2 weeks to find employment. Employment could be nothing in a professional setting, nothing driving, and nothing outside of 9 am to 5 pm unless approved. If you did not have a job at the end of the 2 weeks you were expelled. Needless to say, anxiety was a never-ending occurrence during these intervals. Desperation set in the closer I got to the end of that 2-week period; I was willing to take anything to not be that person asked to pack up and get out. I got a job at Caribou Coffee with maybe 2 days to spare. I have never felt so thankful to get a minimum wage job before in my life. Interestingly, it was as if I was wearing a sign that stated "addict in recovery" because most of the employees were from the same treatment center. When I shared this in group, I was immediately corrected that it was not about the money or the housing; it was about character building. I continued to be full of shame, guilt, and self-doubt. Self-stigma convinced me that no matter what I was able to achieve I was a failure. I hated myself for allowing this to happen to me and I was reminded every day in treatment that I would continue to feel this way if I didn't surrender to knowing that this is the reality of my life. I had no one to blame but myself.

When I completed 11 months of the 12-month program, I was told that they had done all they could do for me; it was time for me to move on to aftercare. Aftercare?! Yes, aftercare was outpatient treatment taken for 18 months after intensive inpatient treatment. I moved into a transitional house in one of the worse neighborhoods in Atlanta but close to my aftercare location and my job. As a matter of fact I had been robbed just about 18 months earlier right down the street. I lived in about 5 different transitional settings during this time, all situated in the worst parts of every city. Why is that? Partially it is because that is all I could afford and partially it is all that I believed at the time that I deserved. Personally, I believe it was more of the latter. I had no idea what self-stigma was at the time, but it often would surface at some of the most unexpected times to remind me of my failings and deserving occasional sadness, depression, and self-pity.

I worked hard at Caribou Coffee for another year and attended aftercare regularly. I paid my bills at the transition house and exercised every chance I got. Working out was my stress management and I looked and felt great. I volunteered and did service work at the treatment center. I was back! Sky was the limit! I was told that ADT Security Services was hiring installers by someone in my aftercare group so I applied and was hired. I was also told that AirTran headquartered in Atlanta was hiring so I applied and was offered that position too. I had options; maybe I wasn't so bad after all. Maybe I wouldn't be doomed to retire from the coffee shop with a college degree in Finance. Okay, so which job would I accept? This was going to be my choice because I was starting to trust myself and my decisions. I chose ADT because I wanted to be a technician. I wanted to be challenged and more than anything, I wanted to prove to myself that I still had the ability to learn things quickly.

I began working at ADT in August of 1999. I quickly rose through the ranks. I reestablished my credit, bought a house and a car, and got into a new relationship. I stopped going to aftercare and 12-step meetings despite everyone in my recovery circle telling me that I was going to regret it. In January of 2001 I relapsed. By September of that same year, when the World Trade Center was being attacked by terrorists, my car had been stolen, I had abandoned my job, and I was in foreclosure. I vowed never to go back to treatment and I entertained suicidal thoughts daily.

What happened? Even writing these words now reminds me of the level of self-loathing and confusion that I felt at that time. My mother allowed me to move into my grandparents' building down the street from her. I hid my relapse for as long as I could but when my mother finally found out, I was evicted by the courts. I went back to treatment again and six more times after that. I was now known as a "chronic relapser," yet another stigmatizing term used for many seeking help. I think that most people believe that active substance users do not deserve a place of their own to call home. Mostly everyone I knew was homeless.

Every time I went back to treatment I downplayed or outright lied about previous treatment. How would it be different this time? You would be singled out in group sessions and watched by staff. The spotlight was shining on you and it was even worse when you went back to the 12-step meetings. I hated coming back after a relapse so I would go to meetings on another side of town for a while until I got my feet under me again. Many times people would just tear the bandage off and say "We know that you put your lab coat back on and went out to experiment." Whenever you returned from a relapse you were told "shut up and sit down," that "you have nothing to say that we want to hear."

Finally, I got serious about recovery after a horrible 18-month relapse in July of 2011. By this time everything I was told about funding cuts was true. Treatment was for alcoholics and heroin addicts. You were out of luck if you used crack. Life became very simple and I enjoyed the recovery journey set out for me to experience. It was not until I began to learn about stigma and the effects it has on individuals that I made a conscious decision to confront my self-stigmatizing views. Stigma had alienated me in one way or another from not only seeking help but from allowing myself to help others who sought after me. I now understand and embrace harm reduction. Total abstinence is not the answer for everyone. To this day when I share this view in my recovery circle, I am viewed as a hypocrite. Harm reduction is not something people want to hear about in a 12-step meeting: it is total abstinence or nothing at all. Abstinence is my chosen form of harm reduction but I understand that others may disagree. My life experiences have shown me that this is the safest route to travel. And I do not isolate myself from people who still use; it is not up to me to decide or judge others and as a result I have made myself available to people at all stages of this journey that we share and for that I am grateful.

CHAPTER 3

Substance Use Stigma and Policy

Emma E. McGinty and Sarah A. White

Introduction

The pervasive stigma surrounding nonmedical substance use (hereafter referred to as "substance use") and substance use disorder relates to policy along multiple pathways (McGinty, Pescosolido, et al., 2018; Tsai et al., 2019). Policy includes both public policies, such as statutes and regulations, as well as institutional policies governing conduct in workplaces, schools, and other organizations (Pollack Porter et al., 2018). In this chapter, we focus on substance use policies in the United States. Following the introduction, this chapter is organized in three sections. First, we introduce a conceptual framework delineating key ways in which stigma and policy relate to one another. Second, we synthesize the evidence on what is known about the relationship between substance use stigma and policy. Third, we discuss the evidence surrounding strategies to reduce stigma and increase support for policies benefiting people who use substances and/or experience substance use disorder.

While substance use disorder encompasses alcohol and other drugs, most of the research this chapter draws upon is focused on drugs other than alcohol, including both illicit drugs (e.g., cocaine) and drugs with mixed licit and illicit status in the United States. Both opioids and cannabis fall into this latter category. In the United States, heroin is an illegal substance, but other versions of opioids can be legally prescribed for pain management and/or used as anesthetics in clinical settings. Further complicating the picture in regards to opioids, synthetic opioids like fentanyl can be both licitly produced for use in healthcare settings and illicitly produced and distributed (Barry, 2018). While cannabis is designated a Schedule I controlled substance under federal law, a category devoted to substances deemed to have no medical use, the United States Justice Department does not enforce this federal prohibition (Cole, 2013); as a result, many states have chosen to legalize use of cannabis for medical and/or adult recreational purposes (National Conference of State Legislatures, 2021). We raise these points to highlight the degree to which public policy deeming some substances legal and others illegal influences stigma. Generally speaking, there is greater stigma toward use of illicit relative to licit substances (Corrigan & Nieweglowski, 2018; Pescosolido & Martin, 2015). While alcohol misuse and alcohol use disorder are stigmatized, there is less stigma surrounding alcohol than other substances (Link et al., 1999; Pescosolido et al., 2010); as a result, most research examining the intersection of stigma and policy has focused on illicit drugs or drugs, like cannabis and opioids, with mixed legal status.

The stigma surrounding substance use and substance use disorder faces a unique intersection with policy due to the stigmatization of evidence-based interventions to address substance use, which is referred to as "interventional stigma" (Madden, 2019); this is highly relevant for policy in that policies govern the implementation of these interventions. For example, evidence-based opioid-agonist medications to treat opioid use disorder are stigmatized independently from addiction itself (Volkow et al., 2014). Stigma toward the opioid-agonist medications methadone and buprenorphine, which are the gold standard to treat opioid use disorder, is driven by the misperception that these medications replace one addiction with another, and that the only acceptable outcome of addiction treatment is abstinence (National Academies of Sciences, Education, and Medicine [NASEM], 2019; Olsen & Sharfstein, 2014; Volkow et al., 2014). In reality, long-term use of these medications is clinically recommended for many individuals with opioid use disorder (Substance Abuse and Mental Health Services Administration [SAMHSA], 2020). Public stigma toward people who use drugs contributes in part to the lack of public and political support for harm reduction strategies like naloxone distribution, syringe services programs, and overdose prevention sites (McGinty, Barry, et al., 2018). The widely held belief that drug use is a moral failing, as opposed to a public health issue, also drives interventional stigma surrounding harm reduction approaches, which seek to minimize the harms of drug use (e.g., fatal overdose, transmission of infectious disease) but do not focus on eliminating drug use itself.

The Relationship between Stigma and Policy

In this section, we describe three mechanisms by which stigma and policy relate to one another: (1) stigma's influence on support for and enactment of policy; (2) stigma's influence on implementation of enacted policies;

and (3) policy's impact on stigma. Before discussing each in depth, it is important to introduce the concept of structural stigma, in which policies are, themselves, a form of stigma. Structural stigma is the societal level conditions, cultural norms, and public and institutional policies that limit the opportunities and well-being of stigmatized groups (Hatzenbuehler, 2016). When we refer to punitive policies throughout the chapter, these are examples of structural stigma.

Stigma Can Influence Support for and Enactment of Policy

First, stigmatizing attitudes toward people who use substances and/or experience substance use disorder can influence support for policy. As is discussed in more detail in the following section, multiple studies have demonstrated that measures of public stigma, such as desire for social distance from people with a substance use disorder or belief that substance use indicates a lack of willpower, are correlated with lower support for evidence-based public health–oriented policies and higher support for punitive policies (Barry & McGinty, 2014; Barry et al., 2014; Corrigan et al., 2009; Kennedy-Hendricks et al., 2017, 2020; Kennedy-Hendricks, Busch, et al., 2016; Kruis & Merlo, 2020; McGinty, Barry, et al., 2018; Mendiola et al., 2018; Murphy & Russell, 2020; Skinner et al., 2007; Stone et al., 2021; Van Boekel et al., 2013). Examples of evidence-based public health policies include budgetary policies allotting additional resources to substance use disorder treatment modalities that are effective but inaccessible to many people, such as medication treatment for opioid use disorder (Beetham et al., 2019; Crotty et al., 2020; Mojtabai et al., 2019; NASEM, 2019; Stein et al., 2016), or policies legalizing harm reduction interventions, like syringe services programs and overdose prevention sites, that research demonstrates can reduce harms associated with drug use such as overdose and HIV and other infections resulting from unsafe needle sharing (Abdul-Quader et al., 2013; Kennedy et al., 2017).

Stigma toward people who use substances and/or experience substance use disorder contributing to low support for beneficial policies and high support for punitive policies is consistent with theory regarding the social construction of public policy target populations, which posits that policies targeting groups with positive social constructions are likely to confer benefits, whereas policies targeting groups with negative social constructions are likely to confer burdens (Schneider & Ingram, 1993). In this context, examples of punitive policies include criminal justice–oriented policies such as mandatory minimum sentencing policies for drug offenses

(Bandara et al., 2020). Many substance use experts also characterize the policy environment surrounding medication treatment for opioid use disorder as punitive (Fiscella et al., 2019; Samet et al., 2018; Tsai et al., 2019; Woodruff et al., 2019). For example, most people prescribed methadone to treat their opioid use disorder must attend a specialty clinic every day to receive their dose in-person (Samet et al., 2018). In contrast, primary care and other office-based prescribers can prescribe methadone for chronic pain the same way that they prescribe antibiotics or antihypertensive medications. Support for policy proposals among the public and key groups of professionals who interact with people with substance use disorder, including clinicians, law enforcement, social workers, child protective services professionals, and others is a key element of policy enactment: policies are much more likely to be enacted when they have widespread support.

Stigma Can Influence Implementation of Policy

We distinguish between enactment of policy, which means putting a policy in place – passing a law, promulgating a regulation, codifying a workplace policy, etc. – versus implementation of policy. By policy implementation, we mean what happens *after* enactment. Once the policy is in place, whether it has its intended effects is enormously dependent on the degree to which the policy is implemented or enforced. Lack of policy implementation is common. For example, many US states have enacted laws requiring prescribers to check their state's prescription drug monitoring program (PDMP), an electronic database of controlled substance prescriptions, prior to prescribing an opioid to a patient. However, evidence shows that these laws have been poorly implemented: in many states, the PDMP is not integrated with the electronic medical systems used by prescribers, limiting the feasibility of accessing the PDMP database (Rutkow et al., 2017). Lack of policy enforcement is also common (Rutkow et al., 2017; Stone et al., 2020; Yuanhong Lai et al., 2019). Continuing the PDMP law example, many states have no system to determine whether a prescriber checked the PDMP prior to prescribing an opioid in accordance with the law, and therefore are unable to fully enforce the law (Rutkow et al., 2017; Stone et al., 2020; Yuanhong Lai et al., 2019).

While implementation and enforcement in the state PDMP law example above seem to be primarily hindered by technical issues, stigma can also be a driving force in policy implementation. If a health system enacts a policy requiring all healthcare providers to refer people with opioid use disorder to clinical guideline–recommended opioid-agonist treatment, healthcare providers who hold stigmatizing attitudes toward people with opioid use disorder may be unlikely to implement the policy (Kennedy-Hendricks, Busch, et al., 2016; Stone et al., 2021). Interventional stigma toward methadone and buprenorphine may further hinder implementation of this policy (Stone et al., 2021). Anticipated stigma among people with opioid use disorder might also impede policy implementation if people are unwilling to disclose their opioid use disorder to clinicians (Bornstein et al., 2020; Luoma et al., 2007; McNeely et al., 2018). In addition to impeding implementation of beneficial, evidence-based policies, stigma might also lead to zealous implementation of punitive policies, for example by influencing healthcare providers' decisions to report a pregnant person using methadone to treat their opioid use disorder (the clinically recommended course of action) to Child Protective Services in a state with a law that deems drug use during pregnancy grounds for child abuse (NASEM, 2019; Terplan et al., 2015; Thomas et al., 2018). Drug-related arrests and prosecutions in the United States are disproportionately concentrated in communities of color, an example of compounded stigma toward substance use and stigma (racism) toward racial and ethnic minorities – particularly the Black community – influencing policy implementation.

Policy Can Influence Stigma

As indicated by our earlier point that use of and addiction to licit substances tends to be less stigmatized than substance use and substance use disorder tied to illicit substances, illegality compounds stigma toward substance use. Other types of punitive policies, like ones emphasizing the need for social control over people with substance use disorder, also have the potential to further promulgate stigma. For example, some experts and advocates assert that in-person methadone dosing requirements and the heavy federal regulation of buprenorphine for the treatment of opioid use disorder in the United States exacerbate already negative views toward people with opioid use disorder and medications to treat this condition (Harris & McElrath, 2012; Samet et al., 2018; Wakeman & Rich, 2018). Federal buprenorphine regulations require prescribers to obtain a special waiver from the US government to prescribe buprenorphine for opioid use disorder (they do not need a waiver to prescribe buprenorphine for chronic pain) and limit the number of patients with opioid use disorder they can treat with buprenorphine (Fiscella et al., 2019; Knopf, 2019; Marino et al., 2019).

Alternatively, policy can also reduce stigma. For example, policies that expand access to effective substance use disorder treatment can reduce public stigma by increasing the likelihood that members of society at large have opportunities to interact with people who have received effective treatment and are thriving as a result (Barry et al., 2014; McGinty et al., 2015; Tsai et al., 2019). Policies that allocate sufficient resources to ensure high-quality implementation of substance use disorder prevention, harm reduction, and treatment interventions are also key stigma reduction tools. When a treatment or harm reduction program moves into a neighborhood, stigma – in this case the not-in-by-my-backyard, or NIMBY phenomenon (Bernstein & Bennett, 2013) – is exacerbated and perpetuated when insufficient resource allocation leads to chaotic or otherwise problematic implementation; for example, dilapidated buildings, lines of people waiting on the street to receive services due to inadequate space, etc. Well-resourced, high-quality implementation, in which these programs serving people with substance use disorder are indistinguishable from other respected businesses, plays an important role in destigmatizing both the people receiving services and the services themselves.

Evidence on the Relationship between Substance Use Stigma and Policy

Survey Research Examining the Correlation between Stigma and Policy Support

A correlation between stigmatizing attitudes and lack of support for policies to expand addiction treatment, harm reduction, and prevention interventions among the United States public has been demonstrated in numerous survey studies (Barry et al., 2014; Kennedy-Hendricks et al., 2017; McGinty, Barry, et al., 2018). This is not specific to the United States, as the relationship between public stigma and support for substance use policies and resource allocation has been shown internationally, including in Scotland, France, Germany, and Canada (Cruz et al., 2007; Jauffret-Roustide et al., 2013; Matheson et al., 2014; Schomerus et al., 2006). Additionally, this relationship has been further demonstrated in the United States among professionals who interact with individuals experiencing addiction, including law enforcement and healthcare providers (Corrigan et al., 2009; Kennedy-Hendricks et al., 2020; Kruis &

Merlo, 2020; Mendiola et al., 2018; Murphy & Russell, 2020; Skinner et al., 2007; Van Boekel et al., 2013). This stigma can influence their support of both public and institutional policies related to their work, such as supporting federal spending on treatment programs (public) or supporting policies/procedures on naloxone distribution in the workplace (institutional) (Kennedy-Hendricks et al., 2020; Kruis & Merlo, 2020). Evidence from survey studies examining the correlation between stigmatizing attitudes and support for drug policies is outlined in the following two sections, first among the public and second among professionals who interact with individuals experiencing addiction.

Most Americans believe that people with substance use disorders are to blame for their problem (Barry et al., 2014, 2016; Kennedy-Hendricks et al., 2017). While substance use includes an element of personal choice, studies show that the public's perspective of an individual with a substance use disorder is heavily stigmatized and has little regard for the societal causes of addiction (Barry et al., 2014; Calabrese & Bell, 2019; Corrigan et al., 2009; Crandall et al., 2002; Luoma et al., 2007). These stigmatizing attitudes then translate into the types of policies that Americans support (Schneider & Ingram, 1993). Stigmatizing attitudes have been shown to be correlated with higher support for punitive policies, such as arresting people getting multiple prescriptions from different doctors and requiring Medicaid enrollees to use a single prescriber and pharmacy if they are suspected of nonmedical use, and lower support of public health–oriented policies, such as expanding Medicaid benefits for treatment, increasing government spending of treatment, and protecting people from criminal charges if they report an overdose (Kennedy-Hendricks et al., 2017). Furthermore, higher stigmatizing attitudes have been shown to decrease the likelihood someone supported overdose prevention sites or syringe service programs, both evidence-based harm reduction strategies (Kulesza et al., 2015; McGinty, Barry, et al., 2018).

Numerous studies have shown that healthcare professionals, from nurses to primary care and emergency room physicians, have negative attitudes toward patients with substance use disorders, in nearly parallel proportion to the public, and that these stigmatizing attitudes are greater than stigma related to other mental health conditions (Kennedy-Hendricks, et al., 2016a, 2020; Mendiola et al., 2018; Skinner et al., 2007; Stone et al., 2021; Van Boekel et al., 2013). These stigmatizing attitudes persist if individuals are using medications for their opioid use disorder, which can have implications on practice as demonstrated by a national survey of primary care providers that found greater stigmatizing attitudes were associated with a lower likelihood to believe these evidence-based medications were effective and a lower likelihood to prescribe any medications for opioid use disorder or provide referrals to other providers who would prescribe these medications (Stone et al., 2021). These stigmatizing attitudes were also associated with a lower likelihood to support key policies: increasing government spending on medication treatment, allowing clinicians to prescribe methadone in primary care settings, and requiring insurance companies to cover medications (Stone et al., 2021). Another recent study found significant differences between primary care physicians and trainees in their support of stigmatizing social distance metrics and for eliminating the federal requirements to prescribe buprenorphine, with trainees demonstrating less stigmatizing attitudes and higher support for eliminating the federal buprenorphine waiver (Kennedy-Hendricks et al., 2020). This suggests that there may be a new generation of providers that support less stigmatizing policies related to drug policy at their institutional level and the federal level.

Law enforcement officers are another critically important group to measure stigma among because they frequently interact with people who use substances and/or have substance use disorders due to the heavy reliance on criminalizing drug use in the United States. Stigmatizing attitudes are high among law enforcement officers (Beletsky et al., 2005; Bessen et al., 2019; Burris et al., 2009; Green et al., 2013; Kruis & Merlo, 2020; Murphy & Russell, 2020). A survey of over 600 police officers in Pennsylvania showed that most law enforcement officers believe naloxone provides individuals an excuse to continue using drugs and feel that tax dollars should not go toward paying for drug treatment (Murphy & Russell, 2020). These stigmatizing attitudes increase among officers who interact more often with individuals experiencing an overdose or administer naloxone and it has been shown that officers that have administered naloxone believe that they should provide less care to persons experiencing an overdose as compared to officers that haven't (Kruis & Merlo, 2020; Murphy & Russell, 2020). However, evidence did show that one way to mitigate these negative attitudes on providing care to persons experiencing an overdose was the existence of a departmental policy on naloxone administration, which led to increased attitudes to provide more help (Kruis & Merlo, 2020). This demonstrates that policy can actually influence stigma because the officers had clear guidelines on naloxone and were trained on the importance of the intervention.

Qualitative Research Exploring Substance Use Stigma

The pathways by which stigma relates to policy support, enactment, and implementation can be illuminated by qualitative research, such as through interviews or focus groups with a particular stakeholder group. Qualitative research has shown that people who use drugs experience breaches of trust in traditional healthcare systems through mistreatment in settings including emergency rooms and pharmacies, as well as disclosures of counseling sessions and drug tests without consent (Ellis et al., 2020; Meyerson et al., 2019), highlighting the importance of enacting and implementing policies to prevent such disclosures.

Multiple qualitative studies exploring the perspectives of people who use drugs have shown that harm reduction interventions enable safer drug use by reshaping social and environmental contexts to injection drug use (Allen et al., 2019; McNeil & Small, 2014), mediating access to health care services like naloxone and HIV testing (Allen et al., 2019; McNeil & Small, 2014), and decreasing risk of bloodborne infections (Allen et al., 2019; McNeil & Small, 2014; Meyerson et al., 2019). However, qualitative research has also identified high levels of anticipated stigma and recognition of widespread public stigma toward harm reduction among people who use drugs, who recognize that large segments of the public view these interventions as encouraging individuals to continue substance use (Allen et al., 2019; Bernstein & Bennett, 2013; NASEM, 2019; Olsen & Sharfstein, 2014; Smith, 2010; Strike & Miskovic, 2017; Volkow et al., 2014). Qualitative research conducted with people who use drugs has shown varying support toward policies to expand medication treatment for opioid use disorder (Harris & McElrath, 2012; Lancaster et al., 2015; Woo et al., 2017; Yarborough et al., 2016). For example, Lancaster and colleagues found that lack of support for expanding access to medication for opioid use disorder among people who use drugs was driven, in part, by the lived experience of interventional stigma surrounding medication and the fact that many people had received treatment from programs that advocated against medication, instead using an abstinence-only approach (Lancaster et al., 2015).

Stigma among the public influences the type of policies and programs that operate within a given community. There is very limited qualitative research examining this relationship between stigma and support for drug policy among members of the public who do not use drugs, but the limited available research focuses on the NIMBY phenomenon (Allen et al., 2019; Bernstein & Bennett, 2013; Smith, 2010; Strike & Miskovic, 2017).

Qualitative research in countries including the United States, Canada, and Australia have found that NIMBY attitudes within a community contribute to zoning policies that do not allow harm reduction services and medication clinics (Bernstein & Bennett, 2013; Lancaster et al., 2015; Smith, 2010; Strike & Miskovic, 2017). One study conducted with Toronto residents revealed that residents' strategy for enacting a zoning policy prohibiting a methadone clinic centered around convincing residents and businesses that the clinic threatened to "contaminate" the area's reputation and that nonproductive people (i.e., people attending the methadone treatment program) are an "inherit threat" to the place itself becoming nonproductive (Smith, 2010). Qualitative research also suggests that stigma contributes to drug court and criminal justice system policies denying people with opioid use disorder access to evidence-based medications (Richard et al., 2020). Interviews with community members in the Appalachian region of Ohio showed that due to interventional stigma, most drug courts in the region did not allow access to medications for opioid use disorder until very recently and that this access was still heavily influenced by the stigmatizing attitudes held by individuals with decision-making power at the county or court levels (Richard et al., 2020).

Qualitative research with healthcare providers yields insights into this group's perspective on how stigma influences healthcare policy enactment and implementation. In one qualitative study, interviews with providers at syringe services programs across the United States suggested that these programs exist in an ever-evolving fragile policy environment (Jones, 2019). This study found that some syringe services programs were operating in states without explicit laws on the issue and were at the will of local regulation. Other syringe services programs were in states with explicit laws allowing them to operate but were still forced to get approval at the local level. Other states had laws explicitly prohibiting syringe services programs; in these states, the programs were forced to operate either entirely underground or with implicit agreements that local law enforcement would not take action against them (Jones, 2019). Other qualitative studies have shown inconsistencies in how pharmacy-level policies concerning the purchase of nonprescription syringes (Meyerson et al., 2019) and dispensing of buprenorphine for opioid use disorder (Cooper et al., 2020) were applied. Qualitative research has also demonstrated that some healthcare providers and pharmacists have high stigma toward and are apprehensive about the use of opioid-agonist medications to treat opioid use disorder, which limits delivery of these medications (Andraka-Christou & Capone, 2018; Cooper et al., 2020).

Strategies to Reduce Stigma and Increase Evidence-Based Policy Support, Enactment, and Implementation

The combination of the survey and qualitative studies discussed thus far demonstrate that stigmatizing attitudes can translate into a lack of evidence-based policies and/or potentially harmful policies at the public and institutional levels. Thus, reducing stigma is one critical component of increasing support for and enactment and implementation of effective policy at the public and institutional levels (Tsai et al., 2019). The most implemented strategy to reduce substance use–related stigma and/or influence support for substance use policies are public communication campaigns. A limited body of research shows that effective communication strategies can change stigmatizing attitudes related to substance use disorders and increase support for policies targeting this group (Bachhuber et al., 2015; Bandara et al., 2020; Goodyear & Chavanne, 2021; Kennedy-Hendricks, McGinty, & Barry, 2016; McGinty, Pescosolido, et al., 2018; McGinty et al., 2015; Romer & Bock, 2008; Tsai et al., 2019), but the specific strategies used are incredibly important because well-intentioned messages can sometimes inadvertently increase stigma and negatively influence policy attitudes (Iyengar, 1990, 1996; Pescosolido et al., 2010). For example, evidence suggests that the national campaign framing mental illness and substance use disorder as "Diseases Like Any Other" disseminated in the United States in the 1990s not only failed to have the intended stigma-reduction effect, by some measures it actually increased stigma, perhaps due to inadvertently increasing audiences' perceptions of the long-term, chronic nature of mental illness and substance use disorders (Mehta & Farina, 2011; Pescosolido et al., 2010; Schnittker, 2008). This cautionary tale highlights the importance of rigorous evaluation of communication strategies, ideally using experimental methods, before they are rolled out in large-scale communication campaigns designed to reduce stigma and increase support for policy (McGinty & Barry, 2020).

Effective messages with the correct "ingredients" have been shown in experimental studies to reduce stigma and increase support for evidence-based, public health–oriented policies. These critical "ingredients" include using person-centered language (Ashford et al., 2018; Kelly et al., 2016), for example, "person with a substance use disorder" as opposed to "substance abuser," and emphasizing the societal versus individual causes of addiction (Gross, 2008; Iyengar, 1990, 1996; Kelly et al., 2016; Kennedy-Hendricks, McGinty, & Barry, 2016; McGinty, Pescosolido, et al., 2018; Niederdeppe et al., 2012, 2014). Research has shown that sympathetic narratives combining a compelling narrative about an individual with substance use disorder with discussion of the societal factors contributing to or causing that individual's addiction can reduce stigma (Niederdeppe et al., 2012, 2014) and increase support for policies to address those societal factors, such as improving limited insurer coverage of substance use disorder treatment (Kennedy-Hendricks, McGinty, & Barry, 2016).

Importantly, evidence suggests that narratives need to be told from the perspective of an individual who resonates with the target audience (Kelly et al., 2016; Kennedy-Hendricks, McGinty, & Barry, 2016; Pescosolido et al., 2010). For example, it has been demonstrated that narratives depicting individuals with low versus high socioeconomic status result in different perceptions of blame for substance use disorder, with the high socioeconomic status leading to reduced perceptions of individual blame and increased perceptions of societal blame, as well as decreased support for punitive policies such as prosecuting a pregnant women addicted to opioid pain relievers on criminal child abuse charges (Kennedy-Hendricks, McGinty, & Barry, 2016). Additional studies have shown that negative attitudes and support for policies vary based on other narrative details like gender, race, the circumstances in which an individual developed a substance use disorder, and if an individual transitioned to drugs perceived as more serious (e.g., from cannabis to cocaine) during the course of their experience with substance use disorder (Gollust & Miller, 2020; Goodyear & Chavanne, 2021; Kennedy-Hendricks, McGinty, & Barry, 2016). One study found that a narrative depicting an individual with opioid use disorder who first used opioids prescribed by a doctor elicited lower stigma and higher support for expanding publicly funded substance use disorder treatment programs than an otherwise identical narrative depicting the individual as first using prescription opioids illicitly supplied by a friend (Goodyear & Chavanne, 2021). This finding highlights how stigma is influenced by the polarizing attitudes toward illicit substances. Additionally, one recent study suggests that messaging frames focusing on the social justice aspects of punitive policies may increase support for eliminating those policies. Specifically, a study by Bandara and colleagues showed that messaging frames that (1) emphasized the fact that in the United States there are major racial differences in criminalization of drug use, despite lack of racial differences in prevalence of drug use and (2) emphasized the adverse effects of punitive drug policies on the children of adults in recovery from substance use disorder increased support for a public policy banning required disclosure of a history of criminal justice system involvement on job applications ("ban the box" policies) (Bandara et al., 2020). The study also found that the messaging frame emphasizing racial differences in criminalization of drug use was also able to significantly increase support for a public policy eliminating mandatory minimum sentences for drug crimes (Bandara et al., 2020).

The evidence on which messages – delivered through which avenues, to which audiences – reduce substance use–related stigma and increase support for effective policies benefiting people who use substances and/or experience substance use disorders is very limited. Given the extremely low access to treatment among people with substance use disorder in the United States (Krawczyk et al., 2017; Mojtabai et al., 2019, 2020; Saloner et al., 2017, 2018), additional research focused on evaluating strategies to increase public and key stakeholder (e.g., healthcare provider, law enforcement) support for expanding evidence-based substance use disorder treatment is needed. Effective strategies need to overcome the widespread perception among the public that people with a substance use disorder have a high degree of control of their condition; in other words, that people can choose to start and stop using substances at will. As alluded to earlier in this chapter in the context of the "Disease Like Any Other" campaign (Pescosolido et al., 2010), some research suggests that messages emphasizing the neurobiological causes of substance use disorders alone may not decrease stigma. However, the evidence surrounding this point is stronger for mental health conditions than for substance use disorders, and some research suggests that biological attributions may be stigma-reducing in the context of substance use. One study found that biological causal explanations were associated with higher acceptance of people with alcohol dependence among a representative sample of German adults (Schomerus et al., 2014). In the same study, biological attributions were associated with lower social acceptance of people with schizophrenia and depression. It is possible that pairing messages about the biological causes of substance use disorder with messages about the effectiveness of treatment, which limited evidence suggests may reduce stigma, might bolster support for expanded treatment; future research should examine this question.

Communication strategies to increase support for harm reduction strategies are another critical area for future research. While policies ensuring first-responder and, in some jurisdictions, public access to the opioid overdose reversal agent naloxone have been widely implemented in the USA, syringe services programs are concentrated in urban areas, and no legally sanctioned overdose prevention sites, in which people can use preobtained drugs under medical supervision, have been implemented. Other nations, particularly Canada, have had more success implementing harm reduction strategies (Kerr et al., 2017). As noted above, lack of support for policies legalizing and funding harm reduction programs is driven by both stigma toward people who use substances and interventional stigma toward harm reduction interventions, stemming from opposition to the fact that harm reduction is designed to reduce the negative consequences of drug use without eliminating drug use itself. To date, one experimental study has provided limited clues about messages that may increase support for harm reduction approaches. Bachhuber and colleagues found that a sympathetic narrative about a young woman who died from a prescription opioid overdose – told from the perspective of her mother – paired with educational messages refuting common misconceptions about naloxone (e.g., that availability of naloxone encourages people to continue nonmedical use of opioids) raised public support for policies that would: train first responders to use naloxone; give family and friends of people at risk of opioid overdose access to naloxone; and pass state laws to (1) legally protect people who administer naloxone and (2) protect people from criminal charges if they call for medical help for an opioid overdose (Bachhuber et al., 2015). This study suggests that messages combining sympathetic narrative depictions of people who use substances and/or experience substance use disorder with educational messages that preemptively refute common misconceptions about harm reduction approaches might reduce the interventional stigma surrounding these approaches, but much more research is needed.

Public communication campaigns disseminating messages through avenues such as radio, television, and online public service announcements and billboards or bus banners are a common strategy to reduce stigma and increase support for and use of the services conferred by substance use disorder policies. However, such campaigns should not be considered the only – or, necessarily, the best – option. The types of effective messages discussed above can be embedded in a wide range of communication strategies beyond those typically used in communication campaigns, including news media editorials and legislative testimony. Ideally communication strategies shown in an experimental context to reduce stigma and increase support for policies benefiting people who use substances and/or experience substance use disorder should be implemented in tandem with other evidence-based interventions, such as the rollout of an addiction consulting service within a healthcare system or integrated delivery of buprenorphine treatment for opioid use disorder in primary care settings (McGinty & Barry, 2020). Adequately funded, well-implemented, evidence-based interventions that help people receive treatment for and recover from substance use disorder, as well as services that reduce the harms associated with substance use, are themselves stigma reduction tools. Meaningful contact with people who use substances, are in treatment for substance use disorder, and/or define themselves as being in recovery from substance use disorder *who are thriving in their lives* – fulfilling and enjoying family and professional roles, contributing to their communities, pursuing creative pursuits, etc. – reduces substance use-related stigma (Kerr et al., 2017; Livingston et al., 2012). It is likely that widespread adoption and rigorous implementation of interventions that help people who use substances and/or have substance use disorder to thrive will also reduce interventional stigma. Public and institutional policies play a critical role in supporting this type of widespread scale-up of effective public health-oriented strategies.

Conclusion

Stigmatizing attitudes toward people who use substances and/or experience substance use disorder and interventional stigma toward key public health interventions – medication treatment for opioid use disorder and harm reduction approaches – contribute to a lack of support for policies scaling up evidence-based approaches. Stigma also impacts implementation of policy, or lack thereof, by driving the degree to which implementation is allocated resources; the degree to which frontline implementers implement the policy as intended; and the degree to which the people targeted by the policy participate as intended. Finally, it is critical to remember that the relationship between stigma and policy is bidirectional. Stigma can influence whether policies are enacted and how they are implemented, but policies can also influence stigma. Punitive policies reinforce widely held stigmatizing attitudes derived from the idea that addiction is a moral failing and sign of deviance. Evidence-based, public health–oriented policies have the potential to reduce substance use–related stigma by helping people who use substances or have substance use disorder to thrive. To meaningfully reduce substance use stigma, we need members of the public to be able to readily identify positive examples of people benefiting from evidence-based substance use services. For the public to become saturated with examples of people thriving, public and institutional policies must shift to support widespread delivery of effective substance use interventions.

References

Abdul-Quader, A. S., Feelemyer, J., Modi, S., et al. (2013). Effectiveness of structural-level needle/syringe programs to reduce HCV and HIV infection among people who inject drugs: A systematic review. *AIDS and Behavior*, *17*(9), 2878–2892.

Allen, S. T., Grieb, S. M., O'Rourke, A., et al. (2019). Understanding the public health consequences of suspending a rural syringe services program: A qualitative study of the experiences of people who inject drugs. *Harm Reduction Journal*, *16*(1), Article 33.

Andraka-Christou, B., & Capone, M. J. (2018). A qualitative study comparing physician-reported barriers to treating addiction using buprenorphine and extended-release naltrexone in U.S. office-based practices. *International Journal of Drug Policy*, *54*, 9–17.

Ashford, R. D., Brown, A. M., & Curtis, B. (2018). Substance use, recovery, and linguistics: The impact of word choice on explicit and implicit bias. *Drug and Alcohol Dependence*, *189*, 131–138.

Bachhuber, M. A., McGinty, E. E., Kennedy-Hendricks, A., Niederdeppe, J., & Barry, C. L. (2015). Messaging to increase public support for naloxone distribution policies in the United States: Results from a randomized survey experiment. *PLOS ONE*, *10*(7), e0130050.

Bandara, S. N., McGinty, E. E., & Barry, C. L. (2020). Message framing to reduce stigma and increase support for policies to improve the wellbeing of people with prior drug convictions. *International Journal of Drug Policy*, *76*, Article 102643.

Barry, C. L. (2018). Fentanyl and the evolving opioid epidemic: What strategies should policy makers consider? *Psychiatric Services*, *69*(1), 100–103.

Barry, C. L., Kennedy-Hendricks, A., Gollust, S. E., et al. (2016). Understanding Americans' views on opioid pain reliever abuse. *Addiction*, *111*(1), 85–93.

Barry, C. L., & McGinty, E. E. (2014). Stigma and public support for parity and government spending on mental health: A 2013 National Opinion Survey. *Psychiatric Services*, *65*(10), 1265–1268.

Barry, C. L., McGinty, E. E., Pescosolido, B. A., & Goldman, H. H. (2014). Stigma, discrimination, treatment effectiveness, and policy: Public views about drug addiction and mental illness. *Psychiatric Services*, *65*(10), 1269–1272.

Beetham, T., Saloner, B., Wakeman, S. E., Gaye, M., & Barnett, M. L. (2019). Access to office-based buprenorphine treatment in areas with high rates of opioid-related mortality. *Annals of Internal Medicine*, *171*(1), 1–9.

Beletsky, L., Macalino, G. E., & Burris, S. (2005). Attitudes of police officers towards syringe access, occupational needle-sticks, and drug use: A qualitative study of one city police department in the United States. *International Journal of Drug Policy*, *16*(4), 267–274.

Bernstein, S. E., & Bennett, D. (2013). Zoned out: "NIMBYism", addiction services and municipal governance in British Columbia. *International Journal of Drug Policy*, *24*(6), e61–e65.

Bessen, S., Metcalf, S. A., Saunders, E. C., et al. (2019). Barriers to naloxone use and acceptance among opioid users, first responders, and emergency department providers in New Hampshire, USA. *International Journal of Drug Policy, 74,* 144–151.

Bornstein, M., Berger, A., & Gipson, J. D. (2020). A mixed methods study exploring methadone treatment disclosure and perceptions of reproductive health care among women ages 18–44 years, Los Angeles, CA. *Journal of Substance Abuse Treatment, 118,* Article 108119.

Burris, S., Beletsky, L., Castagna, C., & Coyle, C. (2009). Stopping an invisible epidemic: Legal issues in the provision of naloxone to prevent opioid overdose. *Drexel Law Review, 1,* 273–340.

Calabrese, C., & Bell, R. A. (2019). Opposition to nonprescription naloxone access: Measurement and psychosocial predictors. *Substance Use & Misuse, 54*(11), 1853–1861.

Cole, J. M. (2013). *Guidance regarding marijuana enforcement* [Memorandum]. United States Department of Justice, Office of the Deputy Attorney General. www.justice.gov/iso/opa/resources/3052013829132756857467.pdf

Cooper, H. L., Cloud, D. H., Freeman, P. R., et al. (2020). Buprenorphine dispensing in an epicenter of the U.S. opioid epidemic: A case study of the rural risk environment in Appalachian Kentucky. *International Journal of Drug Policy, 85,* Article 102701.

Corrigan, P. W., Kuwabara, S. A., & O'Shaughnessy, J. (2009). The public stigma of mental illness and drug addiction. *Journal of Social Work, 9*(2), 139–147.

Corrigan, P. W., & Nieweglowski, K. (2018). Stigma and the public health agenda for the opioid crisis in America. *International Journal of Drug Policy, 59,* 44–49.

Crandall, C. S., Eshleman, A., & O'Brien, L. (2002). Social norms and the expression and suppression of prejudice: The struggle for internalization. *Journal of Personality and Social Psychology, 82*(3), 359–378.

Crotty, K., Freedman, K. I., & Kampman, K. M. (2020). Executive summary of the focused update of the ASAM national practice guideline for the treatment of opioid use disorder. *Journal of Addiction Medicine, 14*(2), 99–112.

Cruz, M. F., Patra, J., Fischer, B., Rehm, J., & Kalousek, K. (2007). Public opinion towards supervised injection facilities and heroin-assisted treatment in Ontario, Canada. *International Journal of Drug Policy, 18*(1), 54–61.

Ellis, K., Walters, S., Friedman, S. R., et al. (2020). Breaching trust: A qualitative study of healthcare experiences of people who use drugs in a rural setting. *Frontiers in Sociology, 5.*

Fiscella, K., Wakeman, S. E., & Beletsky, L. (2019). Buprenorphine deregulation and mainstreaming treatment for opioid use disorder. *JAMA Psychiatry, 76*(3), 229–230.

Gollust, S. E., & Miller, J. M. (2020). Framing the opioid crisis: Do racial frames shape beliefs of whites losing ground? *Journal of Health Politics, Policy and Law, 45*(2), 241–276.

Goodyear, K., & Chavanne, D. (2021). Stigma and policy preference toward individuals who transition from prescription opioids to heroin. *Addictive Behaviors, 115*, Article 106784.

Green, T. C., Zaller, N., Palacios, W. R., et al. (2013). Law enforcement attitudes toward overdose prevention and response. *Drug and Alcohol Dependence, 133*(2), 677–684.

Gross, K. (2008). Framing persuasive appeals: Episodic and thematic framing, emotional response, and policy opinion. *Political Psychology, 29*(2), 169–192.

Harris, J., & McElrath, K. (2012). Methadone as social control. *Qualitative Health Research, 22*(6), 810–824.

Hatzenbuehler, M. L. (2016). Structural stigma: Research evidence and implications for psychological science. *American Psychological, 71*(8), 742–751.

Iyengar, S. (1990). Framing responsibility for political issues: The case of poverty. *Political Behavior, 12*(1), 19–40.

(1996). Framing responsibility for political issues. *The ANNALS of the American Academy of Political and Social Science, 546*(1), 59–70.

Jauffret-Roustide, M., Pedrono, G., & Beltzer, N. (2013). Supervised consumption rooms: The French Paradox. *International Journal of Drug Policy, 24*(6), 628–630.

Jones, C. M. (2019). Syringe services programs: An examination of legal, policy, and funding barriers in the midst of the evolving opioid crisis in the U.S. *International Journal of Drug Policy, 70*, 22–32.

Kelly, J. F., Saitz, R., & Wakeman, S. (2016). Language, substance use disorders, and policy: The need to reach consensus on an "addiction-ary". *Alcoholism Treatment Quarterly, 34*(1), 116–123.

Kennedy, M. C., Karamouzian, M., & Kerr, T. (2017). Public health and public order outcomes associated with supervised drug consumption facilities: A systematic review. *Current HIV/AIDS Reports, 14*(5), 161–183.

Kennedy-Hendricks, A., Barry, C. L., Gollust, S. E., Ensminger, M. E., Chisolm, M. S., & McGinty, E. E. (2017). Social stigma toward persons with prescription opioid use disorder: Associations with public support for punitive and public health–oriented policies. *Psychiatric Services, 68*(5), 462–469.

Kennedy-Hendricks, A., Barry, C. L., Stone, E., Bachhuber, M. A., & McGinty, E. E. (2020). Comparing perspectives on medication treatment for opioid use disorder between national samples of primary care trainee physicians and attending physicians. *Drug and Alcohol Dependence, 216*, Article 108217.

Kennedy-Hendricks, A., Busch, S. H., McGinty, E. E., et al. (2016). Primary care physicians' perspectives on the prescription opioid epidemic. *Drug and Alcohol Dependence, 165*, 61–70.

Kennedy-Hendricks, A., McGinty, E. E., & Barry, C. L. (2016). Effects of competing narratives on public perceptions of opioid pain reliever addiction during pregnancy. *Journal of Health Politics, Policy and Law, 41*(5), 873–916.

Kerr, T., Mitra, S., Kennedy, M. C., & McNeil, R. (2017). Supervised injection facilities in Canada: Past, present, and future. *Harm Reduction Journal, 14*(1), Article 28.

Knopf, A. (2019). ASAM supports eliminating the x-waiver for buprenorphine. *Alcoholism & Drug Abuse Weekly*, *31*(29), 6–7.

Krawczyk, N., Picher, C. E., Feder, K. A., & Saloner, B. (2017). Only one in twenty justice-referred adults in specialty treatment for opioid use receive methadone or buprenorphine. *Health Affairs*, *36*(12), 2046–2053.

Kruis, N. E., & Merlo, A. V. (2020). A preliminary assessment of stigma in law enforcement officers' responses to opioid overdoses. *Journal of Drug Issues*, *51*(2), 301–322.

Kulesza, M., Teachman, B. A., Werntz, A. J., Gasser, M. L., & Lindgren, K. P. (2015). Correlates of public support toward federal funding for harm reduction strategies. *Substance Abuse Treatment, Prevention, and Policy*, *10*(1), Article 25.

Lancaster, K., Santana, L., Madden, A., & Ritter, A. (2015). Stigma and subjectivities: Examining the textured relationship between lived experience and opinions about drug policy among people who inject drugs. *Drugs: Education, Prevention and Policy*, *22*(3), 224–231.

Link, B. G., Phelan, J. C., Bresnahan, M., Stueve, A., & Pescosolido, B. A. (1999). Public conceptions of mental illness: Labels, causes, dangerousness, and social distance. *American Journal of Public Health*, *89*(9), 1328–1333.

Livingston, J. D., Milne, T., Fang, M. L., & Amari, E. (2012). The effectiveness of interventions for reducing stigma related to substance use disorders: A systematic review. *Addiction*, *107*(1), 39–50.

Luoma, J. B., Twohig, M. P., Waltz, T., et al. (2007). An investigation of stigma in individuals receiving treatment for substance abuse. *Addictive Behaviors*, *32*(7), 1331–1346.

Madden, E. F. (2019). Intervention stigma: How medication-assisted treatment marginalizes patients and providers. *Social Science & Medicine*, *232*, 324–331.

Marino, R., Perrone, J., Nelson, L. S., et al. (2019). ACMT position statement: Remove the waiver requirement for prescribing buprenorphine for opioid use disorder. *Journal of Medical Toxicology*, *15*(4), 307–309.

Matheson, C., Jaffray, M., Ryan, M., et al. (2014). Public opinion of drug treatment policy: Exploring the public's attitudes, knowledge, experience and willingness to pay for drug treatment strategies. *International Journal of Drug Policy*, *25*(3), 407–415.

McGinty, E., & Barry, C. L. (2020). Stigma reduction to combat the addiction crisis – developing an evidence base. *New England Journal of Medicine*, *382*(14), 1291–1292.

McGinty, E., Barry, C. L., Stone, E. M., et al. (2018). Public support for safe consumption sites and syringe services programs to combat the opioid epidemic. *Preventive Medicine*, *111*, 73–77.

McGinty, E., Goldman, H. H., Pescosolido, B., & Barry, C. L. (2015). Portraying mental illness and drug addiction as treatable health conditions: Effects of a randomized experiment on stigma and discrimination. *Social Science & Medicine*, *126*, 73–85.

McGinty, E., Pescosolido, B., Kennedy-Hendricks, A., & Barry, C. L. (2018). Communication strategies to counter stigma and improve mental illness and substance use disorder policy. *Psychiatric Services, 69*(2), 136–146.

McNeely, J., Kumar, P. C., Rieckmann, T., et al. (2018). Barriers and facilitators affecting the implementation of substance use screening in primary care clinics: A qualitative study of patients, providers, and staff. *Addiction Science & Clinical Practice, 13*(1), Article 8.

McNeil, R., & Small, W. (2014). 'Safer environment interventions': A qualitative synthesis of the experiences and perceptions of people who inject drugs. *Social Science & Medicine, 106*, 151–158.

Mehta, S., & Farina, A. (2011). Is being "sick" really better? Effect of the disease view of mental disorder on stigma. *Journal of Social and Clinical Psychology, 16*(4), 405–419.

Mendiola, C. K., Galetto, G., & Fingerhood, M. (2018). An exploration of emergency physicians' attitudes toward patients with substance use disorder. *Journal of Addiction Medicine, 12*(2), 132–135.

Meyerson, B. E., Lawrence, C. A., Cope, S. D., et al. (2019). I could take the judgment if you could just provide the service: Non-prescription syringe purchase experience at Arizona pharmacies, 2018. *Harm Reduction Journal, 16*(1), Article 57.

Mojtabai, R., Mauro, C., Wall, M. M., Barry, C. L., & Olfson, M. (2019). Medication treatment for opioid use disorders in substance use treatment facilities. *Health Affairs, 38*(1), 14–23.

(2020). Private health insurance coverage of drug use disorder treatment: 2005–2018. *PLOS ONE, 15*(10), e0240298.

Murphy, J., & Russell, B. (2020). Police officers' views of naloxone and drug treatment: Does greater overdose response lead to more negativity? *Journal of Drug Issues, 50*(4), 455–471.

National Academies of Sciences, Education, and Medicine [NASEM]. (2019). *Medications for opioid use disorder save lives.* Washington, DC: The National Academies Press.

National Conference of State Legislatures. (2021). *State medical marijuana laws.* Retrieved February 24, 2021 from www.ncsl.org/research/health/state-medical-marijuana-laws.aspx

Niederdeppe, J., Kim, H. K., Lundell, H., Fazili, F., & Frazier, B. (2012). Beyond counterarguing: Simple elaboration, complex integration, and counterelaboration in response to variations in narrative focus and sidedness. *Journal of Communication, 62*(5), 758–777.

Niederdeppe, J., Shapiro, M. A., Kim, H. K., Bartolo, D., & Porticella, N. (2014). Narrative persuasion, causality, complex integration, and support for obesity policy. *Health Communication, 29*(5), 431–444.

Olsen, Y., & Sharfstein, J. M. (2014). Confronting the stigma of opioid use disorder – and its treatment. *JAMA, 311*(14), 1393–1394.

Pescosolido, B. A., & Martin, J. K. (2015). The stigma complex. *Annual Review of Sociology, 41*(1), 87–116.

Pescosolido, B. A., Martin, J. K., Long, J. S., Medina, T. R., Phelan, J. C., & Link, B. G. (2010). "A disease like any other"? A decade of change in public reactions to schizophrenia, depression, and alcohol dependence. *American Journal of Psychiatry*, *167*(11), 1321–1330.

Pollack Porter, K. M., Rutkow, L., & McGinty, E. E. (2018). The importance of policy change for addressing public health problems. *Public Health Reports*, *133*(1_suppl), 9S–14S.

Richard, E. L., Schalkoff, C. A., Piscalko, H. M., et al. (2020). "You are not clean until you're not on anything": Perceptions of medication-assisted treatment in rural Appalachia. *International Journal of Drug Policy*, *85*, Article 102704.

Romer, D., & Bock, M. (2008). Reducing the stigma of mental illness among adolescents and young adults: The effects of treatment information. *Journal of Health Communication*, *13*(8), 742–758.

Rutkow, L., Smith, K. C., Lai, A. Y., Vernick, J. S., Davis, C. S., & Alexander, G. C. (2017). Prescription drug monitoring program design and function: A qualitative analysis. *Drug and Alcohol Dependence*, *180*, 395–400.

Saloner, B., Bandara, S., Bachhuber, M., & Barry, C. L. (2017). Insurance coverage and treatment use under the Affordable Care Act among adults with mental and substance use disorders. *Psychiatric Services*, *68*(6), 542–548.

Saloner, B., Stoller, K. B., & Alexander, G. C. (2018). Moving addiction care to the mainstream – improving the quality of buprenorphine treatment. *New England Journal of Medicine*, *379*(1), 4–6.

Samet, J. H., Botticelli, M., & Bharel, M. (2018). Methadone in primary care – one small step for Congress, one giant leap for addiction treatment. *New England Journal of Medicine*, *379*(1), 7–8.

Schneider, A., & Ingram, H. (1993). Social construction of target populations: Implications for politics and policy. *American Political Science Review*, *87*(2), 334–347.

Schnittker, J. (2008). An uncertain revolution: Why the rise of a genetic model of mental illness has not increased tolerance. *Social Science & Medicine*, *67*(9), 1370–1381.

Schomerus, G., Matschinger, H., & Angermeyer, M. C. (2006). Alcoholism: Illness beliefs and resource allocation preferences of the public. *Drug and Alcohol Dependence*, *82*, 204–210.

(2014). Casual beliefs of the public and social acceptance of persons with mental illness: A comparative analysis of schizophrenia, depression, and alcohol dependence. *Psychological Medicine*, *44*, 303–314.

Skinner, N., Feather, N. T., Freeman, T., & Roche, A. (2007). Stigma and discrimination in health-care provision to drug users: The role of values, affect, and deservingness judgments. *Journal of Applied Social Psychology*, *37*(1), 163–186.

Smith, C. B. R. (2010). Socio-spatial stigmatization and the contested space of addiction treatment: Remapping strategies of opposition to the disorder of drugs. *Social Science & Medicine*, *70*(6), 859–866.

Stein, B. D., Sorbero, M., Dick, A. W., Pacula, R. L., Burns, R. M., & Gordon, A. J. (2016). Physician capacity to treat opioid use disorder with buprenorphine-assisted treatment. *JAMA*, *316*(11), 1211–1212.

Stone, E. M., Kennedy-Hendricks, A., Barry, C. L., Bachhuber, M. A., & McGinty, E. E. (2021). The role of stigma in U.S. primary care physicians' treatment of opioid use disorder. *Drug and Alcohol Dependence*, *221*, Article 108627.

Stone, E. M., Rutkow, L., Bicket, M. C., Barry, C. L., Alexander, G. C., & McGinty, E. E. (2020). Implementation and enforcement of state opioid prescribing laws. *Drug and Alcohol Dependence*, *213*, Article 108107.

Strike, C., & Miskovic, M. (2017). Zoning out methadone and rising opioid-related deaths in Ontario: Reforms and municipal government actions. *Canadian Journal of Public Health*, *108*(2), e205–e207.

Substance Abuse and Mental Health Services Administration [SAMHSA] (2020). *Medications for opioid use disorder. Treatment improvement protocol (TIP) series No. 63* (Publication No. PEP20-02-01-006). https://store.samhsa.gov/product/TIP-63-Medications-for-Opioid-Use-Disorder-Full-Document/PEP20-02-01-006

Terplan, M., Kennedy-Hendricks, A., & Chisolm, M. S. (2015). Article commentary: Prenatal substance use: Exploring assumptions of maternal unfitness. *Substance Abuse: Research and Treatment*, *9s2*, Article SART.S23328.

Thomas, S., Treffers, R., Berglas, N. F., Drabble, L., & Roberts, S. C. M. (2018). Drug use during pregnancy policies in the United States from 1970 to 2016. *Contemporary Drug Problems*, *45*(4), 441–459.

Tsai, A. C., Kiang, M. V., Barnett, M. L., et al. (2019). Stigma as a fundamental hindrance to the United States opioid overdose crisis response. *PLOS Medicine*, *16*(11), e1002969.

Van Boekel, L. C., Brouwers, E. P. M., Van Weeghel, J., & Garretsen, H. F. L. (2013). Stigma among health professionals towards patients with substance use disorders and its consequences for healthcare delivery: Systematic review. *Drug and Alcohol Dependence*, *131*(1–2), 23–35.

Volkow, N. D., Frieden, T. R., Hyde, P. S., & Cha, S. S. (2014). Medication-assisted therapies – tackling the opioid-overdose epidemic. *New England Journal of Medicine*, *370*(22), 2063–2066.

Wakeman, S. E., & Rich, J. D. (2018). Barriers to medications for addiction treatment: How stigma kills. *Substance Use & Misuse*, *53*(2), 330–333.

Woo, J., Bhalerao, A., Bawor, M., et al. (2017). "Don't judge a book by its cover": A qualitative study of methadone patients' experiences of stigma. *Substance Abuse: Research and Treatment*, *11*(0), Article 1178221816668508.

Woodruff, A. E., Tomanovich, M., Beletsky, L., Salisbury-Afshar, E., Wakeman, S., & Ostrovsky, A. (2019). *Dismantling buprenorphine policy can provide more comprehensive addiction treatment*. NAM Perspectives. https://nam.edu/dismantling-buprenorphine-policy-can-provide-more-comprehensive-addiction-treatment/

Yarborough, B. J. H., Stumbo, S. P., McCarty, D., Mertens, J., Weisner, C., & Green, C. A. (2016). Methadone, buprenorphine and preferences for opioid agonist treatment: A qualitative analysis. *Drug and Alcohol Dependence, 160,* 112–118.

Yuanhong Lai, A., Smith, K. C., Vernick, J. S., Davis, C. S., Caleb Alexander, G., & Rutkow, L. (2019). Perceived unintended consequences of prescription drug monitoring programs. *Substance Use & Misuse, 54*(2), 345–349.

CHAPTER 4

Experiences of Stigma and Criminal In/Justice among People Who Use Substances

Jamie Livingston, Matthew Bonn, Peter Brown, Steven Deveau, and Anne-Marie Houston

Introduction

Stigma is a vehicle for power that is produced and sustained by the practices and policies of social institutions, including the criminal justice system. People who use substances experience significant issues because of the criminalization of substances. They are criminalized, medicalized, institutionalized, politicized, and ascribed with dehumanizing and disempowering labels rendering them voiceless and powerless. They are socially devalued, rejected, shamed, and excluded because of their substance use. They are often channeled into the criminal justice system, which worsens stigma and diminishes life chances. Increasingly, governments are recognizing the limits of punitive and deterrence-based approaches for addressing substance use, including the serious harms produced by criminalization and stigmatization. This has motivated jurisdictions across the globe, such as Canada, to search for alternatives that prioritize a public health approach to substance use and weaken the criminal justice system's grasp on people who use substances (International Network of People who Use Drugs, 2021; Stevens et al., 2019). In this chapter, we explore the harms created by stigma at the intersection of substance use and criminal justice.

The authors have known each other for several years through their membership in the 7th Step Society of Nova Scotia. The 7th Step Society is a peer support group for people who have experienced criminal justice involvement and are working toward building productive, meaningful, and responsible lives that are free from criminal behavior and the criminal justice system. Most members of the 7th Step Society live with intersecting substance use and criminal justice issues. Matthew, Peter, Steven, and Anne-Marie (the collective "we") are people with lived and

---

The views expressed in this chapter represent those of the individual authors and not views of the organizations to which they are affiliated.

living experiences of substance use issues, repeated criminal justice involvement, criminal desistance, and finding a new way of life. This includes experiencing several short stays in jail, some long stretches in prison, and many community sentences (e.g., probation). Such experiences – combined with their jobs providing peer support, street outreach, harm reduction, and drug policy advocacy – give rich insight into how substance use stigma is expressed at various levels (e.g., self, social, and structural) and intersects with other forms of oppression. Jamie contributes to the 7th Step Society as a community volunteer, which includes offering friendship, support, guidance, and opportunities to members who have experienced criminal justice involvement.

We offer our firsthand experiences to describe how stigma related to substance use and criminal justice issues has shaped our lives. We have lost loved ones from drug poisoning and overdose fueled by substance use stigma. We have had our freedom and liberty taken away from cycling in and out of the criminal justice system, often because of issues related to substances. We have had our health compromised and our lives jeopardized by poor access to services and supports. We have had our self-worth eroded by negative labels (e.g., junkie, drug abuser, drug seeker, and offender), internalized stigma, and social exclusion. Further, our life chances and moral standing have been diminished by criminal convictions and incarcerations. We also have worked hard at staying alive, rebuilding our lives, restoring our social standing, and repairing harms by giving back to our communities.

This chapter builds on the conversations between the authors on the topic of substance use stigma and the criminal justice system. It reflects subjects and issues that we believe are important to highlight. We reflect on intersectional stigma experienced because of having co-occurring health conditions (e.g., mental illness, injective-related infection, HIV, and Hepatitis C), receiving specific treatments (e.g., opioid agonist treatment), consuming certain types of substances (e.g., opioids, methamphetamine), and using substances in particular ways (e.g., intravenous). We also draw from the literature to situate our own experiences in the broader social and international context. Our own experiences are primarily that of cisgender, white European settlers in Canada; therefore, we must acknowledge at the outset that the effects of stigma associated with substance use and criminal justice involvement are amplified by racism, sexism, colonialism, LGBTQ2+ phobia,[1] and other forms of oppression. Additionally, we recognize that the practices and policies of criminal justice systems vary

---

[1] An acronym for lesbian, gay, bisexual, transgender, queer or questioning, two-spirit, and other sexual and gender identities.

in ways that affect the experiences of people who use substances (Sander et al., 2016). Therefore, it is likely that different systems produce distinctive forms and varying levels of substance use stigma. Even within Canada, substance use–related policies and programs (e.g., opioid agonist treatment, sterile drug-using supplies) fluctuate considerably between criminal justice institutions and systems, which limits the generalizability of our personal experiences and observations.

We begin the chapter with a discussion of how stigma creates a social context that channels people who use substances into the criminal justice system. We then explore how substance use stigma is experienced within, and produced by, the criminal justice system and is sustained afterward. We end the chapter by highlighting a range of approaches for reducing stigma at the intersection of substance use and criminal justice.

Stigma Promotes Criminal Justice Involvement

The rate of substance use disorders is high among people in the criminal justice system. Interactions with the police and experiences of incarceration are common among people who use substances (Hughes et al., 2018). Worldwide, it is estimated that at any given time almost half a million people are incarcerated for drug use and possession only, while more than two million people are incarcerated or involuntarily confined for drug-related reasons (Chang et al., 2020). In Canada, half of men entering federal prison have a current substance use disorder and two-thirds have lifetime rates of substance use disorders (Beaudette & Stewart, 2016). The rate of substance use disorders is higher among incarcerated women and Indigenous people in Canada (Derkzen et al., 2017).

A mutually reinforcing relationship exists between substances and crime. Psychopharmacological factors (e.g., impaired cognition), economic factors (e.g., drug-related acquisitive crime), and systemic factors (e.g., illegal drug markets) push people who use substances into lifestyles, situations, and contexts conducive to criminal behavior (Goldstein, 1985). Furthermore, systemic racism promoted by drug laws and enforcement practices criminalize Black, Indigenous, and other racialized people – leading to their gross overrepresentation in the criminal justice system (Maynard, 2017). Stigma is both a cause and effect of criminal justice involvement for people who use substances. It is the inequitable social, political, cultural, and economic glue that binds substances together with crime. Below, we explore how these factors promote criminal justice involvement of people who use substances by highlighting the role that stigma plays in inequitable social conditions, criminalization of substance use, and inadequate funding of substance use services.

Inequitable Social Conditions

Inequitable social conditions increase the likelihood that people who use substances will interact with the criminal justice system; as Rolando et al. (2020) explains: "the link between drug use and offending behaviour cannot be understood without setting it in a context of socio-economic disadvantage" (p. 13). The risk of both substance use disorders and criminal behavior are elevated by the presence of similar experiences such as poverty, childhood neglect and abuse, family dysfunction, domestic violence, familial substance use disorders, antisocial peer relationships, and school difficulties (Whitesell et al., 2013). Stigma weaves its way into the lives of people who use substances through such experiences and inequities.

Anne-Marie, who became involved in organized crime at a young age, traces her experiences all the way back to withdrawing from heroin at birth and then being raised, alongside nine siblings, by parents who sold drugs and struggled with their own issues related to substance use. Peter discusses growing up with a father who sold drugs and was incarcerated: "I watched my father go in and out of prison. I watch him deal with the courts. And, as soon as I turned 18, I was involved with the system – in and out, in and out." Peter started using substances at 13 years of age to cope with traumatic childhood experiences: "Once I started using substances, I found that escape and I was instantly addicted – I just wanted more." Matthew, who drifted into drug use, drug selling, and other mischievous behavior in his teens, observed family members engaging in criminal behavior and interacting with the criminal justice system: "My dad was in trouble and sold dope. He was known to the police. My uncle was incarcerated for a period of time. My stepmom's family were in and out of jail their whole lives." He talks about carrying the lifelong shame caused by social stigma surrounding his, and his family's, substance use: "I know what it's like to be looked at as the drug user. I've experienced that my whole life." Steven, whose first contact with the criminal justice system was when he was 8 years old, describes growing up in an impoverished neighborhood where violence and criminal justice involvement were normalized:

> When you grow up with a single mom and you're the working poor, you're already wearing a stigma and a label from that. And, once you come in contact with the formal system – whether that's through the justice system

or social services or Child Protection Services – then there is another label and a stigma that's put onto you. Where I grew up, alcohol, drugs, and dysfunction were normal.

Steven further describes how the police "targeted me and put me on their list" because of his connection to a marginalized community.

These accounts reveal how the effects of substance use stigma intersect with other forms of exclusion and inequity, taking root in early life and spanning generations. Across multiple life domains, people who use substances face significant barriers to life chances, and discrimination impedes their access to legitimate opportunities (e.g., legal employment). Poverty, unemployment, housing issues, inadequate education, food and income insecurity, stressful life events, and unsafe neighborhoods increase the likelihood that people who use substances will experience routine and recurrent criminal justice involvement.

Criminalization of Substances

The criminalization of substance use and associated activities (e.g., possessing, selling) is a potent source of stigma (Buchman et al., 2017), as Matthew states succinctly: "Criminalization is what fuels the stigma." Prohibition and criminalization operate on the principle that the law can be used to deter people from using substances, thereby preventing potential moral risks, social harms, and health hazards (Room, 2005). However, prohibition laws and drug enforcement efforts have produced substantial health and social harms concentrated in poor, racialized, Indigenous, and disabled communities (Khenti, 2014). Fischer (2020) characterizes drug laws, and resulting labeling and criminalization processes, as a form of structural stigma: "There is no more powerful and impactful social tool to create, and project stigma on a structural level, and its direct and indirect adverse consequences, than through criminalizing a specific behavior and the people such criminalization identifies and targets" (p. 3).

Laws and policies socially construct people who use substances as criminals, which justifies their stigmatization and legally enshrines arbitrary restrictions on their rights and opportunities, making it permissible to discriminate against them (Tsai et al., 2019). Matthew confirms these routine experiences of overt discrimination: "People who use drugs experience blatant, open stigma all the time – really they're experiencing the discrimination because drugs are criminalized." Refusing to hire someone with a criminal record or denying them an apartment are socially acceptable ways to arbitrarily discriminate against, and deny opportunities to people who use substances. Additionally, the criminalization of people who use substances normalizes their involvement with criminal justice agents (e.g., police) and institutions (e.g., prison), which Matthew describes: "By controlling substances and criminalizing the people who use them, they become so stigmatized that it becomes so easy for the system to scoop up lots and lots of people. I don't know too many drug users that haven't ended up in jail."

Criminalization, and the resulting stigma, produces secrecy among people who use substances. Possessing, using, and selling certain substances is illegal, so people engage in such activities with a great deal of secrecy, as Matthew reflects: "They're illegal, so you have to hide to do them. You can't do them around other people because you'd go to jail. It isn't allowed; you become an outcast." Being outcasted diminishes people's self-worth, alters their self-identity, and increases internalized stigma (Radcliffe & Stevens, 2008). Matthew reflects on his own experiences with internalized stigma: "I was battling internalized stigma around drug use – that I shouldn't be doing it and that it was morally wrong. And that was because of the structural and social stigma that I experienced. I started to believe it myself." The separation of "us" from "them" also shapes a person's social network, attachments, and relationships in ways that deepen and stabilize their marginalization, as Matthew discusses: "Stigma really plays with your reality and your concept of honesty. You have to hide it [drug use] from the people you love. And, share it with people who probably don't have your best interest at heart." Secrecy, avoidance, and exclusion from conventional society increases a person's exposure risk factors (e.g., unemployment, criminal peers) conducive to risky and criminal behavior, as Matthew explains: "There's that structural stigma against drug users that forces people away from traditional healthcare, forces us to use alone and not to reach out for help." Therefore, the social processes (e.g., criminalization) and institutions (e.g., criminal justice) created to control substance use and crime may, in fact, contribute to their continuance.

Underfunding of Substance Use Services

Structural stigma is expressed through the chronic and severe underfunding of substance use services (Livingston, 2020). The inequitable allocation of resources results in delayed care, poor quality of care, and dissatisfaction with services, thereby acting as a powerful deterrent for seeking help and accessing care (Clement et al., 2015). Steven notes that the substance use service system "has always been underfunded" causing long waitlists, restricting treatment options, and preventing people from accessing on-demand supports when they need them most. Stigma creates a social context (e.g., devaluing, underfunding, and deprioritizing) that tolerates substandard care and inhibits the provision of evidence-based treatment and harm reduction services. People who use substances experience stigmatizing interactions, such as disrespectful treatment or being denied services, by healthcare practitioners in primary care clinics, hospitals, emergency rooms, and pharmacies (Livingston, 2020). Peter reflects on the stigma faced by people who use substances in healthcare settings: "It runs so deep. The pharmacists, the doctors, and the nurses have no compassion for people using drugs. I hear that story over and over." This, in turn, contributes to the underdiagnosis and undertreatment of substance use disorders and other health conditions, which delays recovery, increases morbidity and mortality, and propels people who use substances into the criminal justice system.

Despite limited evidence about their effectiveness (Werb et al., 2016), support is high among the public for using coercive approaches to manage people who use substances, which is spurred on by the widespread endorsement of negative stereotypes and punitive attitudes toward substance use. Deficiencies in the social welfare and healthcare systems expose people who use substances to coercive and criminalized forms of care that curtail their rights and liberties and ensnare them in the criminal justice system. Steven references this issue when discussing the new courthouse recently built in his hometown: "They built this brand-new beautiful building with beautiful grounds – the new courthouse. That way, we don't have to walk as far to get convicted and sentenced. There's no rehabilitation centre, but there's a multimillion-dollar courthouse." For Steven, the courthouse signals society's willingness to invest in criminal justice approaches, rather than health care, to address issues related to substance use. Moreover, the courthouse's placement in a marginalized community facilitates (i.e., "we don't have to walk as far") the criminalization of poor and racialized people who use substances.

A concerning trend is the growth of hybridized health–justice interventions, such as drug treatment courts and involuntary residential treatment, to address problems caused by social inequities and underfunded substance use service systems. These programs incorporate criminal justice processes (e.g., arrest, criminal charges, and convictions), agents (e.g., police, judges, and probation officers), tools (e.g., treatment contracts and court orders), and surveillance strategies (e.g., electronic monitoring and urine screening) into the substance use service system. Their aim is to divert people from punishment (e.g., incarceration) by supplying access to treatment. However, using the criminal justice apparatus to facilitate access to services (e.g., counseling) and supports (e.g., housing) may widen and deepen the net of criminalization by making it easier to impose coercive practices, involuntary care, and punitive sanctions (e.g., for noncompliance or relapse) onto people who use substances (Burns & Peyrot, 2014). Matthew reflects on his reaction to being offered entry into a drug treatment court program after being denied entry to a diversion program after multiple fentanyl-related arrests: "They offered me drug treatment court and I said 'are you nuts!' I'd rather do four months of house arrest than go on surveillance and urine testing for two or three years." Using components of the criminal justice system as gateways to coercive forms of healthcare services, including police-based diversion programs or drug treatment courts, can worsen the stigmatization of people who use substances.

Stigma Occurs within the Criminal Justice System

The criminal justice system is a major contributor to substance use stigma. Its policies and practices reproduce and reinforce negative stereotypes, social inequities, and injustices causing significant harm to people who use substances. In the criminal justice context, substance use is redefined as a threat to public safety, which shapes how people who use substances are treated and managed. Substance use is routinely assessed and monitored by criminal justice professionals due to its criminalized status and its association with criminal behavior. Approaching substance use through a risk management lens, rather than a health lens, contributes to people who use substances being treated in ways that they experience as nontherapeutic, coercive, punitive, and stigmatizing. Below, we examine how the criminal justice system contributes to substance use stigma through negative police interactions, adverse experiences during incarceration, and inadequate support of people reentering the community following their incarceration.

Policing People Who Use Substances

People who use substances are at increased risk of police interactions, especially for people who are Black or Indigenous, young, poor, homeless, or sex workers (Alberton et al., 2019). Frequent encounters between the police and people who use substances stems from the expansive role assigned to the police for enforcing drug laws, managing social disorder, mitigating substance-related harms (e.g., impaired driving, gang violence), controlling crime, responding to emergency situations (e.g., overdose calls), and enforcing traffic laws. Structural stigma and criminalization processes also contribute to the high rates of police interactions involving people who use substances.

Police practices influence the well-being of people who use substances and are, therefore, considered structural determinants of health (Beletsky et al., 2015). Police interactions can have a positive effect on people who use substances (Hughes et al., 2018) – as Matthew recalls about his recent interactions:

> The two times I've dealt with police in the past year have been when I overdosed and when I responded to an overdose. In both of those times, I was not stigmatized at all by the police officers. I was given privacy and the ability to get my own stuff [drugs]. I left with the drugs that I had. They never searched me. That's not your everyday occurrence.

Matthew further explains, "I've also had really bad experiences with cops as well. I was never abused by them but that's probably my [white] privilege." Mistrust of, and mistreatment by, the police are particularly problematic for racialized, Indigenous, and immigrant communities (Maynard, 2017). Police practices can be harmful and stigmatizing for people who use substances (Collins et al., 2019), as Anne-Marie discusses: "If you're an addict, you're the low of the low. And, the police have no problem calling you a junkie and making you feel worse about yourself than you already do."

Stigmatizing attitudes held by police officers toward people who use substances combined with their wide discretion in handling situations contribute to harmful police practices (Jorgensen, 2018). People who use substances experience arbitrary, degrading, disempowering, and humiliating encounters with the police, which they attribute to being labeled and stigmatized as an "addict" or a "junkie." Repressive police practices include intensive surveillance, harassment, searches (e.g., stop and frisk), confiscation of drugs and drug paraphernalia, neighborhood sweeps, forceful displacement (e.g., while sleeping outside), threats of punitive sanctions (e.g., arrest, fines, or detainment), verbal abuse, and physical violence (McNeil & Small, 2014). Such police practices deter people who use substances from accessing and using health care and harm reduction services (Goldenberg et al., 2020). Peter, who works at a community center that provides opioid agonist treatment, describes the negative effect on his clients: "The police will sit outside the dispensary and watch for people with warrants [for arrest]. It's like shooting fish in a barrel. A lot of our clients have been criminally active, so, when they see the police, they're gone. It throws people off their treatment and then they go into withdrawal." Such police practices can prevent people from using substances safely, thereby increasing the risk of overdose, infectious disease transmission, and death (Baker et al., 2020). Additionally, police practices, such as confiscating drugs, can increase the vulnerability of people who use substances by placing them in a position in which they must commit more crime to pay off debts or to replace their personal supply of drugs (Collins et al., 2019).

People who use substances report being detained by police and held in police cells while enduring painful and dangerous withdrawal symptoms. Anne-Marie recalls her experience of being forced to detoxify from heroin without medical help:

> If the police know you're addicted or you tell them that you're an addict, they hold back on getting you medical attention as long as they possibly can. They will keep you in processing cells until you peak your withdrawal before they let you see a doctor. You're laying on the floor. You're crying. You're literally shitting yourself. And, they just kind of laugh and they tell you "you better fucking clean that up" or "if you didn't put needles in your arms, you wouldn't be in this situation." They avoid helping you.

Such negative police practices and interactions reproduce and reinforce the effects of substance use stigma (Sarang et al., 2010). They elevate fear among people who use substances, which increases their reluctance to report incidents in which they have been criminally victimized. Anne-Marie describes staying in a violent relationship and not seeking help because of the fear associated with her substance use: "Part of the reason why I didn't call the police for so long is because they were not going to believe me." Involving police officers in the response to health-related emergencies (e.g., overdoses, mental health crises) also discourages people who use substances from reaching out for help when needed. For instance, people who have experienced a drug overdose avoid calling emergency services due to worry about being arrested or detained (e.g., for drug possession or outstanding warrants), losing services (e.g., housing), or having their children apprehended (Koester et al., 2017).

Stigma and criminalization invites frequent and recurrent involvement of the police into the lives of people who use substances, which creates harm by driving "people who use drugs underground, acting as a disincentive to seek healthcare and service provision, and further isolating and alienating people who use drugs from normative society"

(Levy, 2014, p. 9). Once they are known to, and stereotyped by, the police, people who use substances report experiencing an inordinate amount of negative attention that makes them susceptible to discrimination, mistreatment, and poor outcomes including arrest and incarceration (Greer et al., 2018).

Incarcerating People Who Use Substances

Incarceration is a stigmatizing event, which Garfinkel (1956) classically termed a status degradation ceremony. It makes people feel disempowered, degraded, devalued, and discredited, which disproportionately affects people who use substances since they are overrepresented in jails and prisons. It upends a person's life, separates them from supports, and disrupts their health care since they can be cut off the medications, including opioid agonist treatment, they were receiving in the community. Additionally, the stigmatizing attitudes and practices of correctional staff intensify the pains of imprisonment for people who use substances, as Anne-Marie suggests: "If you go in a junkie, it's not nice. You are reminded, all the time."

The blending of correctional agendas and health processes in penal institutions creates serious issues for people who use substances. Substances are strictly prohibited, so people who are caught using, possessing, or selling them are punished harshly, as Peter describes: "If they catch someone using substances in prison, they throw them in the hole. They throw you in segregation and leave you there for a little while to think about what you've done." Solitary confinement abruptly cuts a person from the substances they were using, which can cause painful withdrawal symptoms without proper support. People who use substances have similar experiences when they are initially incarcerated, as Peter recalls:

> I was using like $300 a day in opiates when I got arrested. They cut me off cold turkey and I was thrown in jail. It took me three days to get a Tylenol out of them and I was withdrawing cold turkey. I was so sick. I'd just sit there and rock because it would give me a bit of relief from the physical symptoms. That went on for about a week. The second week, it started getting better. I didn't even see a doctor.

People who use substances or are receiving substance use treatment (e.g., methadone maintenance) are watched more closely and searched more often by correctional staff, which Anne-Marie recalls experiencing: "My cell got tossed a whole lot more than everybody else's." Anne-Marie also describes how she was targeted by correctional staff and subjected to humiliating practices, which she attributes to her substance use label:

"They would strip me down right in front of everybody. They wouldn't put me in my cell to strip search me."

Because of the severe consequences, people often hide their substance use during their incarceration, as Peter did for his first prison sentence:

> When I went into prison, I just told the staff "I don't got a substance use problem." People had warned me to "be careful what you say to them because they're going to hold it against you. If you tell them [about substance use], you're not going to be able to have a beer when you get out." And I heeded their advice.

People worry about the negative effect that disclosing their substance use will have on their prison stay and chances of receiving parole. During his second incarceration, Peter's substance use became known and recorded by correctional staff, which he explains created problems for him: "I didn't feel safe because everything that I had ever said was always used against me. As soon as I would make a mistake, everything that I had ever said and done would be thrown on top of it all over again."

The paradox is that people often are required to attend substance use programs as part of their correctional plan, but any substance use they disclose in such programs (including continued use in prison) can result in punitive consequences, such as placement in solitary confinement, increased security classification, or extended time in jail or prison. Anne-Marie describes how her substance use was handled during parole hearings:

> When you go up in front of the parole board, that's the first thing that they talk about: your drug use. Are you going to use? How do we know you're not going to use? Are you going to go drug seeking? Are you going to run away from the halfway house to go use? If you do use, are you going to be honest with your parole officer? If you're an addict, the first half hour of any parole hearing is about drug use.

This illustrates how substance use is viewed as a public safety risk, which can be internalized by people who use substances. Within the correctional context, risk management and punitive practices are prioritized ahead of therapeutic and supportive approaches, which contributes to the stigmatizing experiences of people who use substances.

Penal institutions are notoriously ineffective at meeting people's healthcare needs. Even though most people who are incarcerated have substance use disorders, they often have inadequate access to substance use services and harm reduction supports, as Matthew recalls about one of his short stays in jail: "There were no programs." A similar sentiment is shared by Peter: "I was talking to a guy in prison and he's been in there for almost two years. He still hasn't gotten into the addiction program – and he's in there for drugs!" Anne-Marie describes the inadequate quality of substance use services that she received in prison: "It took me three and a half years to see anybody in addiction services. And then I would see them for 45 minutes once every two months. And, it's not the same person every time. It didn't help. It actually made it worse. I ended up relapsing inside." Steven describes finally receiving proper mental health services during his last incarceration, but this was only after a lifetime of criminal justice involvement that failed to address the underlying factors contributing to his substance use and criminal behavior: "I sat down with a psychiatrist and he said 'have you looked back on your childhood?' And we started putting the pieces together. The trauma had never been treated, so the system was just warehousing me from a young age until an old age." Incarcerating people because of their substance use but not offering adequate services and supports to help them address those issues is one way that structural stigma materializes in penal institutions, which is a frustration shared by Peter: "They're just warehousing them [people who use substances]. They're not helping them do anything different."

People who are incarcerated can sometimes receive opioid agonist treatment (e.g., methadone maintenance) during their incarceration. Although this gives people access to evidence-based treatment that reduces harms (e.g., overdose, infectious disease), it often subjects them to degrading and humiliating security measures. Matthew discusses the routine and normalized strip-searching procedures he experienced and saw in jail:

> Men who are prescribed methadone to treat opioid use disorder are routinely strip-searched every day after receiving their dose. They get you to remove all of your clothes, put your hands through your hair, shake your body, lift up your external genitals, turn around, bend down and cough. In some cases, men in the cells that are across from each other see the search. It becomes so normal in the jail. A lot of these individuals have been sexually abused in their past. Yet, every day, they are stripped down bare-naked to receive a dose of medication that they are dependent on.

Such procedures and the general poor treatment by correctional staff of people on methadone deters them from receiving such treatment, as Anne-Marie recalls about her incarceration: "I weaned off of methadone because I couldn't handle how they [correctional staff] were treating me because of it. They put you in the worst possible cell when they know that you're on methadone, and you're the last one to be picked to go to programs like Narcotic Anonymous." Anne-Marie's experience illustrates the harmful effects, such as disengagement from healthcare services, resulting from coercive, punitive, arbitrary, and stigmatizing correctional practices toward people who use substances.

Community Reentry of People Who Use Substances

The effects of stigma can "keep the revolving door of relapse, recidivism, and incarceration spinning" (van Olphen et al., 2009, p. 3). The issues described earlier – social inequities, criminalization, underfunded services, and frequent police encounters – negatively affect community reintegration and are magnified by new challenges resulting from intensive community supervision, inadequate support, expectations of failure, and the criminal record.

Because substance use is a risk factor for criminal recidivism, people who use substances are required to abstain from substance use while on parole, which is strictly monitored by parole officers through intensive questioning and substance use testing (e.g., urinalysis). People may also be required to avoid associating with others who either are using substances, involved in criminal activity, or have a criminal record, which can significantly diminish a person's support network. Failure to adhere to parole conditions can result in revocation of parole and a person's return to jail or prison. Steven, who struggled with alcohol use disorder, recalls a time when he was swiftly returned to jail because of alcohol use: "I drank one night; I relapsed. I wasn't even out for 24 hours. My parole officer smelled alcohol off me and came back with two cops. I was breached." Steven's experience shows the tendency for the criminal justice system to approach substance use relapse with a punitive response, rather than addressing it through a rehabilitative or harm reduction model. Peter also discusses the punitive approach taken toward people who use substances: "They [correctional staff] need to support people and encourage them. If they fall down, then pick them back up. They don't do that with vulnerable people. They have a punitive approach."

Despite the importance of staying away from substances for formerly incarcerated people to maintain their freedom in the community, few services and supports are available to help them with their substance use needs, as Anne-Marie explains:

> You get out and you have to find programs on your own. They [correctional staff] don't do that for you. You have to do all the research yourself. You have to make all the phone calls yourself. They don't set you up for success. So, you see a lot of people going back to jail or prison very quickly.

Peter describes how people routinely leave courts, jails, and prisons without a change of clothes, a place to go, or something to eat, which propels them back into substance use and criminal behavior: "Most people have nothing when they walk out. Where are they going? They're going right back to where they started or worse." Adhering to parole conditions, including not using substances, is difficult to do when people's basic needs are not being met, as Matthew explains: "It's hard to get out of jail and abide by the rules if you have a substance use disorder and you're homeless and you have nothing." Anne-Marie also discusses the challenge of abiding by parole conditions without adequate support:

> It's hard to stay clean when you feel like you're not enough and you'll never be enough – you hear it so often for so many years. So, all you want to do is get high. You can go to as many programs as you want; the minute they find out you're on parole, everybody runs. Nobody wants to be near you. So, what do you do? You turn around and use.

For many people, mutual support groups, like Alcoholics Anonymous, Narcotics Anonymous, or the 7th Step Society, may be the only source of support in the community to help them manage their substance use and criminal behavior. As Peter explains: "These programs create a community that understand your past, they understand your traumas, and they understand your addiction. They connect you to something bigger than yourself and teach you how to live a prosocial lifestyle." Precariously funded nongovernmental organizations also supply crucial, low-barrier support to people returning to the community by helping them meet their basic needs such as finding shelter, getting food, obtaining identification, accessing medications, and connecting with others.

Correctional supervision in the absence of therapeutic supports sets people up for failure, as Anne-Marie discusses: "People who get out tell you 'I think they [correctional staff] want me to fail. They are always looking for something. Nobody is helping me. They are just making it harder.'" Peter expresses a similar sentiment: "People are just waiting for you to mess up. That is the reality of society. It's like 'oh yeah, he's a junkie or a convict – it's [relapse or reoffending] coming, you just watch.'" Steven also reflects on how relapse and reoffending are expected by correctional staff:

> It doesn't surprise them. The people that work in the system are so desensitized because they see it over and over and over. There's been times they'll say "hope to see you real soon" or "we'll keep a bed open for you." It becomes a joke and a laughing matter because, in reality, they are probably going to see me again.

Matthew shares about a similar experience when he once returned to jail soon after he was released:

> I remember going back vividly because I knew them [correctional staff] all by name and they were kind of treating me as a friend. To them, I became one of the regulars. They said, "just put him back in the same cell." And, I was like "what the hell?"

Feeling like "one of the regulars" who cycles in and out of the criminal justice system is discouraging for people whose reintegration depends on their own self-belief as well as belief from others that success is possible (Best et al., 2017). The widespread pessimism and diminished expectations among correctional staff reveal stigmatizing attitudes toward the ability of people with intersecting substance use and criminal justice issues to redirect their lives in a positive direction. Believing that the criminal justice system is simply waiting for people to fail without offering adequate support also causes significant stress and frustration for people who are under community supervision.

Another significant source of stigma is the criminal record, which has negative effects that persist well after a person has exited the criminal justice system. The criminal record is a barrier for education, since college programs with job placements or practicums are unlikely to admit people with criminal records into their program, as was experienced by Peter: "When I went back to school, I fought tooth and nail. I had to go way beyond anybody else to get into anything except construction." A criminal record also restricts travel options, as Matthew discusses: "A criminal record is a huge barrier. I'd love to go to the United States and one day I'm going to." It is also a significant barrier to employment, as Anne-Marie explains:

> All the things I wanted to be when I grew up, aren't things I can be now. The chances of getting a job are slim-to-none unless you know somebody in that field. The criminal record makes it really, really hard. There aren't a ton of jobs out there that will hire you with a criminal record.

Peer support and advocacy are the few job sectors that will employ people with criminal records. Anne-Marie, Peter, and Steven are currently employed with organizations offering peer services and supports, while Matthew works for a drug user organization. Employers who overlook a person's criminal record are rare. So, with few employment or educational opportunities, people often return to the illegal job market (e.g., selling drugs), continue using substances, and reengage with the criminal justice system, as Steven explains:

> That stuff [criminal history] follows you and it really limits what you can do. So, you're kind of pigeonholed and you go further down the hole into more depression and anxiety, loss of self-worth and you end up on social welfare and then your addiction really takes hold. Then you have no self-worth, so you self-medicate and stay in a vicious cycle in and out of jail and institutions.

After many years without further criminal justice involvement, some people can obtain a criminal record suspension (also known as a pardon) that officially wipes their record clean, but it does not fully cleanse a person's spoiled identity (Goffman, 1963), erase the master status of being an "ex-con" (Becker, 1973), or eliminate the traumatic experiences created by criminal justice involvement – especially incarceration. Steven, who recently received a criminal record suspension, explains the persistence of stigma: "I don't think I'll ever get rid of that label or the stigma. It's always going to be there. Just because you get a piece of paper that says 'we'll give you a pardon or record suspension' is not going to change people that know you." For people who use substances, criminal justice involvement can create an overriding and everlasting stain on their moral character, social identity, and self-image (Erikson, 1962).

Conclusion

This chapter explored the harms created by stigma at the intersection of substance use and criminal justice. Stigma produces a social context contributing to high rates of criminal justice involvement among people who use substances through inequitable social conditions, criminalization of substances, and under-resourcing of substance use services. Substance use stigma is reinforced by harmful police practices, painful imprisonment experiences, and insufficient support offered to formerly incarcerated people living in the community. The issues we have described and the process we have undertaken to write this chapter supply obvious clues to the strategies we believe are key for improving the lives of people who use substances.

Substance use stigma enshrined in criminal law and drug policy produces significant harm (e.g., overdose, infectious disease transmission, violence, and incarceration) that must be addressed, as Matthew explains: "We aren't going to destigmatize substance use until we decriminalize it."

Decriminalizing substance use is recognized as a necessary step toward destigmatizing people who use substances (Bonn et al., 2020; Fischer, 2020). In recognition of the harmful and stigmatizing effects of prohibition and criminalization for people who use substances, especially in relation to the current overdose crisis, many jurisdictions have legalized or decriminalized drugs – most notably, Portugal in 2001. Canada legalized cannabis in 2018 and, in response to the overdose crisis, several major cities (i.e., Vancouver, Montreal) and provinces (i.e., British Columbia) are currently seeking to decriminalize the possession of all illegal substances with the goal of reducing substance use stigma and, thereby, encouraging people's engagement with harm reduction and treatment services. Diminishing the negative effects of repressive police practices on people who use substances can be achieved partially through decriminalizing drug possession; however, research suggests that full legalization of all drugs may be a necessary step toward meaningfully reducing police involvement in the lives of people who use substances (International Network of People who Use Drugs, 2021).

Addressing substance use stigma also requires making significant improvements to the healthcare system. Improving access to voluntary, evidence-based, trauma-informed, and person-centered substance use services, including treatment programs and harm reduction services, is key for reducing the criminal justice involvement for people who use substances (Bondurant et al., 2018). Effectively addressing substance use stigma requires that governments increase the availability and quality of care, which entails making greater investments in publicly funded evidence-based therapies, a continuum of integrated substance use services and harm reduction programs, and a range of peer-delivered services. Working toward removing criminal justice agents and institutions from the substance use service system is also key for addressing substance use stigma. This would help reduce the stigmatizing effects associated with criminalization, coercive practices, compulsory interventions, and punitive consequences. Alongside decriminalizing people who use substances, efforts must be made to ensure that people who are already in the criminal justice system have access to a high standard of substance use treatment and harm reduction services. Increasingly, opioid agonist treatment and needle exchange programs are being made available in penal institutions, but the uptake and growth of such evidence-based services and supports is hampered by political obstacles and ideological resistance (Kolind & Duke, 2016).

Counteracting the exclusionary effects of substance use stigma also entails supporting the meaningful involvement of people who use substances in the healthcare and criminal justice systems, as Anne-Marie states: "We need to have our voices heard. We're human, not just a number. We have souls." This chapter models the "nothing about us, without us" principle by involving people with lived and living experiences in the knowledge creation process as well as valuing both academic and experiential forms of knowledge. Healthcare and criminal justice organizations should ensure that people who use substances are engaged in decision-making processes, such as monitoring service quality, identifying structural barriers, developing policies, and implementing improvements, as Steven suggests: "The relationship between the people with lived experience and people with formal education needs to be strong." Employing and supporting people with lived experiences as peer support workers, peer navigators, advocates, policy advisors, and educators in healthcare and criminal justice systems simultaneously promotes inclusion and produces better outcomes. The experiential knowledge and community relationships possessed by people who use substances are key for offering hope and addressing people's needs, as Peter explains: "They put so much red tape between a client and their needs. We need peers going inside courthouses, jails, and prisons to support people's return." Supporting people who use substances to build productive, meaningful, and responsible lives that are free from crime and criminal justice involvement and providing them with opportunities to give back to their communities are vitally important for addressing stigma at the intersection of substance use and criminal justice.

References

Alberton, A. M., Gorey, K. M., Angell, G. B., & McCue, H. A. (2019). Intersection of Indigenous peoples and police: Questions about contact and confidence. *Canadian Journal of Criminology and Criminal Justice*, *61*(4), 101–119. https://doi.org/10.3138/cjccj.2018-0064

Baker, P., Beletsky, L., Avalos, L., et al. (2020). Policing practices and risk of HIV infection among people who inject drugs. *Epidemiologic Reviews*, *42*(1), 27–40. https://doi.org/10.1093/epirev/mxaa010

Beaudette, J. N., & Stewart, L. A. (2016). National prevalence of mental disorders among incoming Canadian male offenders. *Canadian Journal of Psychiatry*, *61*(10), 624–632. https://doi.org/10.1177/0706743716639929

Becker, H. S. (1973). *Outsiders: Studies in the sociology of deviance*. Free Press.

Beletsky, L., Cochrane, J., Sawyer, A. L., et al. (2015). Police encounters among needle exchange clients in Baltimore: Drug law enforcement as a structural determinant of health. *American Journal of Public Health*, *105*(9), 1872–1879. https://doi.org/10.2105/ajph.2015.302681

Best, D., Irving, J., & Albertson, K. (2017). Recovery and desistance: What the emerging recovery movement in the alcohol and drug area can learn from models of desistance from offending. *Addiction Research & Theory, 25*(1), 1–10. https://doi.org/10.1080/16066359.2016.1185661

Bondurant, S. R., Lindo, J. M., & Swensen, I. D. (2018). Substance abuse treatment centers and local crime. *Journal of Urban Economics, 104*, 124–133. https://doi.org/10.1016/j.jue.2018.01.007

Bonn, M., Palayew, A., Bartlett, S., Brothers, T. D., Touesnard, N., & Tyndall, M. (2020). Addressing the syndemic of HIV, Hepatitis C, overdose, and COVID-19 among people who use drugs: The potential roles for decriminalization and safe supply. *Journal of Studies on Alcohol and Drugs, 81*(5), 556–560. https://doi.org/10.15288/jsad.2020.81.556

Buchman, D. Z., Leece, P., & Orkin, A. (2017). The epidemic as stigma: The bioethics of opioids. *Journal of Law, Medicine & Ethics, 45*(4), 607–620. https://doi.org/10.1177/1073110517750600

Burns, S. L., & Peyrot, M. (2014). Tough love: Nurturing and coercing responsibility and recovery in California drug courts. *Social Problems, 50*(3), 416–438. https://doi.org/10.1525/sp.2003.50.3.416

Chang, J., Agliata, J., & Guarinieri, M. (2020). COVID-19 – Enacting a 'new normal' for people who use drugs. *International Journal of Drug Policy, 83*, Article 102832. https://doi.org/10.1016/j.drugpo.2020.102832

Clement, S., Schauman, O., Graham, T., et al. (2015). What is the impact of mental health-related stigma on help-seeking? A systematic review of quantitative and qualitative studies. *Psychological Medicine, 45*(1), 11–27. https://doi.org/10.1017/S0033291714000129

Collins, A. B., Boyd, J., Mayer, S., et al. (2019). Policing space in the overdose crisis: A rapid ethnographic study of the impact of law enforcement practices on the effectiveness of overdose prevention sites. *International Journal of Drug Policy, 73*, 199–207. https://doi.org/10.1016/j.drugpo.2019.08.002

Derkzen, D., Barker, J., McMillan, K., & Stewart, L. (2017). *Rates of current mental disorders among women offenders in custody in CSC*. Correctional Service Canada. www.csc-scc.gc.ca/research/092/R-406-en.pdf

Erikson, K. T. (1962). Notes on the sociology of deviance. *Social Problems, 9*(4), 307–314.

Fischer, B. (2020). Some notes on the use, concept and socio-political framing of 'stigma' focusing on an opioid-related public health crisis. *Substance Abuse Treatment, Prevention, and Policy, 15*(1), Article 54. https://doi.org/10.1186/s13011-020-00294-2

Garfinkel, H. (1956). Conditions of successful degradation ceremonies. *American Journal of Sociology, 61*(5), 420–424. www.jstor.org/stable/2773484

Goffman, E. (1963). *Stigma: Notes on the management of spoiled identity*. Prentice-Hall.

Goldenberg, S., Watt, S., Braschel, M., Hayashi, K., Moreheart, S., & Shannon, K. (2020). Police-related barriers to harm reduction linked to non-fatal overdose amongst sex workers who use drugs: Results of a community-based cohort in Metro Vancouver, Canada. *International Journal of Drug Policy, 76*, 1–8. https://doi.org/10.1016/j.drugpo.2019.102618

Goldstein, P. J. (1985). The drugs/violence nexus: A tripartite conceptual framework. *Journal of Drug Issues, 15*(4), 493–506. https://doi.org/10.1177/002204268501500406

Greer, A., Sorge, J., Sharpe, K., Bear, D., & Macdonald, S. (2018). Police encounters and experiences among youths and adults who use drugs: Qualitative and quantitative findings of a cross-sectional study in Victoria, British Columbia. *Canadian Journal of Criminology and Criminal Justice, 60*(4), 478–504. https://doi.org/10.3138/cjccj.2017-0044.r1

Hughes, C. E., Barratt, M. J., Ferris, J. A., Maier, L. J., & Winstock, A. R. (2018). Drug-related police encounters across the globe: How do they compare? *International Journal of Drug Policy, 56*, 197–207. https://doi.org/10.1016/j.drugpo.2018.03.005

International Network of People who Use Drugs. (2021). *Drug decriminalisation: Progress or political red herring? Assessing the impact of current models of decriminalization on people who use drugs.* www.inpud.net/en/drug-decriminalisation-progress-or-political-red-herring

Jorgensen, C. (2018). Badges and bongs: Police officers' attitudes toward drugs. *SAGE Open, 8*(4). https://doi.org/10.1177/2158244018805357

Khenti, A. (2014). The Canadian war on drugs: Structural violence and unequal treatment of Black Canadians. *International Journal of Drug Policy, 25*(2), 190–195. https://doi.org/10.1016/j.drugpo.2013.12.001

Koester, S., Mueller, S. R., Raville, L., Langegger, S., & Binswanger, I. A. (2017). Why are some people who have received overdose education and naloxone reticent to call emergency medical services in the event of overdose? *International Journal of Drug Policy, 48*, 115–124. https://doi.org/10.1016/j.drugpo.2017.06.008

Kolind, T., & Duke, K. (2016). Drugs in prisons: Exploring use, control, treatment and policy. *Drugs: Education, Prevention and Policy, 23*(2), 89–92. https://doi.org/10.3109/09687637.2016.1153604

Levy, J. (2014). *The harms of drug use: Criminalisation, misinformation, and stigma.* International Network of People who Use Drugs. www.inpud.net/The_Harms_of_Drug_Use_JayLevy2014_INPUD_YouthRISE.pdf

Livingston, J. D. (2020). *Structural stigma in health-care contexts for people with mental health and substance use issues: A literature review.* Mental Health Commission of Canada. www.mentalhealthcommission.ca/sites/default/files/2020-07/structural_stigma_in_healthcare_eng.pdf

Maynard, R. (2017). *Policing Black lives: State violence in Canada from slavery to the present*. Fernwood.

McNeil, R., & Small, W. (2014). 'Safer environment interventions': A qualitative synthesis of the experiences and perceptions of people who inject drugs. *Social Science & Medicine, 106*, 151–158. https://doi.org/10.1016/j.socscimed.2014.01.051

Radcliffe, P., & Stevens, A. (2008). Are drug treatment services only for 'thieving junkie scumbags'? Drug users and the management of stigmatised identities. *Social Science & Medicine*, *67*(7), 1065–1073. https://doi.org/10.1016/j.socscimed.2008.06.004

Rolando, S., Asmussen Frank, V., Duke, K., et al. (2020). 'I like money, I like many things'. The relationship between drugs and crime from the perspective of young people in contact with criminal justice systems. *Drugs: Education, Prevention and Policy*, *28*(1), 7–16. https://doi.org/10.1080/09687637.2020.1754339

Room, R. (2005). Stigma, social inequality and alcohol and drug use. *Drug and Alcohol Review*, *24*(2), 143–155. https://doi.org/10.1080/09595230500102434

Sander, G., Scandurra, A., Kamenska, A., et al. (2016). Overview of harm reduction in prisons in seven European countries. *Harm Reduction Journal*, *13*(1), Article 28. https://doi.org/10.1186/s12954-016-0118-x

Sarang, A., Rhodes, T., Sheon, N., & Page, K. (2010). Policing drug users in Russia: Risk, fear, and structural violence. *Substance Use & Misuse*, *45*(6), 813–865. https://doi.org/10.3109/10826081003590938

Stevens, A., Hughes, C. E., Hulme, S., & Cassidy, R. (2022). Depenalization, diversion and decriminalization: A realist review and programme theory of alternatives to criminalization for simple drug possession. *European Journal of Criminology*, *19*(1), 29–54, Article 1477370819887514. https://doi.org/10.1177/1477370819887514

Tsai, A. C., Kiang, M. V., Barnett, M. L., et al. (2019). Stigma as a fundamental hindrance to the United States opioid overdose crisis response. *PLoS Medicine*, *16*(11), e1002969. https://doi.org/10.1371/journal.pmed.1002969

van Olphen, J., Eliason, M. J., Freudenberg, N., & Barnes, M. (2009). Nowhere to go: How stigma limits the options of female drug users after release from jail. *Substance Abuse Treatment, Prevention, and Policy*, *4*(1), Article 10. https://doi.org/10.1186/1747-597X-4-10

Werb, D., Kamarulzaman, A., Meacham, M. C., et al. (2016). The effectiveness of compulsory drug treatment: A systematic review. *International Journal on Drug Policy*, *28*, 1–9. https://doi.org/10.1016/j.drugpo.2015.12.005

Whitesell, M., Bachand, A., Peel, J., & Brown, M. (2013). Familial, social, and individual factors contributing to risk for adolescent substance use. *Journal of Addiction*, Article 579310. https://doi.org/10.1155/2013/579310

CHAPTER 5

Substance Use Disorders, Stigma, and Ethics

Laura Williamson

Introduction

As other chapters in the book have shown, substance use disorders (SUDs) are among the most stigmatized of health problems (Room et al., 2001; Schomerus et al., 2011). Many issues that influence the stigmatization of SUDs are values-based or ethical in nature; most simply, ethics is concerned with questions of "how we should live," as individuals and societies (Plato, 2007). The discrediting of people with SUDs through policies, behaviors, structures, or self-stigma is fundamentally a value-laden enterprise. Often at the heart of such values-based ethical concerns are public and professional qualms over the responsibility (or perceived irresponsibility) of individuals for their substance use issues. This, in turn, influences questions about whether and to what extent people with SUDs are worthy of resources, time, and, most fundamentally, respect. Such concerns or judgments about people with SUDs can lead to further instances of stigma, for example, people perceived as having SUDs can experience difficulties securing treatment, stable housing, and employment (National Academies of Sciences, Engineering, and Medicine, 2016). Despite well-documented obstacles that people with SUDs face, key to contemporary ethical discourse on stigma are questions over whether it is always problematic and discriminatory. That is, whether stigma is an obstacle to the fair provision of treatment, or as some have argued, a tool to help improve health in the longer term (Bayer, 2008). In this chapter I argue that the complex issues that influence stigma around SUDs, or the negative stereotyping of undesirable attributes (Jones et al., 1984; Link & Phelan, 2001), require dedicated ethical debate. Unfortunately, for a number of reasons, much civic and professional debate in the field is poorly equipped to make sound ethical judgments.

Efforts to improve the ethical responses to the stigmatization of SUDs must contend with a number of obstacles. Firstly, medical model thinking about SUDs (or addiction) has long rejected the idea that ethics or values have a constructive role to play in preventing or aiding recovery from the condition (Williamson, 2012). Secondly, bioethics has developed in a way that means its primary focus is on the individual, rather than the social dimensions of health. These issues are significant because they influence the scope of the topics thought worthy of attention and the way they are addressed. More specifically, the pull of reductive approaches devoted to either a medical model of addiction, or an individual focus in bioethics, impedes the attention that needs to be given to values-based challenges and the social dimensions of SUDs and stigma. This can overburden individuals with SUDs by making them also most entirely responsible for their recovery and any relapse that they have.

Initially in this chapter I will examine the obstacles to sound ethical civic and professional discourse on stigma in more detail. I will then assess how the individually focused nature of bioethics influences work on SUDs and their stigmatization. The concerns identified will lead to a discussion of the potential for public health ethics to provide an improved values-based response to the stigmatization of SUDs. The final section of the chapter will identify a number of features that need to be afforded more consideration in attitudes toward SUDs and assessments of the stigma around them. It will be argued that these features are central to creating the type of consistent ethical culture needed to inform and sustain meaningful discourse around the stigmatization of SUDs. Such discourse is essential as a foundation for improving the way we respond to stigma and, ultimately, for reducing discrimination.

Ethics and the Medical Model

In 2020 the *American Medical Association Journal of Ethics* published a paper on the "ethical imperative" of addressing the stigma that surrounds SUDs (Adams & Volkow, 2020). The authors, the then surgeon general of the United States, Jerome Adams, and the director of the National Institute on Drug Abuse, Nora Volkow, top and tail their article with the call that it is "ethically incumbent" on all stakeholders to address the negative social stigma toward people with substance use problems (Adams & Volkow, 2020). The authors identify the drivers of this ethical imperative as factors that impede "progress across the entire trajectory of prevention, treatment, and recovery" (Adams & Volkow, 2020, p. E702). The wider literature base supports these concerns by pointing to stigma as impeding people admitting problems with substance use, seeking or accepting treatment, and increasing rates of relapse (Link & Phelan, 2001; Randels & Tracy, 2013; Schomerus & Angermeyer, 2008). Adams and Volkow go on to claim that although stigma is a complex issue to address, "Public education and improving literacy about the medical (rather than the moral) basis of mental illness might lessen the perception of blame and increase care seeking" (Adams & Volkow, 2020, p. E704). However, by rejecting the importance of increasing moral or ethical literacy around SUDs, Adams and Volkow create serious obstacles to helping people to think critically about stigma. This is because their medical model focus essentially curtails debate by placing artificial boundaries on considerations of what are actually complex, biopsychosocial issues.

Leaving people with SUDs, their close contacts, professionals, and concerned citizens to think through questions around issues like responsibility and trust without any guidance, misses opportunities to ensure the debates are soundly based. To better inform debates requires the development of accounts of SUDs and stigma that integrate ethics as part of a more inclusive interdisciplinary venture. Without this type of approach negative judgments about people with SUDs and the resulting discrimination against them goes largely unchallenged. It also means professional and civic discourse about SUDs risks being influenced, not by informed critical debates about values, but uncritical negative stereotypes. Thus, while it is helpful to avoid the "moralizing" sanctimonious remarks that have blighted debates on SUDs, rejecting debates on values also omits consideration of how we should or ought to act in the context of practice and policy. However, as I will now outline, the omission of serious ethical contributions has long characterized debates around SUDs, resulting in an approach that fails to make a meaningful impact on stigma.

Omitting Ethics from Mainstream Policy Debates

Historically, characterizations of SUDs or addiction issues as a character flaw, personal weakness, or failing have been portrayed as a "moral model" (Williamson, 2012). Such condemnations of substance use behaviors can be linked to the moralizing of the temperance movement and similar efforts to control opium use, particularly among lower socioeconomic groups, or classes (Berridge, 1979). Efforts to develop a reputedly value-free, medical approach to SUDs is rooted in the assumption that when people understand SUDs as a disease or medical condition that requires treatment, the stigma around it will lessen. This hope has not been realized – SUDs still remain heavily stigmatized, despite a growing literature base that presents it as a brain disease. It has been argued that the failure to positively transform attitudes is due to an "uneducated" public not understanding complex scientific information and, as a result, still seeing SUDs as a personal weakness (Dackis & O'Brien, 2005). However, this explanation encounters a number of challenges that suggest it misses a more complex set of issues. Firstly, healthcare professionals, who presumably are more able to understand the medical complexities than the general public, also hold negative attitudes toward people with SUDs (Institute of Medicine, 2006; Stone et al., 2021). Secondly, there are concerns that a blinkered medicalizing of the SUDs, and other mental health issues, ties people irrevocably to a condition, and to assumptions that individuals with it will behave badly. As a result, negative attitudes toward SUDs are not usefully challenged by the medical model, but entrenched (Mehta & Farina, 1997). Related to this concern are assertions by exponents of the medical model that "addiction has to be treated" (Volkow, 2020). This claim is imprecise and potentially stigmatizing. This is because research shows more diversity in substance use and recovery patterns than medical model exponents tend to allow for. More specifically, there is evidence of recovery or remission without treatment (Kelly et al., 2017; Mellor et al., 2019; Peele, 1990). Blaming the public for not understanding the implications of science, rather than helping them understand the complexity of the issues around SUDs and stigma – including the ethical dimensions – is a significant obstacle to cultivating a more enlightened and accurate response to the issues involved.

Responsibility and the Medical Model

Of particular importance for the attitudes people hold toward SUDs are questions around the responsibilities different stakeholders have. Although responsibility, an ethical topic, does not naturally fit within the medical model, it is of such importance to stigma that scientists have needed to address it: casting an SUD as a health condition still leads to questions or uncertainty about the responsibilities of substance users. This has led to reassurances that personal responsibility remains relevant. Volkow has claimed it is an "absurdity" to think that people with SUDs don't have the same responsibilities to manage their condition as those who self-manage other conditions (Volkow, 2004). To make her point, Volkow draws an analogy between SUDs and other health conditions or "diseases" like cancer. She claims that "addiction" is like any other health issue, and people with it do not have their responsibilities for managing it removed by its "disease" status.

To inform debates on negative attitudes toward people with SUDs, and the discrimination and stigma they produce, it is critical that arguments in the field are sound and able to win public confidence. Yet it is far from clear that Volkow achieves these standards. The analogy she draws, for example, ignores that people stopping the consumption of addictive substances can prevent the condition from worsening. As a result, continued substance use can still appear "irresponsible" and worthy of being stigmatized. A wider discussion of responsibility is necessary to help highlight the complex individual and social factors that have a bearing on it in the context of SUDs. This illustrates that initiatives to improve literacy around the condition need to go beyond providing scientific information to consistently help professionals and the public discuss the ethical ramifications of such developments. Volkow's focus on the responsibilities of individuals with SUDs in isolation from the responsibilities others have toward them, fails to acknowledge the ethical complexity of the issue. However, as I will now argue, it is not only the role of science in this issue that is problematic for stigma.

The Influence of an Individually Focused Ethics on SUDs

Obstacles to the ethical analysis of the stigmatization of SUDs are not only related to the dominance of the medical paradigm. The focus and priorities of bioethics bring their own limitations to discussions of the negative attitudes and discrimination that surround SUDs. To explain these concerns, it is necessary to briefly outline the development of the field. The development of bioethics was largely driven by the need to react to, and prevent the reoccurrence of, a number of ethical abuses: the Nazi "experiments" during World War II, and the study by the United States Public Health Service in Tuskegee that failed to give available treatment for syphilis to black male study participants. The resulting ethical guidance, the Nuremberg Code and the Belmont Report, marks a commitment to protecting individuals through the promotion of principles like autonomy, respect for persons, and informed consent (National Commission for the Protection of Human Subjects, 1978; Nuernberg Military Tribunals, 1949). Support was given to an individually based ethic with the publication of the first edition of *Principles of Biomedical Ethics* by Beauchamp and Childress (1979). The principlist approach to ethics presented by this now seminal text – based on autonomy, beneficence, nonmaleficence, and justice – became and continues to be central to how ethical issues are approached in health and health care. Now in its eighth edition, the text has evolved (Beauchamp & Childress, 2019), but the individually focused approach to bioethics it inspired remains dominant, particularly because of the commitments of liberal democracies to support individual freedoms and choice.

Bioethics and Substance Use Disorders

The principles and individual focus that have guided work in bioethics impact in a number of ways on debates in ethical literature around SUDs and their stigmatization. For example, ethical literature on SUDs focuses on questions related to the impaired control that can characterize the condition (Williamson, 2012). This includes whether individuals with SUDs have moral capacity, whether having an SUD means people should not be held as morally responsible for the harms that might result from their behavior (Pickard, 2017), whether people with SUDs are able to consent to involvement in clinical research (Foddy & Savulescu, 2006), and whether they can and should be coerced into treatment (Janssens et al., 2004). Such issues are influenced by the focus of bioethics on individuals, their autonomy, and their ability to give informed consent. An inadvertent ramification of this type of focus on SUDs is that it tends to draw attention to topics that can lead to individuals being seen as flawed, unable to give informed consent, and problematic for communities (Williamson, 2021). In short, the focus on bioethics debates on SUDs has often been on issues that can fan the stigmatization of the condition. Less attention has focused on SUDs as a social issue or on discrimination against people with the condition, though exceptions exist (Levy, 2007; Williamson, 2012). I will now examine the implications of this type of ethical focus for discussions of SUDs and stigma and show that, in the context of SUDs, individual responsibility has to be complemented by social responsibility.

Limitations of an Individually Focused Bioethics and Need for Social Responsibility

Despite the obstacles that exist to an inclusive and sound ethical analysis of SUDs and their stigmatization, the individually focused foundations of traditional accounts of bioethics do influence debates in the field. Arguably, this is because of the influence of individual choice in liberal democracies, and not only the reach of bioethics. However, this impact is not necessarily helpful and even has the potential to undermine the reasons for its inclusion. It has been argued, for example, that recovery from SUDs is dependent on individual empowerment supported by autonomy, self-determination, and individual choice (Corrigan et al., 2012; Mancini, 2018). In this respect, Mancini states, drawing on self-determination theory (SDT) (Mancini, 2018), "I would suggest that instilling a sense of autonomy is the *sine qua non* of recovery oriented practice" (Mancini, 2018). This, he continues, is because a "feeling" of autonomy is key to motivation; resisting infringements of autonomy – one assumes through coerced treatment, etc. – is critical to helping those with mental health issues (Mancini, 2018). However, there are significant ethical questions around whether autonomy, without greater specificity, is a sound foundation for empowerment. More specifically, a reliance on an account of autonomy that is tied to self-determination and noninterference is problematic, for a number of reasons that I will now outline.

An individually based focus in debates around SUDs risks exacerbating stigma, rather than necessarily helping to empower people (Williamson, 2021). This is because an individually based ethical foundation has the potential to narrow the scope of discussions and place responsibility for recovery on substance users. In the context of a condition in which relapse is a significant factor (Brandon et al., 2007), a focus on empowering substance users could mean they are solely responsible (and so irresponsible) for any future substance use. Importantly, this focus does not acknowledge the social determinants of SUDs, and without including these it is not feasible to have a meaningful debate on individual responsibility (or stigma). Social scientists have long highlighted that the individual focus of bioethics does not address the social factors that influence health (Fox & Swazey, 1984; Wolpe, 1998). Discussions of empowerment based on autonomy that are not supported by socioethical guidance have the potential to leave stigma lingering around individuals. That is, utilizing a self-determination focus to address stigma risks quickly turning it into a tool with which, practically and ethically, isolated individuals can be blamed. While empowerment may well be an important feature in recovery from SUDs and in efforts to remove stigma, it is important to cultivate ethical foundations that are able to support this commitment appropriately.

Secondly, and linked to the previous point, an individually focused account of ethics has also been criticized for failing to accurately represent how people become autonomous, or empowered. At the root of this issue are disputes over the idea that autonomy can be simply linked to "independence," choice, or simply leaving people alone (O'Neill, 2002). That is, it is ethically questionable whether people become autonomous (or empowered) without support from others. Interpretations of autonomy based on self-determination, or the related ideal of independence, have been criticized in ethical literature for isolating and abandoning people (Gessert, 2008), rather than supporting people in their decision-making and empowerment (O'Neill, 2002; Stoljar, 2011). In this respect, feminist philosophers have argued that autonomy is more relational than often acknowledged (Ells et al., 2011). The central claim at the heart of "relational autonomy" is that people don't actually make decisions in an insular manner, rather they are influenced or supported by their social networks and relationships (O'Neill, 2002). In this respect, Nedelsky (1989) argues for the need to explicitly move away from an account in which the "perfectly autonomous" person is one who is "perfectly isolated." She continues to state it is not isolation that makes people autonomous "but relationships ... that provide the support and guidance necessary" to allow a person to determine their own values (Nedelsky, 1989, p. 12). This more complex understanding of autonomy does appear in literature related to SUDs. More specifically, the self-determination theory on which Mancini draws, suggests that autonomy need not be reduced to independence, or self-determination (Ryan, 1995). In this respect, Ryan notes a high perception of "relatedness" can lead to an increased, not reduced, sense of autonomy (Ryan, 1995). Unfortunately, Mancini does not engage sufficiently with this alternative reading of autonomy (Mancini, 2018). In this way, his reliance on an unnuanced understanding of autonomy, like Volkow's discussion of responsibility, suggests a need for more considered, interdisciplinary engagement with health ethics (Volkow, 2004). The shortcomings of both contributions relate to a failure to engage rigorously and consistently with the social dimensions of SUDs, and, also, with a more sophisticated ethical approach that problematizes placing responsibility for recovery on the shoulders of individual substance users. As I have argued elsewhere, given the complex challenges that exist in the field, a social ecological approach could provide a more useful foundation for discussing SUDs and stigma than individualism that tends to dominate debates (Williamson, 2012). But given the important role of values within these debates, this alternative approach to SUDs needs to fully integrate an account of health ethics not reliant on individualism.

Ethics and Person-centered Care

Thirdly, another issue that indicates the importance of gaining more precision in how ethics can and should influence debates on SUDs and its stigmatization is the use of person-centered care (PCC) in the field. The importance of PCC in health care has been growing since the late 1970s (World Health Organization, 1978), and it is now well established across health systems in developed countries (Institute of Medicine, 2001). While it has a number of aims, fundamentally it endeavors to improve the quality of health care by giving service users a voice in decisions that impact on them, particularly by attending to their preferences and values (Institute of Medicine, 2001). It has been argued that PCC has an important role to play in the context of SUDs in helping to ensure people receive respectful, quality, tailored treatment when needed (Institute of Medicine, 2006). Although stigma can lead to an assumption that people with SUDs are not able to play a significant role in their treatment, the Institute of Medicine argues it is both possible and desirable for them to influence their treatment (Institute of Medicine, 2006). People having an active role in their treatment and recovery is important for helping to challenge stigma – it signals that they are able and willing to function in that way. In addition, PCC is particularly important in the context of SUDs given research that shows relational factors like a good working relationship or alliance and empathic exchange with therapists is important for recovery (Norcross & Wampold, 2011). Relationships with therapists have been argued to be more important than the treatment they provide (Miller et al., 1998).

However, caution is needed when seeking to deliver on the ethical commitments at the heart of PCC. More specifically, while reliance on autonomy in bioethics developed as a move away from paternalism, it also requires – as does PCC – real engagement with the specific preferences of services users. It is insufficient for healthcare providers or researchers to imagine what might seem to them worthy of autonomy, and then seek to implement that course. In this respect, the attempt of Schwartz and colleagues to study the value of PCC in the context of SUDs by artificially creating a treatment environment they imagined to be more supportive of service user autonomy, misses the importance of authentic patient values (Schwartz et al., 2017). That is, their effort to mimic PCC by creating environments that are, for example, more relaxed about service users breaking rules does not necessarily make services more autonomy promoting or respectful of service user preferences or values. In addition, it suggests that people with SUDs would prioritize the easing of rule-breaking penalties, and implies they cannot play a meaningful role in determining what type of care and support they want. Both assumptions risk exacerbating the stigma around SUDs, and illustrate the ethical challenges that debates in the area must contend. As the following section will now illustrate, the focus of PCC on the values of service users must work alongside an approach to health ethics that prioritizes public rather than individual health.

Public Health, Ethics, and Stigma

Ethics Lessons from the HIV/AIDS Pandemic

Developments in bioethics have tended to be reactive in nature and led by contemporary challenges. As noted above, the individually focused account of bioethics was driven by events that prioritized the need to protect individuals. This primacy was challenged in the 1980s by the emergence of HIV infection and cases of AIDS that required a response that prioritized public health. Important for ethical treatments of stigma, HIV rates were high among stigmatized groups – gay men and intravenous drug users in developed countries – and much attention focused on protecting public health while not exacerbating problems for these hard-to-reach groups. More specifically, there was concern that using traditional public health measures among these groups, like mandatory testing, screening, and case reporting, could drive infection underground and make it harder to treat. Early in the HIV/AIDS pandemic, this led to calls for the civil liberties or rights of those impacted to be respected and not overridden by public health policies. The resulting health and human rights focus contended that to respond to public health challenges effectively and ethically, it is important to work through human rights requirements that individuals are respected (Mann et al., 1994). In this respect, architect of the health and human rights approach, Jonathan Mann (and colleagues), argued that HIV/AIDS was marked by "a consistent pattern through which discrimination, marginalization, stigmatization and, more generally, a lack of respect for human rights and dignity of individuals and groups heightens their vulnerability to becoming exposed to HIV" (Mann et al., 1994, p. 20f.).

It appeared that demands public health should work through human rights (and autonomy), and not override them, had been established as central to protecting community well-being. But soon scientific developments that allowed for the testing and treatment of HIV meant that regarding HIV/AIDS as an "exception" to traditional public health measures became questionable and began to be challenged (Oppenheimer & Bayer, 2009; Smith & Whiteside, 2010). More specifically, debates moved away from a focus on human rights and protection of individual liberty, and toward traditional public health requirements that individual wishes can be overridden to protect the community (Childress et al., 2002). As Bayer notes, once HIV/AIDS was perceived to be less of a threat to the wider community, "exceptionalist" policies began to "lose their force" (Bayer, 1991). Importantly, this was not, as Wynia explains, because it was thought a good idea to deliberately stigmatize HIV or AIDS, but because it was hoped that making screening and testing "widespread" would normalize the practice and lead to a decline in stigma (Wynia, 2006). It is significant that, even when the intensity of debates around HIV cooled, plans to deliberately stigmatize gay men as a way to control infection would have led to heated objections. This is not least because community activism – particularly among politically active gay men – played a significant role in influencing policy around HIV/AIDS (Parker, 2011). However, in the next phase of the development of public health ethics, the deliberate use of stigma or moral condemnation is discussed and recommended as a viable option for managing certain behavior-related health issues.

The Development of Public Health Ethics

Public health ethics began to develop in a systematic manner around the year 2000. Its development was promoted by a number of public health challenges that required a response different to that offered by traditional bioethics. These challenges include HIV/AIDS and other infectious diseases, but also, chronic health conditions such as heart disease, diabetes, and cancers. The development of public health ethics is iterative, and a number of frameworks are available (Kass, 2004; Upshur, 2002). However, its foundational values include: the protection of public interest(s); solidarity (we are all in this together); proportionate constraints on individual autonomy or freedoms; and an interest in social justice, rather than the allocation of resources for individual service users (Childress et al., 2002). Human rights is still part of public health ethics (Childress et al., 2002). However, like public health itself, ethical debate in the field is focused on public interests, needs, and utility.

Stigma: A Public Health Resource?

This broader focus on issues like public interest and solidarity appears to offer a better foundation from which to address the social responsibilities and other determinants of SUDs and the stigma that surrounds them.

However, when scholars with an interest in public health ethics have addressed stigma and issues relating to SUDs, their work has not always tried to remove negative social attitudes toward such health conditions. In 2008 Bayer published a paper that interrogated "the orthodoxy" on the role of stigma in public health (Bayer, 2008). More specifically, he challenged assumptions that stigma could only be problematic for health. He suggested that the role of stigma in attempts to promote smoking cessation led to the "denormalization" of smoking. This suggested that stigma should be examined more closely to determine its value. Bayer acknowledges that the impact of using stigma in the context of SUDs is variable. That is, while smoking did decrease among some due to efforts to denormalize it (Evans-Polce et al., 2015), smoking came to be concentrated among those in lower socioeconomic groups (Bayer, 2008). Bayer also acknowledges another failure of using stigma in the context of illicit drug use through the War on Drugs and the resulting "destructive pattern of mass incarcerations" (Bayer & Fairchild, 2015; Williamson et al., 2014). While it is easy to move past these shortcomings and back to the (restricted) success of stigma among smokers, their ethical implications merit more attention.

The prospect of deliberately using stigma to control health-related behaviors risks layering additional stigma or disenfranchisement onto people who are already socially marginalized and disadvantaged; this might be referred to as "'stigma-max." Although the selective use of stigma can be mooted, in reality the general nature of public health policies means the impacts of "denormalization" strategies risk being felt beyond the intended targets. This could include people who, for a variety of reasons, struggle to trust the health systems they need to rely on. In addition, it is also feasible that if their behaviors are considered undesirable, stigma could be deliberately used against those already vulnerable. If health issues like SUDs are partly influenced by social and environmental factors, the deliberate use of measures that stigmatize lead to concerns about "victim-blaming" (Faden et al., 2020), or the reprimanding or shunning of people for things they cannot, alone, change. Related to this are concerns that the deliberate use of stigma is blind to the impact that social disadvantage can have on people's health and well-being. In this respect, Callahan has also argued that the use of stigma can be ethically acceptable to impact obesity. He notes that stigma helped him to stop smoking. However, it is notable that Callahan was a senior academic and a key player in the development of bioethics as a field (Callahan, 2013). Thus, his personal experience of stigma is likely much different from people in lower socioeconomic groups.

This point leads to another concern about who will be stigmatized, or more specifically, about who it is thought acceptable to stigmatize. As noted above, even when HIV exceptionalism was phased out, the approach adopted by policy was to make HIV testing usual or normal through greater availability. It was not to deliberately stigmatize or shame gay men to get them to test. This makes it important to consider what it is about groups like the obese and people with SUDs that means it is acceptable to target them with stigma, or in some cases "stigma-max." In this respect, there are concerns such people are simply easy targets because, unlike gay men, they often lack the support needed to defend their interests. Although increasingly people with SUDs are joining visible advocacy groups, many still seek support through organizations in which they are anonymous (Alcoholics or Narcotics Anonymous). This makes it difficult for them to articulate publicly (and powerfully) the impacts of stigma or social marginalization on their lives, and, importantly, they will often lack the advocacy support to object to their public shaming.

Other concerns with the deliberate use of stigma also exist. Key to Bayer's argument on the ethics of stigma are the categorizations of stigma employed by Link and Phelan to argue that ethical assessments of stigma require a careful analysis, rather than blanket condemnations (Bayer, 2008; Bayer & Fairchild, 2015; Link & Phelan, 2001). More specifically, Link and Phelan (2001) argue that stigma is a "matter of degree" and its negative effects vary. Bayer and Fairchild take this to support their argument that not all stigmatization is necessarily ethically unacceptable because there are "differences between stigma that causes discomfort and that which deeply wounds" (Bayer & Fairchild, 2015, p. 614), and it can potentially be used to "reintegrate" people into society, not simply exclude them from it (Bayer, 2008; Braithwaite, 1989). I have already suggested that the population focus of public health makes the targeting of stigma difficult given its potential for collateral damage. In addition, other aspects of Link and Phelan's work are pertinent: following their discussion of degrees of stigmatization they consider how stigma can be alleviated. They reject the idea of focusing on particular issues as a way to break down the "morass of interconnecting stigma-facets into a more tractable problem" (Link & Phelan, 2001, p. 380). This is because it "leaves the broader context untouched," and they argue for a "multifaceted and multilevel" approach and one that addresses the "fundamental cause of stigma" (Link & Phelan, 2001, p. 381). This suggestion, that a joined-up approach to stigma is important, problematizes the use of Link and Phelan's work to argue that ad hoc stigmatization may be desirable and ethically justifiable.

Rather, the multifaceted approach recommended by Link and Phelan leads to a need to emphasize that health contexts and experiences are interconnected. The idea that stigma can be used when convenient overlooks the impact this will have more widely. Policy makers, healthcare professionals or close contacts behaving like a 'capricious parent' towards people with SUDs risks fracturing peoples' much-needed trust in health systems (Williamson et al., 2014). Service user trust is fragile. It is concerning that what efforts to deliberately use stigma show is that the moralizing of the moral model of addiction – which we thought long since discredited – is alive and well. This is not a good foundation from which to encourage health scientists to engage more consistently with ethicists.

Looking Forward: Ethical Literacy, Engagement, and Consistency

We have seen that ethical issues are important determiners of negative attitudes toward people with SUDs and the stigma-driven discrimination that results. Also ethically significant for SUDs is the deliberate use of stigma to control socially undesirable behaviors. In this final section of the chapter, I will identify a number of features that require more attention in ethical debates around SUDs and their stigmatization. As the initial examination of the obstacles to ethical assessment of SUDs and stigma revealed, mainstream science contributions to the field can sideline the importance of ethical debate. I have suggested that a ramification of this is that civic and professional debates on stigma require much greater ethical support to ensure they are well grounded. Thoroughgoing interdisciplinarity must be embraced. The need to cultivate ethics literacy is led by a number of issues including the need to provide ethical support for contextually aware engagement between stakeholders with interests in SUDs and stigma, and the importance of considering how ethical inconsistency influences trust when addressing health issues relating to stigmatized conditions like SUDs.

Contextually Aware Engagement

We have seen that relational factors, such as a good working alliance and empathy with service users, are important for the success of SUDs treatment (Norcross & Wampold, 2011), and, critically, familiarity or contact with people impacted by SUDs can help to address stigma. More generally, commitment to PCC also requires greater relational support. I have argued that the individually based ethic that dominates work on SUDs is not well equipped to support or inform exchange or engagement. This is important because focusing on individuals, and not the contextual factors that influence them, can skew debates toward blaming substance users. To correct this focus, it is necessary to increase the ethical significance of relationships, engagement, and the contexts in professional and civic discourse on stigma and SUDs. Placing people and issues in their wider context provides a route to seeing their complexity. Providing context can, where appropriate, diffuse the blame (stigma) that falls on individuals. This is significant because SUDs, like other health conditions, develop in and are either reduced or exacerbate by exchanges with others and the environments in which they take place. The individualism that dominates bioethics and liberal democracies is often too blinkered to appreciate the need to respond to these influences that are fundamental to more accurately assessing the responsibilities around SUDs. We have seen that an alternative understanding of autonomy has been presented by feminist philosophers, who argue that we become autonomous or empowered through relationships. Only by introducing more diverse ethical knowledge into debates, on this and other points, is it feasible to have meaningful, accurate exchanges on the role of stigma and the diverse responsibilities that exist in respect of SUDs.

Ethical Consistency

Initially I highlighted that medical model approaches to SUDs suggest that, as a health problem, they require a response that is science led and essentially value-free. I have argued that this approach is insufficient given the ethical challenges and questions integral to responding to stigmatization. We have seen that public health ethicists have argued that SUDs might be worthy of deliberate stigmatization. These two prominent approaches don't fit easily together. One rejects stigma, the other opens the way to sanctioning it. Such contradictory approaches are not a good foundation for cultivating useful and respectful civic debate around SUDs.

Other ethical inconsistencies on the issue also exist. For example, commitments to PCC point to the importance of service user values and opinions, including the importance of this approach in the context of SUDs. But again, the failure to address the stigmatization of SUDs, and especially arguments for its deliberate use, undermine the veracity of claims across health services that there is an ethical requirement to consistently respect the people that use them. Even if stigma changes behaviors in a way that leads to people being healthier, the colleterial damage to trust requires serious consideration. As with empowerment efforts in the context of SUDs, it is debatable precisely what ethical support PCC requires from principles like autonomy (e.g., relational, rather than noninterference). However, such questions do not undermine the basic ethical commitments to not eroding the innate value of the people who need to have access to reliable, trustworthy health services.

Conclusion

Substance use disorders are among the most stigmatized of health problems. It is unfortunate that the important role of ethics in alleviating stigma is impeded by a number of obstacles. This includes the lack of interdisciplinary work, and the dominance of an individually based ethic that cannot do justice to the complexity of the issues. Also significant are attempts to deliberately use stigma as a public health tool. I have indicated that, even if such proposals have some positive outcomes, their negative impacts are ethically concerning. Proposals to use stigma risk loading further marginalization onto people who are already socially disadvantaged. This carries implications for service users' trust. In addition, the use of stigma keeps the moral model of addiction alive, and so impedes the much-needed collaboration between science and ethics. This point is critical because there are many important ethical debates that need to be had around SUDs, responsibilities – individual and social – and empowerment. But while ethics remains marginal to much mainstream science and policy work these debates cannot take place in a meaningful way. Yet while ethicists continue to flirt with the deliberate use of stigma, science has good reason to keep its distance.

References

Adams, J. M., & Volkow, N. D. (2020). Ethical imperatives to overcome stigma against people with substance use disorders. *AMA Journal of Ethics*, 22(1), E702–E708. https://doi.org/10.1001/amajethics.2020.702

Bayer, R. (1991). Public health policy and the AIDS epidemic. An end to HIV exceptionalism? *New England Journal of Medicine*, 324(21), 1500–1504. https://doi.org/10.1056/nejm199105233242111

  (2008). Stigma and the ethics of public health: Not can we but should we. *Social Science & Medicine*, 67(3), 463–472. https://doi.org/10.1016/j.socscimed.2008.03.017

Bayer, R., & Fairchild, A. L. (2015). Stigma: Time for a hard conversation. *International Journal on Drug Policy*, 26(7), 613–614. https://doi.org/10.1016/j.drugpo.2015.01.017

Beauchamp, T., & Childress, J. (1979). *The principles of biomedical ethics*. Oxford University Press.

(2019). *The principles of biomedical ethics* (8th ed.). Oxford University Press.

Berridge, V. (1979). Morality and medical science: Concepts of narcotic addiction in Britain, 1820–1926. *Annals of Science, 36*(1), 67–85. https://doi.org/10.1080/00033797900200131

Braithwaite, J. (1989). *Crime, shame, and reintegration*. Cambridge University Press.

Brandon, T. H., Vidrine, J. I., & Litvin, E. B. (2007). Relapse and relapse prevention. *Annual Review of Clinical Psychology, 3*, 257–284. https://doi.org/10.1146/annurev.clinpsy.3.022806.091455

Callahan, D. (2013). Obesity: Chasing an elusive epidemic. *Hastings Center Report, 43*(1), 34–40. https://doi.org/10.1002/hast.114

Childress, J. F., Faden, R. R., Gaare, R. D., et al. (2002). Public health ethics: Mapping the terrain. *Journal of Law, Medicine & Ethics, 30*(2), 170–178. https://doi.org/10.1111/j.1748-720x.2002.tb00384.x

Corrigan, P. W., Angell, B., Davidson, L., et al. (2012). From adherence to self-determination: Evolution of a treatment paradigm for people with serious mental illnesses. *Psychiatric Services, 63*(2), 169–173. https://doi.org/10.1176/appi.ps.201100065

Dackis, C., & O'Brien, C. (2005). Neurobiology of addiction: Treatment and public policy ramifications. *Nature Neuroscience, 8*(11), 1431–1436. https://doi.org/10.1038/nn1105-1431

Ells, C., Hunt, M. R., & Chambers-Evans, J. (2011). Relational autonomy as an essential component of patient-centered care. *International Journal of Feminist Approaches to Bioethics, 4*(2), 79–101. https://doi.org/10.3138/ijfab.4.2.79

Evans-Polce, R. J., Castaldelli-Maia, J. M., Schomerus, G., & Evans-Lacko, S. E. (2015). The downside of tobacco control? Smoking and self-stigma: A systematic review. *Social Science & Medicine, 145*, 26–34. https://doi.org/10.1016/j.socscimed.2015.09.026

Faden, R., Bernstein, J., & Shebaya, S. (2020). Public health ethics. In E. N. Zalta (Ed.), *Stanford encyclopedia of philosophy* (Fall 2020 ed.). Stanford University. https://plato.stanford.edu/archives/fall2020/entries/publichealth-ethics/

Foddy, B., & Savulescu, J. (2006). Addiction and autonomy: Can addicted people consent to the prescription of their drug of addiction? *Bioethics, 20*(1), 1–15. https://doi.org/10.1111/j.1467-8519.2006.00470.x

Fox, R. C., & Swazey, J. P. (1984). Medical morality is not bioethics – medical ethics in China and the United States. *Perspectives in Biology and Medicine, 27*(3), 336–360. https://doi.org/10.1353/pbm.1984.0060

Gessert, C. E. (2008). The problem with autonomy. *Minnesota Medicine, 91*(4), 40–42.

Institute of Medicine. (2001). *Crossing the quality chasm: A new health system for the 21st century*. National Academy Press.

(2006). *Improving the quality of healthcare for mental and substance use conditions: The quality chasm series*. National Academies Press.

Janssens, M. J., Van Rooij, M. F., ten Have, H. A., Kortmann, F. A., & Van Wijmen, F. C. (2004). Pressure and coercion in the care for the addicted: Ethical perspectives. *Journal of Medical Ethics*, *30*(5), 453–458. https://doi.org/10.1136/jme.2002.002212

Jones, E. E., Farina, A., Hastorf, A. H., Markus, H., Miller, D. T., & Scott, R. A. (1984). *Social stigma: The psychology of marked relationships*. Freeman Press.

Kass, N. E. (2004). Public health ethics: From foundations and frameworks to justice and global public health. *Journal of Law, Medicine & Ethics*, *32*(2), 232–242. https://doi.org/10.1111/j.1748-720x.2004.tb00470.x

Kelly, J. F., Bergman, B., Hoeppner, B. B., Vilsaint, C., & White, W. L. (2017). Prevalence and pathways of recovery from drug and alcohol problems in the United States population: Implications for practice, research, and policy. *Drug and Alcohol Dependence*, *181*, 162–169. https://doi.org/10.1016/j.drugalcdep.2017.09.028

Levy, N. (2007). The social: A missing term in the debate over addiction and voluntary control. *American Journal of Bioethics*, *7*(1), 35–36. https://doi.org/10.1080/15265160601064173

Link, B. G., & Phelan, J. C. (2001). Conceptualizing stigma. *Annual Review of Sociology*, *27*, 363–385. https://doi.org/10.1146/annurev.soc.27.1.363

Mancini, A. D. (2018). Self-determination theory: A framework for the recovery paradigm. *Advances in Psychiatric Treatment*, *14*(5), 358–365. https://doi.org/10.1192/apt.bp.107.004036

Mann, J. M., Gostin, L., Gruskin, S., Brennan, T., Lazzarini, Z., & Fineberg, H. V. (1994). Health and human rights. *Health and Human Rights*, *1*(1), 6–23.

Mehta, S., & Farina, A. (1997). Is being 'sick' really better? Effect of the disease view of mental disorder on stigma. *Journal of Social and Clinical Psychology*, *16*(4), 405–419. https://doi.org/10.1521/jscp.1997.16.4.405

Mellor, R., Lancaster, K., & Ritter, A. (2019). Systematic review of untreated remission from alcohol problems: Estimation lies in the eye of the beholder. *Journal of Substance Abuse Treatment*, *102*, 60–72. https://doi.org/10.1016/j.jsat.2019.04.004

Miller, W., Andrews, N., Wilbourne, P., et al. (1998). A wealth of alternatives: Effective treatments for alcohol problems. In W. R. Miller & N. Heather (Eds.), *Treating addictive behaviors: Processes of change* (pp. 203–210). Plenum Press.

National Academies of Sciences, Engineering, and Medicine. (2016). *Ending discrimination against people with mental and substance use disorders: The evidence for stigma change*. National Academies Press. https://doi.org/10.17226/23442

National Commission for the Protection of Human Subjects of Biomedical and Behavioral Research. (1979). *The Belmont report: Ethical principles and guidelines for the protection of human subjects of research*. Department of

Health, Education, and Welfare. www.hhs.gov/ohrp/regulations-and-policy/belmont-report/index.html

Nedelsky, J. (1989). Reconceiving autonomy: Sources, thoughts, and possibilities. *Yale Journal of Law and Feminism, 1*(1), 7–36. https://digitalcommons.law.yale.edu/yjlf/vol1/iss1/5/

Norcross, J. C., & Wampold, B. E. (2011). Evidence-based therapy relationships: Research conclusions and clinical practices. *Psychotherapy, 48*(1), 98–102. https://doi.org/10.1037/a0022161

Nuernberg Military Tribunals. (1949). *Trials of war criminals before the Nuernberg Military Tribunals under Control Council Law No. 10 – permissible medical experiments*. US Government Printing Office. www.loc.gov/rr/frd/Military_Law/pdf/NT_war-criminals_Vol-II.pdf

O'Neill, O. (2002). *Autonomy and trust in bioethics*. Cambridge University Press. https://doi.org/10.1017/CBO9780511606250

Oppenheimer, G., & Bayer, R. (2009). The rise and fall of AIDS exceptionalism. *The Virtual Mentor, 11*(12), 988–992. https://doi.org/10.1001/virtualmentor.2009.11.12.mhst1-0912

Parker, R. (2011). Grassroots activism, civil society mobilization, and the politics of the global HIV/AIDS epidemic. *The Brown Journal of World Affairs, 17*(2), 21–37. www.jstor.org/stable/24590789

Peele, S. (1990). What works in addiction treatment and what doesn't: Is the best therapy no therapy? *International Journal of the Addictions, 25*(12a), 1409–1419. https://doi.org/10.3109/10826089009088552

Pickard, H. (2017). Responsibility without blame for addiction. *Neuroethics, 10*(1), 169–180. https://doi.org/10.1007/s12152-016-9295-2

Plato. (2007). *The Republic* (D. Lee, Trans.). Penguin Classics.

Randles, D., & Tracy, J. L. (2013). Nonverbal displays of shame predict relapse and declining health in recovering alcoholics. *Clinical Psychological Science, 1*(2), 149–155. https://doi.org/10.1177/2167702612470645

Room, R., Rehm, J., Trotter, R., Paglia, A., & Ustun, T. (2001). Cross-cultural views on stigma, valuation, parity, and social values towards disability. In T. Ustun, S. Chatterji, & J. Rehm (Eds.), *Disability and culture: Universalism and diversity* (pp. 247–291). Hogrefe & Huber Publishing.

Ryan, R. M. (1995). Psychological needs and the facilitation of integrative processes. *Journal of Personality, 63*(3), 397–427. https://doi.org/10.1111/j.1467-6494.1995.tb00501.x

Schomerus, G., & Angermeyer, M. C. (2008). Stigma and its impact on help-seeking for mental disorders: What do we know? *Epidemiology and Psychiatric Sciences, 17*(1), 31–37. https://doi.org/10.1017/s1121189x00002669

Schomerus, G., Lucht, M., Holzinger, A., Matschinger, H., Carta, M. G., & Angermeyer, M. C. (2011). The stigma of alcohol dependence compared with other mental disorders: A review of population studies. *Alcohol and Alcoholism, 46*(2), 105–112. https://doi.org/10.1093/alcalc/agq089

Schwartz, R. P., Kelly, S. M., Mitchell, S. G., et al. (2017). Patient-centered methadone treatment: A randomized clinical trial. *Addiction, 112*(3), 454–464. https://doi.org/10.1111/add.13622

Smith, J. H., & Whiteside, A. (2010). The history of AIDS exceptionalism. *Journal of the International AIDS Society, 13*(1), 47. https://doi.org/10.1186/1758-2652-13-47

Stoljar, N. (2011). Informed consent and relational conceptions of autonomy. *Journal of Medicine and Philosophy, 36*(4), 375–384. https://doi.org/10.1093/jmp/jhr029

Stone, E. M., Kennedy-Hendricks, A., Barry, C. L., Bachhuber, M. A., & McGinty, E. E. (2021). The role of stigma in U.S. primary care physicians' treatment of opioid use disorder. *Drug and Alcohol Dependence, 221*, Article 108627. https://doi.org/10.1016/j.drugalcdep.2021.108627

Upshur, R. E. (2002). Principles for the justification of public health intervention. *Canadian Journal of Public Health, 93*(2), 101–103. https://doi.org/10.1007/bf03404547

Volkow, N. (2004). Nora Volkow: Motivated neuroscientist. *Molecular Interventions, 4*(5), 243–247. https://doi.org/10.1124/mi.4.5.2

(Expert). (2020, September 30). *Dr. Volkow explains the basics of drugs & addiction* [Online video]. National Institute on Drug Abuse. www.drugabuse.gov/videos/dr-volkow-explains-basics-drugs-addiction

Williamson, L. (2012). Destigmatizing alcohol dependence: The requirement for an ethical (not only medical) remedy. *American Journal of Public Health, 102*(5), e5–e8. https://doi.org/10.2105/ajph.2011.300629

(2021). Creating an ethical culture to support recovery from substance use disorders. *Journal of Medical Ethics, 47*(12), e9. https://doi.org/10.1136/medethics-2020-106661

Williamson, L., Thom, B., Stimson, G. V., & Uhl, A. (2014). Stigma as a public health tool: Implications for health promotion and citizen involvement. *International Journal of Drug Policy, 25*(3), 333–335. https://doi.org/10.1016/j.drugpo.2014.04.008

Wolpe, P. R. (1998). The triumph of autonomy in American bioethics: A sociological view. In R. De Vries & J. Subedi (Eds.), *Bioethics and society: Constructing the ethical enterprise* (pp. 38–59). Prentice Hall.

World Health Organization. (1978, September 12). *Declaration of Alma-Ata: International Conference on Primary Health Care, Alma-Ata, USSR.* https://www.who.int/publications/almaata_declaration_en.pdf

Wynia, M. K. (2006). Routine screening: Informed consent, stigma and the waning of HIV exceptionalism. *American Journal of Bioethics, 6*(4), 5–8. https://doi.org/10.1080/15265160600843536

CHAPTER 6

Intersectional Stigma in Substance Use Disorders

Daniel Dittrich and Georg Schomerus

Introduction

The stigma process, as described by Bruce Link and Jo Phelan (Link & Phelan, 2001), begins by distinguishing and labeling human differences, based on certain attributes like having a diagnosis of a substance use disorder (SUD). However, people usually have more than one attribute that distinguishes them from others, and, not infrequently, several of their attributes can lead to stigmatization. SUDs in particular often occur in companion to other stigmatized characteristics – as causes for substance use, or consequences of substance use, or just incidentally. Someone with an SUD might be stigmatized because of their economic status, employment status, criminal record, race, gender, sexual orientation, or due to having a comorbid physical condition, just to name a few. Isolating each of these conditions when addressing stigma might miss the complexity of injustice and discrimination in our society. The concept of intersectionality addresses this complexity. Intersectionality is often about issues we have not yet fully realized (Purdie-Vaughns & Eibach, 2008). In a frequently used metaphor, intersectionality provides a lens through which findings become visible, which have previously been hard to see. To better understand how a perspective of intersectionality is necessary to understand the stigma of SUDs fully, we start this chapter with a very brief exploration of the concept's history.

A Brief History of Intersectionality

In 1976, five black women brought discrimination charges against General Motors in *Degraffenreid* v. *General Motors* (1976). GM had hired black women only after 1960 and had later laid them off under a "last hired – first fired" policy. The court had refused to recognize that discrimination on the combined ground of being black and female was within "what the drafters of the relevant statutes intended." It declined statutory remedies, as GM did employ white women and black males. Kimberlé Crenshaw, a black female American lawyer and nowadays professor of law, argued against this use of antidiscrimination law and coined the term intersectionality, introducing it with a metaphor (Crenshaw, 1989):

> Consider an analogy to traffic in an intersection, coming and going in all four directions. Discrimination, like traffic through an intersection, may flow in one direction, and it may flow in another. If an accident happens in an intersection, it can be caused by cars traveling from any number of directions and, sometimes, from all of them. Similarly, if a Black woman is harmed because she is in the intersection, her injury could result from sex discrimination or race discrimination. ... [P]roviding legal relief only when Black women show that their claims are based on race or on sex is analogous to calling an ambulance for the victim only after the driver responsible for the injuries is identified. (Crenshaw, 1989, p. 149)

Since these establishing arguments, intersectionality has come a long way. It has become a "gold standard" multidisciplinary approach for analyzing subjects' experiences of identity and oppression (Nash, 2008). It has become a "scholarly buzzword" (Nash, 2008) and has been criticized in sociopolitical debate (Sullivan, 2017, 2019) and suggestions for further developments have been made (Nash, 2008, 2019). But, as Crenshaw has concluded in an interview: "it stands, because it resonates with people's lives, but because it resonates with people's lives, it's under attack" (Steinmetz, 2020). This chapter aims to show what benefits a look through the intersectionality lens holds for the understanding associated with the stigma of SUDs.

What Is Intersectional Stigma?

The detrimental effect of combined disadvantageous positions on different identity axes was evident to researchers before intersectionality entered the scientific stage. Terminologically, "double," "layered," or "overlapping stigma" have been used to emphasize areas where focusing on one form of stigma at a time falls short of capturing the lived experience of stigmatization. These terms, however, have been criticized for prematurely implying an additive interaction effect for different forms of stigma (Turan et al., 2019), where the very nature of the interaction effects should be subject to scientific investigation. "Intersectional stigma," introduced by Michele Berger (2006), has emerged as the term under which thinking about intersectionality in stigma has come together. The question of how multiple low-status identities interact, however, has no consistent answer. On the one hand, many findings conform to a "risk model" (Vargas et al., 2020). This approach (also referred to as the "multiple jeopardy perspective" or "multiple-hierarchy stratification approach" [Vu et al., 2019]) assumes that different forms of marginalized identities add up so that the individuals with the highest number of low-status identities will experience the most severe form of stigmatization. In some cases, discrimination is even more severe than the "mere" sum of its parts – intersectionality's point of departure. This includes "intersectionality paradoxes," where an advantage of a high-status identity is paradoxically repealed by its intersection with a stigmatized identity. The relation between higher socioeconomic status (SES) and better health outcomes, for example, is clearly documented. Nevertheless, high rates of infant mortality among highly educated black women and higher homicide rates among black middle-class men persist (Bowleg, 2012). These paradoxes have been called the most noteworthy contributions of intersectionality (Vu et al., 2019) because they bring realities to light that otherwise would have remained obscured.

On the other hand, it is contended that processes and effects of intersectional stigma will differ not only in degree but in kind (Ciftci et al., 2013) and in some cases might even entail favorable outcomes. For example, Mereish and Bradford (2014) found that in a sample of a US urban community health center, sexual minority men of color had lower odds of substance use problems than white sexual minority men. By being exposed to multiple minority stressors, sexual minority men of color might have developed coping resources that made them more resilient to stressors and thereby against substance use. Findings like this have been humorously addressed as "the bright side of stigma" (Wang et al., 2016), or, more dryly, as conforming to a "resilience model" (Vargas et al., 2020).

However, in a review of studies on the combined effect of multiple types of discrimination on mental health, the authors found mostly support for the risk model, while fewer studies supported the resilience model (Vargas et al., 2020).

One important observation for structuring the numerous findings on intersectional stigma has been made by Vargas et al. (2020): the multiple literature on SUD stigma answers related, but different questions: (a) whether it increases a person's chances of poor mental health, and (b) how much of a person's mental health problems are explained by different types of discrimination.

Intersectional SUD Stigma

To revisit Crenshaw's metaphorical image: the four-way crossroads of race, gender, sexual orientation, and class has been intersectionality's traditional focus (Crenshaw, 1989; Nash, 2008). This section will provide an overview of findings on SUD stigma at these intersections. Later we will ask what other categories of marginalization should be considered.

Racialized Drug Stigma

An abundance of evidence shows how racism affects the stigma of people with SUDs in North America. This could easily fill a chapter itself (which others have written: Mendoza et al., 2019). Public stigma in the form of judicial discrimination evidenced by sentencing research has repeatedly refuted the "no discrimination thesis," which contends that once there are adequate controls for other factors (i.e., criminal history and severity of the current offense), unwarranted racial disparity ceases to exist. In a meta-analysis of 71 studies conducted in the USA, Mitchell (2005) found that African Americans generally were sentenced more harshly than whites for substance-related crimes.

Lee and Rasinski (2006) examined racialized public drug stigma in a nationally representative telephone survey in the USA of white Americans. They asked about appropriate sanctions for being caught for the first time with five grams of cocaine. Though the predicted direct relationship between racism and severity of sanction was not found, a strong indirect relationship was found as racism operated through morality, blame, and beliefs about racial group use of cocaine. But racialized public drug stigma is not merely an abandoned phenomenon of a darker past. When the opioid epidemic in North America occurred, it coincided with growing scientific awareness for differential effects of race. The initial constellation itself can be considered as a special subtype of intersectional paradox (cf. section "What Is Intersectional Stigma?"), where intersecting privilege turned to disadvantage: Hansen and Netherland (2016) gave a detailed account of how racially stratified insurance coverage and access to physicians, which was primarily a privilege of US whites, led to an unparalleled increase of nonmedical use of prescription opioids being primarily a phenomenon of white communities. As a consequence of this epidemic, the life expectancy of US whites ultimately declined. The public response, however, is an impressive example of how race and class determine the stigma associated with nonmedical opioid use. While opioid dependency in the form of heroin and crack had been centered in communities of color, and, via harsher penalties and criminalization, had led to an "epidemic of incarcerations of young black men" (Hansen & Netherland, 2016) the response to the opioid epidemic was of a totally different nature:

> Rather than arresting opioid users, regulators mandated physicians to use Prescription Drug Monitoring Programs, instituted voluntary take-back programs for unused medication, and disseminated the opioid overdose reversal medication naloxone.... The arrest rate for sale or possession of manufactured drugs was one-quarter that for the sale or possession of heroin or cocaine, even though prescription opioid misuse far exceeded heroin use. (Hansen & Netherland, 2016, p. 2128)

This inequality, of course, was not only mediated by race, but represents a truly intersectional phenomenon, as the 91% of the US patients taking buprenorphine three years after the FDA's approval were not only white, but also college-educated and employed (Hansen & Netherland, 2016). Mendoza et al. (2019, p. 132) summarize: the "criminalization of addiction among nonwhites and medicalization of addiction among whites deeply influenced and differentiated the experiences of stigma among these groups."

Gender and SUD Stigma

Do men or women who use drugs experience more severe SUD stigma? A recent review of studies on this question exposed a remarkable difference in results depending on whether qualitative or quantitative methodology was used (Meyers et al., 2021). Quantitative literature was equivocal regarding the influence of gender on SUD stigma, with 55% of the quantitative studies finding no association between gender and SUD stigma, 10% identifying women who use drugs as more stigmatized, and 5% finding men to be more stigmatized. In contrast, nearly all (97%) of the qualitative articles demonstrated that women who use drugs experienced greater levels of drug use-related stigma. From this discrepancy, the authors deduce the need for tailoring drug use–related stigma measures for women who use drugs.

Reasons discussed for a heightened female stigma are mainly twofold. For one thing, women's drug use is associated with a perceived inability to fulfill traditional gender roles, such as taking care of dependent children (Becker et al., 2016; Sorsdahl et al., 2012). Women with an SUD, therefore, might be morally sanctioned for not following cultural scripts of selfless nurturing, and supposedly endangering their children. Secondly, women can be subject to increased blame due to conservative beliefs about appropriate behavior in patriarchal culture, as drug use is associated with fantasies of female sexual availability and "immoral" behavior (Sorsdahl et al., 2012).

The finding of a more severe SUD stigma is not homogenous, though, and some studies even suggest the contrary. This is in line with findings on mental-illness stigma in general, where women are subjected to somewhat less mental-illness stigma than men (Farina, 1981). Regarding SUD stigma, men have higher rates than females for opioid use disorder (Goodyear et al., 2018; Sattler et al., 2017) and alcohol use disorder (Sattler et al., 2017). This is contextualized in light of stereotypic gender traits and the ensuing affective reactions (Ottati et al., 2005; Sattler et al., 2017). In this line of reasoning, addiction in men might be seen as having more negative consequences such as aggressive or dangerous behavior and therefore be perceived as more harmful and threatening (Sattler et al., 2017). Women with an SUD, on the other hand, might elicit impressions of requiring protection and help, which could amount to "benevolence stigma" (Corrigan & Wassel, 2008; Flaskerud & Winslow, 1998). In support, a vignette study on a large sample by Goodyear et al. (2018) found higher SUD stigma rates and higher negative affect ratings for male drug users.

These conflicting findings suggest that in addition to the question of whether men or women experience more severe SUD stigma, it will be fruitful to assess differences in their respective SUD stigma experience. They are not alike because they are rooted in varying societal gender norms. Overall, the interactions of gender and SUD stigma do not seem clear-cut, and an intersectional perspective will help to explain opposing findings.

Sexual Orientation and SUD Stigma

Although most studies examine the influence of femininity and masculinity on SUD stigma under the politically correct gender headline, it is mostly operationalized as a gender binary. This approach has been criticized as "reinstating the very stereotypes it was meant to remedy" (Sandelowski et al., 2009, p. 283). Where aspects of nonbinary gender and self-identification are addressed, it is under the category of sexual orientation.

People who identify with sexual minorities experience significant stigma. With this group in mind, Meyer proposed the concept of minority stress (Meyer, 2007), which has much common ground with intersectionality. It assumes being a sexual minority is linked with chronic stress by social processes that are additive to general stressors as experienced by all people. Intersectional minority stress through stigmatization has been repeatedly linked to greater risk of substance use problems among sexual minorities compared to heterosexuals (Green & Feinstein, 2012; King et al., 2019; Marshal et al., 2008) and is mainly interpreted as a way to cope with sexual minority stress.

There are substance use disparities among the different subgroups of LGBTQIA+ communities. Sexual minority women have a higher risk for substance use compared with heterosexual women. For sexual minority men, the risk seems to be smaller, and less pervasive (Burgard et al., 2005; Cochran & Mays, 2000; Cochran et al., 2007; Drabble et al., 2005). An intersectional analysis showed how substance use disparities become more nuanced when race is included as an additional axis of identity (Mereish & Bradford, 2014). In a sample of an urban community health center in northeast America, lifetime substance use problems were higher for sexual minority men than for heterosexual men and sexual minority women than for heterosexual women. When examining the interaction with race, a pronounced difference was found wherein sexual minority women of color had much higher odds of substance use problems than heterosexual women of color. In contrast, no difference was found for sexual minority men of color with heterosexual men of color.

Access to SUD treatment is hampered for sexual minorities in various ways (Lombardi, 2007; Ross & Setchell, 2019). This emphasizes the need to specifically consider LGBTQIA+ inclusive interventions, and their needs in treatment environments. There is debate, though, that this might entail "mixed-blessings," as has been the case previously with other well-intentioned antistigma campaigns (Haslam & Kvaale, 2015). In a critical analysis of drug policies in Australia, Pienaar et al. caution that while it might be well intentioned to highlight the needs of LGBTQIA+ people, this might result in an unwarranted problematization of substance use among them (Pienaar et al., 2018). They fear it might constitute them as a targeted minority, justifying policy and state intervention into their lives. This touches the critical dynamics of inclusion and exclusion in antistigma action as a dynamic and simultaneous process (Hunting et al., 2015). It is a genuinely intersectional task to work out the nature of experience at individual intersections such as this one.

Socioeconomic Status and SUD Stigma

What Crenshaw referred to as "class" is mainly operationalized as SES in empiric research. However, the two constructs do not produce identical results in their relation with mental disorders (Muntaner et al., 2004).

Research whether people with lower SES have a higher risk for SUD is mixed. On the one hand, a broad body of research suggests higher substance use among people with lower SES (Potts & Henderson, 2020; Spooner, 2009). Higher stress levels caused by a shortage of money favor substance use (Spooner, 2009). Access to high-quality mental health care might be limited, making people with mental health disorders more prone to comorbid SUDs (Yang et al., 2019). Additionally, adolescents in low SES communities grow up more often in neighborhoods that are characterized by higher rates of unemployment, drug use, and drug availability, which is conducive for initiation of drug use (Spooner, 2009). On the other hand, there are examples of how a privileged SES can be a risk factor for increased substance use, too. Among several studies, higher family background SES was associated with higher rates of alcohol and marijuana consumption (Humensky, 2010; Patrick et al., 2012), as well as cocaine consumption (Humensky, 2010) among adolescents. These heterogeneous findings illustrate how exploring addiction stigma as a risk factor for SUDs needs to be addressed in more specific scenarios, for example by examining separate scenarios of drug initiation, use habits, cessation, abstinence, and relapse, as well as contrasting groups of substances (e.g., smoking and alcohol versus illicit drugs; Galea et al., 2004).

Apart from a risk factor perspective, do lower SES people experience more SUD stigma by people in their environment? The higher incidence of addiction in conjunction with findings that low-income neighbourhoods express more stigmatizing views suggest so (Potts & Henderson, 2020). This would be especially impactful, as there is considerable transgenerational stability of low SES (Senia et al., 2016) , making it challenging for low SES drug users to evade these surroundings. Potts and Henderson (2020) note that higher incidence of mental illness and higher levels of stigma experienced in lower SES environments would be at odds with another consistent finding in stigma research: familiarity with mental illness is strongly related to lower stigmatization levels. Among a UK national survey sample it was found that the positive effect of familiarity on stigma outcomes is weaker among lower socioeconomic groups. Possible mechanisms discussed are higher prognostic pessimism levels due to prior unfavorable experiences with mental disorders and the understanding that mental health problems result from social issues that are difficult to resolve in psychotherapy. Although this study addresses the broader field of mental illness in general, it is likely to be worse for people with SUDs, as attitudes toward persons with drug addiction, compared to those with mental illness, are more negative (Barry et al., 2014).

Another aspect of addiction stigma through class is the association of poverty with poorer treatment outcomes. This has been confirmed by meta-analysis for depression and anxiety disorders (Finegan et al., 2018), but single studies suggest the same for addiction (Saloner & Lê Cook, 2013). Another salient aspect of class is highlighted by an intersectional study on racial discrimination, socioeconomic position, and illicit drug use among blacks in the USA (Carliner et al., 2016). While there was no significant association between self-reported racial discrimination and frequent drug use for black people with low SES, this relationship was strong among people with higher SES. This is an intersectional paradox, as a risk model would suggest occupying two disadvantaged positions would create greater discrimination risk for people with low SES. It might be explained by the theory of relative deprivation (Carliner et al., 2016). For black people with higher SES, the opportunity for comparison may be more common due to more interaction with white neighbors and colleagues, producing higher perceptions of stigmatization. These experiences might increase higher awareness of inequity and exacerbate the insult of racial discrimination, resulting in greater psychosocial stress and increased risk for drug use as a coping behavior in black people with higher SES.

More Intersections

In addition to intersectionality's "big four" (race, gender, sexual orientation, and class), are there other critical intersections of identity for SUD stigma? We suggest adopting the utilitarian approach of harm reduction for the choice of additional intersectional locations in SUD stigma. Harm reduction is a public health approach that provides practical remedies for those issues in drug use that convey the actual harm (Roe, 2005), for example, needle and syringe programs for intravenous drug users that help avoid transmission of blood-borne diseases. Harm reduction is characterized by a utilitarian approach that refrains from moral judgment. So wherever intersecting identities result in higher risk for developing an SUD or in having difficulties getting into therapy, these axes of identity merit attention. One way to identify the intersecting locations of these "sororities that no one wants to join" (Steinmetz, 2020) is by looking at sociodemographic variables associated with unmet need for mental health treatment. A recent analysis of a representative national US survey points to a number of additional intersections important for addiction stigma (Yang et al., 2019). First, the findings underline the urgency of this issue, with alcohol and pain reliever use disorder being the categories with the highest odds for unmet need for treatment. Stigmatization was the second most-often cited cause, preceded only by cost. Second, while female gender and lower SES were associated with higher odds of unmet need for mental health treatment, interestingly, of seven race categories, only Non-Hispanic Mixed was associated with higher unmet need. Third, *living in nonurban* areas and reporting *poor physical health* were associated with higher odds for unmet need and stigmatization as an access barrier. Fourth, looking at which groups have fallen through the study's cracks suggests they will easily fall through the cracks of mental health care, too: not included were *homeless people* and people living at institutions, which encompasses many people with *mental or physical disabilities*.

Sixth and last, the study assessed unmet need as a self-report variable. Therefore, it reflects levels of desired care instead of objective unmet need. Stigma may interfere early on in the help-seeking process and diminish perceived need for help (Schomerus et al., 2019). As there is evidence that hints at higher prognostic pessimism in lower socioeconomic groups (Potts & Henderson, 2020), this would likely render professional treatment less desirable and lower expressed need. A possible solution would be to make healthcare options more attractive and accessible to those who need them most, which would necessitate participatory research in groups underserved by current SUD health care.

Intersectionality in Interventions and Healthcare Provision

Intersectionality scholars, embedded in an activist and idealist background, have always linked their theoretical debates with concern for practical societal change. It is one of the core tenets of intersectionality to build coalitions among different groups and to work toward social justice (Hankivsky, 2014). As Nash (2008, p. 11) remarks, it was one thing to identify particular intersections as undertheorized or unacknowledged - but "so what?"

As "intersectionality is widely used but defined in different ways," (Hunting et al., 2015, p. 103) a first step is developing common concepts as to how to put intersectional theory into practice. Recently, intersectional frameworks have been published for interventions and policies that target mental illness and addiction stigma (Hunting et al., 2015; Stangl et al., 2019; Turan et al., 2019).

On a hands-on level, knowledge and teaching resources on intersectionality have been made freely available. Notable examples of high-quality low-threshold information include the "fun guide" (Dobson, 2013), and

"Intersectionality 101" (Hankivsky, 2014). Online platforms provide learning modules and promote a grasp of the breadth of individual experiences (Canadian Observatory on Homelessness, 2021). Group exercises can be found to induce personal reflection about their own intersectional constitution (Canadian Observatory on Homelessness, 2020). Coverage of model projects – for example, how intersectional analysis was brought in the development of women-centered supportive housing (Canadian Observatory on Homelessness, 2017) – can help to inform future projects. Although these examples do not specifically address intersectional SUD stigma, they are applicable for this field, too, and are recommended for everyone looking for ways to implement an intersectional perspective.

Implications

In many ways, the stigma of SUDs is a prototypical field to be examined through the intersectional lens. The broad array of substances encompassed by "SUD" accounts for enormous intracategorical diversity. Intersectionality as a methodological tool has been designed to cut through this myriad of different identities to reveal where our efforts to address addiction problems remain partial and exclusionary.

In addition to the classic intersectional categories of race, gender, class, and sexual orientation, we suggest addressing additional categories whenever there is theory and evidence pointing to unique intersections of hardship that require more tailored approaches. We need to go where the most significant amounts of hardship persist. For this purpose, we discuss the role of physical and intellectual disabilities, obesity and overweight, homelessness, living in a suburban or rural area, and citizenship versus immigrant status for research on intersectional SUD stigma. In any case, relevant categories will have to be "updated" concerning selection and meaning, as this is bound to vary over time. Although the stigma of SUDs seems more stable over time than the stigma of other mental disorders (Angermeyer et al., 2013; Schomerus et al., 2014), stigma is a volatile sociocultural phenomenon, demonstrated for example by the rise in hate crime against Asian Americans in the wake of the political framing of the COVID pandemic.

An overview of existing research on this subject shows dearth and abundance at the same time. Several studies touch on the intersections of SUD stigma by examining additional covariates relevant to intersectional stigma, but fall short of systematically comparing different intersectional identities. There is still a lack of systematic and aggregating studies that explicitly address intersectionality aspects. At the time of writing, new research on this topic is emerging continuously; we are amid an era of interest in intersectional problems. Recently, suggestions for integrating intersectional frameworks in research, intervention development, and policy have been made (Stangl et al., 2019), and challenges and opportunities have been mapped (Turan et al., 2019) that should inform further research. So far, studies have addressed intersectional SUD stigma not as a separate domain but included in the broader category of mental health diseases (MHD), which adds to the problem of unwarranted categorical homogeneity. What can we learn from the intersectional stigma of MHDs for SUDs? Where do they differ, and are they alike? How does intersectional stigma for SUDs depend on which specific substance is under discussion?

What can be gained from using an intersectional framework and analysis of SUDs as a separate category is demonstrated by a study of Vu et al. (2019). Men who identified as white sexual minority had higher depressive symptoms and odds of using marijuana compared to men identifying as white heterosexual. In contrast, no significant higher risks were observed for black heterosexual or sexual minority men. Women who identified as white sexual minority had higher risks for a range of negative outcomes compared to those who identified as white heterosexual, while black sexual minority women had higher odds only for using tobacco products and marijuana (Vu et al., 2019). A practical application of this would be to specifically address sexual minority stress in tailoring interventions that address SUD stigma.

Another area of shortage is the replication of current findings for different nationalities and cultures. Corrigan has emphasized the need for interventions to be local, culturally specific, and carefully targeted (Corrigan, 2011). It has to be assumed that most cultural backgrounds will give additional meaning to intersectional SUD stigma and determine which intersections of identity merit particular scrutiny (Schomerus & Angermeyer, 2021). Findings from distinct cultures are just starting to assemble (Eylem et al., 2020; Husain et al., 2020; Rai et al., 2020).

In light of the immense intragroup diversity that intersectional findings entail, it is essential not to become daunted or overwhelmed by their complexity. As Crenshaw has emphasized, intersectionality is not "a blanket term to mean, 'well, it's complicated'" and cause paralysis (Columbia

Law School, 2017). Of the same importance as adding intracategorical complexity is to address the question of common denominators of intersectional SUD stigma. Are there common drivers and/or salient pathways that can be addressed with broader benefit (Turan et al., 2019)? There are likely to be common elements of SUD stigma that are valid and relevant across different identities, like blaming someone for their substance use and feelings of shame. While South Asian students reported significantly less positive public attitudes toward help-seeking than Caucasians (Loya et al., 2010), ethnicity's effect on help-seeking attitudes was significantly reduced by including personal stigma variables as mediators. The difference caused by an ethnicity could be traced back to differences in self-stigma, a variable that stigma researchers are acquainted with and have experience on how to address it. Differences in stigma level and content have also been identified stemming from class and educational attainment (Phelan et al., 1998) and specific religious beliefs (Wesselmann & Graziano, 2010).

Due to its multifaceted nature, SUD stigma is a prototypical field for the application of an intersectional framework. However, it differs from the stigma of gender or race in ways that might hamper intersectional analysis. With the inception of intersectionality, black feminists brought their case of discrimination to attention. By doing so, they voted with their feet to spotlight the intersection of race and gender. Participatory action has remained a characteristic of intersectionality (see how women's studies have employed intersectionality to advance gender issues). It may even be a prerequisite, because intersectional positions are easily overlooked by those not concerned and might therefore require the perspective of those who cannot ignore the intersectional problem because it is where they find themselves every day in society's matrix of opportunity and oppression. The nature of stigma engendered by SUDs differs in its covert, shameful nature. Self-stigma is a more critical factor (Matthews et al., 2017; Schomerus et al., 2011). Social and legal repercussions have to be feared when publicly protesting being at an overseen intersection. As opposed to race, gender, and sexual orientation, there is no denying that SUDs are unwanted features of identity. In a qualitative research paper titled "That's Not Me Anymore," Gunn et al. point out how women with substance use and incarceration histories resort to disowning their former identity as part of resistance strategies for managing their intersectional stigma (Gunn et al., 2018). Participation of people with lived experience of SUDs in research to point out overseen intersections of stigma thus is challenging; it requires particular courage and wisdom. However, allowing people to understand their individual experiences by framing them as part of intersecting marginalized identities might help in easing the normative pressure that is ingrained in SUD stigma. It might help to develop novel narratives of empowerment and, thus, become more resilient to stigmatization.

REFERENCES

Angermeyer, M. C., Matschinger, H., & Schomerus, G. (2013). Attitudes towards psychiatric treatment and people with mental illness: Changes over two decades. *The British Journal of Psychiatry: The Journal of Mental Science*, *203*(2), 146–151.

Barry, C. L., McGinty, E. E., Pescosolido, B. A., & Goldman, H. H. (2014). Stigma, discrimination, treatment effectiveness, and policy: Public views about drug addiction and mental illness. *Psychiatric Services*, *65*(10), 1269–1272.

Becker, J. B., McClellan, M., & Reed, B. G. (2016). Sociocultural context for sex differences in addiction. *Addiction Biology*, *21*(5), 1052–1059.

Berger, M. T. (2006). *Workable sisterhood: The political journey of stigmatized women with HIV/AIDS*. Princeton University Press.

Bowleg, L. (2012). The problem with the phrase women and minorities: Intersectionality – an important theoretical framework for public health. *American Journal of Public Health*, *102*(7), 1267–1273.

Burgard, S. A., Cochran, S. D., & Mays, V. M. (2005). Alcohol and tobacco use patterns among heterosexually and homosexually experienced California women. *Drug and Alcohol Dependence*, *77*(1), 61–70.

Canadian Observatory on Homelessness. (2017). *Designing common spaces for women centred supportive housing: A practical application of intersectional feminist analysis.* www.homelessnesslearninghub.ca/library/resources/designing-common-spaces-women-centred-supportive-housing-practical-application

(2020). *Intersectionality – power shuffle exercise.* www.homelessnesslearninghub.ca/learning-materials/2slgbtqia-toolkit/intersectionality-power-shuffle-exercise

(2021). *Intersectionality – homelessness learning hub.* www.homelessnesslearninghub.ca/learning-materials/2slgbtqia-toolkit/2slgbtqia-youth-programming/intersectionality

Carliner, H., Delker, E., Fink, D. S., Keyes, K. M., & Hasin, D. S. (2016). Racial discrimination, socioeconomic position, and illicit drug use among US Blacks. *Social Psychiatry and Psychiatric Epidemiology*, *51*(4), 551–560.

Ciftci, A., Jones, N., & Corrigan, P. W. (2013). Mental health stigma in the Muslim community. *Journal of Muslim Mental Health*, *7*(1).

Cochran, S. D., & Mays, V. M. (2000). Relation between psychiatric syndromes and behaviorally defined sexual orientation in a sample of the US population. *American Journal of Epidemiology*, *151*(5), 516–523.

Cochran, S. D., Mays, V. M., Alegria, M., Ortega, A. N., & Takeuchi, D. (2007). Mental health and substance use disorders among Latino and Asian American lesbian, gay, and bisexual adults. *Journal of Consulting and Clinical Psychology, 75*(5), 785–794.

Columbia Law School. (2017). *Kimberlé Crenshaw on intersectionality, more than two decades later.* www.law.columbia.edu/news/archive/kimberle-crenshaw-intersectionality-more-two-decades-later

Corrigan, P. W. (2011). Best practices: Strategic stigma change (SSC): Five principles for social marketing campaigns to reduce stigma. *Psychiatric Services, 62*(8), 824–826.

Corrigan, P. W., & Wassel, A. (2008). Understanding and influencing the stigma of mental illness. *Journal of Psychosocial Nursing and Mental Health Services, 46*(1), 42–48.

Crenshaw, K. (1989). Demarginalizing the intersection of race and sex: A Black feminist critique of antidiscrimination doctrine, feminist theory and antiracist politics. *The University of Chicago Legal Forum, 1,* 139–167.

DeGraffenreid v. General Motors Assembly Div., etc., 413 F. Supp. 142 (E.D. Mo. 1976). https://law.justia.com/cases/federal/district-courts/FSupp/413/142/1660699/

Dobson, M. (2013). *Intersectionality: A fun guide.* https://miriamdobson.com/2013/04/24/intersectionality-a-fun-guide/

Drabble, L., Midanik, L. T., & Trocki, K. (2005). Reports of alcohol consumption and alcohol-related problems among homosexual, bisexual and heterosexual respondents: Results from the 2000 National Alcohol Survey. *Journal of Studies on Alcohol, 66*(1), 111–120.

Eylem, O., Wit, L. de, van Straten, A., et al. (2020). Stigma for common mental disorders in racial minorities and majorities: A systematic review and meta-analysis. *BMC Public Health, 20*(1), Article 879.

Farina, A. (1981). Are women nicer people than men? Sex and the stigma of mental disorders. *Clinical Psychology Review, 1*(2), 223–243.

Finegan, M., Firth, N., Wojnarowski, C., & Delgadillo, J. (2018). Associations between socioeconomic status and psychological therapy outcomes: A systematic review and meta-analysis. *Depression and Anxiety, 35*(6), 560–573.

Flaskerud, J. H., & Winslow, B. J. (1998). Conceptualizing vulnerable populations health-related research. *Nursing Research, 47*(2), 69–78.

Galea, S., Nandi, A., & Vlahov, D. (2004). The social epidemiology of substance use. *Epidemiologic Reviews, 26,* 36–52.

Goodyear, K., Haass-Koffler, C. L., & Chavanne, D. (2018). Opioid use and stigma: The role of gender, language and precipitating events. *Drug and Alcohol Dependence, 185,* 339–346.

Green, K. E., & Feinstein, B. A. (2012). Substance use in lesbian, gay, and bisexual populations: An update on empirical research and implications for treatment. *Psychology of Addictive Behaviors: Journal of the Society of Psychologists in Addictive Behaviors, 26*(2), 265–278.

Gunn, A. J., Sacks, T. K., & Jemal, A. (2018). "That's not me anymore": Resistance strategies for managing intersectional stigmas for women with substance use and incarceration histories. *Qualitative Social Work*, *17*(4), 490–508.

Hankivsky, O. (2014). *Intersectionality 101*. The Institute for Intersectionality Research & Policy, SFU.

Hansen, H., & Netherland, J. (2016). Is the prescription opioid epidemic a white problem? *American Journal of Public Health*, *106*(12), 2127–2129.

Haslam, N., & Kvaale, E. P. (2015). Biogenetic explanations of mental disorder. *Current Directions in Psychological Science*, *24*(5), 399–404.

Humensky, J. L. (2010). Are adolescents with high socioeconomic status more likely to engage in alcohol and illicit drug use in early adulthood? *Substance Abuse Treatment, Prevention, and Policy*, *5*, Article 19.

Hunting, G., Grace, D., & Hankivsky, O. (2015). Taking action on stigma and discrimination: An intersectionality-informed model of social inclusion and exclusion. *Intersectionalities: A Global Journal of Social Work Analysis, Research, Polity, and Practice*, *4*(2), 101–125.

Husain, M. O., Zehra, S. S., Umer, M., et al. (2020). Stigma toward mental and physical illness: Attitudes of healthcare professionals, healthcare students and the general public in Pakistan. *BJPsych Open*, *6*(5), e81.

King, T. L., Shields, M., Shakespeare, T., Milner, A., & Kavanagh, A. (2019). An intersectional approach to understandings of mental health inequalities among men with disability. *SSM – Population Health*, *9*, Article 100464.

Lee, R. D., & Rasinski, K. A. (2006). Five grams of coke: Racism, moralism and White public opinion on sanctions for first time possession. *International Journal of Drug Policy*, *17*(3), 183–191.

Link, B. G., & Phelan, J. C. (2001). Conceptualizing stigma. *Annual Review of Sociology*, *27*, 363–385.

Lombardi, E. (2007). Substance use treatment experiences of transgender/transsexual men and women. *Journal of LGBT Health Research*, *3*(2), 37–47.

Loya, F., Reddy, R., & Hinshaw, S. P. (2010). Mental illness stigma as a mediator of differences in Caucasian and South Asian college students' attitudes toward psychological counseling. *Journal of Counseling Psychology*, *57*(4), 484–490.

Marshal, M. P., Friedman, M. S., Stall, R., et al. (2008). Sexual orientation and adolescent substance use: A meta-analysis and methodological review. *Addiction*, *103*(4), 546–556.

Matthews, S., Dwyer, R., & Snoek, A. (2017). Stigma and self-stigma in addiction. *Journal of Bioethical Inquiry*, *14*(2), 275–286.

Mendoza, S., Hatcher, A. E., & Hansen, H. (2019). Race, stigma, and addiction. In J. D. Avery & J. J. Avery (Eds.), *The stigma of addiction: An essential guide* (pp. 131–152). Springer International Publishing.

Mereish, E. H., & Bradford, J. B. (2014). Intersecting identities and substance use problems: Sexual orientation, gender, race, and lifetime substance use problems. *Journal of Studies on Alcohol and Drugs*, *75*(1), 179–188.

Meyer, I. H. (2007). Prejudice and discrimination as social stressors. In I. H. Meyer & M. E. Northridge (Eds.), *The health of sexual minorities: Public health perspectives on lesbian, gay, bisexual and transgender populations* (pp. 242–267). Springer Science+Business Media LLC.

Meyers, S. A., Earnshaw, V. A., D'Ambrosio, B., Courchesne, N., Werb, D., & Smith, L. R. (2021). The intersection of gender and drug use-related stigma: A mixed methods systematic review and synthesis of the literature. *Drug and Alcohol Dependence, 223*, Article 108706.

Mitchell, O. (2005). A meta-analysis of race and sentencing research: Explaining the inconsistencies. *Journal of Quantitative Criminology, 21*(4), 439–466.

Muntaner, C., Eaton, W. W., Miech, R., & O'Campo, P. (2004). Socioeconomic position and major mental disorders. *Epidemiologic Reviews, 26*, 53–62.

Nash, J. C. (2008). Re-thinking intersectionality. *Feminist Review, 89*(1), 1–15.

(2019). *Black feminism reimagined: After intersectionality*. Duke University Press.

Ottati, V., Bodenhausen, G. V., & Newman, L. S. (2005). Social psychological models of mental illness stigma. In P. W. Corrigan (Ed.), *On the stigma of mental illness: Practical strategies for research and social change* (1st ed., pp. 99–128). American Psychological Association.

Patrick, M. E., Wightman, P., Schoeni, R. F., & Schulenberg, J. E. (2012). Socioeconomic status and substance use among young adults: A comparison across constructs and drugs. *Journal of Studies on Alcohol and Drugs, 73*(5), 772–782.

Phelan, J. C., Bromet, E. J., & Link, B. G. (1998). Psychiatric illness and family stigma. *Schizophrenia Bulletin, 24*(1), 115–126.

Pienaar, K., Murphy, D. A., Race, K., & Lea, T. (2018). Problematising LGBTIQ drug use, governing sexuality and gender: A critical analysis of LGBTIQ health policy in Australia. *The International Journal on Drug Policy, 55*, 187–194.

Potts, L. C., & Henderson, C. (2020). Moderation by socioeconomic status of the relationship between familiarity with mental illness and stigma outcomes. *SSM – Population Health, 11*, Article 100611.

Purdie-Vaughns, V., & Eibach, R. P. (2008). Intersectional invisibility: The distinctive advantages and disadvantages of multiple subordinate-group identities. *Sex Roles, 59*(5–6), 377–391.

Rai, S. S., Peters, R. M. H., Syurina, E. V., Irwanto, I., Naniche, D., & Zweekhorst, M. B. M. (2020). Intersectionality and health-related stigma: Insights from experiences of people living with stigmatized health conditions in Indonesia. *International Journal for Equity in Health, 19*(1), Article 206.

Roe, G. (2005). Harm reduction as paradigm: Is better than bad good enough? The origins of harm reduction. *Critical Public Health, 15*(3), 243–250.

Ross, M. H., & Setchell, J. (2019). People who identify as LGBTIQ+ can experience assumptions, discomfort, some discrimination, and a lack of knowledge while attending physiotherapy: A survey. *Journal of Physiotherapy, 65*(2), 99–105.

Saloner, B., & Lê Cook, B. (2013). Blacks and Hispanics are less likely than whites to complete addiction treatment, largely due to socioeconomic factors. *Health Affairs (Project Hope), 32*(1), 135–145.

Sandelowski, M., Barroso, J., & Voils, C. I. (2009). Gender, race/ethnicity, and social class in research reports on stigma in HIV-positive women. *Health Care for Women International, 30*(4), 273–288.

Sattler, S., Escande, A., Racine, E., & Göritz, A. S. (2017). Public stigma toward people with drug addiction: A factorial survey. *Journal of Studies on Alcohol and Drugs, 78*(3), 415–425.

Schomerus, G., & Angermeyer, M. C. (2021). Blind spots in stigma research? Broadening our perspective on mental illness stigma by exploring 'what matters most' in modern Western societies. *Epidemiology and Psychiatric Sciences, 30*, e26. doi.org/10.1017/S2045796021000111

Schomerus, G., Corrigan, P. W., Klauer, T., Kuwert, P., Freyberger, H. J., & Lucht, M. (2011). Self-stigma in alcohol dependence: Consequences for drinking-refusal self-efficacy. *Drug and Alcohol Dependence, 114*(1), 12–17.

Schomerus, G., Matschinger, H., & Angermeyer, M. C. (2014). Attitudes towards alcohol dependence and affected individuals: Persistence of negative stereotypes and illness beliefs between 1990 and 2011. *European Addiction Research, 20*(6), 293–299.

Schomerus, G., Stolzenburg, S., Freitag, S., et al. (2019). Stigma as a barrier to recognizing personal mental illness and seeking help: A prospective study among untreated persons with mental illness. *European Archives of Psychiatry and Clinical Neuroscience, 269*(4), 469–479.

Senia, J. M., Neppl, T. K., Gudmunson, C. G., Donnellan, M. B., & Lorenz, F. O. (2016). The intergenerational continuity of socioeconomic status: Effects of parenting, personality, and age at first romantic partnership. *Journal of Family Psychology: JFP: Journal of the Division of Family Psychology of the American Psychological Association (Division 43), 30*(6), 647–656.

Sorsdahl, K., Stein, D. J., & Myers, B. (2012). Negative attributions towards people with substance use disorders in South Africa: Variation across substances and by gender. *BMC Psychiatry, 12*(1), Article 101.

Spooner, C. (2009). Social determinants of drug use – barriers to translating research into policy. *Health Promotion Journal of Australia: Official Journal of Australian Association of Health Promotion Professionals, 20*(3), 180–185.

Stangl, A. L., Earnshaw, V. A., Logie, C. H., et al. (2019). The Health Stigma and Discrimination Framework: A global, crosscutting framework to inform research, intervention development, and policy on health-related stigmas. *BMC Medicine, 17*(1), Article 31.

Steinmetz, K. (2020, February 20). She coined the term 'intersectionality' over 30 years ago. Here's what it means to her today. *Time.* https://time.com/5786710/kimberle-crenshaw-intersectionality/

Sullivan, A. (2017, March 10). Is intersectionality a religion? *Intelligencer.*

Sullivan, A. (2019, November 15). A glimpse at the intersectional left's political endgame. *Intelligencer.*

Turan, J. M., Elafros, M. A., Logie, C. H., et al. (2019). Challenges and opportunities in examining and addressing intersectional stigma and health. *BMC Medicine*, *17*(1), Article 7.

Vargas, S. M., Huey, S. J., & Miranda, J. (2020). A critical review of current evidence on multiple types of discrimination and mental health. *The American Journal of Orthopsychiatry*, *90*(3), 374–390.

Vu, M., Li, J., Haardörfer, R., Windle, M., & Berg, C. J. (2019). Mental health and substance use among women and men at the intersections of identities and experiences of discrimination: Insights from the intersectionality framework. *BMC Public Health*, *19*(1), Article 108.

Wang, K., Rendina, H. J., & Pachankis, J. E. (2016). Looking on the bright side of stigma: How stress-related growth facilitates adaptive coping among gay and bisexual men. *Journal of Gay & Lesbian Mental Health*, *20*(4), 363–375.

Wesselmann, E. D., & Graziano, W. G. (2010). Sinful and/or possessed? Religious beliefs and mental illness stigma. *Journal of Social and Clinical Psychology*, *29*(4), 402–437.

Yang, J. C., Roman-Urrestarazu, A., McKee, M., & Brayne, C. (2019). Demographic, socioeconomic, and health correlates of unmet need for mental health treatment in the United States, 2002–16: Evidence from the national surveys on drug use and health. *International Journal for Equity in Health*, *18*(1), Article 122.

CHAPTER 7

International Perspectives on Stigma toward People with Substance Use Disorders

Jakob Manthey, Vivek Benegal, Carolin Kilian, Jayant Mahadevan, Juliana Mejía-Trujillo, Neo Morojele, Pratima Murthy, Maria Neufeld, Augusto Pérez-Gómez, and Jürgen Rehm

The Dimension of Substance Use and Substance Use Disorders around the World

Humans have a long-standing, active, and functional relationship with substance use (Sullivan & Hagen, 2015). In modern times, alcohol and tobacco are by far the most commonly used substances, with about half of the global adult population estimated to have had at least one drink in 2017 (Manthey et al., 2019) and about one in five people having smoked in 2015 (World Health Organization, 2018b). For both substances, the prevalence of use is highest in high-income countries. While alcohol consumption is on the rise in many low- and middle-income countries (see, e.g., Rehm et al., 2019; Sornpaisarn et al., 2020), the use of tobacco has been declining in most regions worldwide for decades (World Health Organization, 2018b).

For other substances, the picture is more blurry since the legal status varies across jurisdictions. In 2018, an estimated 250 million people used substances other than alcohol and tobacco, including cannabis, opioids, cocaine, and stimulants (henceforth termed "illegal substances" despite the nonuniform legal status of these substances across countries). Globally, about 4% of the population aged 15–64 used cannabis in 2018, with considerably higher rates reported in North America (15%), Oceania (11%), and West/Central Africa (9%), while most Asian countries report lower than average use rates. For opioids, the regional pattern is more mixed. Globally, prevalence of use was estimated at 1% of the population aged 15–64, with higher rates reported in North American, Oceanian, Middle Eastern, as well as West/Central African countries.

Maria Neufeld is a staff member of the World Health Organization. The authors alone are responsible for the views expressed in this publication and these do not necessarily represent the decisions or the stated policy of the World Health Organization.

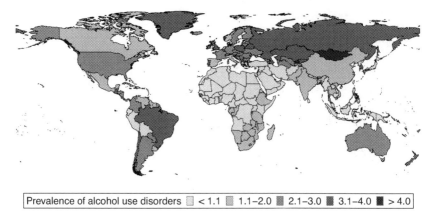

Figure 3 Prevalence of alcohol use disorders in 2019, globally. Data obtained from Institute for Health Metrics and Evaluation (2021)

Injecting substance use is one special form of substance use administration and of particular relevance given high rates of adverse health outcomes for users, particular in low- and middle-income countries (Mathers et al., 2013). Globally, there are an estimated 16 million people who inject drugs (Degenhardt et al., 2017), with a substantial share of users living with human immunodeficiency viruses (HIV; 18%) or hepatitis C virus (HCV; 52%). Prevalence of injecting drug use is highest in Eastern European and Northern American countries (about 1% of the population aged 15–64 years) and lowest in South Asian, North African, and Middle Eastern countries (around 0.1%, [Degenhardt et al., 2017]).

Among those who use substances, there is a subgroup of people with particularly high levels of use including those meeting criteria for substance use disorder (SUD). Globally, about 280 million people or 5% of the adult population are affected by alcohol use disorder (AUD) (World Health Organization, 2018a) and 35 million people meeting criteria for at least one illegal SUD (United Nations Office on Drugs and Crime, 2020). The geographical distribution matches that of prevalence of use, as illustrated in Figure 3 for AUD and Figure 4 for illegal SUD, with high SUD rates above the global average in European and North American countries.

People with SUD are in need of professional treatment for their substance use but also for comorbid health problems. However, the proportion of affected people receiving appropriate care is lower than for other mental disorders (for alcohol and mental disorders in Europe, see Alonso et al., 2004; Mekonen et al., 2020); for US estimates for other substances,

International Perspectives on Stigma

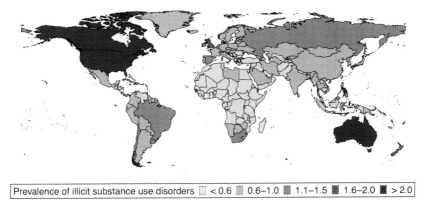

Figure 4 Prevalence of illegal substance use disorders in 2019, globally. Data obtained from Institute for Health Metrics and Evaluation (2021)

see Grant et al., 2016). Barriers to treatment provision vary across countries and substances and may relate to a lack of resources among affected persons, a lack of capacities in the health care system or to insufficient training of health care providers. One recurring and key barrier to SUD treatment is the stigmatization of affected people (van Boekel et al., 2013). As elaborated in other chapters of this book, SUD stigma is complex and interacts with the legal status of the substances, established cultural norms, and prevailing socioeconomic inequalities (Room, 2005). Therefore, it is reasonable to assume that the manifestations of SUD stigma also vary across regions and societies.

In this chapter, we attempt to take an international perspective on SUD stigma to outline regional differences and possible societal particularities. We focus on six exemplary regions around the world and review the local literature to identify regional perspectives on SUD stigma. The selection of regions is not comprehensive, but they differ widely with respect to economic development, cultural traditions, and social norms. Methodological differences between studies prohibit a direct comparison of stigma levels or qualities across regions. However, this narrative review identifies both recurring and regionally specific themes related to the stigma of people with SUD and provides a nuanced picture of the global reality of SUD stigma, which we summarize and discuss at the end of this chapter.

High-Income North America

High-income North America (Canada and the USA) is characterized by comparatively high levels of both legal and illegal substance use and SUDs

(Global Health Data Exchange (GHDx), 2020; Manthey et al., 2019; Peacock et al., 2018). Canada and several US states have legalized the recreational use of cannabis in recent years, making this region unique as a sizeable proportion of the population has legal access to alcohol, tobacco, and cannabis.

Stigma seems to be mainly against people with AUD, tobacco use, and illegal substance use (Yang et al., 2017) whereas alcohol and cannabis use are usually seen positively (American Addiction Centers, 2019). In a recent overview of stigma against people with SUD, 6 out of the 18 studies identified were from high-income North America, with few differences between countries (Yang et al., 2017).

The Unique Characteristics of Structural Discrimination in the USA

Structural discrimination, including the denial of health services, is one important aspect of SUD stigma and might be particularly high in high-income North America. In fact, the World Health Organization has defined the human right to health as "a legal obligation on states to ensure access to timely, acceptable, and affordable health care of appropriate quality as well as to provide for the underlying determinants of health, such as safe and potable water, sanitation, food, housing, health-related information and education, and gender equality" (World Health Organization, 2017). Consequently, the provision of treatment for people with SUD is included as an indicator for the Sustainable Development Goals, with which the United Nations agreed (United Nations Department of Economic and Social Affairs: Statistics Division, 2018; Indicator 3.5.1).

A recent workshop of the US National Academies of Sciences, Engineering, and Medicine (National Academies of Sciences, Engineering, and Medicine, 2020) revealed clear structural discrimination for people with any kind of behavioral health conditions in the United States, which are not restricted to people with SUD, but which include mental health and SUDs. While behavioral health conditions are highly prevalent in the general population (National Academies of Sciences, Engineering, and Medicine, 2016), and despite this high prevalence and frequent use of emergency health services, few receive specialist behavioral health care (Klein & Hostetter, 2014). In other words, people with SUD are present in health care systems, however, they do not receive adequate treatment for their conditions (Hasin & Grant, 2015).

In addition, socioeconomic status, race, ethnicity, and sexual orientation may further decrease access to care in countries without universal health care such as the USA. These factors also increase the likelihood that people will use substances and experience SUD in the first place (e.g., Carliner et al., 2016; Case & Deaton, 2020; Desalu et al., 2019). To give but one example (Yang et al., 2017): African-Americans and African-Canadians have been highly stigmatized and have been subject to discrimination. For many years, addiction to opioids was seen as a condition largely affecting this disadvantaged minority, and addiction treatment was not a high priority for most policymakers in North America. However, in recent years, addiction first to prescription opioids and later to heroin and fentanyl has spread to subgroups of the European descent population, and the public and politicians have been vocal in demanding appropriate treatments. Thus, some stigma associated with SUDs could be due to, or worsened by, assumptions about the race/ethnicity of drug-addicted populations (e.g., Yang et al., 2017, see also Chapter 6 on intersectionality of SUD stigma). As well, the type of illegal substance used was found to be related to discrimination. In North America, discrimination is traditionally stronger against heroin than against cocaine (Crawford et al., 2012).

Moreover, more than two-thirds of primary care providers in the USA report that they are unable to connect patients with behavioral health providers because of a shortage of mental health providers and health insurance barriers (Alliance for Health Policy, 2017; Cunningham, 2009). As the organizers of the above-mentioned workshop report in their introduction, part of the explanation for the lack of access to care lies in a historical legacy of discrimination and stigma that has made people reluctant to seek help and has also led to segregated and inhumane services for those facing SUDs and other mental health conditions (Storholm et al., 2017). Moreover, although the Affordable Care Act ("Obamacare") strengthened insurance coverage for, and access to, SUD treatment, considerable gaps remain (Abraham et al., 2017); health insurance programs often still provide limited coverage for services for these disorders compared to services for other conditions. For instance, a study in Massachusetts noted that the percentage of uninsured patients with substance use problems remained relatively high – and that when patients did become insured, requirements for copayments for their care deterred them from seeking treatment. Expanded coverage alone seemed to be insufficient to increase treatment for SUD. More systemic changes in eligibility, services, financing, system design, and policy may also be required (Capoccia et al., 2012). In their 2014 overview, Klein and Hostetter found that two years later, even when services were legally covered by the Affordable Care Act, inadequate reimbursement or lack of available health care services in a region might still limit access for any treatment of SUD and mental disorders (Klein & Hostetter, 2014).

While there are certainly barriers to the use of health services in Canada as well (Murney et al., 2020), the overall situation is superior given the provision of universal health care. Nevertheless, overall treatment rates have remained low for AUD (Larsen et al., 2015).

While denial of the right for health care is an important aspect of structural discrimination of people with SUD, it is only one aspect. People with SUD are discriminated against in other ways and structural stigma encompasses policies within corporations, the judicial system, government, professional groups (including health care), schools and universities, and social service agencies, which may affect health care, employment, and educational opportunities (National Academies of Sciences, Engineering, and Medicine, 2016). Most importantly in this respect may be the legal prosecution for the use of illegal substances, resulting in a situation where a substantial proportion of people in North American prisons have been incarcerated as punishment for their substance use (see Chapter 4 on SUD stigma and the criminal justice system). The decriminalization of drug use and possession has been proposed as a public health strategy as well as a strategy to protect the human rights of those with substance use problems and SUD (Wogen & Restrepo, 2020), underlying some of the initiatives to legalize and/or decriminalize cannabis use in North America (Crépault et al., 2016); the other reasons were economic (Krane, 2020). While decriminalization of illegal drugs has not been limited to high-income North America, it has become more prominent given the current opioid crisis being the cause of a high number of overdose deaths in this region (Imtiaz et al., 2020). Related to the use of illegal substances, the Joint United Nations Programme on HIV/AIDS (UNAIDS) asserts that "decriminalization of drug use and possession for personal use reduces the stigma and discrimination that hampers access to health care, harm reduction and legal services ... people who use drugs need support, not incarceration" (Joint United Nations Programme on HIV/AIDS (UNAIDS), 2019). As prisons in North America are filled with people with SUD, not restricted to people who were incarcerated solely for their use of illegal substances, efforts have been made to provide treatment interventions in prisons, and these have been shown to be effective (De Andrade et al., 2018).

Conclusion

In sum, despite the high prevalence of substance use and SUD in North America, stigma is high as well. Of particular importance seems the structural discrimination against SUD, with no right for treatment of these conditions in the USA.

Latin America

In Latin America, studies on SUD stigma were conducted in Argentina, Colombia, Chile, Uruguay, Brazil, Peru, and Mexico. Here, alcohol and other illegal substance use is less prevalent than in most European or North American countries (Manthey et al., 2019; United Nations Office on Drugs and Crime, 2020). However, there is a serious problem of binge drinking and heavy drinking on weekends among adults (World Health Organization, 2018a) and alcohol use is common among minors. The use of cannabis and cocaine is particularly prevalent in Chile, Argentina, and Uruguay and less so in Colombia, Peru, and Mexico. Importantly, cannabis is legal in Uruguay, however, small doses for personal use are decriminalized in some countries; lately, Mexico legalized the recreational use of marihuana (Lopez, 2021).

As in other regions, high levels of stigmatization constitute an important obstacle for health care access in Latin American countries (Abeldaño et al., 2016; Bard et al., 2016; International Drug Policy Consortium (IDPC), 2019; TNI, 2014). Stigmatization of people with SUD is interdependent with lack of treatment and in many cases appropriate SUD treatment is not offered by official entities. Where it is offered, as happens in Colombia, the treatment uptake remains very low because people feel that going into those facilities implies strong social rejection; for that reason, they prefer the more anonymous and less formal treatment services, for example, those offered by Alcoholics Anonymous (Ministerio de Salud y Protección Social de Colombia, 2016).

In spite of large similarities, research has revealed distinct nuances across Latin American countries regarding stigma. Due to the lack of comparative studies, however, it remains unclear whether these differences represent genuine country differences or different research interest or methodologies.

Nuances in SUD Stigma across Latin American Countries

In Mexico, one of the main reasons for stigmatization is that users are considered responsible for their problem: in a study carried out in Tijuana (Paris et al., 2009), using a mixed methodology (qualitative and quantitative) it was shown that in addition to the difficulty in accessing treatment, consumers were subjected to mistreatment and abuse by the authorities, especially in public spaces. In another study (IDPC, 2019), results showed that women consumers would be victims of more barriers and would be the object of domestic and sexual violence.

In Argentina, there seems to be a somewhat atypical situation, as the literature suggests that AUD stigma is higher than the stigma toward users of other substances, which is usually the opposite in Latin America. Thereby, negative stereotypes are likely to increase the risk of facing additional problems beyond consumption itself, including social rejection. As in Mexico, people who use drugs in Argentina are often rejected because many people attribute the responsibility for their condition to the persons themselves (Vázquez, 2014). Furthermore, stigmatization is likely to go beyond substance use in Argentina and is in particular associated with poverty, marginalization, and crime (Vázquez, 2014). In other words, people may be stigmatized because of socioeconomic circumstances and their substance use only aggravates these experiences.

In Peru, only 8.5% of all the resources used in the field of drugs are invested in prevention and treatment, while the remaining resources are spent on repression, which further fuels stigmatization of people who use drugs (TNI, 2014). However, other Latin American countries, such as Colombia, report even lower spending on prevention and treatment, albeit without higher levels of SUD stigma (elpacientecolombiano.com, 2018). Yet, the absence of harm prevention policies may increase the risks of stigma.

In Brazil, there is a tendency to associate illegal substance use with crime, indignity, undesirability, and unproductiveness (Bard et al., 2016). In other words, stigma affects the social hierarchy, considering people who use drugs inferior and undesirable, and stimulating what in Latin America has been called "social cleansing" – a term that covers the murder of street dwellers or homeless people. They are also considered dangerous, incapable of self-regulation, unpredictable, violent, and unreliable (Ventura et al., 2017). As such, people participating in a general population survey in São Paulo found people with AUD to be highly associated with violent behavior (Peluso Ede & Blay, 2008).

Finally, in Colombia, stigmatization of people with SUD has been identified as a "deterrent" to drug use, explaining the paradox of high availability, few legal restrictions, and relatively low rates of use in this country. It has been argued that this was especially relevant for young people fearing to be labeled "drug addicts" and excluded from their families, to which bonds are particularly strong (Lende, 2003). However, the stigmatization of people with SUD does have negative implications. In 2020, the Ministry of Health raised concerns about the role of SUD stigma during the public health crises related to the COVID-19 pandemic (Minsalud, 2020). Specifically, people who use drugs living on the streets may carry a greater infection risk for other people. The stigma related to their substance use would act as a barrier to health care access if affected persons hid the disease, thus putting both themselves and others at a higher risk and provoking reduced solidarity with substance users in communities.

Conclusion

People with SUD face high levels of public stigma in Latin American countries, which often intersects with socioeconomic marginalization.

High-Income Europe

In this section, we summarize the literature of SUD stigma in selected high-income European countries (henceforth: Europe), including studies from Finland, France, Germany, Italy, Netherlands, Poland, Portugal, Sweden, Spain, and the United Kingdom. Both legal and illegal substance use is widely prevalent in Europe. Alcohol and tobacco use have a long-standing tradition in Europe, with alcohol being granted a status of a cultural heritage, boasting an exceptional art of brewing beer, award-winning wine, and great distilleries, which is celebrated in diverse events in many countries. In sharp contrast to substance use being part of everyday life for the majority of Europeans, high levels of stigmatization toward people with AUD have been reported. Prevalence of illegal substance use is also among the highest in the world in Europe and some countries, such as Czechia, the Netherlands, and Portugal have decriminalized possession of cannabis and other substances.

Stigma of AUD in Europe

The most recent systematic review summarizing research on the public stigma of AUD compared to other substance-related and unrelated disorders, published after 2010, included seven studies based in four European countries (Kilian et al., 2021). According to this review, people with AUD were generally perceived as more dangerous, more responsible for their condition, and more avoided than people with substance-unrelated mental health disorders, corroborating findings from a previous review (Schomerus et al., 2011). Importantly, the systematic review failed to identify substantial differences in stigmatizing attitudes or discriminatory behavior toward people with AUD and people with other SUDs.

However, single studies conducted in European countries find meaningful differences between substances (e.g., Blomqvist, 2012; Tikkinen et al., 2012).

The prevailing public stigma toward people with AUD in Europe is of public health concern, as it has been identified as a key barrier for health care provision. In a six-country study, primary care patients with AUD were asked whether they sought professional help for their problems and to indicate the reasons for not doing so (Probst et al., 2015). Patients with a higher AUD severity were less likely to deny their problems but more likely to cite various barriers to treatment seeking, including fear of stigma and shame. To fully understand the way stigma acts on health care provision, one should consider the perspective of those affected but also the perspective of health care professionals. For example, in a survey of general practitioners in five European countries, stigma was cited as a key barrier to routine alcohol screening among patients with hypertension (Hanschmidt et al., 2017). Among Italian and French practitioners, every second respondent found it difficult to discuss alcohol use with their patients or mentioned other stigma-related issues as a reason for not engaging in alcohol screening. In fact, the uneasiness of discussing alcohol with patients may be one explanation for lower screening (Demmert et al., 2011) and brief intervention rates (Angus et al., 2019; Demmert et al., 2011) for risky drinkers as compared to tobacco smokers.

Stigma of Illegal SUD in Europe

Discrimination and other stigmatizing experiences are also commonly reported among people receiving SUD treatment in Europe (Pelullo et al., 2019; van Boekel et al., 2016). Both internalized as well as enacted stigma has been repeatedly linked to delayed or impaired access to SUD treatment (e.g., United Kingdom: Cornford et al., 2019; Luty et al., 2018; Medina-Perucha et al., 2019). A notable exception to this pattern was a Portuguese study in which the majority of patients reported high levels of satisfaction with opioid substitution treatment, and both general practitioners and patients rated opioid substitution treatment to be easily accessible (Goulão, 2013). It should be noted that Portugal has decriminalized possession of small amounts of all illegal substances in 2001 in response to high rates of overdose deaths from illegal substance use (Greenwald, 2009). The limited evidence available suggests that the Portuguese way has led to protecting users from facing criminal charges, thus eliminating a major source of discrimination, while facilitating access to treatment for people with opioid use disorder.

In fact, drug prohibition has been identified as an important driver for stigmatizing people who use drugs, enacted via social rejection and structural discrimination (Stöver, 2016). Importantly, this does not only concern people with SUD but all users who face criminal justice sanctions and their wider implications, for example, losing one's drivers' license even if not driving under the influence of illegal substances (European Monitoring Centre for Drugs and Drug Addiction, 2021). The association of stigma experiences and repressive policies was also studied in a sample of cannabis users from seven European countries. In this study, the lowest levels of stigmatization were reported in the Netherlands, while Greek users reported highest levels of stigmatization (Skliamis et al., 2020). The level of stigmatization thus roughly corresponded to the legal status of cannabis, which can be bought in licensed coffeeshops in the Netherlands, while sentencing practices for possession of cannabis in Greece are among the strictest in Europe.

Conclusion

In summary, people with AUD face high levels of negative attitudes of the public – despite alcohol use being highly prevalent in Europe. For people with illegal SUD, stigma experiences seem to be aggravated by more repressive drug policies.

Sub-Saharan Countries

In this section, we outline the literature of stigma toward people with SUD in sub-Saharan African countries, including studies from South Africa, Botswana, Nigeria, Senegal, Sierra Leone, Kenya, Tanzania, Uganda, Gabon, Democratic Republic of Congo, and Mauritius. In sub-Saharan Africa, alcohol use is relatively common in most countries, barring Muslim-majority countries. It was restricted during the precolonial period primarily to ceremonial occasions, and women of childbearing age and children were prohibited from consuming alcohol. Although women have started drinking increasingly, the majority of women are still abstainers (World Health Organization, 2018a). In most parts of the region heavy episodic drinking is common, as approximately 50% of drinkers aged 15 years and above engage in this pattern of drinking (World Health Organization, 2018b). Apart from alcohol, the other most widely used dependence-producing substances include tobacco and cannabis (United Nations Office on Drugs and Crime, 2018; World Health Organization,

2019b), and less commonly, cocaine, opiates and opioids, and amphetamines and prescription stimulants depending on the region (United Nations Office on Drugs and Crime, 2018).

Internalized Stigma among People with SUD in Sub-Saharan Africa

In sub-Saharan Africa, AUD treatment coverage is low and ranges between 3.5% (95% confidence interval: 0.6–19.0) and 13.1% (95% confidence interval: 5.9–26.5) (Rathod et al., 2016; Zewdu et al., 2019), and thus lower than average (Mekonen et al., 2020). Reasons that are often cited for this large treatment gap include external/structural factors (such as distances to health facilities and costs of treatment) and internal/psychosocial factors (such as stigma, and illness and treatment perceptions; Zewdu et al., 2019). Furthermore, the training of health workers on SUDs is seldom prioritized. For example, one study among emergency physician consultants and junior registrars in South Africa found that only 2.9% had received formal training in the "substance use field" (Kalebka et al., 2013).

Studies that have investigated the stigmatization of people with SUDs in sub-Saharan Africa have tended to focus on people living with HIV in HIV care settings simultaneously focusing on people who engage in harmful or hazardous drinking or with AUD (e.g., Regenauer et al., 2020; Satinsky et al., 2020), while others have considered tuberculosis patients (Møller et al., 2010), and noted high levels of internalized and structural stigma among people who inject drugs (e.g., Duby et al., 2018; Scheibe et al., 2017). The predominance of research focused on people living with HIV is likely to be attributable to the high volume of research on HIV in sub-Saharan Africa; the region of the world with the highest prevalence of HIV (Joint United Nations Programme on HIV/AIDS, 2020). Unlike other regions, sexual risk behavior is the main form of HIV transmission (Joint United Nations Programme on HIV/AIDS, 2020) and is fueled to a large extent by alcohol (Hahn et al., 2011; Scott-Sheldon et al., 2013; Woolf-King et al., 2013). Studies have identified internalized stigma and anticipated stigma among patients, and enacted stigma (or discriminatory behaviors) in the form of scolding or threats to withhold antiretroviral medication from HIV care providers (Regenauer et al., 2020). Some consequences of this anticipated stigma have been patients' failure to access or engage in HIV care and to disclose the true extent of their alcohol problems when interacting with health care providers (Regenauer et al., 2020). Similar reluctance to access tuberculosis treatment due to health workers' stigmatizing attitudes has been reported by individuals with alcohol problems (Møller et al., 2010).

Enacted Stigma toward People with SUD in Sub-Saharan Africa

Community attitudes toward people who use alcohol and other drugs or with SUDs have been investigated in quantitative and qualitative studies in sub-Saharan Africa (Sorsdahl et al., 2012). In a mixed methods study in South Africa, community members were found to assign negative attributes to people who "smoke and drink a lot" (Møller et al., 2010). They tended to be scapegoated and blamed for spreading tuberculosis and HIV, and to be blamed for their ill health. In a household survey that was conducted as part of this mixed-methods study, 71% of community members indicated that people who drink and smoke a lot were the most important risk factor leading to tuberculosis infection. Just under 50% considered people who drink and smoke to be nonadherent to their tuberculosis medication and the same percentage (47%) agreed that "abstaining from drinking and smoking was a recipe for success in completing tuberculosis treatment." In a semantic differential task, community members tended to select negative characteristics as being associated with "typical" drinkers and smokers (Møller et al., 2010).

One study in Moshi, Tanzania (Griffin et al., 2020), examined community members' and injury patients' stigma toward "former alcoholics" using the Perceived Alcohol Stigma scale (PAS), which was adapted from the Perceived Devaluation-Discrimination scale. The participants had generally high levels of perceived alcohol-related stigma, with a mean total PAS score of 51.9 (SD = 7.8) (Griffin et al., 2020), which was much higher than the average total PAS scores observed in studies in Germany (37.2, SD = 8.1) in 2011 (Schomerus et al., 2014) and the United States (37.8, SD = 8.47) in 2004/2005 (Glass et al., 2013).

One study in Cape Town in which community members were required to rate depictions of men and women with alcohol and other drug (cannabis, heroin, and methamphetamine) use disorders in terms of nine stereotypes on the Attribution Questionnaire Short Form (AQ-9) identified high levels of stigma (Sorsdahl et al., 2012). There were few significant differences in the participants' attributions regarding users of different types of drugs, except that the cannabis users were deemed less dangerous than the alcohol users.

Several studies have examined the attitudes of health workers toward people who have an SUD. For example, a study in South Africa found that 55.1% of emergency physician consultants and junior registrars agreed with the statement that "most alcohol and drug dependent persons are unpleasant to work with as patients," while 36.2% disagreed and a further

8.7% indicated that they were uncertain (Kalebka et al., 2013). Qualitative studies have identified health workers' negative stigmatizing views of people with SUDs (Møller et al., 2010; Regenauer et al., 2020), and a tendency to blame people with an SUD for their health problems. Regenauer et al. (2020) found that AUD stigma was less common than illegal SUD–related stigma.

Gender and Stigma toward People with SUD in Sub-Saharan Africa

Alcohol and other substance use–related stigma, involving both internalized and enacted stigma, is experienced more by women than men. This difference may stems from adolescence when the use of alcohol by girls is stigmatized much more than is the case for boys (Sommer et al., 2020). Sommer and colleagues found that community members tended to associate adolescent boys' alcohol consumption to supposed positive male attributes, such as masculinity, whereas girls' drinking tended to be linked to risky outcomes (e.g., sexual assault) and girls who drink alcohol were ascribed negative attributes and considered "morally loose", to have a reduced chance of getting married, and were seen to bring shame upon a family.

In the above-cited study conducted in Moshi, Tanzania (Griffin et al., 2020), based on their responses on items on the discrimination subscale of the PAS (e.g., "Most employers will pass over the application of a former alcoholic in favour of another applicant") women reported more discriminatory attitudes than men with regards to people with a former AUD. In other words, women were more likely than men to think that members of their community would discriminate against "former alcoholics." However, with regards to judging "former alcoholics" negatively (devaluation), there was no significant sex difference among respondents of this community. An example item from the devaluation subscale of the PAS used in the study is as follows: "Most people think less of a person who has been in alcohol treatment."

In the study described above in which community members rated vignettes of men and women with SUDs it emerged that community members were more likely to rate women than men with an AUD as being in need of help, but less likely to consider it appropriate to coerce women with an AUD into treatment. In contrast, community members' score on the AQ-9 suggested that they were more likely to avoid women who were cannabis users and more likely to consider it appropriate to coerce women who were methamphetamine users into treatment (Sorsdahl et al., 2012).

Conclusion

SUD stigmatization seems to be most common among and toward women and people who have other stigmatized health conditions such as HIV and tuberculosis. SUD stigma leads to reduced help seeking among people with SUDs and poorer service delivery by health care providers. The stigmatization of people with an AUD by community members has been observed even for those who have undergone treatment for an AUD.

Former Soviet Union Countries

In this section, we summarize the literature of stigma toward people with SUD in Russia and other former Soviet Union countries, including studies from Armenia, Azerbaijan, Belarus, Estonia, Georgia, Kazakhstan, Latvia, Lithuania, Kyrgyzstan, Moldova, Russia, Tajikistan, Turkmenistan, Ukraine, and Uzbekistan. Based on a summary of the historic roots of SUD treatment in the Soviet Union, we outline how these roots continue to contribute to SUD stigma in many of these countries.

The Soviet Narcological System

In order to understand the stigmatization of people with SUD, it is crucial to outline the current state and the history of respective treatment systems in this region. In many former Soviet Union countries, today's regulatory frameworks and treatment provision of AUD and other SUD are rooted in legislation that were developed during the time of the Soviet Union (Shields, 2009), although they have been developed and strongly changed ever since.

In the Soviet Union, the medical discipline of narcology was formed as a subspecialty of psychiatry in the 1970s. At that time, a country-wide network of so-called narcological centers was established in urban and narcological stations in rural areas. This network was based on a territorial-hierarchical principle, according to which patients were assigned to district narcologists (Golichenko & Chu, 2018; Nemtsov, 2011). Once registered as a "narcological patient," individuals were subsequently monitored for at least five years (three years after 1988), depending on the doctor's decision. Many of the narcological in-patient facilities were created by factories and production sites, often right next to workers' housing facilities and dormitories, using patients as a cheap source of labor (Nemtsov, 2011). Patients with heavy and chronic forms of SUD and, in particular, those with a record of "violation of labor discipline or rules of the socialist order" could also be sent to Occupational Therapy Rehabilitation Centres (лечебно-трудовые профилактории), which constituted a network of de facto work camps for people with SUDs, established across the entire Soviet Union (Bobrova et al., 2006; Morozov & Egorysheva, 2014; Shields, 2009; World Health Organization Regional Office for Europe, 2019). In these camps, forced labor as the primary method of "treatment" could be mandated for up to two years without any social contacts. The decisions were made by the People's Court, following the request of trade unions, the administration of factories and enterprises, the police, or the narcological service (Kirn, 1987; Morozov & Egorysheva, 2014). In order to transfer someone's case to the People's Court, a medical examination was required, which was conducted by a commission consisting of three doctors – a narcologist, a neurologist, and a therapist (i.e., general practitioner). Case documents were prepared by the Department of Internal Affairs and if patients failed to appear before the commission, they were brought in by the police, using force. The court decision on the mandated length of stay at the center was final and not subject to appeal (Morozov & Egorysheva, 2014; Nemtsov, 2011). Moreover, criminal liability was imposed on people who were convicted to labor treatment but escaped the centers without being formally released (Nemtsov, 2011).

Taken together, the Soviet Union narcology system was designed to control people with SUD rather than provide treatment options according to their needs, which can also be viewed in the broader context of Soviet punitive psychiatry as a tool for coercion (Elovich & Drucker, 2008; Raikhel, 2010). Overall, it is estimated that more than two million people were sent to these labor camps in the 1970s and 1980s, most of them being people with AUD (Shields, 2009). It is well documented that the camps were not only ineffective in their approaches, but also ridden with human rights violations, including forced treatment of people who did not formally meet the indication criteria (Zhirnov, 2013). The entire narcology system was set up to closely collaborate with governmental mechanisms of social control, with narcologists routinely cooperating and sharing information with law enforcement agencies and the police because, by law, confidentiality was reserved only for cooperative patients "firmly committed to treatment" (Human Rights Watch, 2007).

Current State of Narcology/SUD Treatment Systems: Russia as Example

This uneasy heritage of the narcological system lives on in many former Soviet Union countries, although the implications are probably best documented for the Russian Federation (Bobrova et al., 2006; Elovich & Drucker, 2008; Sarang et al., 2010). According to today's legislation, a narcological registration of monitoring of patients with AUD and other SUDs in Russia is still mandatory if the person wants to receive specialized treatment in a governmental health care facility.

In Russia, two types of monitoring exist: 1) "preventive" monitoring for the duration of one year of patients who potentially qualify in the category "harmful use," but do not yet fulfill the clinical criteria of dependence as per the tenth revision of the International Classification of Diseases (ICD-10; World Health Organization, 2019a) and 2) "narcological" monitoring of patients who were diagnosed with dependence by a narcologist with three years of monitoring time for AUD and five years for illegal SUD. Starting from 2019 and following a "modernization strategy," these procedures now require informed consent and patients under the "preventive" monitoring provision can be removed from the narcological register if they obtain written consent and approval of their treating and monitoring narcologist. However, so far, no data exist on how often patients actually use this possibility and how aware they are of these changes and there is no effort to collect this information (Incossi.ru, 2021; Neufeld, Bunova, et al., 2020). For individuals seeking anonymous treatment on their own, a contingent of anonymous treatment places was created as mandated by law, however, capacities are in reality very limited and access further hindered by favoritism and nepotism (Neufeld, Bunova, et al., 2020; Zakonbase.ru, 1999).

Avoiding the narcological registration is considered important for many patients, because the registration would imply the impossibility of applying for or renewing a driver's license and it bars affected people from holding various professions, such as professional drivers, pilots, electricians, mechanics, firefighters, law enforcement officers, or other security personnel carrying handguns. Moreover, if a person commits an administrative violation while being monitored, they will be denied official employment at any institution and the patient's criminal record can be cited as a reason to not hire this person. Clearly, this practice acts as an important barrier to early treatment and intervention because the legal and social implications of monitoring can initiate a vicious circle of substance use, social decline, and marginalization (Bobrova et al., 2006). Moreover, affected individuals often face situations that compromise their health and well-being, such as dangerous work (Shields, 2009). At the same time, private and costly treatment options that are often questionable and not evidence-based are thriving (Jargin, 2017; Raikhel, 2016). This only adds to the vulnerability of socioeconomically disadvantaged people with an SUD, who want to avoid narcological treatment as long as possible resulting in avoidable chronification of the condition and occurrence of comorbidities (Bobrova et al., 2006; Neufeld et al., 2017).

In Russia, the former Soviet network of Occupational Therapy Rehabilitation Centers and the forced labor provisions have been eliminated. However, these are still in place in Belarus and Turkmenistan (Neufeld, Bobrova, et al., 2020; Popova, 2015) and there were attempts to reintroduce the occupational centers in Russia in the 2000s and the idea of forced treatment of different population groups, for instance drunk drivers, regularly resurfaces in national debates (Moskva24.ru, 2020; Zelenskaya, 2010).

Taken together, people with SUD in Russia face punitive rather than supportive health care services and hardly any professional support outside of the state-run narcological network, at least when looking at intervention options that do not require out-of-pocket payments for services. In fact, the mandatory registration procedure as a "narcological patient" and thus as a state-certified "addict" and the automatic removal of various citizenship rights resonates – symbolically and literally – with the origins of the stigma concept as a process of marking of undesired individuals, who should be avoided and separated from the community (Goffman, 2009).

Different Approaches to Superseding the Narcological System in Former Soviet Union Countries

Since the dissolution of the Soviet Union, former Soviet Union countries took quite different paths in terms of the legislative regulation of substance use and treatment, allowing for some very interesting comparisons today. For instance, the Baltic countries have abolished the Soviet narcology system and its forced treatment and monitoring procedures soon after becoming independent in 1991 and introduced anonymous treatment soon after (Ahven, 2000). A study that compares experiences of stigma among people who inject drugs with HIV from an Estonian and a Russian city concludes that while internalized and experienced stigma was high in both samples, stigma was more strongly associated with adverse health outcomes in Russia than in Estonia (Burke et al., 2015).

Different approaches were also chosen in relation to opioid substitution treatment. While various former Soviet Union countries have introduced opioid substitution treatment in the 2000s, it is currently prohibited by law in Russia, Turkmenistan, and Uzbekistan (Aizberg, 2008; Harm

Reduction International, 2020; Latypov et al., 2012). In Russia, opioid substitution treatment remains hotly debated and despite an international law case involving activists, non-governmental organizations, and the European Court of Human Rights, the government's position remains unchanged (Larsson, 2016; Ministry of Health of the Russian Federation, 2016). Evidence from countries like Ukraine, which have introduced opioid substitution treatment but kept their narcological registration in place, suggests that the stigma associated with the registration remains a specific barrier to accessing opioid substitution treatment (Bojko et al., 2015).

Stigma in Former Soviet Union Countries Today: Perspectives and Experiences of People with SUD

In modern times, the type of substance used is highly relevant for the stigma of SUD in former Soviet Union countries. While alcohol is a well-accepted and normalized substance, illegal substance use and SUD are associated with greater danger, reflecting the predominance of the global discourses on safety and the "War on Drugs" (Erofeeva, 2016). People who inject drugs are particularly vulnerable, often because of the intersecting stigma of illegal substance use and HIV, but also because of legality issues and their exposure to the police and the authorities (Aleksandrov, 2006; Shields, 2009). In Russia, violations of human rights of people who use drugs were frequently documented in the past, against the background of the government's deep skepticism toward harm reduction approaches and an official policy of "social intolerance" of drug use, aimed at legitimizing and encouraging stigmatization and ill treatment of people who use drugs (Golichenko & Chu, 2018; Golichenko & Sarang, 2013; Human Rights Watch, 2007; Levinson & Torban, 2009). Unsanctioned police brutality toward people who use drugs and specifically people who inject drugs is one of the many ramifications of this stance. For instance, a study in three Russian cities highlights how law enforcement practices created an atmosphere of fear and contributed to the reproduction and experience of stigma, specifically by reinforcing processes of internalized self-blame, lack of self-worth, and fatalism regarding one's own life. The personal accounts of people who use drugs tell of routine and mundane day-to-day harassment through drug planting, unjustified arrest, money extortion, and coercion into being police informants, up to incidence of extreme violence, torture and organized rape, and sexual assault by the police (Sarang et al., 2010). A study from Belarus also highlights how people who use drugs do not perceive the narcology system as helpful and as a place to seek for help, but as something that inflicts fear, first and foremost the fear of narcological registration and monitoring. Moreover, people who use drugs criticized the (in their view) outdated treatment methods and low professional skills of narcologists as well as their indifference and lack of care for patients and wish for less restrictive and punitive drug policies, meaning to replace imprisonment by treatment (Kondratenya, 2016).

A similar passive and helpless stance to alcohol, AUD treatment, and general health as well as fatalistic attitudes toward one's life, paired with self-neglect and marginalization, were also frequently voiced by people with AUD in different Russian cities, including patients of narcology clinics, highlighting the impact of internalized stigma (Bobrova et al., 2009; Neufeld et al., 2019; Saburova et al., 2011).

Conclusion

The perspective from former Soviet Union countries highlights that people with SUD have faced, and in some countries still face, severe forms of discrimination, including stigmatizing practices from state-run health services, the legislative framework, and law enforcement authorities. The practice of narcological registration and monitoring that still exists in many former Soviet Union countries is often perceived as not only a barrier to treatment and health services but also as a control instrument to strip affected persons from civic rights and societal participation.

India and South Asia

In this section, we summarize the literature on stigma toward people with SUD in India and neighboring South Asian countries, including India, Pakistan, Nepal, Bangladesh, and Sri Lanka.

Patterns of Substance Use in South Asia

The use of different substances is prevalent in South Asia, but recent population-level epidemiological data are only available for India and Pakistan. There has been a long tradition of alcohol use in the region with several locally brewed beverages, particularly in India and Sri Lanka (Murthy, 2015). However, the prevalence of lifetime abstainers is also high with wide support for temperance-based and prohibitionist approaches. Overall, this has contributed to an ambivalent culture surrounding alcohol use (Benegal, 2005). With regard to tobacco, its smokeless form is more prevalent than smoked tobacco across South Asia with local tobacco preparations being popular in most regions (Sreeramareddy et al., 2014). Other substances such as cannabis have been culturally and religiously accepted including medical applications that are outlined in traditional texts (Touw, 1981). This trend has also been seen with regard to opium and opium-based preparations that find widespread recreational and medical uses (Ganguly et al., 1995). The scenario has changed considerably after all the countries became signatories of the three United Nations Conventions of 1961, 1971, and 1988 on drug abuse and trafficking. This has introduced a tight legal framework for supply reduction and stringent laws that even have provisions for the death penalty for drug-related offenses.

There has been a relative paucity of scientific literature evaluating the various dimensions of stigma among individuals with SUD from South Asia. The majority of the studies have been conducted in India, recruited individuals from hospitals, and focused on opioid use disorder.

SUD and Self-Stigma in South Asia

In the domain of self-stigma, most studies have evaluated perceived and internalized stigma. These have shown that in general there is significant stigma associated with all types of SUD (Hawlader et al., 2020; Sarkar et al., 2019). Two studies that compared levels of stigma between individuals with SUD and other psychiatric illnesses found significantly higher levels of internalized stigma in the former group (Garg et al., 2012; Modi et al., 2018).

Studies comparing levels of stigma between individuals with AUD and opioid use disorder have yielded contrasting findings. Contradictory to what would typically be expected, it was seen that perceived stigma was greater among individuals with AUD than those with opioid use disorder. This was explained by the authors as being due to a longer duration of use in the AUD group, more overt manifestations of alcohol intoxication, and a degree of cultural acceptance of opium use (Mattoo et al., 2015), in certain parts of northwestern India. This finding was replicated in another study of male opium users, in north India, where levels of internalized stigma were less than those of individuals using alcohol or heroin from the same center (Gupta et al., 2019). This points to the role of cultural mores in influencing the development of stigmatizing attitudes toward individuals with SUD. A descriptive study that evaluated the correlates of stigma among treatment-seeking individuals with AUD and opioid use disorder found that stigma was not influenced by sociodemographic and clinical characteristics of the study sample, except for being from a rural area, which was linked to perceiving greater stigma (Gyawali et al., 2018). All studies that examined the impact of stigma on quality of life found that greater levels of perceived and internalized stigma were associated with poorer quality of life across physical, psychological, and environmental domains (Sarkar et al., 2019; Singh et al., 2018). Internalized stigma was also seen to be a predictor of greater disability in individuals with opioid use disorder (Kumar et al., 2018). As with other parts of the world, people who inject drugs indicated high levels of self-stigma, including shame related to being a drug user and a fear of rejection by friends and family. The level of stigma was also seen to be positively associated with higher levels of unsafe injection practices (Latkin et al., 2010), such as sharing equipment, which is a matter of great concern. Two community-based studies of enacted stigma among people who inject drugs that measured the impact of acts of discrimination found that denial of health care services, experiencing physical/verbal abuse, and being arrested for carrying needles or syringes/using drugs was associated with poorer quality of life in psychological and social domains (Sarin et al., 2013). Previous experiences of refusal of health care or harm reduction services, arrests for possession of syringes, and greater experiences of social exclusion were also associated with lower health care utilization, which included general health care, harm reduction, and detoxification services (Sarin & Kerrigan, 2012).

SUD and Public as well as Structural Stigma in South Asia

The literature on public stigma toward SUD in the South Asian context is limited and has focused mainly on families of individuals with SUD. It was seen that female family members (wives, sisters, and daughters) of individuals with SUD perceived significant stigma and this predicted poorer mental health in the sample (Rafiq & Sadiq, 2019). This observation was replicated by a study where family stigma was associated with poorer quality of life (Garg et al., 2019). A qualitative study among adolescent offspring of men with AUD also underlined the social ostracism and stigma encountered, particularly by women from such families (Nattala et al., 2020). Surprisingly, a study contrasting perceived stigma between individuals with SUD and their family members found no differences, which the authors ascribe to shared cultural values (Mattoo et al., 2015). Despite this seemingly tolerant attitude of families toward individuals with

SUD, individuals in the community who do not use substances exhibited significantly greater rejection and avoidance of people who use drugs (Arun et al., 2010).

This is also compounded by stigmatizing attitudes of health care professionals, a fact that strongly influences treatment seeking. A study among undergraduates and doctors found that AUD and other illegal SUDs were associated with the greatest amount of stigma (Fernando et al., 2010) among all mental illness. This was mirrored by two studies among nursing students where SUDs were once again the most stigmatized mental health condition (Sreeraj et al., 2017), a fact that alarmingly seemed to get accentuated despite training in the area (Aggarwal et al., 2012).

There is no scientific literature available on the role of structural discrimination toward individuals with SUD from South Asia. However, treatment of individuals with SUD is not covered by most private and government insurance schemes in India. Further, the treatment gap for SUDs is the highest among all mental illnesses (Gururaj et al., 2016). There is also a moral undertone that characterizes the institutional discourse on management of SUD that may magnify preexisting stigmatizing attitudes (Murthy, 2015). This is typified by systemic attitudes toward opioid substitution treatment that range from scorn (government as an "official" drug dealer and money being "wasted" on undeserving people) to fear and mistrust (Rao, 2017). The coverage for opioid substitution treatment also remains low (Ambekar et al., 2013; Bergenstrom et al., 2015) and is limited in its scope to include only injecting drug users.

Gender and Stigma toward People with SUD in South Asia

In terms of gender, women with SUD in South Asia are subject to greater stigma (Benegal et al., 2005) than their male counterparts in the community (Murthy, 2008). This also extends to the health care system and contributes to reduced help seeking (Thomas et al., 2018). This emphasizes the need to address stigma in treatment of women with SUD and the need for provision of women-centric services (Ahluwalia et al., 2020).

Conclusion

We find significant self-stigma among individuals with SUD in South Asia that was more pronounced than among people with other mental illnesses. Greater stigma was consistently associated with poorer quality of life, greater disability, and inadequate help seeking, and seems to be significantly more for women with SUD. Further, families of individuals with SUD, particularly women, while themselves facing significant stigma, did not seem to harbor a greater degree of stigma toward individuals with SUD. Interestingly, stigma did not differ between users of legal and illegal substances. This appears to be different from Southeast Asian countries, such as Philippines, Singapore, and Indonesia, which are marked by criminalization of drug-related offences, including capital punishment in many cases. This section does not cover Southeast Asia, where the experience of stigma among individuals with SUD is likely to vary.

Linking Perspectives: Global Implications of SUD Stigma

Reviewing studies on SUD stigma from six world regions, we have covered large parts of the available literature but have also excluded some regions, such as Australasia, Southeast and East Asia, as well as Northern Africa and the Middle East. Acknowledging these limitations, we find that the available evidence converges on the fact that people with SUD do experience high levels of stigmatization. However, manifestations do differ depending on the region and the substance in play.

Most importantly, SUD stigma both constitutes a problem and creates problems not only with regards to treatment access but also for societal participation at large. Discriminatory consequences, the most impactful manifestation of stigma, are present in all world regions, yet with varying nuances. While social rejection from communities was reported in South Asia and sub-Saharan Africa to some extent, lack of treatment access or even treatment denial has emerged as a key theme in the Americas. In some former Soviet Union countries, people with SUD experience even more severe consequences, including denial of human rights. Further, the impact of SUD stigma is more severe for women and ethnic minorities, and consequences are further aggravated for economically disadvantaged people. In addition, the issue of intersectionality is clearly evident from sub-Saharan Africa, where the stigma enacted toward people with SUDs seems to be compounded when such individuals also have other stigmatized conditions such as HIV or tuberculosis.

While the current situation for people with SUD may appear grim, there is some reason for hope. The manifestation of SUD stigma appears to vary not only with prevailing cultural norms that are constantly changing but also with policy approaches. As reported in Colombia, the free-of-charge provision of health care for people with AUD may not work from one day to the next; however, such approaches may pave the way for a sustainable change of both public attitudes and internal beliefs. In Portugal, ten years after decriminalizing all illegal substances, opioid substitution treatment provision was rated satisfactorily by both providers and patients. Lastly, abolishment of the Soviet narcological system, and thus lowering barriers to care, may have contributed to weaken the link of stigma and health outcomes in select former Soviet Union countries.

References

Abeldaño, R. A., Gallo, V., Burrone, M. S., & Fernández, A. R. (2016). Estigma internalizado en consumidores de drogas en Córdoba, Argentina [Internalized stigma among drug users in Cordoba, Argentina]. *Acta de investigación psicológica, 6*(2), 2404–2411.

Abraham, A. J., Andrews, C. M., Grogan, C. M., et al. (2017). The Affordable Care Act transformation of substance use disorder treatment. *American Journal of Public Health, 107*(1), 31–32.

Aggarwal, M., Ghai, S., & Basu, D. (2012). Attitude of nursing students towards psychoactive substance use: Does training matter. *International Journal of Nursing Education, 4*(2), 146–150.

Ahluwalia, H., Chand, P. K., & Suman, L. (2020). Therapeutic focus for women with substance use disorders: Views of experts and consumers in a tertiary hospital in India. *Professional Psychology: Research and Practice, 51*(1), 34–50.

Ahven, A. (2000). Social problems in official statistics in Estonia in the 1980s and 1990s. *NAD PUBLICATION, 37*, 17–58.

Aizberg, O. (2008). *Opioid substitution therapy in selected countries of Eastern Europe and Central Asia.* International AIDS Society. https://citeseerx.ist.psu.edu/viewdoc/download?doi=10.1.1.536.3075&rep=rep1&type=pdf

Aleksandrov, A. A. (2006). Stigmatizacija v narkologii [Stigmatization in narcology]. *Medicinskaja panorama, 6*, 42–46.

Alliance for Health Policy. (2017). *Chapter 8 – Mental health and substance abuse.* https://www.allhealthpolicy.org/sourcebook/mental-health-and-substance-abuse/

Alonso, J., Angermeyer, M. C., Bernert, S., et al. (2004). Use of mental health services in Europe: Results from the European Study of the Epidemiology of Mental Disorders (ESEMeD) project. *Acta Psychiatrica Scandinavica, 109*, 47–54.

Ambekar, A., Rao, R., Pun, A., Kumar, S., & Kishore, K. (2013). The trajectory of methadone maintenance treatment in Nepal. *International Journal of Drug Policy, 24*(6), e57–e60.

American Addiction Centers. (2019). *Americans' perceptions of alcohol vs. marijuana.* https://americanaddictioncenters.org/learn/perceptions-of-alcohol-vs-marijuana/

Angus, C., Brown, J., Beard, E., et al. (2019). Socioeconomic inequalities in the delivery of brief interventions for smoking and excessive drinking: Findings from a cross-sectional household survey in England. *BMJ Open, 9*(4), e023448.

Arun, P., Singh Chavan, B., & Bhargava, R. (2010). Attitudes towards alcoholism and drug taking: A survey of rural and slum areas of Chandigarh, India. *International Journal of Culture and Mental Health*, *3*(2), 126–136.

Bard, N. D., Antunes, B., Roos, C. M., Olschowsky, A., & Pinho, L. B. (2016). El estigma y el prejuicio: la experiencia de los consumidores de crack [Internalized stigma among drug users in Cordoba, Argentina]. *Revista Latino-Americana de Enfermagem*, *24*.

Benegal, V. (2005). India: Alcohol and public health. *Addiction*, *100*(8), 1051–1056.

Benegal, V., Nayak, M., Murthy, P., Chandra, P., & Gururaj, G. (2005). Women and alcohol in India. In I. S. Obot & R. Room (Ed.), *Alcohol, gender and drinking problems: Perspectives from low and middle income countries* (pp. 89–124). World Health Organization.

Bergenstrom, A., Achakzai, B., Furqan, S., ul Haq, M., Khan, R., & Saba, M. (2015). Drug-related HIV epidemic in Pakistan: A review of current situation and response and the way forward beyond 2015. *Harm Reduction Journal*, *12*(1), 1–7.

Blomqvist, J. (2012). Perceptions of addiction and recovery in Sweden: The influence of respondent characteristics. *Addiction Research & Theory*, *20*(5), 435–446.

Bobrova, N., Rhodes, T., Power, R., et al. (2006). Barriers to accessing drug treatment in Russia: A qualitative study among injecting drug users in two cities. *Drug and Alcohol Dependence*, *82*(Suppl. 1), S57–S63.

Bobrova, N., West, R., Malutina, D., Koshkina, E., Terkulov, R., & Bobak, M. (2009). Drinking alcohol surrogates among clients of an alcohol-misuser treatment clinic in Novosibirsk, Russia. *Substance Use & Misuse*, *44*(13), 1821–1832.

Bojko, M. J., Mazhnaya, A., Makarenko, I., et al. (2015). "Bureaucracy & beliefs": Assessing the barriers to accessing opioid substitution therapy by people who inject drugs in Ukraine. *Drugs: Education, Prevention and Policy*, *22*(3), 255–262.

Burke, S. E., Calabrese, S. K., Dovidio, J. F., et al. (2015). A tale of two cities: Stigma and health outcomes among people with HIV who inject drugs in St. Petersburg, Russia and Kohtla-Järve, Estonia. *Social Science & Medicine*, *130*, 154–161.

Capoccia, V. A., Grazier, K. L., Toal, C., Ford, J. H., & Gustafson, D. H. (2012). Massachusetts's experience suggests coverage alone is insufficient to increase addiction disorders treatment. *Health Affairs*, *31*(5), 1000–1008.

Carliner, H., Delker, E., Fink, D. S., Keyes, K. M., & Hasin, D. S. (2016). Racial discrimination, socioeconomic position, and illicit drug use among US Blacks. *Social Psychiatry and Psychiatric Epidemiology*, *51*(4), 551–560.

Case, A., & Deaton, A. (2020). *Deaths of despair and the future of capitalism*. Princeton University Press.

Cornford, C., Fraser, L., & Wright, N. (2019). Deep vein thromboses in injecting drug users: Meanings, bodily experiences, and stigma. *Qualitative Health Research*, *29*(11), 1641–1650.

Crawford, N. D., Rudolph, A. E., Jones, K., & Fuller, C. (2012). Differences in self-reported discrimination by primary type of drug used among New York City drug users. *The American Journal of Drug and Alcohol Abuse, 38*(6), 588–592.

Crépault, J.-F., Rehm, J., & Fischer, B. (2016). The Cannabis Policy Framework by the Centre for Addiction and Mental Health: A proposal for a public health approach to cannabis policy in Canada. *International Journal on Drug Policy, 34*, 1–4.

Cunningham, P. J. (2009). Beyond parity: Primary care physicians' perspectives on access to mental health care: More PCPs have trouble obtaining mental health services for their patients than have problems getting other specialty services. *Health Affairs, 28*(Suppl. 1), w490–w501.

De Andrade, D., Ritchie, J., Rowlands, M., Mann, E., & Hides, L. (2018). Substance use and recidivism outcomes for prison-based drug and alcohol interventions. *Epidemiologic Reviews, 40*(1), 121–133.

Degenhardt, L., Peacock, A., Colledge, S., et al. (2017). Global prevalence of injecting drug use and sociodemographic characteristics and prevalence of HIV, HBV, and HCV in people who inject drugs: A multistage systematic review. *The Lancet Global Health, 5*(12), e1192–e1207.

Demmert, A., Grothues, J. M., & Rumpf, H. J. (2011). Attitudes towards brief interventions to reduce smoking and problem drinking behaviour in gynaecological practice. *Public Health, 125*(4), 182–186.

Desalu, J. M., Goodhines, P. A., & Park, A. (2019). Racial discrimination and alcohol use and negative drinking consequences among Black Americans: a meta-analytical review. *Addiction, 114*(6), 957–967.

Duby, Z., Nkosi, B., Scheibe, A., Brown, B., & Bekker, L. G. (2018). 'Scared of going to the clinic': Contextualising healthcare access for men who have sex with men, female sex workers and people who use drugs in two South African cities. *Southern African Journal of HIV Medicine, 19*(1), Article 701.

Elovich, R., & Drucker, E. (2008). On drug treatment and social control: Russian narcology's great leap backwards. *Harm Reduction Journal, 5*, Article 23.

elpacientecolombiano.com. (2018). *Inversión en salud mental en Colombia disminuye aunque aumentan violencias [Investment in mental health in Colombia decreases although violence increases]*. https://elpacientecolombiano.com/salud-mental/la-inversion-en-salud-mental-en-colombia-disminuye-aunque-aumentan-violencias/

Erofeeva, P. A. (2016). Stigmatizacija alkohol'noj i narkoticheskoj zavisimosti: parametry i posledstvija [Stigmatization of alcohol and drug addiction: Parameters and consequences]. *Zhurnal issledovanij social'noj politiki, 14*(3), 377–392.

European Monitoring Centre for Drugs and Drug Addiction. (2021). *Legal approaches to drugs and driving*. https://www.emcdda.europa.eu/publications/topic-overviews/legal-approaches-to-drugs-and-driving/html_en

Fernando, S. M., Deane, F. P., & McLeod, H. J. (2010). Sri Lankan doctors' and medical undergraduates' attitudes towards mental illness. *Social Psychiatry and Psychiatric Epidemiology, 45*(7), 733–739.

Ganguly, K. K., Sharma, H. K., & Krishnamachari, K. A. (1995). An ethnographic account of opium consumers of Rajasthan (India): Socio-medical perspective. *Addiction, 90*(1), 9–12; discussion 13–21.

Garg, R., Chavan, B., & Arun, P. (2012). Stigma and discrimination: How do persons with psychiatric disorders and substance dependence view themselves? *Indian Journal of Social Psychiatry 28*, 3–4.

Garg, R., Gupta, A., & Kundal, D. (2019). Comparison of impact of family stigma on quality of life among caregivers of male inpatients with alcohol and opioid use disorder. *Industrial Psychiatry Journal, 28*(2), 278–285.

Glass, J. E., Kristjansson, S. D., & Bucholz, K. K. (2013). Perceived alcohol stigma: Factor structure and construct validation. *Alcoholism: Clinical & Experimantal Research, 37*(Suppl. 1), E237–246.

Global Health Data Exchange (GHDx). (2020). *GBD Results Tool for the Global Burden of Disease 2017 Study*. Institute for Health Metrics and Evaluation. Retrieved April 12, 2020 from http://ghdx.healthdata.org/gbd-results-tool

Goffman, E. (2009). *Stigma: Notes on the management of spoiled identity*. Simon & Schuster.

Golichenko, M., & Chu, S. K. H. (2018). Human rights in patient care: Drug treatment and punishment in Russia. *Public Health Reviews, 39*(1), 1–12.

Golichenko, M., & Sarang, A. (2013). Atmospheric pressure: Russian drug policy as a driver for violations of the UN Convention against Torture and the International Covenant on Economic, Social and Cultural Rights. *Health & Human Rights Journal, 15*, E135–E143.

Goulão, J. (2013). Atitudes e percepções relativas ao tratamento de manutenção com opiáceos em Portugal: Um inquérito a médicos, doentes e utilizadores [Attitudes and beliefs regarding opioid maintenance treatment in Portugal: A survey to physicians, patients and opioid users]. *Acta Medica Portuguesa, 26*(5), 537–548.

Grant, B. F., Saha, T. D., Ruan, W. J., et al. (2016). Epidemiology of DSM-5 drug use disorder: Results from the National Epidemiologic Survey on Alcohol and Related Conditions-III. *JAMA Psychiatry, 73*(1), 39–47.

Greenwald, G. (2009). *Drug decriminalization in Portugal: Lessons for creating fair and successful drug policies*. Cato Institute Whitepaper Series.

Griffin, S. M., Karia, F. P., Zimmerman, A., et al. (2020). A mixed-methods study: Sex differences in experiences of stigma associated with alcoholism and alcohol use disorders among injury patients in Tanzania. *Alcoholism: Clinical and Experimental Research, 44*(8), 1700–1707.

Gupta, P., Panda, U., Parmar, A., & Bhad, R. (2019). Internalized stigma and its correlates among treatment seeking opium users in India: A cross-sectional observational study. *Asian Journal of Psychiatry, 39*, 86–90.

Gururaj, G., Varghese, M., Benegal, V., et al. (2016). *National mental health survey of India, 2015–16: Summary*. National Institute of Mental Health and Neurosciences.

Gyawali, S., Sarkar, S., Balhara, Y. P. S., Kumar, S., Patil, V., & Singh, S. (2018). Perceived stigma and its correlates among treatment seeking alcohol and opioid users at a tertiary care centre in India. *Asian Journal of Psychiatry, 37,* 34–37.

Hahn, J. A., Woolf-King, S. E., & Muyindike, W. (2011). Adding fuel to the fire: Alcohol's effect on the HIV epidemic in Sub-Saharan Africa. *Current HIV/AIDS Reports, 8*(3), 172–180.

Hanschmidt, F., Manthey, J., Kraus, L., et al. (2017). Barriers to alcohol screening among hypertensive patients and the role of stigma: Lessons for the implementation of screening and brief interventions in European primary care settings. *Alcohol and Alcoholism, 52*(5), 572–579.

Harm Reduction International. (2020). *The global state of harm reduction* (7th ed.). https://www.hri.global/files/2021/03/04/Global_State_HRI_2020_BOOK_FA_Web.pdf

Hasin, D. S., & Grant, B. F. (2015). The National Epidemiologic Survey on Alcohol and Related Conditions (NESARC) Waves 1 and 2: Review and summary of findings. *Social Psychiatry and Psychiatric Epidemiology, 50*(11), 1609–1640.

Hawlader, M. D. H., Nabi, M. H., Hussain, A., Al Amin, S. U., Zaman, S., & Masud, I. (2020). Legal and social consequences of substance use: Results from a nationwide study in Bangladesh. *Journal of Ethnicity in Substance Abuse,* 1–11.

Human Rights Watch. (2007). *Rehabilitation required: Russia's human rights obligation to provide evidence-based drug dependence treatment* (Vol. 19). Human Rights Watch.

Imtiaz, S., Shield, K. D., Fischer, B., et al. (2020). Recent changes in trends of opioid overdose deaths in North America. *Substance Abuse Treatment, Prevention, and Policy, 15*(1), Article 66.

Incossi.ru. (2021). *Registered with a narcologist.* Retrieved March 11, 2021 from https://incossi.ru/na-uchete-u-narkologa/

Institute for Health Metrics and Evaluation. (2021). *GBD results tool* http://ghdx.healthdata.org/gbd-results-tool

International Drug Policy Consortium (IDPC). (2019). *Women who use drugs and access to treatment in Mexico: Between violence and stigma.* https://idpc.net/blog/2019/12/women-who-use-drugs-and-access-to-treatment-in-mexico-between-violence-and-stigma

Jargin, S. (2017). Alcohol and alcoholism in Russia: Policies and their effects. *Archives Medical Review Journal, 26,* 207–222.

Joint United Nations Programme on HIV/AIDS (UNAIDS). (2019). *Health, rights, and drugs: Harm reduction, decriminalization and zero discrimination for people who use drugs.* https://www.unaids.org/sites/default/files/media_asset/JC2954_UNAIDS_drugs_report_2019_en.pdf

Joint United Nations Programme on HIV/AIDS (UNAIDS). (2020). *UNAIDS data 2020.* https://www.unaids.org/sites/default/files/media_asset/2020_aids-data-book_en.pdf

Kalebka, R., Bruijns, S., & Van Hoving, D. (2013). A survey of attitudes towards patient substance abuse and addiction in the Emergency Centre. *African Journal of Emergency Medicine, 3*(1), 10–17.

Kilian, C., Manthey, J., Carr, S., et al. (2021). Stigmatisation of people with alcohol use disorders: An updated systematic review of population studies. *Alcoholism: Clinical and Experimental Research*, *45*(5), 899–911.

Kirn, T. F. (1987). Branch of medicine called 'narcology' spearheads aggressive Soviet campaign against alcoholism. *JAMA*, *258*(7), 885–886.

Klein, S., & Hostetter, M. (2014). *In focus: Integrating behavioral health and primary care.* The Commonwealth Fund.

Kondratenya, K. A. (2016). Narkologicheskaja sluzhba glazami potrebitelej narkotikov [Drug service through the eyes of drug users]. 70-ja Mezhdunarodnaja nauchno-prakticheskaja konferencija studentov i molodyh uchjonyh "Aktual'nye problemy sovremennoj mediciny i farmacii – 2016." *Sbornik materialov konferencii*, 1512–1517. Retrieved March 11, 2021, from http://rep.bsmu.by/bitstream/handle/BSMU/11229/1.pdf?sequence=1&isAllowed=y

Krane, K. (2020, May 26). Cannabis legalization is key to economic recovery, much like ending alcohol prohibition helped us out of the Great Depression. *Forbes.* https://www.forbes.com/sites/kriskrane/2020/05/26/cannabis-legalization-is-key-to-economic-recovery-much-like-ending-alcohol-prohibition-helped-us-out-of-the-great-depression/?sh=4c3a0cc53241

Kumar, S., Singh, S., Sarkar, S., & Balhara, Y. P. S. (2018). Disability among patients with opioid use disorders and its relationship with stigma toward substance use. *Indian Journal of Social Psychiatry*, *34*(1), 30–36.

Larsen, E., Gheorghe, P., Rehm, M. X., & Rehm, J. (2015). Treatment for alcohol use disorders in Canada. *Journal of Addiction Medicine and Therapy*, *3*(1), Article 1013.

Larsson, N. (2016, September 14). How three drug users took on the might of the Russian state. *The Guardian.* https://www.theguardian.com/global-development-professionals-network/2016/sep/14/how-three-drug-users-took-on-the-might-of-the-russian-state

Latkin, C., Srikrishnan, A. K., Yang, C., et al. (2010). The relationship between drug use stigma and HIV injection risk behaviors among injection drug users in Chennai, India. *Drug and Alcohol Dependence*, *110*(3), 221–227.

Latypov, A., Bidordinova, A., & Khachatrian, A. (2012). *Opioid substitution therapy in Eurasia: How to increase the access and improve the quality.* IDPC Briefing Series on Drug Dependence Treatment No. 1. International Drug Policy Consortium.

Lende, D. H. (2003). *Pattern and paradox: Adolescent substance use and abuse in Bogotá, Colombia.* Emory University.

Levinson, L., & Torban, M. (2009). Narkouchet: Po zakonu ili po instrukcii? Regulirovanie registracii potrebitelej narkotikov v Rossijskoj Federacii [Drug registration: By law or by instruction? Regulation of registration of drug users in the Russian Federation]. *Anaharsis.* http://www.biblioteka.freepress.ru/e_books/narkouchet/narkouchet.html

Lopez, O. (2021, March 10). Mexico set to legalize marijuana, becoming world's largest market. *The New York Times.* https://www.nytimes.com/2021/03/10/world/americas/mexico-cannabis-bill.html

Luty, J., Kumar, P., & Stagias, K. (2018). Stigmatised attitudes in independent pharmacies associated with discrimination towards individuals with opioid dependence. *The Psychiatrist, 34*(12), 511–514.

Manthey, J., Shield, K. D., Rylett, M., Hasan, O. S. M., Probst, C., & Rehm, J. (2019). Alcohol exposure between 1990 and 2017 and forecasts until 2030: A global modelling study. *The Lancet, 393*(10190), 2493–2502.

Mathers, B. M., Degenhardt, L., Bucello, C., Lemon, J., Wiessing, L., & Hickman, M. (2013). Mortality among people who inject drugs: A systematic review and meta-analysis. *Bulletin of the World Health Organization, 91*(2), 102–123.

Mattoo, S. K., Sarkar, S., Gupta, S., Nebhinani, N., Parakh, P., & Basu, D. (2015). Stigma towards substance use: Comparing treatment seeking alcohol and opioid dependent men. *International Journal of Mental Health and Addiction, 13*(1), 73–81.

Medina-Perucha, L., Scott, J., Chapman, S., Barnett, J., Dack, C., & Family, H. (2019). A qualitative study on intersectional stigma and sexual health among women on opioid substitution treatment in England: Implications for research, policy and practice. *Social Science and Medicine, 222*, 315–322.

Mekonen, T., Chan, G. C. K., Connor, J., Hall, W., Hides, L., & Leung, J. (2020). Treatment rates for alcohol use disorders: A systematic review and meta-analysis. *Addiction, 116*(10), 2617–2634.

Ministerio de Salud y Protección Social de Colombia. (2016). *Modelo de atención integral por uso de sustancias psicoactivas en Colombia*. Government of Columbia.

Ministry of Health of the Russian Federation. (2016). *Pozicija Minzdrava Rossii v otnoshenii zamestitel'noj opioidnoj podderzhivajushhiej terapii* [Position of the Russian Ministry of Health on opioid substitution maintenance therapy]. https://minzdrav.gov.ru/news/2016/03/11/2832-pozitsiya-minzdrava-rossii-v-otnoshenii-zamestitelnoy-opioidnoy-podderzhivayuschiey-terapii

Minsalud. (2020). *Estigma social asociado a COVID 19 [Stigma associated with COVID 19]*. Consejo Nacional de Salud Mental. https://www.minsalud.gov.co/sites/rid/Lists/BibliotecaDigital/RIDE/VS/PP/recomendaciones-sm-covid-19-prevencion-stigma.pdf

Modi, L., Gedam, S. R., Shivji, I. A., Babar, V., & Patil, P. (2018). Comparison of total self-stigma between schizophrenia and alcohol dependence patients. *International Journal of High Risk Behaviors and Addiction, 7*(3), 14–18.

Møller, V., Erstad, I., & Zani, D. (2010). Drinking, smoking, and morality: Do 'drinkers and smokers' constitute a stigmatised stereotype or a real TB risk factor in the time of HIV/AIDS? *Social Indicators Research, 98*(2), 217–238.

Morozov, A. V., & Egorysheva, I. V. (2014). K 40-letiju sozdanija narkologi-cheskoj sluzhby v strane [To the 40th anniversary of the drug service in the country]. *Problemy social'noj gigieny, zdravoohranenija i istorii mediciny, 6*(6), 55–57.

Moskva24.ru. (2020). *V GD ne schitajut, chto prinuditel'noe lechenie ot alkogolizma prineset plody [The State Duma does not believe that compulsory treatment for *alcoholism will bear fruit]*. https://www.m24.ru/news/obshchestvo/ 21012020/104407?utm_source=CopyBuf

Murney, M. A., Sapag, J. C., Bobbili, S. J., & Khenti, A. (2020). Stigma and discrimination related to mental health and substance use issues in primary health care in Toronto, Canada: A qualitative study. *International Journal of Qualitative Studies on Health and Well-being, 15*(1), Article 1744926.

Murthy, P. (2008). *Women and drug use in India: Substance, women and high-risk assessment study*. United Nations Office on Drugs and Crime. https://www.unodc.org/documents/southasia/reports/UNODC_Book_Women_and_Drug_Use_in_India_2008.pdf

(2015). Culture and alcohol use in India. *World Cultural Psychiatry Research Review, 10*, 27–39.

National Academies of Sciences, Engineering, and Medicine. (2016). *Ending discrimination against people with mental and substance use disorders: The evidence for stigma change*. National Academies Press.

(2020). *Caring for people with mental health and substance use disorders in primary care settings: Proceedings of a workshop*. National Academies Press.

Nattala, P., Murthy, P., Weiss, M. G., et al. (2020). Experiences and reactions of adolescent offspring to their fathers' heavy drinking: A qualitative study from an urban metropolis in India. *Journal of Ethnicity in Substance Abuse*, 1–20.

Nemtsov, A. V. (2011). *A contemporary history of alcohol in Russia*. Södertörns högskola.

Neufeld, M., Bobrova, A., Davletov, K., et al. (2020). Alcohol control policies in Former Soviet Union countries: A narrative review of three decades of policy changes and their apparent effects. *Drug and Alcohol Review, 40*(3), 350–367.

Neufeld, M., Bunova, A., Gornyi, B., et al. (2020). Russia's national concept to reduce alcohol abuse and alcohol-dependence in the population 2010–2020: Which policy targets have been achieved? *International Journal of Environmental Research and Public Health, 17*(21), Article 8270.

Neufeld, M., Wittchen, H.-U., & Rehm, J. (2017). Drinking patterns and harm of unrecorded alcohol in Russia: A qualitative interview study. *Addiction Research & Theory, 25*(4), 310–317.

Neufeld, M., Wittchen, H.-U., Ross, L. E., Ferreira-Borges, C., & Rehm, J. (2019). Perception of alcohol policies by consumers of unrecorded alcohol: An exploratory qualitative interview study with patients of alcohol treatment facilities in Russia. *Substance Abuse Treatment, Prevention, and Policy, 14*(1), 1–14.

Paris, M., Pérez, L., & Medrano, G. (2009). *Estigma y discriminación hacia las y los usuarios de drogas y sus familiares [Stigma and discrimination toward drug users and their families]*. Consejo Nacional para Prevenir la Discriminación.

Peacock, A., Leung, J., Larney, S., et al. (2018). Global statistics on alcohol, tobacco and illicit drug use: 2017 status report. *Addiction, 113*(10), 1905–1926.

Pelullo, C. P., Curcio, F., Auriemma, F., et al. (2019). The discrimination against, health status and wellness of people who use drugs in Italian services: A survey. *Medicina (Kaunas, Lithuania), 55*(10), 662.

Peluso Ede, T., & Blay, S. L. (2008). Public perception of alcohol dependence. *Brazilian Journal of Psychiatry*, *30*(1), 19–24.

Popova, I. (2015, December 17). Inside Belarus's 'rehab prisons' for alcoholics – in pictures. *The Guardian*. https://www.theguardian.com/world/gallery/2015/dec/17/belarus-soviet-jail-for-alcoholics-irina-popova

Probst, C., Manthey, J., Martinez, A., & Rehm, J. (2015). Alcohol use disorder severity and reported reasons not to seek treatment: A cross-sectional study in European primary care practices. *Substance Abuse Treatment, Prevention, and Policy*, *10*, Article 32.

Rafiq, M., & Sadiq, R. (2019). Caregiver stress, perceived stigma and mental health in female family members of drug addicts: Correlational study. *JPMA*, *69*(9), 1300–1303.

Raikhel, E. (2010). Post-Soviet placebos: Epistemology and authority in Russian treatments for alcoholism. *Culture, Medicine, and Psychiatry*, *34*(1), 132–168.

(2016). *Governing habits: Treating alcoholism in the post-Soviet clinic*. Cornell University Press.

Rao, R. (2017). The journey of opioid substitution therapy in India: Achievements and challenges. *Indian Journal of Psychiatry*, *59*(1), 39–45.

Rathod, S. D., De Silva, M. J., Ssebunnya, J., et al. (2016). Treatment contact coverage for probable depressive and probable alcohol use disorders in four low-and middle-income country districts: The PRIME cross-sectional community surveys. *PLOS ONE*, *11*(9), e0162038.

Regenauer, K. S., Myers, B., Batchelder, A. W., & Magidson, J. F. (2020). "That person stopped being human": Intersecting HIV and substance use stigma among patients and providers in South Africa. *Drug and Alcohol Dependence*, *216*, Article 108322.

Rehm, J., Manthey, J., Shield, K. D., & Ferreira-Borges, C. (2019). Trends in substance use and in the attributable burden of disease and mortality in the WHO European Region, 2010–16. *European Journal of Public Health*, *29*(4), 723–728.

Room, R. (2005). Stigma, social inequality and alcohol and drug use. *Drug and Alcohol Review*, *24*(2), 143–155.

Saburova, L., Keenan, K., Bobrova, N., Leon, D. A., & Elbourne, D. (2011). Alcohol and fatal life trajectories in Russia: Understanding narrative accounts of premature male death in the family. *BMC Public Health*, *11*(1), 1–10.

Sarang, A., Rhodes, T., Sheon, N., & Page, K. (2010). Policing drug users in Russia: Risk, fear, and structural violence. *Substance Use & Misuse*, *45*(6), 813–864.

Sarin, E., & Kerrigan, D. (2012). The impact of human rights violations and perceptions of discrimination on health service utilization among injection drug users in Delhi, India. *Substance Use & Misuse*, *47*(3), 230–243.

Sarin, E., Samson, L. J., & Sweat, M. D. (2013). Impact of acts of discrimination on quality of life among injecting drug users in Delhi, India. *Social Indicators Research*, *113*(1), 319–334.

Sarkar, S., Balhara, Y. P. S., Kumar, S., et al. (2019). Internalized stigma among patients with substance use disorders at a tertiary care center in India. *Journal of Ethnicity in Substance Abuse, 18*(3), 345–358.

Satinsky, E. N., Myers, B., Andersen, L. S., Kagee, A., Joska, J., & Magidson, J. F. (2020). "Now we are told that we can mix": Messages and beliefs around simultaneous use of alcohol and ART. *AIDS and Behavior, 24*(9), 2680–2690.

Scheibe, A., Shelly, S., Versfeld, A., Howell, S., & Marks, M. (2017). Safe treatment and treatment of safety: Call for a harm-reduction approach to drug-use disorders in South Africa. *South African Health Review, 2017*(1), 197–204.

Schomerus, G., Lucht, M., Holzinger, A., Matschinger, H., Carta, M. G., & Angermeyer, M. C. (2011). The stigma of alcohol dependence compared with other mental disorders: A review of population studies. *Alcohol and Alcoholism, 46*(2), 105–112.

Schomerus, G., Matschinger, H., Lucht, M. J., & Angermeyer, M. C. (2014). Changes in the perception of alcohol-related stigma in Germany over the last two decades. *Drug and Alcohol Dependence, 143*, 225–231.

Scott-Sheldon, L. A., Walstrom, P., Carey, K. B., Johnson, B. T., Carey, M. P., & Team, M. R. (2013). Alcohol use and sexual risk behaviors among individuals infected with HIV: A systematic review and meta-analysis 2012 to early 2013. *Current HIV/AIDS Reports, 10*(4), 314–323.

Shields, A. (2009). *The effects of drug user registration laws on people's rights and health: Key findings from Russia, Georgia, and Ukraine*. Open Society Institute. https://www.opensocietyfoundations.org/uploads/def77bbe-43fd-46ad-9f91-b1b8bd26a221/drugreg_20091001.pdf

Singh, S., Kumar, S., Sarkar, S., & Balhara, Y. P. S. (2018). Quality of life and its relationship with perceived stigma among opioid use disorder patients: An exploratory study. *Indian Journal of Psychological Medicine, 40*(6), 556–561.

Skliamis, K., Benschop, A., & Korf, D. J. (2020). Cannabis users and stigma: A comparison of users from European countries with different cannabis policies. *European Journal of Criminology*.

Sommer, M., Kaaya, S., Kajula, L., Marwerwe, G., Hamisi, H., & Parker, R. (2020). Social and structural determinants of youth alcohol use in Tanzania: The role of gender, social vulnerability and stigma. *Global Public Health*, 1–13.

Sornpaisarn, B., Shield, K., Manthey, J., et al. (2020). Alcohol consumption and attributable harm in middle-income South-East Asian countries: Epidemiology and policy options. *International Journal of Drug Policy, 83*, 102856.

Sorsdahl, K., Stein, D. J., & Myers, B. (2012). Negative attributions towards people with substance use disorders in South Africa: Variation across substances and by gender. *BMC Psychiatry, 12*, Article 101.

Sreeraj, V. S., Parija, S., Uvais, N., Mohanty, S., & Kumar, S. (2017). Indian nursing students' attitudes toward mental illness and persons with mental illness. *Industrial Psychiatry Journal, 26*(2), 223–227.

Sreeramareddy, C. T., Pradhan, P. M. S., Mir, I. A., & Sin, S. (2014). Smoking and smokeless tobacco use in nine South and Southeast Asian countries: Prevalence estimates and social determinants from demographic and health surveys. *Population Health Metrics, 12*(1), Article 22.

Storholm, E. D., Ober, A. J., Hunter, S. B., et al. (2017). Barriers to integrating the continuum of care for opioid and alcohol use disorders in primary care: A qualitative longitudinal study. *Journal of Substance Abuse Treatment, 83*, 45–54.

Stöver, H. (2016). Drogenprohibition, soziale Ausgrenzung, Stigmatisierung und Kriminalisierung [Drug prohibition, social exclusion, stigmatization and criminalization]. *Suchttherapie, 17*(3), 124–130.

Sullivan, R. J., & Hagen, E. H. (2015). Passive vulnerability or active agency? An evolutionarily ecological perspective of human drug use. In P. Anderson, J. Rehm, & R. Room (Eds.), *Impact of addictive substances and behaviours on individual and societal well-being*. Oxford University Press.

Thomas, R., Pandian, R. D., & Murthy, P. (2018). Treatment service related needs and concerns of women with substance use disorders: A qualitative study. *International Journal of Culture and Mental Health, 11*(2), 123–133.

Tikkinen, K. A., Leinonen, J. S., Guyatt, G. H., Ebrahim, S., & Jarvinen, T. L. (2012). What is a disease? Perspectives of the public, health professionals and legislators. *BMJ Open, 2*(6), e001632.

TNI. (2014). *Reforma de la ley de drogas en Perú: guía básica [About drug law reform in Peru]*. TNI. https://www.tni.org/es/publicacion/reforma-de-la-ley-de-drogas-en-peru-guia-basica#7

Touw, M. (1981). The religious and medicinal uses of cannabis in China, India and Tibet. *Journal of Psychoactive Drugs, 13*(1), 23–34.

United Nations Department of Economic and Social Affairs: Statistics Division. (2018). *SDG Indicators: Metadata Repository, Goal 3, Target 3.5 Ensure healthy lives and promote well-being for all at all ages*. Retrieved February 18, 2021 from https://unstats.un.org/sdgs/metadata?Text=&Goal=3&Target=3.5

United Nations Office on Drugs and Crime. (2018). *World drug report 2018*. https://www.unodc.org/wdr2018/

United Nations Office on Drugs and Crime. (2020). *World drug report 2020*. https://wdr.unodc.org/wdr2020/index.html

van Boekel, L. C., Brouwers, E. P., van Weeghel, J., & Garretsen, H. F. (2013). Stigma among health professionals towards patients with substance use disorders and its consequences for healthcare delivery: Systematic review. *Drug and Alcohol Dependence, 131*(1–2), 23–35.

(2016). Experienced and anticipated discrimination reported by individuals in treatment for substance use disorders within the Netherlands. *Health and Social Care in the Community, 24*(5), e23–e33.

Vázquez, A. (2014). Políticas públicas en materia de drogas en Argentina: políticas de estigmatización y sufrimiento [Public policies regarding drugs in

Argentina: Policies on stigmatization and suffering]. *Saúde em Debate, 38*, 830–839.
Ventura, C. A. A., Carrara, B. S., Bobbili, S., et al. (2017). General beliefs and stigma regarding illicit drug use: Perspectives of family members and significant others of drug users in an inner city in Brazil. *Issues in Mental Health Nursing, 38*(9), 712–716.
Wogen, J., & Restrepo, M. T. (2020). Human rights, stigma, and substance use. *Health and Human Rights, 22*(1), 51–60.
Woolf-King, S. E., Steinmaus, C. M., Reingold, A. L., & Hahn, J. A. (2013). An update on alcohol use and risk of HIV infection in sub-Saharan Africa: Meta-analysis and future research directions. *International Journal of Alcohol and Drug Research 2*(1), 99–110.
World Health Organization. (2017, December 29). *Fact sheet: Human rights and health.* https://www.who.int/news-room/fact-sheets/detail/human-rights-and-health

(2018a). *Global status report on alcohol and health 2018.* https://www.who.int/substance_abuse/publications/global_alcohol_report/en/

(2018b). *WHO global report on trends in prevalence of tobacco smoking 2000–2025* (2nd ed.). https://www.who.int/tobacco/publications/surveillance/trends-tobacco-smoking-second-edition/en/

(2019a). *International statistical classification of diseases and related health problems 10th revision.* https://icd.who.int/browse10/2019/en

(2019b, July 25). *WHO report on the global tobacco epidemic, 2019.* https://www.who.int/publications/i/item/9789241516204

World Health Organization Regional Office for Europe. (2019). *Alcohol policy impact case study: The effects of alcohol control measures on mortality and life expectancy in the Russian Federation.* http://www.euro.who.int/en/health-topics/disease-prevention/alcohol-use/publications/2019/alcohol-policy-impact-case-study-the-effects-of-alcohol-control-measures-on-mortality-and-life-expectancy-in-the-russian-federation-2019
Yang, L. H., Wong, L. Y., Grivel, M. M., & Hasin, D. S. (2017). Stigma and substance use disorders: An international phenomenon. *Current Opinion in Psychiatry, 30*(5), 378–388.
Zakonbase.ru. (1999). *Prikaz Minzdrava rf ot 23 avgusta 1999 g. N 327 "ob Anonimnom Lechenii v Narkologicheskih Uchrezhdenijah (Podrazdelenijah)" [Order of the Ministry of Health of the Russian Federation of 23 August 1999 n 327 "on Anonymous Treatment in Narcological Institutions (Divisions)"].* https://zakonbase.ru/content/base/33411/
Zelenskaya, E. L. (2010). Prinuditel'noe lechenie alkogolizma v lechebno-trudovyh profilaktorijah: Istoriko-pravovoj aspekt [Compulsory treatment of alcoholism in medical and labor dispensaries: Historical and legal aspect]. *Sibirskoe juridicheskoe obozrenie, 13*, 21–22.
Zewdu, S., Hanlon, C., Fekadu, A., Medhin, G., & Teferra, S. (2019). Treatment gap, help-seeking, stigma and magnitude of alcohol use disorder

in rural Ethiopia. *Substance Abuse Treatment, Prevention, and Policy*, *14*(1), 1–10.

Zhirnov, E. (2013). "Izoljacija alkogolikov i narkomanov ne obespechivaetsja": Chto Genprokuratura SSSR obnaruzhila v LTP ["Isolation of alcoholics and drug addicts is not ensured": What the USSR Prosecutor General's Office found in the LTP]. *Kommersant.ru.* https://www.kommersant.ru/doc/2115648

CHAPTER 8

Using Community-Based Participatory Research to Address the Stigma of Substance Use Disorder

Lindsay Sheehan, Aaron Graham, and Chris White

The stigma against those with substance use disorders (SUD) and its resulting harm has been well documented in previous chapters of this volume. Stigma interferes with research and public health agendas that address SUD, leading to segregation, isolation, and disenfranchisement (Corrigan & Nieweglowski, 2018). A review commissioned by the National Academy of Sciences (NAS) identified an overall lack of research and initiatives for SUD stigma (Sheehan, 2015). Furthermore, our own literature scan identified a gap in community-involved research on SUD stigma. Thus, the goal of this chapter is to provide practical knowledge and resources for community-based participatory research (CBPR) in SUD stigma. Although CBPR provides a framework for addressing health inequities, systemic power differentials between researchers and community stakeholders result in implementation challenges. In this chapter we describe CBPR, apply a case example, and suggest ways that community members can be directly involved in research on SUD stigma. Drawing on the CBPR literature from other stigmatized health conditions, we suggest issues to consider during implementation of CBPR projects and suggest models that can guide CBPR work.

Defining CBPR

CBPR is a type of action-based research that emphasizes collaboration with community members as equal partners in all phases of the research process (Minkler & Wallerstein, 2011). CBPR often focuses on health inequities faced by a particular group and includes peer researchers – members of the affected community – in research tasks such as planning, recruitment, and data collection (Graham et al., 2019). Knowledge gained through the use of CBPR is typically used to benefit the community in which the research has been conducted (Israel et al., 2001). In addition to CBPR, other terms refer to similar research practices such as *participatory action research (PAR)*, *community engaged research (CER)*, or *coproduction* (Holkup et al., 2004). While the aforementioned terms typically describe research that is initiated or directed by academia, *service user research* and *user-controlled research* describe a process whereby service users (such as people with SUD) control all stages of the research process, with little or no support from professional researchers (Langston, 2006; Syrett, 2011). While we use the term CBPR in this chapter, we acknowledge that regardless of the term used, community involvement in research occurs on a continuum and within a variety of contexts.

The following (fictional) case study provides an example of how a CBPR project on the stigma of SUD could be implemented. Note that the case study is merely one model of how CBPR might be implemented rather than an "ideal" of what CBPR should entail. In this case study, the research project is initiated by the representative of an SUD treatment agency; in other instances, CBPR could be initiated by professional researchers, service users, advocacy groups, collaboratives, or private foundations. Similarly, this case study describes a project that is grant funded and relatively large in scope; CBPR projects could entail smaller endeavors that involve less funding. We use the case study to illustrate the principles of CBPR.

Case Study: Using CBPR to Reduce the Stigma of Substance Use Disorder

Dr. Josie Piper, the executive director at Beyond Recovery, an outpatient SUD treatment center, believes that self-stigma is preventing some clients from moving forward in their recovery. She wants to implement an antistigma program at the center and consults with Dr. Joyce Long at the local university about how best to address the self-stigma of substance use. Dr. Long reviews the literature and finds some evidence-based programs for self-stigma of mental illness, but nothing specific to SUD. Given the lack of research in this area, she suggests that they could adapt the curriculum from a mental illness program and evaluate the program's effectiveness in a research study. Dr. Long suggests that they use CBPR to ground the project and that they seek funding for the project.

Dr. Piper approaches the consumer advisory board (which is composed of service users with lived experience of SUD) at Beyond Recovery to see if members have an interest in the project. She presents the initial idea and three advisory board members indicate that they would like to work on the project, including Mr. Carl Lalitha, who is a person with lived experience of SUD and wants to be coleader on the project. Mr. Lalitha suggests a private foundation that they could seek funding from.

The team of five decides to meet once a week to prepare a grant submission and to start adapting the curriculum. Dr. Long takes the lead in writing the grant submission and Mr. Lalitha and Dr. Piper begin work on the curriculum development with the help of the advisory board. The team decide they will do mixed methods research to evaluate the program and they will put money in the budget to pay a CBPR team for their work on the project. Once the grant proposal is submitted, they put the project on hold until they hear about the funding.

Five months later, they find out they have received funding for the project. Mr. Lalitha and Dr. Piper recruit three additional service users with lived experience of SUD to work on the team. They put a call out to Beyond Recovery's service users, and ask interested people to complete a short application and interview for the team. The also decide to include an SUD counselor on the team, and Dr. Piper nominates a member of her staff to attend meetings.

The team prepares for about 25 meetings along the course of the two-year project. They will meet weekly during project start-up, and then monthly during the data collection phase. The team members will be paid as consultants for their time in meetings and for work outside of meetings. The team completes some initial training modules about CBPR, research methods, and research ethics. They decide that meetings will be coled by Mr. Lalitha and Dr. Piper.

Dr. Long drafts the materials for institutional review board (IRB) approval through her university and presents these to the team. The team makes several suggestions for changes:

(1) They want several parts of the consent form rewritten in lay language.
(2) They suggest changes to the flyer to appeal more to potential participants.
(3) They want to add a fact sheet for staff of the agency to better understand the study for recruitment purposes.
(4) They want some extra questions added to the qualitative interviews.
(5) They want participants to fill out surveys using pen and paper rather than electronically.

Mr. Lalitha presents a draft of the curriculum to the team and the team provides feedback. Dr. Piper gives a presentation to her staff about the upcoming study. Mr. Lalitha and select CBPR members train staff who will run the program. Dr. Long recruits a student research assistant to work with several members of the CBPR team on data collection. The CBPR team members are trained in conducting individual interviews with program participants.

Once the data are collected, Dr. Long does the quantitative analyses and CBPR members are trained to help with the qualitative analyses. They spend several meetings discussing the results and implications of results. They decide to submit results for an upcoming conference and begin work on a journal article. The team members give several informal presentations to agency staff and discuss their project at a local event.

Dr. Long searches for grant funding to pursue a larger study. Dr. Piper consults with the group about implementation of the program within the organization.

Principles of CBPR

Israel and colleagues (2017) identify ten principles of CBPR, which are outlined in Table 1. In the second column of Table 1, we provide examples from the case study that illustrate each principle. The first two principles (P1 and P2) state that CBPR begins with a community of interest, using the assets of that community to conduct the research. In our case example, the community is defined as service users from the Beyond Recovery treatment center, and the strengths of that community include an existing advisory board and the lived experiences of its members. Ideally, CBPR should be an inclusive, collaborative, and equitable process that empowers team members to impact their community (P3; Israel et al., 2017). When conducted through true partnership and power-sharing, this type of research has the potential to reduce inequity and produce research that is culturally credible and relevant to key stakeholders. For example, services users from the CBPR case study were involved in project decision-making throughout the research process, giving input through their lived experiences of self-stigma. Additionally, one service user (Mr. Lalitha) occupied a leadership position on the project.

CBPR also facilitates learning and growth of team members, such that academic researchers learn about the community, and community stakeholders learn about and conduct research (P4). Further, CBPR projects pursue a balance between research and community action (P5); CBPR teams gather data that highlights inequalities or suggests solutions for change, which communities can then use to implement programming or policy. CBPR teams tackle local issues, recognizing that health problems originate from complex social environments (P6) and require a "cyclical and iterative process" (Israel et al., 2017, p. 34) to elicit system-level changes (P7). This type of in-depth engagement will require multiple meetings between team members that occur over an extended period of time (P9). Thus, academic researchers and community stakeholders alike

Table 1. *CBPR principles and application to case study*

	Principle	Case Study Application
P1	"Recognizes community as a unit of identity" (p. 32)	Community of focus is service users at the Beyond Recovery SUD treatment center.
P2	"Builds on strengths and resources within community" (p. 32)	Beyond Recovery helps identify service users for the team through the existing advisory board and provides a milieu to implement the self-stigma program. Service users use their connections with the community for recruitment and data collection. Service users utilize their lived experiences through curriculum development.
P3	"Facilitates collaborative, equitable partnership in all research phases and involves an empowering and power-sharing process that attends to social inequities" (p. 33)	Service users are involved in research design, curriculum development, conduct and dissemination of research, including in leadership roles (Mr. Lalitha is coinvestigator). Major project decisions are made during team meetings with opportunity for discussion.
P4	"Promotes co-learning and capacity building among all partners" (p. 33)	The team completes training modules together. Team members are paid for their time on the project. Researchers and service providers on the team learn about lived experience perspectives.
P5	"Integrates and achieves a balance between research and action for the mutual benefit of all partners" (p. 33)	The project focuses on creating a program that represents the needs of service users. Researchers publish and disseminate to the academic community.
P6	"Emphasizes public health problems of local relevance and ecological perspectives that attend to the multiple determinants of health and disease" (p. 33)	The problem of self-stigma within Beyond Recovery was identified as one of local relevance.
P7	"Involves systems development through a cyclical and iterative process" (p. 34)	CBPR team members engage in considerable dialogue over 25 meetings to develop curriculum and conduct research.
P8	"Disseminates findings and knowledge gained to all partners and involves all partners in dissemination process" (p. 34)	The CBPR team gives community presentations, writes a journal article, and gives academic presentations.

Table 1. (cont.)

	Principle	Case Study Application
P9	"Requires long-term process and commitment to sustainability" (p. 34)	The entire team is committed to the two-year process from the start, and a proper team was established from the beginning.
P10	Addresses issues of race, ethnicity, racism, and social class and embraces cultural humility (p. 34)	The self-stigma project addresses issues of internalized ableism. Researchers and service providers were open to learning about the service user perspectives on SUD stigma.

Source: Principles from Israel and colleagues (2017, pp. 32–34).

must commit to the duration of the project in order to sustain the collaboration over time.

CBPR efforts also extend toward disseminating findings in both real-world and academic settings (P8). As in the case study, this could include dissemination through a variety of means, including community presentations, policy recommendations, press releases, or journal articles. Finally, CBPR team members should aim to confront multiple forms of discrimination and approach each other (and the research project) from a place of cultural humility (P10). These efforts can help bridge cultural differences and build trust between academic researchers and communities.

Given that CBPR principles call for long-term, iterative interactions between stakeholders – who enter the project with differing, and often conflicting agendas – CBPR is complicated to implement effectively (Minkler & Wallerstein, 2011). Equitable partnerships are not easy to achieve within the context of structural injustice. While we discuss more of the issues specific to SUD research later in the chapter, Harrison (2001) suggests some general guidelines for researchers who engage in CBPR. These include 1) maintain flexibility while recognizing the limits of yourself and the team; 2) be open to sharing power, responsibility, and recognition for the research; 3) sustain awareness of ethical dilemmas; 4) be culturally open, curious, and respectful within interactions.

Ways CBPR Can Address Gaps in SUD Stigma Research

While CBPR teams include perspectives of community stakeholders, including family members, service providers, and policymakers, the most disenfranchised stakeholders, people with lived experience of SUD, will be essential to include in antistigma efforts. While peer-involved CBPR has been used extensively in mental health research (Nieweglowski et al., 2021), it has less commonly been applied to SUD research. We were unable to locate published studies in which people with lived experience of SUD used CBPR to study SUD stigma. However, CBPR with SUD service users *has* been used for other research purposes, such as to better understand perceptions of harm reduction in people who inject drugs (Boucher et al., 2017) and for a smoking cessation intervention (Andrews et al., 2012).

CBPR teams that involve people with lived experience of SUD and other stakeholders have a role in addressing stigma on multiple levels, using a multitude of research methodologies. On the individual level, CBPR teams can explore the impact of internalized stigma (i.e., self-stigma) of SUD. People with lived experience of SUD have essential perspectives on questions to best elicit experiences of peers with SUD and then develop interventions that address self-stigma on the individual level. The concept of intersectionality is similarly essential to consider – how do multiple stigmatized identities converge and interact with the self-stigma of SUD? For example, a person with SUD could also be living with HIV, be a person of color, and have criminal justice involvement. How does that person experience stigma differently from, for example, a Mormon woman who has SUD and has attempted suicide? CBPR teams composed of these intersectional identities are better prepared to engage with these issues and communities than academic researchers (Wallerstein et al., 2019).

People with SUD who have experienced prejudice and discrimination personally, can use these experiences in developing interventions for public stigma. Research on mental health stigma has shown that the most effective antistigma interventions for public stigma include 1) educating the public about stereotypes and unfair behaviors and practices, and 2) meaningful contact with the stigmatized individual (Corrigan et al., 2012). People with lived experience of SUD can share experiences in contact- and education-based interventions. Research also suggests that stigma programs work best when tailored to specific locations, populations, and cultures – what works in New York City might not work in rural Florida (Corrigan, 2011). People with lived experience and other stakeholders have an important role in cultural adaptations. Furthermore, they have a role in implementation and dissemination if they become involved with promoting and facilitating evidence-based antistigma programming as it emerges. Comprehensive, nationwide antistigma programs addressing the stigma of mental illness (e.g., beyondblue in Australia) have utilized people with lived experience in development and evaluation of these efforts.

On the structural level, findings that emerge through the CBPR process might support changes in broader policies and practices that impact SUD treatment. Lived experience researchers could advocate for legislative changes to reduce stigma: for example, expanded insurance coverage for SUD, availability of recovery homes, and decriminalization of substance use. Personal stories that are backed by research can make more of a difference in advocacy work and protest-based actions. Targets for anti-stigma interventions include SUD treatment providers, law enforcement/criminal justice professionals, mental health professionals, and family members. By engaging people with lived experience in the research process, this provides an opportunity for researchers and other stakeholders involved in the research project to have meaningful contact, view peer researchers as equitable partners, and thereby reduce their own biases.

Stakeholder Engagement

Identifying and Selecting Stakeholders

Individuals who wish to use CBPR for stigma research should consider which stakeholders to involve on their team. Stakeholders might include addiction counselors, addiction program managers, people with previous SUD, people with current SUD, family members, physicians, nurses, policymakers, statisticians, police, probation officers, insurance company representatives, or others. The inclusion of people with lived experience of SUD on the team is especially important, given that they are the primary target of SUD stigma, and have been traditionally marginalized and excluded from leadership and decision-making in research. Furthermore, teams should match the purpose of the project and be diverse in terms of age, race/ethnicity, gender, and other characteristics relevant to the project. For example, if the overall goal of the project is developing and testing a program to reduce the opioid-related stigma among paramedics, the CBPR might involve individuals involved in training paramedics, paramedic workers, individuals with opioid use disorder, and family members, in addition to one or two academic researchers. Similarly, if the purpose of the research is to understand self-stigma experienced by construction workers with alcohol use disorder, the team might include a diverse group

Table 2. *Examples of stakeholder involvement at each stage of research*

Study Planning and Design	Conduct of the Study	Dissemination and Implementation of Findings
Serve as coinvestigators on research grants and cowrite grants or contract proposals.	Write or give feedback on the research protocol, consent form, recruitment flyers, or other study materials.	Coauthor academic papers.
Develop research questions, hypotheses, and/or study design.	Assist with recruitment of research participants.	Identify creative avenues and mechanisms for dissemination to nonacademic communities.
Facilitate community partnerships and involvement of additional stakeholders.	Collect and/or analyze data.	Advocate for implementation of evidence-based practices stemming from research.
Select research outcomes and measures.	Pilot test the study intervention or research protocol.	Present seminars, webinars, or poster sessions about study findings.
Develop study inclusion/exclusion criteria.	Conduct research fidelity audits.	Advocate for social or legislative change stemming from study findings.

Source: Adapted from PCORI Engagement Rubric (Sheridan et al., 2017).

of construction workers with lived experience, a union representative, safety professional, addiction clinician, and researcher.

Continuous Stakeholder Engagement

Researchers, advocates, and funders have recently called for involvement of community stakeholders throughout the entire course of the research project, from inception of the research idea to dissemination of findings. It is especially important to bring stakeholders together early, in order to build a working relationship and establish shared goals. For example, the Patient-Centered Outcomes Research Institute (PCORI) has created a rubric to guide researchers with engagement of patients in the context of healthcare research, specifying how patients can be involved in study planning, conduct of the study, and dissemination of findings (Sheridan et al., 2017). In Table 2, we use the overall structure of the PCORI

Engagement Rubric to suggest ways for people with lived experience of SUD or other stakeholders to be involved at each stage of stigma research. We discuss engagement during these three stages in detail below.

Study Planning and Design: During this research stage, CBPR team members might work with academic researchers to develop research questions and hypotheses around the stigma for SUD (e.g., "Are people with SUD discriminated against in the public housing voucher system?"). Stakeholders might initiate research projects and solicit involvement from an academic researcher, as in our case study, or the academic researcher could initiate contact with community members. People with lived experience of SUD or other SUD stakeholders can assist with grant submissions or use their connections in the community to access samples for data collection, or additional stakeholders to be involved on the CBPR team. At this stage, stakeholders give valuable input on study design (e.g., qualitative, quantitative, or mixed methods), and what research outcomes and measures will be most important.

Conduct of the Study: Once the study is initiated, CBPR teams can compose a research protocol that is sensitive to the needs of participants. This might include developing a script to explain the study, and making sure the consent form language is culturally sensitive and that recruitment materials are clear and appealing to the target audience. A mock administration of protocol and survey measures to the CBPR team might reveal questions or situations that could be amended such as moving demographic questions to the end of the survey, asking participants about SUD using alternative language (e.g., slang terms) and assuring participants about confidentiality protocols. Within their network in the community, CBPR team members have a valuable role in recruitment, such as sending emails, passing out flyers, calling community leaders, or making recruitment presentations at community events. In terms of data collection, CBPR can be trained to conduct data collection activities and research participants may feel more comfortable disclosing sensitive topics to community peers, especially if this involves reporting illegal activities such as drug use. If an intervention is involved, CBPR members can pilot the intervention and make changes necessary for a specific culture or situation.

Dissemination and Implementation: Stakeholders have particularly vital roles at the end of the project that may extend beyond the scope of traditional research studies. While an academic researcher would typically publish a paper and proceed to a subsequent project, community members can identify more creative and public-friendly modes of dissemination (e.g., social media campaign or storytelling event). Stakeholders can also participate with the researcher in more traditional modes of dissemination such as academic papers and seminars. In terms of implementation, CBPR members could use findings to advocate for changes in laws or policy, and initiate evidence-based antistigma interventions with their organization or community. CBPR is especially helpful in translating research to practice (Dari et al., 2019).

CBPR in SUD Research

Thus far we have introduced CBPR and discussed strategies to engage the community in addressing SUD stigma. Due to the history of systemic stigma and criminalization, individuals with SUD may be particularly distrustful of researchers and expect that researchers may exploit them (Souleymanov et al., 2016). These attitudes may also be reflected in the CBPR team. Likewise, stigma may play out within the CBPR team (Jozaghi et al., 2018), such as if team members with lived experience of SUD are not trusted with managing money, are viewed as unreliable, or are seen as at greater risk of inappropriate behaviors. Now we discuss specific issues that may arise in conducting CBPR work on SUD.

Inclusion of People with Lived Experience in CBPR

While involving community members in research that impacts them is an ethical and moral imperative (Case et al., 2014), stigma can impede the inclusion of people with SUD in the research process (Jozaghi et al., 2018). The academic researcher or SUD agency representative is likely to serve in a gatekeeping role for the entry of lived experience team members into the project. Individuals who initiate CBPR should prospectively consider how they will recruit and select team members, and who will make decisions about inclusion on the team. For example, will the team involve people who are currently using substances or only people in recovery? If leaders exclude people from the group, what is the rationale for doing so and how does it reflect principles of inclusion? The ideal CBPR team will strive for diverse representation, but how that will manifest for each project must be decided by leaders going into the project. Project leaders might also consider the unique needs of people with SUD on the team when scheduling and planning meetings and when communicating with the team, including the need to offer accommodations to team members. If team members attend a day treatment program, meetings may need to be scheduled in the evening, or if a team member misses a meeting, leaders should be prepared to meet individually to cover materials. Inherent in CBPR is a sense of reciprocity and bidirectional learning between researchers and the community (Maiter et al., 2008). Project leaders should consider how they can foster this spirit and emphasize the value of community members on the team. In the dissemination phase, research articles should transparently report on how community members were involved throughout the process, including how many were involved, how much they were compensated, and what they contributed to the project (Nieweglowski et al., 2021).

Confidentiality and Dual Roles

CBPR team members are research partners rather than research participants and thus are not typically protected under confidentiality guidelines for the protection of human subjects. Team members who disclose their lived experiences of SUD risk negative consequences in the form of prejudice and discrimination, both within the confines of the research project and in the larger community. Given that individuals with lived experience are encouraged to openly share their valuable first-hand knowledge of SUD, team members should understand this expectation, along with the possible risks. When individuals with SUD disclose use of illegal drugs or other illicit activities during the project, they also risk legal implications. CBPR leaders can request that personal information shared within the team be kept confidential but will not be able to guarantee confidentiality or privacy of team members and should explicitly make team members aware of this at the beginning of the project. CBPR teams are often comprised of diverse stakeholders including researchers, clinicians, family members, and people with lived experience. Projects embedded in tight-knit communities, community organizations, or rural areas have a greater risk of team members who have dual relationships with one another (Souleymanov et al., 2016). Dual relationships, or dual roles, occur when a team member has a relationship with another team member in a different context, in addition to their professional relationship working together on the research project. For example, an SUD clinician might work on the research team alongside a former client, or the researcher may know an individual with lived experience through their religious community. The existence and implications of dual relationships should be discussed at the beginning of the project; relationships wherein CBPR team members are providing direct clinical services to another team member should be avoided. In other cases, individuals in the dual relationship should discuss whether or not they will acknowledge their work on the CBPR project in another setting (e.g., within their religious community) and team leaders might help with negotiating challenges that emerge therein. Individuals with lived experience who are recruiting participants or collecting data in the community might have dual relationships with research participants (Guta & Voronka, 2020; Souleymanov et al., 2016). The research participant might experience recruitment by someone they know and respect in the community as coercive (Guta & Voronka, 2020). Therefore, the CBPR team should have a protocol for addressing dual relationships (e.g., having another peer researcher conduct the interview).

Protection of Research Participants

Community stakeholders who are involved in CBPR projects often have difficulty receiving official recognition through institutional review boards (IRB) (Souleymanov et al., 2016). Academic institutions may lack protocols for training community members on research ethics and including them in the IRB process (Hatcher & Schoenberg, 2007). Investigators might educate their IRB in advance of the project and problem-solve around requirements for community-based researchers. Human subject protection trainings have been developed for community members who have minimal research background; however, these may not be recognized by all IRBs (Hatcher & Schoenberg, 2007). If community members will be collecting data, IRBs might require additional protocols for protecting such data, especially if data collection will take place in community settings. Lived experience researchers who are collecting data should be trained in protecting confidentiality and reducing the risk of coercion. Furthermore, researchers should make sure they understand any struggles that peer researchers may have with recruitment, such as pressures to recruit a large sample, difficulties ensuring that participants understand the consent, and the burden of administering lengthy surveys (Souleymanov et al., 2016; True et al., 2017). Due to these concerns, involving people with lived experience as research partners requires a proactive approach that includes flexibility and creative solutions (Guta & Voronka, 2020).

Protection of Lived Experience Researchers

People with lived experience of SUD who are in the community recruiting or collecting data for the project could, depending on the nature of the project, be in unsafe conditions, such as traveling in dangerous neighborhoods or interviewing research participants in their homes (True et al., 2017). People with lived experience who conduct research interviews could be traumatized or triggered by participant responses. Furthermore, people with lived experience may experience pressure or burnout from being a gatekeeper to resources (e.g., social services or money for participating in the study; True et al., 2017). CBPR members with lived experience might experience frustration around the limitations of the research study and inability to provide essential services that are unrelated to the research. CBPR leaders should reflect on and discuss these issues with the team, and put protocols in place to protect lived experience researchers and ensure they are not taking on an unfair burden of risk for the study. This might include training on trauma-informed interviewing, debriefing after an interview, interviewing research participants in public spaces, or ongoing support groups for lived experience researchers.

Power Sharing

Some stakeholders – often researchers and healthcare providers – have a power differential over individuals with lived experience in terms of social resources, control of project finances, education, and research experience (Duran et al., 2019). They may make decisions about participation and inclusion, about entry onto the team, payments for team members, and accommodations for team members with lived experience. This includes decisions about how team members are paid, whether team members can be actively using substances, whether they are welcome at team meetings while intoxicated, and under what circumstances they might be asked to leave the team. When stakeholders are intimidated or marginalized within the team (whether intentionally or unintentionally), the project can suffer from surface-level involvement of team members or tokenism, and the reinforcement of stigmatizing attitudes toward people with SUD. When team members feel marginalized, this may manifest in the team dynamics; people reduce efforts at participation and become disengaged, resulting in the loss of knowledge, skills, and experience.

One way to address power differential is through explicit acknowledgment of this dynamic at the beginning of the working relationship, and efforts on the part of those with greater social power to share this power (Wallerstein et al., 2019). To this end, academic researchers can encourage team members to be critical and challenge their ideas, provide explanations for research terms, seek opportunities to hear perspectives of team members, and take an active listening approach during meetings (rather than dominating the discussion and using directive communication strategies). A strategy to reduce tokenism is the involvement of multiple individuals representing each marginalized stakeholder group (e.g., women with opioid addiction) so that one person will not have the burden of representing all people from that group. Small group activities or subcommittees around specific tasks (e.g., recruitment) can increase the comfort level and partnership development for those more hesitant to speak out in larger group meetings.

Another way to address power differential is involving at least one person with lived experience in a leadership role on the project, such as coinvestigator (e.g., see Sheehan et al., 2017). A lived experience research leader could work under an employment contract or as consultant to an academic institution or community organization, and could cofacilitate research meetings, with a focus on engaging stakeholders and ensuring that there are equitable contributions and benefits from the project (Vaughn et al., 2018). This may require capacity-building, including the funding and training necessary to support this position. People with lived experience of SUD who take on leadership positions may also benefit from ongoing supervision and mentorship.

Benefit to CBPR Members and Community

Advocates have proposed that just as with the protection of research participants, it is an ethical issue to ensure CBPR team members benefit and do not take on undue risk or burden (True et al., 2017). In past research, people with lived experience of SUD sometimes fail to see the impact or benefit of research that they collaborate on (Souleymanov et al., 2016). For stigma research in particular, the CBPR approach challenges stigma and highlights value, dignity, and equity for people with SUD. For team members with lived experience, benefits might mean job experience, recommendation for future projects, or recognition in the community. For each person these benefits will be unique, so the team might take time in initial meetings to discuss the benefits that each team member hopes to obtain. However, the benefits desired by the researcher or healthcare provider (e.g., finishing the project as quickly as possible) could be in conflict with those of the community (e.g., spend time building relationships). The team can plan regular process evaluations of team satisfaction and engagement, with the aim of continuous improvement in benefit to team members and community.

Access to Compensation and Resources

The support of lived experience researchers can also be viewed through an ethical lens, including how they are treated by human resources and finance departments and how they are paid (Guta & Voronka, 2020). In the absence of equitable and transparent distribution of compensation and resources, team rapport can quickly erode and derail the project. CBPR team leaders should develop and share the project budget with team members, including detail of who will be paid, at what times, the work expectations, and the type of payment method. Compensation could include formal employer–employee contract, cash, gift cards, monthly stipend checks, transportation cards, meals, or food vouchers. Payment methods should align with CBPR team member preferences and may require administrative planning to ensure feasibility of payment methods. Team members might also require access to other resources such as electronic devices, Wi-Fi, private work space, telephone lines, or project-related training. These should be anticipated and negotiated in advance.

Models for CBPR Implementation

Researchers should consider a model to guide efforts and structure the process of CBPR (Vaughn et al., 2018). This ensures that researchers adequately address essential issues of CBPR such as equitable recruitment and inclusion practices and human protections training. Many of these can be adapted from research with other health conditions, especially mental illness. For example, the *Inspiring Change* CBPR curriculum provides structure and tools for engaging African Americans with mental illness in health research (Sheehan et al., 2015), which includes an accompanying leadership training for lived experienced leaders (Sheehan et al., 2017; see curriculum at www.chicagohealthdisparities.org). The Inspiring Change model calls for a triumvirate of leaders (academic researcher, healthcare provider, person with lived experience) and provides guidance and structure for research meetings, including topics such as forming the team, engaging the team, research ethics, and research methods. In a large research study on women with HIV, Kaida and colleagues (2019) developed a method for hiring, training, and supporting people with lived experience, including those with SUD, to recruit and collect data for the project. A training model of peer researcher from studies on HIV in Canada used blended action learning (online and in-person) which included an explanation of study purpose, consents, how to conduct research interviews, practice interviews, self-care, data, and logistics (Eaton et al., 2018). User-led research models in the UK also provide frameworks that can be applied to SUD; the National Institute on Health Research in the UK has standards for involving the community in research, which include specific questions that project investigators can use to evaluate their involvement in each of six domains: 1) communications, 2) working together, 3) inclusive opportunities, 4) impact, 5) governance, and 6) support and learning (see https://sites.google.com/nihr.ac.uk/pi-standards/home).

Conclusion

While CBPR is a promising way to enhance research on the stigma of SUD, it has been critically underutilized. In this chapter, we introduced the concept of CBPR, using a case study to illustrate the guiding principles of CBPR. We suggested ways that CBPR might address gaps in research on the stigma of SUD and provided guidelines to engaging stakeholders in CBPR. Finally, we highlighted issues that are likely to emerge for those who undertake CBPR and suggested models to guide CBPR implementation. Clearly, implementation of CBPR is a complex process that will require the long-term development of strong community partnerships and structural changes (Vaughn et al., 2018). Individuals who aspire to undertake CBPR should carefully consider their motivations for pursuing CBPR, the underlying CBPR principles, how their project can achieve fidelity to these principles, and how they will evaluate partnership engagement at each stage of the process.

References

Andrews, J. O., Newman, S. D., Heath, J., Williams, L. B., & Tingen, M. S. (2012). Community-based participatory research and smoking cessation interventions: A review of the evidence. *Nursing Clinics*, *47*(1), 81–96.

Boucher, L. M., Marshall, Z., Martin, A., et al. (2017). Expanding conceptualizations of harm reduction: Results from a qualitative community-based participatory research study with people who inject drugs. *Harm Reduction Journal*, *14*(1), 1–18.

Case, A. D., Byrd, R., Claggett, E., et al. (2014). Stakeholders' perspectives on community-based participatory research to enhance mental health services. *American Journal of Community Psychology*, *54*(3–4), 397–408.

Corrigan, P. W. (2011). Best practices: Strategic stigma change (SSC): Five principles for social marketing campaigns to reduce stigma. *Psychiatric Services*, *62*(8), 824–826.

Corrigan, P. W., Morris, S. B., Michaels, P. J., Rafacz, J. D., & Rüsch, N. (2012). Challenging the public stigma of mental illness: A meta-analysis of outcome studies. *Psychiatric Services, 63*(10), 963–973.

Corrigan, P. W., & Nieweglowski, K. (2018). Stigma and the public health agenda for the opioid crisis in America. *International Journal of Drug Policy, 59*, 44–49.

Dari, T., Laux, J. M., Liu, Y., & Reynolds, J. (2019). Development of community-based participatory research competencies: A Delphi study identifying best practices in the collaborative process. *Professional Counselor, 9*(1), 1–19.

Duran, B., Oetzel, J., Magarati, M., et al. (2019). Toward health equity: A national study of promising practices in community-based participatory research. *Progress in Community Health Partnerships: Research, Education, and Action, 13*(4), 337–352.

Eaton, A. D., Ibáñez-Carrasco, F., Craig, S. L., et al. (2018). A blended learning curriculum for training peer researchers to conduct community-based participatory research. *Action Learning: Research and Practice, 15*(2), 139–150.

Graham, I. D., McCutcheon, C., & Kothari, A. (2019). Exploring the frontiers of research co-production: The Integrated Knowledge Translation Research Network concept papers. *Health Research Policy and Systems, 17*(1), Article 88.

Guta, A., & Voronka, J. (2020). Ethical issues in community-based, participatory, and action-oriented forms of research. In R. Iphofen (Ed.), *Handbook of research ethics and scientific integrity* (pp. 561–576). Springer.

Harrison, B. (2001). *Collaborative programs in indigenous communities: From fieldwork to practice*. AltaMira Press.

Hatcher, J., & Schoenberg, N. E. (2007). Human subjects protection training for community workers: An example from "Faith Moves Mountains." *Progress in Community Health Partnerships: Research, Education, and Action, 1*(3), 257–265.

Holkup, P. A., Tripp-Reimer, T., Salois, E. M., & Weinert, C. (2004). Community-based participatory research. *ANS: Advances in Nursing Science, 27*(3), 162–175.

Israel, B. A., Schulz, A. J., Parker, E. A., et al. (2017). Critical issues in developing and following CBPR principles. In N. Wallerstein et al. (Eds.), *Community-based participatory research for health: Advancing social and health equity* (pp. 32–35). Wiley.

Israel, B. A., Schulz, A. J., Parker, E. A., Becker, A. B., & Community-Campus Partnerships for Health. (2001). Community-based participatory research: Policy recommendations for promoting a partnership approach in health research. *Education for Health (Abingdon, England), 14*(2), 182–197.

Jozaghi, E., Buxton, J. A., Thomson, E., Marsh, S., Gregg, D., & Bouchard, M. (2018). Building new approaches to risk reduction with social networks and people who smoke illegal drugs from participatory community-based research. *International Journal of Qualitative Methods, 17*(1), 1609406918771247.

Kaida, A., Carter, A., Nicholson, V., et al. (2019). Hiring, training, and supporting peer research associates: Operationalizing community-based research principles within epidemiological studies by, with, and for women living with HIV. *Harm Reduction Journal, 16*(1), 1–13.

Langston, A. (2006). User controlled research: Its meanings and potential. *Health Expectations: An International Journal of Public Participation in Health Care and Health Policy, 9*(3), 301–302.

Maiter, S., Simich, L., Jacobson, N., & Wise, J. (2008). Reciprocity: An ethic for community-based participatory action research. *Action Research, 6*(3), 305–325.

Minkler, M., & Wallerstein, N. (Eds.). (2011). *Community-based participatory research for health: From process to outcomes*. John Wiley & Sons.

Nieweglowski, K., Sheehan, L., & Despande, A. (2021). A systematic review of community-based participatory studies involving individuals with mental illness. *Psychiatric Rehabilitation Journal* [in review].

Sheehan, L. (2015). *Strategies for changing the stigma of behavioral healthcare*. Commissioned paper for the National Academy of Sciences: Committee on the Science of Changing Behavioral Health Norms. http://sites.nationalacademies.org/DBASSE/BBCSS/DBASSE_170049

Sheehan, L., Ballentine, S., Agnew, L., et al. (2015). *The Inspiring Change manual: A community-based participatory research manual for involving African Americans with serious mental illness in research*. Illinois Institute of Technology.

Sheehan, L., Ballentine, S., Cole, S., et al. (2017). *Inspiring Change leadership training manual: A leadership curriculum for African Americans with serious mental illness in community-based participatory research*. Illinois Institute of Technology.

Sheridan, S., Schrandt, S., Forsythe, L., Hilliard, T. S., & Paez, K. A. (2017). The PCORI engagement rubric: Promising practices for partnering in research. *The Annals of Family Medicine, 15*(2), 165–170.

Souleymanov, R., Kuzmanović, D., Marshall, Z., et al. (2016). The ethics of community-based research with people who use drugs: Results of a scoping review. *BMC Medical Ethics, 17*(1), 1–13.

Syrett, M. (2011). Service user involvement in mental health research: A user's perspective. *Advances in Psychiatric Treatment, 17*(3), 201–205.

True, G., Alexander, L. B., & Fisher, C. B. (2017). Supporting the role of community members employed as research staff: Perspectives of community researchers working in addiction research. *Social Science & Medicine, 187*, 67–75.

Vaughn, L. M., Whetstone, C., Boards, A., et al. (2018). Partnering with insiders: A review of peer models across community-engaged research, education and social care. *Health & Social Care in the Community, 26*(6), 769–786.

Wallerstein, N., Muhammad, M., Sanchez-Youngman, S., et al. (2019). Power dynamics in community-based participatory research: A multiple-case study analysis of partnering contexts, histories, and practices. *Health Education & Behavior, 46*(1_suppl), 19S–32S.

CHAPTER 9

Three Competing Agendas of Addressing Stigma of Substance Use Disorder

Carla D. Kundert and Patrick W. Corrigan

The demand for stigma reduction is described by three sometimes-competing agendas: (1) the services agenda, which aims to reduce the public stigma that often serves as a barrier to treatment-seeking; (2) the rights agenda, which aims to replace stigma with rightful opportunity and full social inclusion; and (3) the self-worth agenda, which centers empowerment and self-determination over shame and blame. While all three share goals, the methods of action and values informing each differ greatly, contributing to sometimes contradictory efforts. There is potential, however, for these agendas to be complementary, explored more in depth at the end of this chapter. As a note, research on the stigma of substance use disorder (SUD) is quite limited so these agendas are largely based on models from mental illness stigma literature.

The Services Agenda: Engaging People with SUD in Evidence-Based Treatment

According to the National Survey on Drug Use and Health, 21.2 million people over the age of 12 needed treatment for substance use in 2018, but only 11.1% of them actually availed themselves of services (Substance Abuse and Mental Health Services Administration, 2019). Of those who did not receive SUD treatment, 14.9% reported concerns about what their community and peers would think of them. Stigma is an oft-cited barrier to entering treatment for people with mental health or substance use challenges (Barney et al., 2006; Cunningham et al., 1993; Hingson et al., 1982; Klingemann, 1991; Luoma, 2011; Schober & Annis, 1996; Tuchfeld, 1981). Label avoidance, to borrow from mental health stigma literature (Ben-Zeev et al., 2012; Clement et al., 2015; Corrigan et al., 2014), occurs when an individual delays or avoids treatment or withdraws from services to evade a stigmatizing label such as a diagnosis. For example, Marcos is worried that people who see him leaving the substance use clinic will think "Wow, Marcos is in treatment for drug use? He must be really out of control and dangerous – better stay away from that guy!" Thus, Marcos decides not to seek out treatment to evade the stereotypes, prejudice, and discrimination that may come with the label of "substance use disorder." In addition, people with SUD may avoid self-labeling in an effort to evade self-stigmatizing attitudes, as demonstrated in the mental illness literature (Stolzenburg et al., 2017).

Stigma can also impede sustained engagement in evidence-based treatment. Higher levels of public stigma have been associated with poorer retention and outcomes in treatment for SUD (Crapanzano et al., 2018; Simpson, 1981; Stark, 1992). A 2013 meta-analysis of provider stigma identified that providers generally held negative attitudes toward people with SUD that was associated with less engagement in treatment and worse health outcomes (Van Boekel et al., 2013). In mental illness stigma literature, internalized stigma contributes to decreased empowerment in making decisions and acting, including engaging in care (Rüsch et al., 2010; Thornicroft, 2013).

Education and Public Health Messaging

The stigma that contributes to label avoidance has typically been addressed through education, namely public health campaigns that educate the public on facts about a condition and treatment options. Highlighting treatment benefits and educating the public on how to recognize when oneself or a loved one may have an SUD may contribute to stigma reduction from a services perspective (Corrigan, Schomerus, Shuman, et al., 2017). In the mental illness realm, the beyondblue campaign in Australia does just that, framing depression as a treatable illness that can be addressed with proper care. It has become a widely recognizable program that has improved the public's awareness of mental illness and the benefits of treatment (Corrigan, 2016; Highet et al., 2006; Jorm et al., 2005). Effectiveness of such programs in eliminating stigma that contributes to label avoidance, however, is rather limited.

Essential to the notion that stigma reduction is necessary to facilitate treatment-seeking is the idea that evidence-based interventions are universally beneficial and necessary for those who fall along the continuum of substance use and SUD. This is not to say that some treatments are ineffective and should not be pursued; it is simply unclear what interventions an effective public health campaign might recommend given the wide continuum of substance use. Additionally, definitions of recovery –

usually the goal of treatment – vary widely as it is personal and often a moving target. Many assert that recovery from SUD is an outcome that obligates abstinence from substance use, while a few others define recovery as making positive change toward managing use and its consequences (Corrigan, Qin, et al., 2019). Another consideration regarding this agenda is the question of what kind of substance use would be targeted by public health messaging. Some substance use is legal and largely accepted (e.g., drinking alcohol at a sporting event or wedding). Furthermore, use of substances that may be illegal or socially unacceptable does not imply functional limitation or harm to goals, social roles, and expectations. However, limiting messaging to only those who meet criteria for an SUD may also be problematic. This arbitrary binary of SUD diagnosis or no diagnosis does not consider everyone along the continuum of use and may deepen the divide between "us" and "them" that contributes to public stigma. Messaging that embraces the concept of a continuum of substance use may more effectively reduce public stigma and increase problem recognition among people who use substances (Morris et al., 2020; Schomerus et al., 2013).

Prevention of Substance Use as Part of the Services Agenda

The public health goals of the services agenda may be extended to include substance use prevention. Perhaps one of the most popular prevention programs in the USA is Drug Abuse Resistance Education or DARE, as it is known. DARE aims to engage adolescents in conversations with law enforcement officers about the dangers of drug use and concludes with a pledge to abstain from drug use – emphasizing the potential legal consequences of substance use and perhaps strengthening stereotypes of criminality. DARE's impacts are incredibly limited, and as is research on other effective prevention efforts (Corrigan, Schomerus, Shuman, et al., 2017; Ennett et al., 1994). Stigma against people who use drugs may further impede prevention efforts. People may not support prevention programs because of prejudice against and perceived difference from people with SUD (e.g., "People who get addicted to drugs and alcohol are losers with no self-control. That kind of thing would never happen to my kids or in my community!").

Impact of Language on Label Avoidance

Negative stereotypes that contribute to label avoidance can be mitigated by the language we choose. Changing the lexicon surrounding SUD to avoid

Table 3. *Recommendations to reduce potentially stigmatizing language surrounding substance use*

Potentially stigmatizing language	Recommended word choice
"Drop dirty/clean"	Positive/negative drug screen
"Abuser"	Person who uses substances/drugs
"Addict"	Person with a substance use disorder
"Dope sick"	Experiencing withdrawal
"Relapsed"	Resumed use
"Substance misuse"	Nonmedical use

connotations of shame, blame, or willful misconduct to be more neutral (e.g., "substance use" instead of "abuse" or "test positive for substances" rather than "a dirty drop") has been demonstrated to reduce public stigma (J. F. Kelly et al., 2010; Kelly & Westerhoff, 2010; M. P. Kelly et al., 2015). Recommendations to adapt language around substance use as such have been issued for providers via the Substance Abuse and Mental Health Services Administration (SAMHSA, 2018), for scientists via the International Society of Addiction Journal Editors (ISAJE, 2015), and for the US government via the Office of National Drug Control Policy (ONDCP, 2017). Table 3 includes recommendations for more neutral language surrounding substance use.

A note, however, about the limitations of suppressing word use, borrowed from mental illness stigma literature. Focusing on word choice may distract from efforts toward real change; expending energy on changing language rather than condemning harmful discriminatory action and making change at the policy level (Corrigan, 2019). Furthermore, many marginalized groups choose to use or even reclaim the power of once-stigmatizing language. The LGBTQ community often does this by referring to themselves as queer. People with SUD or in recovery, for example, may identify as an "addict" or "alcoholic." One should use caution in censoring word use of others, especially among those who are on the spectrum of substance use.

The Rights Agenda: Replacing Stigma with Rightful Opportunity

The rights agenda aims at reducing stigma to promote the rights of people with SUD to participate in all aspects of an independent, autonomous life, including safe, integrated housing, opportunity to work, and access to compassionate and evidence-based health care. These echo many of the goals of the disability rights movement and mental health advocates, as demonstrated by the UN Convention on Rights of Persons with Disabilities and in the US New Freedom Commission (Hogan, 2003; United Nations, 2006). The legal prohibition of many substances proves a particular challenge to the rights agenda. People who endorse stereotypes of criminality report higher levels of stigma toward people who use substances (West et al., 2014). Incarceration for drug-related offenses serves as an obvious disruption to participating fully in one's family, community, and the economy. In the USA alone, 500,000 life-years are spent incarcerated each year for drug-related offenses (Caulkins & Chandler, 2006; Caulkins et al., 2014). Furthermore, discrimination against people who use drugs is often legally justified and culturally sanctioned (Corrigan, Schomerus, & Smelson, 2017). Justice involvement for drug crimes can create barriers to employment, voting in elections, accessing public and private housing, and receiving federal student loans for higher education (Federal Student Aid, n.d.; Mooney et al., 2019; Walter et al., 2017).

Advancing the Rights Agenda through Education, Protest, and Advocacy

The use of education-based interventions to advance the rights agenda has largely been researched in healthcare access and equity. For example, education interventions for physician assistants-in-training demonstrated a statistically significant reduction in stigmatizing attitudes toward people who use heroin, though effect sizes were small and attitudes were still rather negative (Crapanzano et al., 2014). Similarly, an education program for medical and nursing students contributed to more knowledge of and comfort in discussing substance use with patients, but there was no significant change in stigma (Bland et al., 2001; Cadiz et al., 2012).

Similar to other marginalized groups, individuals may engage in protest and advocacy to advance the rights of individuals who use drugs. Advocacy for the rights agenda goes beyond providing information by serving as a call to action to energize stakeholders to create positive change. This kind of advocacy may target both public awareness and legislative concerns (National Academies of Sciences, Engineering, and Medicine, 2016). On the legislative front, drug prohibition laws have contributed to significant discrimination against and disenfranchisement of people with SUD and led to excessive rates of incarceration (Corrigan, Schomerus, & Smelson, 2017). Advocates for legalization or decriminalization of drugs often look to Portugal, which legalized all drug use in 2001. The country has seen a significant decrease in the negative consequences (e.g., incarceration, violence, overdose) and an increase in treatment-seeking for substance use, all the while rates of use have remained relatively stable (Laqueur, 2015).

In the USA, the state of Oregon decriminalized possession of all drugs in late 2020 after activists, with the support of the Drug Policy Alliance (DPA), collected voter signatures in support of the legislation (Lopez, 2020). The DPA and similar advocacy organizations work in advocacy and protest for the rights of people who use drugs, calling on legislative change to minimize the negative impacts of drug use and its criminalization (DPA, 2020).

For those using protest to raise public awareness and decrease stigma, there is a dearth of evidence about its effectiveness in the behavioral health realm. National Alliance on Mental Illness members may act as "stigma busters" to challenge stereotypes of people with mental illness, and mental health professionals' social media platforms have been identified as potentially beneficial in challenging public stigma through protest and advocacy (National Academies of Sciences, Engineering, and Medicine, 2016). Similarly, academic drug researchers are considering their role as activists to reduce stigma by "coming out" as people who use drugs to challenge public perceptions and further the rights of their research's focal communities (Ross et al., 2020). While protest and confrontation of public stigma may be effective in some instances for achieving instrumental change, there is evidence of an unintended rebound effect where protest leads people to grasp even more firmly to their negative beliefs (Corrigan et al., 2001).

Contact-Based Interventions

In the mental illness stigma literature, contact-based interventions – where people with lived experience share their experiences with mental health challenges, stigma, and recovery – have largely demonstrated robust and longer-lasting effects in diminishing stigma (Corrigan et al., 2012; Corrigan, Michaels, & Morris, 2015; Corrigan, Schomerus, Shuman, et al., 2017; Griffiths et al., 2014). Far fewer studies have investigated the effects of contact-based interventions for reducing public stigma of SUD, and results of its benefits compared to education remain unclear (Livingston et al., 2012; McGinty et al., 2015, Sanders, 2012). However, from a rights perspective, contact-based interventions may be preferred as they center the lived experiences of people in recovery from and/or living with SUD, allowing for more active participation in rights advancement – to borrow from the disability rights community, this allows for "nothing about us without us." Furthermore, contact-based interventions that allow for peers in recovery to share their stories and come "out" with their experiences may have additional benefits for people with SUD, explored more later in this chapter and in Chapter 10.

Diminishing Shame: The Self-Worth Agenda

In a study by Birtel and colleagues (2017) of individuals in treatment for SUD, perceived public stigma had deleterious effects on self-esteem, depression, anxiety, and even sleep. The relationship between perceived stigma and these indicators of well-being were mediated by internalized shame (Birtel et al., 2017). The self-worth agenda, as translated from the mental health literature, aims to diminish stigma associated with SUD to minimize the shame and instead foster empowerment and self-determination.

Peer Support to Bolster Self-Worth

In the mental health realm, peer support has been identified as crucial for reducing stigma to promote self-worth (Corrigan, Larson, et al., 2019a; Corrigan, Schomerus, Shuman, et al., 2017). Peer relationships are mutually beneficial that offer both emotional and instrumental or practical support in navigating one's life with a behavioral health condition, services, and identity. People with lived experience of substance use have long been a part of both formal and informal services for SUD, both as peer support staff and in mutual support groups (Reif et al., 2014). A recent meta-analysis of peer services in SUD treatment demonstrated its positive impacts, including on increasing self-efficacy and decreasing stress (Eddie et al., 2019). Similar to contact-based interventions among the general public, contact with peers who have lived with SUD (and its accompanying stigma) and continue to thrive may bolster the hope, self-determination, and empowerment that the self-worth agenda seeks.

A visible presence of people being "out" with their lived experience of SUD in the community at large could further this agenda as well. Peer voices need not be tied to healthcare services or treatment may serve to empower and promote the worth of those who are not interested in reducing or ceasing use, as neither the self-worth agenda nor peer support hinge on abstinence, moderation, or treatment. This openness of lived experience to normalize substance use along the continuum may include more people "coming out" as people who use substances or are in recovery. Contact-based interventions that discuss disclosure of one's mental health condition may have benefits for the individual (e.g., diminished self-stigma, improvement in depression and anxiety; Corrigan, Larson, et al., 2015; Rüsch et al., 2014) that may extend to people with SUD – this is discussed in detail in Chapter 10.

Additionally, the principles of harm reduction align well with the self-worth agenda as they are centered on the inherent value of people who use drugs, regardless of intention to stop using substances. Among the principles of harm reduction, the movement aims to reduce the negative consequences of substance use and its criminalization by "empower[ing] people who use drugs to share information and support each other in strategies which meet their actual conditions of use" (National Harm Reduction Coalition, 2020). Harm reduction advocates have moved to create safer consumption sites, facilities where people can use substances and access supplies or resources in a safe, supervised space. These may well be an ideal space for peers to connect and offer community, safety, and promote dignity (Barry et al., 2019).

Conflicting Agendas to Decrease Stigma of SUD

In many ways, the goal remains the same across agendas but methods of achieving them may differ and even contradict one another. First, strategies utilized by those prioritizing the services agenda, such as education programs that frame substance use disorder as a treatable health condition like any other to encourage treatment-seeking, may unintentionally undermine the goals of the self-worth agenda. In mental health stigma research, emphasis on the medical model contributes to stereotypes of permanence and undermines stories of recovery. As well, these campaigns may underline the differences between people with SUD and people without, rather than promoting empowerment and recovery (Corrigan, Schomerus, Shuman, et al., 2017). In mental health stigma research, the limitations of education programs are evident. A randomized controlled trial comparing the impact of the beyondblue educational campaign in Australia with a recovery-oriented video demonstrated that the recovery video results in greater change in stigma and empowerment outcomes than the public service announcement (Corrigan, Powell, & Al-Khouja, 2015). More research is needed to determine how this may translate for SUD educational campaigns.

Furthermore, health messaging for prevention of substance use often plays on negative stereotypes of people with SUD to deter substance use.

For example, campaigns by Mothers Against Drunk Driving in the past often associated alcohol and drug use with the dangers of drunk driving, depicting deadly car crashes, guilt, and shame. A 2002 Superbowl commercial compared purchasing illicit drugs to terrorism, associating the harms of clandestine narcotrafficking markets with everyday drug purchases by individual users (Corrigan, Schomerus, & Smelson, 2017). Public service announcements (PSAs) may attempt to promote prevention messages by drawing the connection between substance use and worsened health and wellness. The quintessential 1980s PSA that likens a fried egg to "your brain on drugs" creates graphic imagery about the harms of substance use on brain health. The National Institute for Drug Abuse (NIDA) launched a series of PSAs in the early aughts to convey similar messages, warning of the dangers of contracting HIV through the story of a couple named "Jack & Jill" and urging viewers to "Keep Your Brain Healthy" as people who use drugs are not often considered "bright" (NIDA, n.d.). Evidence of the effectiveness of these messaging campaigns is very limited despite their continued use for prevention efforts (Werb et al., 2011; Westat, 2006). Furthermore, repeated messaging from "experts" warning that using substances makes someone dangerous, criminal, unhealthy, or unintelligent is likely to have detrimental impacts on the self-worth of people with SUD.

Conversely, the self-worth agenda may be perceived as undermining the goals of the services agenda when self-worth is not predicated on desire for treatment, moderation, or abstinence. However, these ideas are not mutually exclusive. Approaches like harm reduction, that prioritize the inherent value and worth of people with SUD, are sometimes characterized as incremental steps toward treatment or abstinence as a long-term goal, depending on the desires and needs of the individual (Corrigan et al., 2020; Kellogg, 2003; Kellogg & Kreek, 2005). Harm reduction interventions may aim to increase contact with safe and supportive resources and opportunities to access treatment (National Harm Reduction Coalition, 2020).

Potential for Overlap and Coordination

Despite the tension between agendas and strategies to achieve stigma reduction for people with SUD, there exists great overlap between these priorities where they may complement one another. Perhaps the most glaring among these is the use of contact to reduce stigma. Contact-based interventions may be utilized to reduce the public stigma that keeps people from treatment. Similarly, these lived experience stories may be impactful in advocacy and protest efforts to effect policy change for the rights agenda (e.g., "I am a person with SUD and deserve the right to access equitable health care."). Finally, fostering hope and empowerment through connection over shared experiences is critical to the concept of peer support in the self-worth agenda. Centering the lived experience voice may be critical to advancing each agenda with minimal harm to the others.

Additionally, advancing stigma reduction via the rights agenda may inadvertently further goals for self-worth and services agendas. As people with SUD are extended more opportunities and access into society vis-à-vis the rights agenda, their perceived self-worth may be bolstered. Looking to inclusion in gainful employment as an example, recent expansion of programs such as individualized placement and support (IPS) to people with substance use disorder has led to improved rates of employment, increased hours worked, and wages earned (LePage et al., 2016; Lones et al., 2017). The robust body of research supporting the use of IPS for other groups, namely serious mental illness, indicates that gainful competitive employment is associated with greater life satisfaction, well-being, and self-esteem (Luciano et al., 2014). This relationship between self-worth and rightful opportunity may function in the opposite direction as well. Individuals who are valued, respected, and do not face shame for their choices may be more willing to advocate for and seek out opportunities to participate in their communities. Rightful, equitable inclusion in employment, especially in countries where health insurance is linked to one's employer, may also increase access to treatment. In countries without universal public health insurance, people with SUD who are employed will likely have more money and insurance coverage to seek out services as needed.

Finally, strategies utilized in promoting the self-worth agenda may improve treatment access and outcomes. A recent systematic review by Eddie and colleagues (2019) identified the potential benefits of peer support services for people with SUD, which include improved engagement and treatment retention, reduced use and relapse, and treatment satisfaction. Harm reduction strategies including safer consumption sites and peer support communities may also play a role in offering information on SUD treatment when desired to individuals who are not yet in contact with other treatment providers (Barry et al., 2019). The potential of peer support has also been extended to hospital emergency departments to not only support empowerment and hope but also provide linkage to care (McGuire et al., 2020).

Conclusion

Stigma reduction efforts originate from one of three agendas: the services agenda, the rights agenda, or the self-worth agenda. As researchers, advocates, and people with lived experience work to understand and reduce the stigma of SUD, each must be intentional with their efforts to ensure that their pursuit in the name of one agenda does not impede the progress of the others. There is significant overlap in the goals and strategies of the three agendas, namely efforts that center the voices of people with lived experience of substance use. Interventions that consider treatment, rightful inclusion, and the inherent worth of those with SUD simultaneously can effectively reduce stigma to further the pursuit of meaningful and hopeful lives of people with SUD.

References

Barney, L. J., Griffiths, K. M., Jorm, A. F., & Christensen, H. (2006). Stigma about depression and its impact on help-seeking intentions. *Australian & New Zealand Journal of Psychiatry*, *40*(1), 51–54. https://doi.org/10.1080/j.1440-1614.2006.01741.x

Barry, C. L., Sherman, S. G., Stone, E., et al. (2019). Arguments supporting and opposing legalization of safe consumption sites in the US. *International Journal of Drug Policy*, *63*, 18–22. https://doi.org/10.1016/j.drugpo.2018.10.008

Ben-Zeev, D., Corrigan, P. W., Britt, T. W., & Langford, L. (2012). Stigma of mental illness and service use in the military. *Journal of Mental Health*, *21*(3), 264–273. https://doi.org/10.3109/09638237.2011.621468

Birtel, M. D., Wood, L., & Kempa, N. J. (2017). Stigma and social support in substance abuse: Implications for mental health and well-being. *Psychiatry Research*, *252*, 1–8. https://doi.org/10.1016/j.psychres.2017.01.097

Bland, E., Oppenheimer, L. W., Oppenheimer, L., et al. (2001). Influence of an educational program on medical students' attitudes to substance use disorders in pregnancy. *The American Journal of Drug and Alcohol Abuse*, *27*(3), 483–490. https://doi-org.ezproxy.gl.iit.edu/10.1081/ADA-100104513

Cadiz, D. M., Butell, S. S., Epeneter, B. J., Basin, B., & O'Neill, C. (2012). Quasi-experimental evaluation of a substance use awareness educational intervention for nursing students. *Journal of Nursing Education*, *51*(7), 411–415. https://doi.org/10.3928/01484834-20120515-02

Caulkins, J. P., & Chandler, S. (2006). Long-run trends in incarceration of drug offenders in the US. *Crime and Delinquency*, *52*(4), 619–641. https://doi-org.ezproxy.gl.iit.edu/10.1177/0011128705284793

Caulkins, J. P., Kasunic, A., Kleiman, M., & Lee, M. A. C. (2014). Understanding drug legalization. *International Public Health Journal*, *6*(3), 283–294.

Clement, S., Schauman, O., Graham, T., et al. (2015). What is the impact of mental health-related stigma on help-seeking? A systematic review of quantitative and qualitative studies. *Psychological Medicine, 45*(1), 11–27. https://doi.org/10.1017/S0033291714000129

Corrigan, P. W. (2016). Lessons learned from unintended consequences about erasing the stigma of mental illness. *World Psychiatry, 15*(1), 67–73. https://doi-org.ezproxy.gl.iit.edu/10.1002/wps.20295

(2019). Beware the word police. *Psychiatric Services, 70*(3), 234–236. https://doi.org/10.1176/appi.ps.201800369

Corrigan, P. W., Druss, B. G., & Perlick, D. A. (2014). The impact of mental illness stigma on seeking and participating in mental health care. *Psychological Science in the Public Interest, 15*(2), 37–70. https://doi-org.ezproxy.gl.iit.edu/10.1177/1529100614531398

Corrigan, P. W., Larson, J. E., Michaels, P. J., et al. (2015). Diminishing the self-stigma of mental illness by coming out proud. *Psychiatry Research, 229*(1–2), 148–154. https://doi.org/10.1016/j.psychres.2015.07.053

Corrigan, P. W., Larson, J. E., Smelson, D., & Andra, M. (2019). Recovery, peer support and confrontation in services for people with mental illness and/or substance use disorder. *The British Journal of Psychiatry, 214*(3), 130–132. https://doi.org/10.1192/bjp.2018.242

Corrigan, P. W., Morris, S. B., Michaels, P. J., Rafacz, J. D., & Rüsch, N. (2012). Challenging the public stigma of mental illness: A meta-analysis of outcome studies. *Psychiatric Services, 63*(10), 963–973. https://doi.org/10.1176/appi.ps.201100529

Corrigan, P. W., Michaels P. J., & Morris, S. B. (2015). Do the effects of anti-stigma programs persist over time? Findings from a meta-analysis. *Psychiatric Services, 66,* 543–546. https://doi.org/10.1176/appi.ps.201400291

Corrigan, P. W., Powell, K. J., & Al-Khouja, M. A. (2015). Examining the impact of public service announcements on help seeking and stigma: Results of a randomized controlled trial. *Journal of Nervous and Mental Disease, 203,* 836–842. https://doi.org/10.1097/NMD.0000000000000376

Corrigan, P. W., Qin, S., Davidson, L., Schomerus, G., Shuman, V., & Smelson, D. (2019). How does the public understand recovery from severe mental illness versus substance use disorder? *Psychiatric Rehabilitation Journal, 42*(4), 341–334. https://doi.org/10.1037/prj0000380

(2020). Recovery from mental illness versus substance use disorder. *Advances in Dual Diagnosis, 13*(3), 101–110. https://doi.org/10.1108/ADD-10-2019-0012

Corrigan, P. W., River, L. P., Lundin, R. K., et al. (2001). Three strategies for changing attributions about severe mental illness. *Schizophrenia Bulletin, 27*(2), 187–195. https://doi.org/10.1093/oxfordjournals.schbul.a006865

Corrigan, P. W., Schomerus, G., Shuman, V., et al. (2017). Developing a research agenda for reducing the stigma of addictions, part II: Lessons from the mental health stigma literature. *American Journal on Addictions, 26*(1), 67–74. https://doi-org.ezproxy.gl.iit.edu/10.1111/ajad.12436

Corrigan, P., Schomerus, G., & Smelson, D. (2017). Are some of the stigmas of addictions culturally sanctioned?. *The British Journal of Psychiatry, 210*(3), 180–181. https://doi.org/10.1192/bjp.bp.116.185421

Crapanzano, K. A., Hammarlund, R., Ahmad, B., Hunsinger, N., & Kullar, R. (2018). The association between perceived stigma and substance use disorder treatment outcomes: A review. *Substance Abuse and Rehabilitation, 10*, 1–12. https://doi.org/10.2147/SAR.S183252

Crapanzano, K., Vath, R. J., & Fisher, D. (2014). Reducing stigma towards substance users through an educational intervention: Harder than it looks. *Academic Psychiatry, 38*(4), 420–425. https://doi.org/10.1007/s40596-014-0067-1

Cunningham, J. A., Sobell, L. C., & Chow, V. M. C. (1993). What's in a label? The effects of substance types and labels on treatment considerations and stigma. *Journal of Studies on Alcohol, 54*(6), 693–699. https://doi.org/10.15288/jsa.1993.54.693

Drug Policy Alliance. (2020). *About us.* https://drugpolicy.org/about-us#vision-mission

Eddie, D., Hoffman, L., Vilsaint, C., et al. (2019). Lived experience in new models of care for substance use disorder: A systematic review of peer recovery support services and recovery coaching. *Frontiers in Psychology, 10*, Article 1052. https://doi.org/10.3389/fpsyg.2019.01052

Ennett, S. T., Tobler, N. S., Ringwalt, C. L., & Flewelling, R. L. (1994). How effective is drug abuse resistance education? A meta-analysis of Project DARE outcome evaluations. *American Journal of Public Health, 84*(9), 1394–1401. https://doi.org/10.2105/AJPH.84.9.1394

Federal Student Aid. (n.d.). *Students with criminal convictions have limited eligibility for federal student aid.* Office of the US Department of Education. https://studentaid.gov/understand-aid/eligibility/requirements/criminal-convictions

Griffiths, K. M., Carron-Arthur, B., Parsons, A., & Reid, R. (2014). Effectiveness of programs for reducing the stigma associated with mental disorders: A meta-analysis of randomized controlled trials. *World Psychiatry, 13*(2), 161–175. https://doi-org.ezproxy.gl.iit.edu/10.1002/wps.20129

Highet, N. J., Luscombe, G. M., Davenport, T. A., Burns, J. M., & Hickie, I. B. (2006). Positive relationships between public awareness activity and recognition of the impacts of depression in Australia. *Australian & New Zealand Journal of Psychiatry, 40*(1), 55–58. https://doi-org.ezproxy.gl.iit.edu/10.1080/j.1440-1614.2006.01742.x

Hingson, R., Mangione, T., Meyers, A., & Scotch, N. (1982). Seeking help for drinking problems: A study in the Boston Metropolitan Area. *Journal of Studies on Alcohol, 43*(3), 273–288. https://doi.org/10.15288/jsa.1982.43.273

Hogan, M. F. (2003). New Freedom Commission Report: The President's New Freedom Commission: Recommendations to transform mental health care in America. *Psychiatric Services, 54*, 1467–1474. https://doi.org/10.1176/appi.ps.54.11.1467

International Society of Addiction Journal Editors. (2015). *Statements and guidelines: Addiction terminology.* www.isaje.net/addiction-terminology.html

Jorm, A. F., Nakane, Y., Christensen, H., Yoshioka, K., Griffiths, K. M., & Wata, Y. (2005). Public beliefs about treatment and outcome of mental disorders: A comparison of Australia and Japan. *BMC Medicine, 3*(1), 1–14. https://doi.org/10.1186/1741-7015-3-12

Kellogg, S. H. (2003). On 'gradualism' and the building of the harm reduction-abstinence continuum. *Journal of Substance Abuse Treatment, 25*(4), 241–247. https://doi.org/10.1016/S0740-5472(03)00068-0

Kellogg, S. H. & Kreek, M. J. (2005). Gradualism, identity, reinforcements, and change. *International Journal of Drug Policy, 16*(6), 369–375. https://doi.org/10.1016/j.drugpo.2005.08.001

Kelly, J. F., Dow, S. J., & Westerhoff, C. (2010). Does our choice of substance-related terms influence perceptions of treatment need? An empirical investigation with two commonly used terms. *Journal of Drug Issues, 40*(4), 805–818. https://doi.org/10.1177/002204261004000403

Kelly, J. F., & Westerhoff, C. M. (2010). Does it matter how we refer to individuals with substance-related conditions? A randomized study of two commonly used terms. *The International Journal on Drug Policy, 21*(3), 202–207. https://doi.org/10.1016/j.drugpo.2009.10.010

Kelly, M. P., Heath, I., Howick, J., & Greenhalgh, T. (2015). The importance of values in evidence-based medicine. *BMC Medical Ethics, 16*(1), 69. https://doi.org/10.1186/s12910-015-0063-3

Klingemann, H. K.-H. (1991). The motivation for change from problem alcohol and heroin use. *Addiction, 86*(6), 727–744. https://doi.org/10.1111/j.1360-0443.1991.tb03099.x

Laqueur, H. (2015). Uses and abuses of drug decriminalization in Portugal. *Law & Social Inquiry, 40*(3), 746–781. https://doi.org/10.1111/lsi.12104

LePage, J. P., Lewis, A. A., Crawford, A. M., et al. (2016). Incorporating individualized placement and support principles into vocational rehabilitation for formerly incarcerated veterans. *Psychiatric Services, 67*(7), 735–742. https://doi.org/10.1176/appi.ps.201500058

Livingston, J. D., Milne, T., Fang, M. L., & Amari, E. (2012). The effectiveness of interventions for reducing stigma related to substance use disorders: A systematic review. *Addiction, 107*(1), 39–50. https://doi-org.ezproxy.gl.iit.edu/10.1111/j.1360-0443.2011.03601.x

Lones, C. E., Bond, G. R., McGovern, M. P., et al. (2017). Individual placement and support (IPS) for methadone maintenance therapy patients: A pilot randomized controlled trial. *Administration and Policy in Mental Health and Mental Health Services Research, 44*(3), 359–364. https://doi.org/10.1007/s10488-017-0793-2

Lopez, G. (2020, November 11). *America's war on drugs has failed. Oregon is showing a way out.* www.vox.com/future-perfect/21552710/oregon-drug-decriminalization-marijuana-legalization

Luciano, A., Bond, G. R., & Drake, R. E. (2014). Does employment alter the course and outcome of schizophrenia and other severe mental illnesses? A systematic review of longitudinal research. *Schizophrenia Research, 159* (2–3), 312–321. https://doi.org/10.1016/j.schres.2014.09.010

Luoma, J. B. (2011). Substance use stigma as a barrier to treatment and recovery. In B. A. Johnson (Ed.), *Addiction medicine: Science and practice* (pp. 1195–1215). Springer. https://doi.org/10.1007/978-1-4419-0338-9_59

McGinty, E. E., Goldman, H. H., Pescosolido, B., & Barry, C. L. (2015). Portraying mental illness and drug addiction as treatable health conditions: Effects of a randomized experiment on stigma and discrimination. *Social Science & Medicine, 126,* 73–85. https://doi.org/10.1016/j.socscimed.2014.12.010

McGuire, A. B., Powell, K. G., Treitler, P. C., et al. (2020). Emergency department-based peer support for opioid use disorder: Emergent functions and forms. *Journal of Substance Abuse Treatment, 108,* 82–87. https://doi.org/10.1016/j.jsat.2019.06.013

Mooney, A. C., Neilands, T. B., Giannella, E., Morris, M. D., Tulsky, J., & Glymour, M. M. (2019). Effects of a voter initiative on disparities in punishment severity for drug offenses across California counties. *Social Science & Medicine, 230,* 9–19. https://doi.org/10.1016/j.socscimed.2019.03.010

Morris, J., Albery, I. P., Heather, N., & Moss, A. C. (2020). Continuum beliefs are associated with higher problem recognition than binary beliefs among harmful drinkers without addiction experience. *Addictive Behaviors, 105,* Article 106292. https://doi.org/10.1016/j.addbeh.2020.106292

National Academies of Sciences, Engineering, and Medicine. (2016). *Ending discrimination against people with mental and substance use disorders: The evidence for stigma change.* The National Academies Press. https://doi.org/10.17226/23442

National Harm Reduction Coalition. (2020). *Principles of harm reduction.* https://harmreduction.org/hrc2/wp-content/uploads/2020/08/NHRC-PDF-Principles_Of_Harm_Reduction.pdf

National Institute on Drug Abuse. (n.d.) *Public service announcements.* National Institutes of Health. www.drugabuse.gov/news-events/public-education-projects/public-service-announcements

Office of National Drug Control Policy. (2017). *Memorandum to heads of executive departments and agencies: Changing federal terminology regarding substance use and substance use disorders.* https://obamawhitehouse.archives.gov/sites/whitehouse.gov/files/images/Memo%20-%20Changing%20Federal%20Terminology%20Regrading%20Substance%20Use%20and%20Substance%20Use%20Disorders.pdf

Reif, S., Braude, L., Lyman, D. R., et al. (2014). Peer recovery support for individuals with substance use disorders: Assessing the evidence. *Psychiatric Services, 65*(7), 853–861. https://doi.org/10.1176/appi.ps.201400047

Ross, A., Potter, G. R., Barratt, M. J., & Aldridge, J. A. (2020). "Coming out": Stigma, reflexivity and the drug researcher's drug use. *Contemporary Drug Problems*, *47*(4), 268–285. https://doi-org.ezproxy.gl.iit.edu/10.1177/0091450920953635

Rüsch, N., Abbruzzese, E., Hagedorn, E., et al. (2014). Efficacy of coming out proud to reduce stigma's impact among people with mental illness: Pilot randomised controlled trial. *British Journal of Psychiatry*, *204*(5), 391–397. https://doi.org/10.1192/bjp.bp.113.135772

Rüsch, N., Corrigan, P. W., Todd, A. R. & Bodenhausen, G. V. (2010). Implicit self-stigma in people with mental illness. *Journal of Nervous and Mental Disease*, *198*(2), 150–153. https://doi.org/10.1097/nmd.0b013e3181cc43b5

Thornicroft, G. (2013). Premature death among people with mental illness. *British Medical Journal*, *346*, Article F2969. https://doi.org/10.1136/bmj.f2969

Sanders, J. M. (2012). Use of mutual support to counteract the effects of socially constructed stigma: Gender and drug addiction. *Journal of Groups in Addiction & Recovery*, *7*(2–4), 237–252. https://doi-org.ezproxy.gl.iit.edu/10.1080/1556035X.2012.705705

Schober, R., & Annis, H. M. (1996). Barriers to help-seeking for change in drinking: A gender-focused review of the literature. *Addictive Behaviors*, *21*(1), 81–92. https://doi.org/10.1016/0306-4603(95)00041-0

Schomerus, G., Matschinger, H., & Angermeyer, M. C. (2013). Continuum beliefs and stigmatizing attitudes towards persons with schizophrenia, depression and alcohol dependence. *Psychiatry Research*, *209*(3), 665–669. https://doi.org/10.1016/j.psychres.2013.02.006

Simpson, D. D. (1981). Treatment for drug abuse: Follow-up outcomes and length of time spent. *Archives of General Psychiatry*, *38*(8), 875–880. https://doi.org/10.1001/archpsyc.1981.01780330033003

Stark, M. J. (1992). Dropping out of substance abuse treatment: A clinically oriented review. *Clinical Psychology Review*, *12*(1), 93–116. https://doi.org/10.1016/0272-7358(92)90092-M

Stolzenburg, S., Freitag, S., Evans-Lacko, S., Muehlan, H., Schmidt, S., & Schomerus, G. (2017). The stigma of mental illness as a barrier to self labeling as having a mental illness. *The Journal of Nervous and Mental Disease*, *205*(12), 903–909. https://doi.org/10.1097/NMD.0000000000000756

Substance Abuse and Mental Health Services Administration. (2018). *Overcoming stigma, ending discrimination resource guide*. www.samhsa.gov/sites/default/files/programs_campaigns/02._webcast_1_resources-508.pdf

(2019). *2018 National Survey of Drug Use and Health (NSDUH)*. www.samhsa.gov/data/release/2018-national-survey-drug-use-and-health-nsduh-releases

(2013). Premature death among people with mental illness. *British Medical Journal*, *346*, Article F2969. https://doi.org/10.1136/bmj.f2969

Tuchfeld, B. S. (1981). Spontaneous remission in alcoholics: Empirical observations and theoretical implications. *Journal of Studies on Alcohol, 42*(7), 626–641. https://doi.org/10.15288/jsa.1981.42.626

United Nations (2006). *Convention on the rights of persons with disabilities.* Department of Economic and Social Affairs. www.un.org/development/desa/disabilities/convention-on-the-rights-of-persons-with-disabilities.html

Van Boekel, L. C., Brouwers, E. P. M., Van Weeghel, J., & Garretsen, H. F. L. (2013). Stigma among health professionals towards patients with substance use disorders and its consequences for healthcare delivery: Systematic review. *Drug and Alcohol Dependence, 131*(1–3), 23–35. https://doi.org/10.1016/j.drugalcdep.2013.02.018

Walter, R. J., Viglione, J., & Tillyer, M. S. (2017). One strike to second chances: Using criminal backgrounds in admission decisions for assisted housing. *Housing Policy Debate, 27*(5), 734–750. https://doi-org.ezproxy.gl.iit.edu/10.1080/10511482.2017.1309557

Werb, D., Mills, E. J., DeBeck, K., Kerr, T., Montaner, J. S., & Wood, E. (2011). The effectiveness of anti-illicit-drug public-service announcements: A systematic review and meta-analysis. *Journal of Epidemiology and Community Health, 65*(10), 834–840. http://dx.doi.org/10.1136/jech.2010.125195

West, M. L., Yanos, P. T., & Mulay, A. L. (2014). Triple stigma of forensic psychiatric patients: Mental illness, race, and criminal history. *International Journal of Forensic Mental Health, 13*(1), 75–90. https://doi-org.ezproxy.gl.iit.edu/10.1080/14999013.2014.885471

Westat. (2006). *Evaluation of the National Youth Anti-Drug Media Campaign: 2004 report of findings executive summary.* National Institute on Drug Abuse, National Institutes of Health. https://archives.drugabuse.gov/sites/default/files/execsumvolume.pdf

CHAPTER 10

The Benefits of Disclosure

Sai Snigdha Talluri and Patrick W. Corrigan

Disclosure is the process by which an individual shares personal information with others. Disclosure is thought to help reduce self-stigma and lead to improved self-esteem and self-efficacy (Corrigan et al., 2010). It involves sharing both stories of struggles and of recovery and empowerment. Disclosure varies in terms of the amount of information that is shared, as well as the extent of information shared (Omarzu, 2000). The important notion to emphasize here is that disclosure is a choice. Using this approach, people can be open and share all their experiences or people can test the waters. Disclosure can lead to improvements in both mental and physical health outcomes (Broman-Fulks et al., 2007; Ruggiero et al., 2004).

Lessons learned from disclosure experiences in the mental health arena may be helpful in understanding the process for substance use disorder (SUD). Both groups have experienced considerable stigma because of society-wide misperceptions. For instance, having a mental illness has been attributed to being possessed by a demon or having an SUD meant the person was "weak." Given these commonalities, this chapter aims to connect the literature surrounding disclosure of mental health conditions to the experiences of people with SUD.

Identity and Mental Illness or SUD

In order for disclosure to occur, individuals are required to identify with the health condition (Corrigan, 2018). Identifying with a health condition is not a clear-cut decision – for example, the person either identifies with the condition or does not. Instead, people may identify with some aspects of the condition (e.g., the cravings experienced while trying to cut down/ reduce the use of substances) but not others (e.g., being regarded as a criminal when seeking help). Research on identifying with a mental illness is contradictory. One study found a positive correlation between group-identification and self-efficacy in people with mental illness (Watson et al., 2007). In another, individuals reported reduced hope and diminished self-esteem when they identified with their mental health condition and also embraced the stigma associated with it (Rüsch et al., 2006, 2009). Thus, it can be said that identifying with a mental illness does not automatically lead to more stress; rather it is the perceived legitimacy of the stigma that has potentially negative consequences for identity and emotional health (Lysaker et al., 2007).

Research about identity and its relationship to addiction mirrors studies about the ill-effects of disease identification and mental illness. In some cases, identification with addiction may exacerbate drug use. An alcohol or marijuana use identity reflects the extent to which alcohol or marijuana use is a central part of how one sees oneself (Montes et al., 2021). Stephens and McBride (1976) interviewed 50 people who use heroin in inpatient treatment and observed that increased identification with and commitment to the "addict" role was associated with increased drug use. Thus, individuals who identify with their addiction have worse outcomes (Hughes, 2007; Walters, 1996). Hence, an adaptive goal of SUD treatment might be to replace addiction identity with recovery identity (Buckingham et al., 2013). Identifying with one's addiction is required in 12-step Programs such as Alcoholics Anonymous and Narcotics Anonymous ("I'm Marie and I'm an alcoholic"). Research suggests that during the course of these meetings, a new identity associated with "recovery" will be formed in comparison to the existing identity associated with addiction (Oakes, 1987). While the "addict" identity may include alcohol/drug use, the "recovery" identity may include abstinence or controlled use.

Further studies suggest that, in the context of addiction, preference for the identity associated with recovery in comparison to the identity associated with addiction may lead to increased beliefs that one can achieve their goal of decreasing substance use. Higher levels of abstinence were observed in participants who strongly endorsed a recovery identity relative to an addiction identity (Dingle et al., 2015).

Pride and Identity

People who appreciate their identity have pride in it (Corrigan et al., 2013; Sullivan, 2014). Pride has several meanings. It is a sense of contentment or satisfaction derived from achieving standards recognized by one's culture or set by one's self. People with behavioral health challenges may experience pride when they overcome hurdles associated with their condition. For instance, an individual with depression might experience pride in graduating from college despite recurring bouts of depression. This does not necessarily mean that people need to be symptom-free to claim accomplishment. Instead, accomplishment involves meeting one's personally defined goals despite the challenges that they experience. A sense of agency and self-determination in the face of symptoms and disabilities fosters self-esteem and contributes to an identity about which a person might be proud.

Pride is also authenticity that involves expressing any part of one's identity in the face of an imposing world. Authenticity is the answer to the question, "Who am I?" It involves more than just embracing who one is – it may explain SUD as an identity that one might be proud of. Being authentic includes embracing how SUD has shaped one's worldview or life experiences. This does not mean people must publicly acclaim their SUD experiences, only that they have the option to do so with whom they choose.

Disclosure of Mental Illness or SUD Identity

Corrigan et al. (2010) conducted a quantitative assessment of people's experience with disclosure and demonstrated that disclosure of mental illness identity seems to be a protective factor against self-stigma's effects on quality of life; disclosure augments a sense of personal empowerment that enhances well-being. Individuals who disclose their mental health condition experience more supportive and less stigmatizing responses (Bos et al., 2009). Research on disclosure of one's addiction experiences and consequent decrease in stigma is contradictory. Individuals who were the most "out" about their substance use reported the highest levels of internalized stigma (Quinn et al., 2014). Being out was measured on a scale ranging from almost nobody knowing the identity to nearly everyone knowing about the identity. However, higher levels of concealing one's substance use was associated with lower levels of psychological flexibility, lower quality of life, more experiences of stigma-related rejection in the past, and higher internalized shame (Luoma et al., 2007).

Honest Open Proud for Behavioral Health

Honest Open Proud (HOP) was developed by Corrigan et al. (2017) and a team consisting of people with behavioral health challenges to help

Table 4. *The costs and benefits of disclosing for Jane Smith*

Setting: At the office	
Benefits	Costs
May find support in coworkers.	Discrimination and disapproval from supervisor/other coworkers.
Can be more open about day-to-day affairs.	Others at work may gossip.
Builds relationships with coworkers who may have had similar experiences.	Worry about what coworkers will think of me.
Promotes a sense of power by telling story.	Worry that coworkers will pity me.
Reduces feelings of shame and guilt.	
Challenges negative stereotypes about people with mental health conditions.	

individuals disclose their experiences with stigmatized health conditions. HOP is meant to help people identify and challenge self-stigmatizing beliefs. The central tenet of HOP is that strategic decision and actions regarding disclosure *may* significantly diminish self-stigma. Let us be clear, however, HOP is not meant to encourage people to disclose but rather to inform them of their disclosure options and help them decide if and when they may choose to disclose. HOP is typically led by individuals with lived experience. The objectives of HOP are threefold. First, the program helps participants weigh the costs and benefits of disclosing aspects of their behavioral health condition. Second, the program teaches relatively safe ways to disclose. Third, it provides a format for telling one's story. The following sections discuss the foundation of HOP. We then explore its potential to be adapted for people with SUD.

Costs and Benefits of Disclosing

Disclosing one's experiences with a mental illness is a complex decision that is likely to be influenced by many factors. People with similar experiences may perceive differences in the costs and benefits of disclosure. Costs are reasons why one might choose not to disclose their experiences with mental illness and benefits are reasons why disclosure might be helpful. Costs and benefits can vary depending on the setting; for example, at work versus in a faith-based community. Table 4 lists the costs and benefits for disclosing at office for Jane Smith.

There are benefits to disclosure: people who talk openly about their experiences may find support in coworkers, peers, and family members. Disclosing may help people be more open about day-to-day experiences. They may be able to build relationships with those who have had similar experiences. Disclosure can be the first step to finding an entire support network of family, friends, and coworkers who have had similar experiences and might be available to help in the future. Individuals who have a supportive network report less self-stigma that in turn has positive effects on health (Birtel et al., 2017).

Disclosing experiences can help people realize that they no longer have to worry about keeping their experiences with their mental health condition a secret. Keeping a secret about a mental health condition may foster feelings of shame or guilt. By telling their story, people are promoting a sense of personal power and can eliminate feelings of shame or guilt. This sense of power over one's life is a major step toward ending stigma. Disclosure directly challenges many of the negative stereotypes that individuals have about mental health conditions.

Still, there are many risks to disclosing. People may choose not to disclose due to potential repercussions from others or from society. Some people may disapprove of others sharing their experiences with mental illness as they may fear individuals with mental illness or are offended by people who have been hospitalized. As a result, some who hear stories may shun an individual who discloses at social gatherings. Worse, some people may actively exclude the individual from work or housing opportunities. A supervisor might keep a person with a mental health condition from a promotion because they believe stereotypes that people with mental health conditions are untrustworthy. People who disclose may worry how others perceive them. They may wonder what people mean when they ask, "How are you?" or say, "Can't join you for lunch." Others may be concerned that people may pity them.

There is no easy way to weigh costs and benefits and subsequently arrive at a decision. Clearly, individuals will identify some costs or benefits as more important and that will impact their decision to disclose. Another aspect to consider is that the impact of costs and benefits is sometimes immediate, while at other times the impact is delayed. It might be helpful to identify both short-term benefits and costs and compare these to long-term benefits and costs. Generally, people tend to be more immediately influenced by short-term costs and benefits because of the immediate impact. However, long-term costs and benefits frequently have greater implications for the future.

Table 5. *Five strategies people might use to disclose their experiences*

Approach	Definition
Social avoidance	Avoiding situations outside the mental health community where others might discover one's condition
Nondisclosure	Keeping experiences private
Selective disclosure	Sharing experiences with a few trusted individuals
Indiscriminant disclosure	Sharing experiences with the public. Not trying to actively conceal experiences
Broadcasting one's experience	Actively seeking out people to share experiences and educate people about mental health conditions

Adding to the complexity is knowing that disclosure is not a one-time decision. Interests in disclosing change depending on life circumstances. People who decide to disclose today may change their mind in a few weeks. Although disclosure helps eradicate the stigma around mental health conditions, HOP encourages conservatism. Once the person is out, it is hard to go back.

Approaches to Disclosure

Research summarized in the HOP program shows that disclosure is described by five approaches (Herman, 1993); see Table 5. Each approach to disclosure also has its own costs and benefits. The first way to handle disclosure is social avoidance; namely, not telling anyone about one's experiences and actively avoiding situations where people may accidentally find out. People who choose social avoidance opt only to socialize and interact with others who have had similar experiences. However, social avoidance has risks because it perpetuates the belief that people with behavioral health challenges are different from the rest of the world and need to be kept away from others in society. Avoiding the outside world completely will result in limited access to a wide variety of opportunities and support systems.

A second approach is nondisclosure that involves keeping experiences private. By their very nature, mental illness and SUD are concealable identities. That is, one cannot tell just by looking at someone if they have a mental illness or SUD. Hence instead of avoiding situations altogether, people may choose the nondisclosure approach and keep their experiences private. A third approach to disclosure, selective disclosure involves disclosing experiences to a small set of people. This approach enables people to receive the support of others. Using this approach may also result in the person feeling "relieved" because they no longer have to conceal their experiences.

The next approach is the indiscriminant approach where individuals make no effort to hide their history and experiences. This does not involve telling everyone about addiction experiences. Instead, in this approach, people are comfortable discussing experiences when they come up naturally or when the time is right. People who choose this approach abandon the notion of secrecy and shame. They are not affected by potential negative consequences of their disclosure. For instance, "I got tired of wondering who knew and who didn't. I finally got to the point where I didn't care. I stopped trying to keep my past a secret. I stopped concealing my meds and doctors' appointments." Last is broadcasting one's experience. This kind of disclosure involves actively seeking out individuals with whom people can share their experiences. It also means educating the public about mental illness and addiction. Similar to the costs and benefits of disclosing, different approaches to disclosure have their own costs and benefits that should be carefully considered.

Testing Someone for Disclosure

People might choose to "test" someone to determine if they are a good person for disclosure. They can do this making a note of examples from recent news stories, magazine articles, or TV shows or movies related to mental illness or SUD and sharing it with a friend. The goal is to share something small: "Did you see the TV show *This is Us* with Justin Hartley? He portrayed a man who experiences a Vicodin addiction in attempts to manage his pain." This provides an opportunity to find out what the person thinks about SUD. The key is to share something benign; sharing something drastic like a death because of overdose can evoke strong stigmatizing reactions.

If they respond, "You know, I am sick and tired of these kinds of shows where they make addictions look so benign," they might not be a good candidate for disclosure. People who react negatively by showing disrespect, denial, or by gossiping may not be good candidates for disclosure. Alternatively, if someone responds, "I thought Justin Hartley portrayed struggles with addiction honestly," they might be a good person to disclose to. Generally, people with whom you have developed a supportive or empathic relationship are good candidates for disclosure. Supportive or empathic people are willing to listen and react with concern.

Crafting a Story

HOP also provides an outline that summarizes important elements of an impactful disclosure story. Disclosure stories contain two types of narratives: on-the-way-down versus on-the-way-up. On-the-way-down narratives include experiences of diagnoses, symptoms, and history. On-the-way-up stories are messages of recovery. Important details to include in a disclosure story are concrete personal experiences, listing achievements and accomplishments, and specifying how stigma has been a hurdle on the path to achieving goals. Providing specific examples enables listeners of the story to truly imagine what the experience must have been like. It also reinforces the belief that people with behavioral health conditions are capable and can attain life goals just like anybody else.

Research on HOP

A number of randomized controlled trials (RCTs) have demonstrated support for HOP as a way to reduce self-stigma in individuals with behavioral health conditions. HOP was shown to lead to reduction in participants' applying stigma messages to themselves, self-stigma harm, and stigma stress in adults who self-reported as having a mental health condition (Corrigan et al., 2015). Another RCT demonstrated that HOP participants experienced significant stigma stress reductions with the idea of disclosure, perceived benefits of disclosing, and the need to keep their identity a secret compared to the control group (Rüsch et al., 2014). An RCT of a modified HOP in people who had attempted suicide showed that participants who had completed HOP-suicide showed improvements in self-stigma, self-esteem, and depression (Sheehan et al., 2021). HOP has also been shown to be beneficial in young adults. It improved outcomes related to stigma stress, self-stigma, help seeking, disclosure intentions, and depression in young adults and college students (Conley et al., 2020; Mulfinger et al., 2018).

Adapting HOP for SUD

Although HOP was originally developed to address self-stigma in adults with mental illness, it has been adapted for different conditions like Tourette's syndrome and dementia (Corrigan et al., 2018). Community-based participatory research (CBPR) is used to facilitate such kinds of adaptations. In CBPR, community members with lived experience guide the research team through the adaptation process. Hence, programs meant to erase the stigma of addiction should be led by people with SUD. This could include people who are actively using and those in recovery. CBPR teams also include allies such as family and friends as well as service providers. Researchers bring the technical skills necessary to complete antistigma program development in a reliable and valid manner.

Disclosure of SUD is complicated by the criminalization of substances. Disclosing current use of controlled substances such as cocaine, opioids, or methamphetamines can result in facing legal actions and/or penalties. The criminalization of addictions worsens the stigma and often makes disclosure of SUD nearly impossible in some contexts. Further, under the Americans with Disabilities Act (ADA; 1990) people with mental health conditions who disclose can request accommodations such as taking time off for mental health appointments. However, the same opportunities are not available for people with SUDs. Individuals with addictions only qualify for ADA protections if they are enrolled in a treatment program or are no longer using substances (Corrigan et al., 2017).

There is also the issue of disclosure perceived differently across cultures. Research suggests that disclosure experiences may be influenced by local culture, for example individuals from individualistic countries in the West versus more collectivist countries in Asia (Berry-Cyprian et al., 2017). Researchers in China, for example, described how concealing mental health experiences preserves face (*lian*) and it preserves one's (and by extension, one's family's) dignity and reputation (Chen et al., 2013). As a result, disclosure may be discouraged because it is thought to disrupt social harmony and may burden another person, namely the listener. Collectivist cultures show a tendency for members to be more concerned with the consequence of one's behaviors to others and hence the costs and benefits of disclosure are likely to be viewed through this lens.

Another key issue that needs to be considered is the issue of intersectionality. In 2015, HOP was conducted for inmates in the Cook County Jail (CCJ). CCJ is one of the largest providers of behavioral health services in the United States. Findings highlighted how intersectionality challenges HOP. In addition to mental illness, many incarcerated participants had a co-occurring SUD, belonged to the LGBTQ community, and/or had HIV-AIDS. Stigma experienced by an African American with SUD and HIV who is incarcerated is more than the sum of their stigmatized identities. These identities and associated stigma are likely to interact in ways that may worsen the stigma of one condition over another. People may be more open to discussing costs and benefits of disclosing their mental illness but might be concerned about the stigma of SUD. Programs designed to address self-stigma of SUD should include considerations on intersectionality.

Disclosure and age are also an important factor to consider in the adaptation process. Young people might use online video chat or social media websites to share their experiences. Using online video platforms like Skype or Facetime gives people the ability to express emotion and to observe listener reactions. Another kind of social media is text messages, emails, or private messages on Facebook or Instagram. This medium makes disclosure less stressful because the person does not have to "look the other in the eye" to disclose; instead, they can disclose their experiences through a carefully thought-out message. However, these written messages can be passed on without the sender's knowledge.

A final category of social media is websites such as Twitter, Instagram, Facebook, blog posts, and TikTok. These kinds of websites allow the person to broadcast their experiences to a large/small group of people. Social media disclosure can result in receiving a lot of negative comments and disapproval from others and hence should only be used if the person is not fazed by who knows about their mental illness. Given the pros and cons of different e-disclosure options, individuals can decide how they wish to proceed with disclosure.

Other Interventions for Self-Stigma in SUD

Other efforts exist to reduce the self-stigma for SUD beyond disclosure. Livingston et al. (2012) conducted a review on stigma change interventions and found three interventions that targeted self-stigma. Luoma et al. (2008) demonstrated that group-based acceptance and commitment therapy (ACT) led to significant reductions in shame and internalized stigma in individuals with SUDs. ACT focuses on increasing psychological acceptance, and cognitive diffusion through techniques of mindfulness (Hayes et al., 1999). It teaches individuals to respond to thoughts of self-stigma in a way that does not obstruct recovery. An RCT by the National Institute on Drug Abuse (NIDA, 1978) tested the effects of an employment skills training intervention along with substance use treatment and found that it improved participants' view of society and decreased feelings of social alienation. Finally, an observational study by Shuster and Lewin (1968) suggested that surgically removing needle track marks may be beneficial for injection drug users in recovery.

Conclusion

The essence of disclosure is talking about one's experience with mental illness or substance use. Disclosure begins with identity. Identity may worsen or improve substance use and recovery. Identity also includes pride: being proud of one's accomplishments and authenticity. Given these factors, we developed HOP as a peer-led program to help people decide whether and how to disclose. HOP consists of three aims: weigh costs and benefits of disclosure, learn different approaches to disclosure, and learn ways to craft one's story. HOP has been supported by research from multiple studies.

References

Berry-Cyprian, D., Nelson, R., & Yang, B. (2017). Self-disclosure, culture and situational influence: An analysis of interracial interaction. *Concordia Journal of Communication Research*, *4*(1), Article 2.

Birtel, M. D., Wood, L., & Kempa, N. J. (2017). Stigma and social support in substance abuse: Implications for mental health and well-being. *Psychiatry Research*, *252*, 1–8.

Bos, A. E., Kanner, D., Muris, P., Janssen, B., & Mayer, B. (2009). Mental illness stigma and disclosure: Consequences of coming out of the closet. *Issues in Mental Health Nursing*, *30*(8), 509–513.

Broman-Fulks, J. J., Ruggiero, K. J., Hanson, R. F., et al. (2007). Sexual assault disclosure in relation to adolescent mental health: Results from the National Survey of Adolescents. *Journal of Clinical Child and Adolescent Psychology*, *36*(2), 260–266.

Buckingham, S. A., Frings, D., & Albery, I. P. (2013). Group membership and social identity in addiction recovery. *Psychology of Addictive Behaviors*, *27*(4), 1132–1140.

Chen, F. P., Lai, G. Y. C., & Yang, L. (2013). Mental illness disclosure in Chinese immigrant communities. *Journal of Counseling Psychology*, *60*(3), 379–391.

Conley, C. S., Hundert, C. G., Charles, J. L., et al. (2020). Honest, Open, Proud–College: Effectiveness of a peer-led small-group intervention for reducing the stigma of mental illness. *Stigma and Health*, *5*(2), 168–178.

Corrigan, P. W. (2018). *The stigma effect: Unintended consequences of mental health campaigns*. Columbia University Press.

Corrigan, P. W., Kosyluk, K. A., & Rüsch, N. (2013). Reducing self-stigma by coming out proud. *American Journal of Public Health*, *103*(5), 794–800.

Corrigan, P. W., Larson, J. E., Michaels, P. J., et al. (2015). Diminishing the self-stigma of mental illness by coming out proud. *Psychiatry Research*, *229*(1–2), 148–154.

Corrigan, P. W., Morris, S., Larson, J., et al. (2010). Self-stigma and coming out about one's mental illness. *Journal of Community Psychology, 38*(3), 259–275.

Corrigan, P. W., Rüsch, N., & Scior, K. (2018). Adapting disclosure programs to reduce the stigma of mental illness. *Psychiatric Services, 69*(7), 826–828.

Corrigan, P. W., Schomerus, G., & Smelson, D. (2017). Are some of the stigmas of addictions culturally sanctioned?. *The British Journal of Psychiatry, 210*(3), 180–181.

Dingle, G. A., Cruwys, T., & Frings, D. (2015). Social identities as pathways into and out of addiction. *Frontiers in Psychology, 6*, Article 1795.

Hayes, S. C., Strosahl, K., & Wilson, K. G. (1999). *Acceptance and commitment therapy: An experiential approach to behavior change*. Guilford.

Herman, N. J. (1993). Return to sender: Reintegrative stigma-management strategies of ex psychiatric patients. *Journal of Contemporary Ethnography, 22*(3), 295–330.

Hughes, K. (2007). Migrating identities: The relational constitution of drug use and addiction. *Sociology of Health & Illness, 29*(5), 673–691.

Livingston, J. D., Milne, T., Fang, M. L., & Amari, E. (2012). The effectiveness of interventions for reducing stigma related to substance use disorders: A systematic review. *Addiction, 107*(1), 39–50.

Luoma, J. B., Twohig, M. P., Waltz, T., et al. (2007). An investigation of stigma in individuals receiving treatment for substance abuse. *Addictive Behaviors, 32*(7), 1331–1346.

Luoma, J. B., Kohlenberg, B. S., Hayes, S. C., Bunting, K., & Rye, A. K. (2008). Reducing self-stigma in substance abuse through acceptance and commitment therapy: Model, manual development, and pilot outcomes. *Addiction Research & Theory, 16*(2), 149–165.

Lysaker, P. H., Davis, L. W., Warman, D. M., Strasburger, A., & Beattie, N. (2007). Stigma, social function and symptoms in schizophrenia and schizoaffective disorder: Associations across 6 months. *Psychiatry Research, 149*(1–3), 89–95.

Montes, K. S., Cruz, M. D., Weinstein, A. P., et al. (2021). Alcohol and marijuana protective behavioral strategies mediate the relationship between substance use identity and use-related outcomes: A multi-sample examination. *Addictive Behaviors, 112*, Article 106613.

Mulfinger, N., Müller, S., Böge, I., et al. (2018). Honest, Open, Proud for adolescents with mental illness: Pilot randomized controlled trial. *Journal of Child Psychology and Psychiatry, 59*(6), 684–691.

National Institute on Drug Abuse. (1978). *Services research report. Skills training and employment for ex-addicts in Washington, DC: A report on TREAT*. US Department of Health, Education, and Welfare. US Government Printing Office.

Oakes, P. J. (1987). The salience of social categories. In J. C. Turner, M. A. Hogg, P. J. Oakes, S. D. Rieche, & M. S. Wetherell (Eds.), *Rediscovering the social group: A self categorization theory* (pp. 117–141). Sage Publications.

Omarzu, J. (2000). A disclosure decision model: Determining how and when individuals will self-disclose. *Personality and Social Psychology Review, 4*(2), 174–185.

Quinn, D. M., Williams, M. K., Quintana, F., et al. (2014). Examining effects of anticipated stigma, centrality, salience, internalization, and outness on psychological distress for people with concealable stigmatized identities. *PLoS ONE, 9*(5), e96977.

Ruggiero, K. J., Smith, D. W., Hanson, R. F., et al. (2004). Is disclosure of childhood rape associated with mental health outcome? Results from the National Women's Study. *Child Maltreatment, 9*(1), 62–77.

Rüsch, N., Abbruzzese, E., Hagedorn, E., et al. (2014). Efficacy of Coming Out Proud to reduce stigma's impact among people with mental illness: Pilot randomised controlled trial. *The British Journal of Psychiatry, 204*(5), 391–397.

Rüsch, N., Corrigan, P. W., Wassel, A., et al. (2009). Self-stigma, group identification, perceived legitimacy of discrimination and mental health service use. *The British Journal of Psychiatry, 195*(6), 551–552.

Rüsch, N., Lieb, K., Bohus, M., & Corrigan, P. W. (2006). Self-stigma, empowerment, and perceived legitimacy of discrimination among women with mental illness. *Psychiatric Services, 57*(3), 399–402.

Sheehan, L., Oexle, N., Bushman, M., et al. (2021). To share or not to share? Evaluation of a strategic disclosure program for suicide attempt survivors. *Death Studies* [in press].

Shuster, M. M., & Lewin, M. L. (1968). Needle tracks in narcotic addicts. *New York State Journal of Medicine, 68*(24), 3129–3134.

Stephens, R. C., & McBride, D. C. (1976). Becoming a street addict. *Human Organization, 35*(1), 87–93.

Sullivan, G. B. (Ed.). (2014). *Understanding collective pride and group identity: New directions in emotion theory, research and practice*. Routledge.

Walters, G. D. (1996). Addiction and identity: Exploring the possibility of a relationship. *Psychology of Addictive Behaviors, 10*(1), 9–17.

Watson, A. C., Corrigan, P., Larson, J. E., & Sells, M. (2007). Self-stigma in people with mental illness. *Schizophrenia Bulletin, 33*(6), 1312–1318.

CHAPTER 11

The Role of Peers in SUD Stigma Change
A Personal Perspective

David McCartney

This chapter outlines the contribution of people with lived experience in combatting the stigma of substance use disorders (SUDs). A consistent finding of stigma research is that contact is important for change. Contact and peer involvement are very personal – both for those who make contact with someone they perceive to belong to a stigmatized group and, arguably, even more so for those who share their lived experience. In this chapter, it seemed appropriate for me to use my own lived experience to connect the available evidence on the role of peers in SUD stigma change.

Public Stigmatization

"Junkie Doc" – that's what the newspapers called me. When I saw my name in headlines and my picture on the front page of a national newspaper as I was about to start a new job ("Fury as addict lands key NHS post"), I plunged into a dark pool of shame. It didn't matter that I'd had a 20-year career as a general practitioner. It didn't matter that, at the time, I was developing a novel drug and alcohol rehabilitation program with the Scottish Government and setting up a team of nurses, therapists, and administrators. It didn't matter that I was more than two years into my recovery from substance dependence or that I had gone back to university to do a master's degree in alcohol and drug studies. All that mattered at that moment was the shame of having been a "junkie." I felt humiliated, worthless, and did not want to show my face in public. Worse, despite myself, a significant part of me felt that the stigmatization was deserved.

This scrutiny wasn't the only time I was stigmatized in the press. The same newspaper described me in a separate article as an "addict doctor." A broadsheet described me as "an ex-addict" who had been "clean for two years." The BBC described me as an "ex-addict." A Sunday tabloid, on which I was also front-page news, was so full of inaccuracies and discriminatory language that on receiving a complaint from me, the UK newspaper regulator, the Press Complaints Commission, forced an apology and the paper agreed to remove the article from its website.

The reason for the attention was related to the tragic death of a patient in whose care I had been involved. Press interest in the case was legitimate. However, I had been one of four doctors and several nurses involved in the care of the patient, but the only one paraded as an "addict" in the press, something that had no bearing on the circumstances. Was my experience typical? An analysis of representations of drug use and drug users in the British press (UK Drug Policy Commission, 2010) suggested that Scottish newspapers were no worse than elsewhere in the UK, but also found that professionals were mentioned more often than others, that drug users were more likely to be condemned than empathized with, and that the tabloids were the most critical.

Thirteen years later, I found myself sharing my personal story of addiction and recovery to an audience of academics, policymakers, and alcohol use disorder specialists at a European conference on alcohol policy. This time there was no shame – indeed I received positive and affirming feedback. A consequence of this self-disclosure was that I was asked to use my experience and contribute a chapter to this book. Traversing the distance between these two points has been quite a journey, moving to recovery while negotiating the stigma of SUD, and, to a lesser extent, the stigma applied to those in recovery.

The Journey

Many of my nonprofessional peers have experienced far more stigmatization than I have, and may have had fewer coping resources, but in this chapter I want to use my own observations, experience, and learning, as well as published evidence, to illustrate some of the problems and some potential remedies that I hope will be relevant more widely. The circumstances, context, and extent of the stigma I've experienced may be different from that of my patients, but how stigma has made me and them feel is the same. We are together in this.

Variations accepted, almost everyone suffering from an SUD will know stigma's pernicious touch – either from self-stigma or social or institutional stigma. Scotland has the worst drug death rate in Europe and much effort has gone into trying to tackle this. "Rights, Respect and Recovery," the Scottish Government's drug and alcohol strategy, identifies the barrier that stigma represents in tackling our nation's drug problems. The strategy says,

People who experience alcohol or drug problems, either through use or by association, often experience the most stigma in our society. Negative attitudes and stigma from society, from professionals within services, and self-stigmatisation, can be one of the biggest barriers to accessing treatment, community services and other activities. Stigma needs to be challenged across the sector and society. (The Scottish Government, 2018)

When thinking of personal examples of stigmatization, I struggled with two things. The first was which ones to use as examples, for there are plenty, and the second was how to narrate these in an even and balanced way without sounding like a victim. After all, these experiences are suffused with emotional resonances, even with the passing of time.

Stigma in Institutions

My recovery from SUD began properly during a four-month stay in a residential treatment setting. When I returned home there were multiple challenges to face. One of these was financial insecurity. Since I'd been a junior doctor, I'd had a sickness insurance policy with a medical insurer to provide income in the event of my being unable to work through illness. When I needed to call on it, during my treatment and early recovery, the insurers refused to pay out, despite medical certification from my general practitioner, meaning I had to go onto state benefits. Was that because I was suffering from an SUD rather than something more acceptable – a form of institutional stigma? Alcohol and other SUDs are not considered impairments that would qualify for protection under the United Kingdom's Equality Act 2010. SUDs with severe consequences that require long residential treatment and prevent return to work are by definition disabling, so does the law discriminate through stigmatizing legislation?

When I went for a medical examination to evidence that I was not fit to return to work, I had a taste of another example of institutional stigma that I'd heard about many times from my patients with SUDs. The medical certificate from my GP that I had presented to the Benefits Agency gave "addiction" as the reason for my inability to work. The doctor I saw did not make eye contact with me throughout the interview or during the cursory physical examination. There was no warmth or small talk. I recognized what was likely going on, but I was curious and wanted to see it and experience it as a patient. At the end of the interview, he asked me about my normal occupation. I told him I was a GP. Everything changed – eye contact, sympathy, and warmth were suddenly on show.

I was fascinated by this and although it was unpleasant, I felt quite humbled to have experienced it.

The journey back to work can be hard for anyone in recovery, but the regulatory hurdles (e.g., from the General Medical Council) that doctors and other professionals face are a specific part of the challenge. As I navigated uncharted waters, I was keen to get good advice from those I respected. One of these people I identified was a senior medic in a powerful role whom I'd known for many years. I knew he had heard about what I'd been going through. I tried to contact him on the phone, but he did not return my calls. I spoke with his secretary and asked for an appointment. He declined to see me several times, citing a variety of reasons, none of which made sense to me, but I persevered. Communicating through an intermediary, he set out several milestones he felt I had to reach before he would see me.

When I finally met with him, several months had passed. He told me that in his view "with your history" I'd never get back to working in general practice again. His counsel was to go back to training as a junior doctor in a different specialty and work my way back up the professional ladder. As Corrigan et al. (2005) point out, stigma can deny people opportunities, including those centrally important to most people – as well as employment. I was 44 years old at the time, had been a partner in practice for 15 years, an honorary senior clinical lecturer at Glasgow University, a medical writer, and an innovator in primary care. Retraining seemed incongruous and a waste of my skills. I realized quickly I was talking to the wrong person – this was bad advice, likely coming from a bad place.

Within a few weeks of my disheartening meeting, I was working in general practice once more. As the kind GP leader (the "right" person this time) who helped facilitate this said, "If we can't help our own when they are sick, how can we hope to effectively look after our patients?" As I write this, I am filled with emotion and gratitude toward my gracious and compassionate GP colleague. These two very different approaches highlight how stigmatizing attitudes can block recovery and how humanizing and supportive responses can catalyze it.

As I got back to work in primary care, I did start to retrain, but I did this by keeping my GP identity, experience, and skills, while developing a special interest in SUDs. I wanted to turn my own lived experience to some sort of good. My recovery had been transformational for me, but the patients I was treating in general practice did not have access the sort of expensive, intense, and lengthy residential treatment that I was privileged to receive. This sat uncomfortably with me.

I started a master's degree in alcohol and drug studies that led to my securing the position of tutor in a national training program for the management of drug dependence in primary care, run by the Royal College of General Practitioners in Scotland. Shortly after I'd been accepted, my appointment was questioned by the leader of my college on the grounds that my history of addiction and exposure in the newspapers could bring the college "into disrepute." Fortunately, a brave colleague spoke up on my behalf and I was able to go ahead.

Self-Stigmatization and the Role of Peers

Experiences like this reinforced for me that some saw my SUD as a moral failing from which there was no way back. I was in established recovery by this time, still being monitored and supported by an SUD psychiatrist. Despite this, it seemed recovery was not to be trusted. I felt that I slotted in nicely to Goffman's (1963) conceptualization of stigma - as if I had been "reduced from a whole person ... to a discounted one" (p. 3). Each time I had one of these experiences, a part of me regressed, my self-belief faltered, and a very vulnerable part of me spoke up in my head and said, "you are worthless." Such experiences and resulting self-stigmatization can lead to what Corrigan and colleagues (2009) call the "why try?" effect – a disempowering paralysis, limiting progress in various domains.

What got me through these early experiences of shame and what stopped me being paralyzed by them? I was beginning to understand that my self-stigmatization was reinforced by structural and social stigma. My self-efficacy was growing, and I was getting better at recognizing those negative self-messages as being unreliable and not to be trusted. But there was more to be addressed. I'd experienced a bewildering and terrifying loss of values as my addiction took hold. I'm not inherently dishonest, unreliable, uncommitted, and disloyal, but I became that way. In the late actor Robin William's words, I found that, in active addiction, "I was violating my standards faster than I could lower them." My behaviors were unacceptable to me, never mind to others. When you live like that, shame becomes a bedfellow.

Birtel and colleagues (2017) found that internalized shame and stigma for those with SUDs in treatment were mediators for both stigma and support, and that social support – for instance from family and friends – may reduce internalized stigma leading to improvements in self-esteem. This seemed to be true for me too, but by far the biggest help for me was the support of peers with lived experience of SUDs and recovery. While in residential treatment, I had become a member of an organization called the British Doctors and Dentists Group (BDDG) – a UK-wide system of peer support groups for doctors, dentists, and medical/dental students seeking or maintaining recovery from SUDs. In my local group there were other doctors who had suffered discrimination at the hands of the press in relation to their SUDs. There were still others who had faced employment discrimination but had surmounted the barriers. Because they had already been in the hole I found myself in and had managed to climb out of it, they were able to help me do the same.

Although the evidence base is emergent, there is evidence of mitigation of harms through peer support and a theoretical understanding has been developed. William White references this theoretical basis of peer support (White, 2009) laying out the conceptual frameworks and the "active ingredients." These include social psychology (commitment to change), group psychotherapy (altruism), social learning theory (enactive attainment), cognitive consistency theory (resolution of ambivalence), and self-psychology (alteration of personal identity). It is not hard to see that insights developed through personal experience of SUD and recovery may then help others going through similar circumstances. As White writes, "peer recovery support helps to remedy the inequality of power/authority, perceived invasiveness, role passivity, cost, inconvenience, and social stigma associated with professional help for severe alcohol or other drug problems" (p. 67).

It's not surprising that peer support may help in different ways to professional interventions in addressing stigma. Mead and MacNeil (2006), make the point that "in general, peer support has been defined by the fact that people who have like experiences can better relate and can consequently offer more authentic empathy and validation" (p. 29).

Contact (e.g., with peers) has been reliably found to be the most effective way of reducing stigma (Corrigan & Penn, 1999). In mental health research, contact has been found to have an immediate effect, which also persists in the short and medium term (Maunder & White, 2019) and this is being translated, to some extent, in policy and practice. In her report for the Scottish Government on drug user stigmatization, Nicola Singleton (2011) lays out a series of actions that may positively impact on the problem. One of these is the suggestion that government "support and promote self-help and mutual aid bodies and the nascent drug-user recovery communities as vehicles for reintegration" (p. 8). She makes the point, "Peer support is often a key component in achieving and sustaining recovery. Recovery communities can also provide a way of making recovery more visible and in this way challenging stigma and promoting greater public understanding of recovery" (p. 8).

Lived experience peer involvement can take place in treatment settings, at mutual aid groups, through advocacy and activism, and by sharing stories on social, written, and broadcast media. Many SUD treatment settings have now adopted peer support as an important component of the delivery model. According to Mead et al. (2001), "Peer support is a system of giving and receiving help founded on key principles of respect, shared responsibility, and mutual agreement of what is helpful" (p. 135). Distinct from medical models and mental health diagnostic labels, peer support depends on empathy and understanding through shared experiences.

Although there is a deficit of high-quality studies, evidence already exists to support the value of peer recovery support in individuals recovering from SUDs. In their review of published studies from 1995 to 2012, Sharon Reif and colleagues (2014), found that studies, "demonstrated reduced relapse rates, increased treatment retention, improved relationships with treatment providers and social supports, and increased overall satisfaction with the treatment experience" (p. 860).

Peer advocacy for, and by, those marginalized by SUDs (and even lived experience/recovery) is often done in tandem with family members and "visionary addiction treatment professionals" and owes much to the mental health recovery and advocacy movement (White, 2007). One of the goals of the new recovery advocacy movement is to "counter public attempts to dehumanise, objectify and demonise those with alcohol and other drug problems" (p. 698).

Lived Experience and Stigma

Looking at this from the other side, the Scottish Government acknowledges the role of people with lived experience in helping to highlight the impact of stigma.

> We have seen the rapid growth of recovery communities in Scotland which have grown up alongside existing peer-led mutual aid groups. This has added a new dimension to Scotland's response to alcohol and drug problems. It has enabled those involved to socialise, reduce isolation and support each other. It has also improved the overall understanding of addiction, and recovery, and the impact of stigma and discrimination. (The Scottish Government, 2018, p. 15)

In 2018, an advisory group to the Scottish Government invited representatives from the 120+ nonmutual aid indigenous recovery groups across

Scotland to an event to explore stigma and its impact. Two-thirds of the 350 participants self-identified as being in recovery. The other third identified as being "influencers." They discussed structural stigma (relating to harms coming from laws and policies), public stigma (negative responses to the stigmatized group), stigma by association with a stigmatized group, and internalized self-stigma (Partnership for Action on Drugs in Scotland [PADS], 2018). At the end of the event, there was consensus on actions that were likely to tackle stigma effectively. Peers in recovery determined that they would work with influencers, including teachers, employers, public services, and young people by sharing their stories. The "power of example" and meeting others in recovery could help with self-stigmatization, as could high visibility of lived experience in homelessness, and in treatment and recovery settings. Joining mutual aid fellowships and participating in national events, like recovery walks, were also seen as valid interventions.

Such activities may impact on stigma more widely, but could the very act of participation in advocacy and peer support actually provide some individual cushioning from stigma and discrimination? Ashford and colleagues found evidence suggesting that those individuals who believe they are stigmatized have less recovery capital and self-esteem than those who do not hold this belief (Ashford et al, 2019). Engaging in advocacy had impacts across a range of domains (e.g., reduced stigma, increased sense of self, sense of purpose and meaning) and was linked to both perceived benefits and harms. Benefits included mechanisms to change self and systems and support others, but also identified were the benefits to the public of witnessing successful recovery and helping to reduce societal stigma. There are downsides too. Harms included experiencing further stigma during advocacy, lack of self-care as a result of time spent on advocacy, and wider harms to the larger recovery movement and community when things went wrong.

Recovery with and without Peer Involvement

When I think of my own experience of recovery initiation, I can divide it into two phases, one with no peer involvement and one suffused with peer support. Initially when I asked for help through my GP, I entered a medical model of treatment where the focus was on detoxification, medications to assist abstinence, and support sessions with a nurse using cognitive behavioral therapy techniques. I was advised against engaging with mutual aid. The BDDG was not mentioned to me despite a meeting taking place close to the clinic I was attending. I asked about psychotherapy as I was aware that my early life experiences might be relevant, but it wasn't felt to be the right approach. Although I was grateful for the help I received, and some things got a bit better, sobriety at that point was a very unpleasant experience – with the anxiety and craving feeling intolerable over many months. I was not able to sustain my faltering recovery and I returned to use.

On relapse, when my problems increased precipitously, I took a different tack. I phoned a helpline that I'd seen advertised in the *British Medical Journal* – The Sick Doctors Trust. This time a doctor with lived experience of addiction and recovery answered my call. He empathized, told me his story, and in the telling gave me hope. I'm ashamed to say that other than a few encounters with patients in practice over the years, I'd never met anyone else who identified as being in recovery, never mind another recovering medical professional. This was a bit of a revelation; a few days later, at his suggestion I was in a therapeutic community residential treatment center where, after detox, the emphasis was on connecting with peers, holistic healing, and the generation of self-awareness. Essentially, the community of peers was the treatment. In groups and as a larger community, we shared our stories, we identified with one another, we worked on our problems, we challenged and supported each other, and we laughed, cried, and hugged. All of this was foreign to me, and I initially resisted it, but it turned out that it was exactly what I needed. My SUD had left me disengaged from myself and from others, my spirit low, my self-esteem in my boots; I needed reconnection. Residential treatment was one of the hardest things I've ever done, but in a few months, I felt transformed in my thinking, feelings, and behavior.

I had powerful experiences of the easing of shame and self-stigmatization through hearing others' stories. I was accepted and not judged by my peers. I began to feel reconnected with others. My fractured identity was beginning to heal and to change for the better. This experience of recovery as a process of beginning to heal, feeling shame diminish, and feeling reconnected to others more widely is clearly not restricted to middle-class doctors. In mutual aid meetings across the world, and in lived experience recovery organizations, people seeking recovery, and those in established recovery, meet to support and affirm each other and shame is dissolved in the process.

Shame can be a risk factor for relapse, but the management of shame takes place in community recovery programs (Sawer et al., 2019). That ability of peer support to help ease shame and stigma is powerful, in my experience. One of the main principles of progressing on the recovery journey is the process of moving out of drinking and using networks and transitioning to new networks supportive of recovery (Longabaugh et al., 2010). This allows the development of a positive identity and offers protection against exclusion and stigma. I have my own evidence of contact being the most effective way of tackling stigma. When I think back to my first ever attendance at the Doctors and Dentists mutual aid group, when I was still in residential treatment, there was a moment of epiphany. A member of the group shared his story. It was almost identical to my own. At the time, I was shackled into my own self-stigma. I felt I had let the profession down, that I was a bad doctor and a bad person. I wasn't only ashamed of my behavior; I was ashamed of who I was. When I heard a version of my own story, told honestly and without evidence of shame, I was astonished. I identified with this colleague and as a result I experienced the genesis of hope. The same experiences happened in nonprofessional mutual aid. Hope is not something that is easily manufactured or measured, but it is an essential element to the recovery journey and not always accessible in all of our treatment settings.

It is not only the shared experiences of SUDs and recovery that make the difference – other values and principles are at play. As White (2009) writes, "the most important dimensions of the peer relationship are emotional authenticity, humility, and the capacity to offer support from a position of moral equality" (p. 72).

Wider Impacts

There is evidence then that peer support and mutual aid can help in reducing self-stigma, but what part do peers and those with lived experience play in reducing professional, public, and institutional stigma?

Balasanova and colleagues (2020), noting the tendency for negative perspectives toward patients with SUDs to develop in in medical school students, found that attending an Alcoholics Anonymous meeting could challenge the students' stigmatizing attitudes. I have had my own opportunities to "come out" to medical students as a doctor in recovery.

Peer support had helped the process of my starting to speak up tentatively about my experiences – initially in the safe setting of places like the BDDG – but paradoxically so did the public outing of my SUD history in the newspapers. Once I'd recovered from the initial emotional turmoil, it seemed to me that there was little left to lose from talking publicly about my experiences of SUD and recovery. The first time I did so, in front of

200 medical students at Edinburgh University, I was nervous, but the shame was not overwhelming. I discovered from student feedback that some had been moved by my story and, like Balasavanova's medical students, it had challenged their thoughts around alcohol and drug dependence. Despite having given my talk many times over the years I still feel somewhat anxious about such personal disclosure. I feel it as I write this chapter. It can be a struggle to make decisions about if and when is the right time and place to disclose recovery stories. Earnshaw and colleagues (2019) found that recovering people grew more comfortable with disclosure over time and that it was easier with family and friends than with coworkers, the media, and in public settings. Those in recovery from opioid use disorder had the greatest reluctance to disclose, suggesting hierarchies of shame.

In my current work post, there is a fair amount of teaching for me and my colleagues. We routinely invite well-supported volunteers with lived experience to come with us when we are teaching medical, nursing, and psychology students. We encourage medical students to attend open mutual aid meetings. Elsewhere in Edinburgh, medical colleagues have included people with lived experience in the delivery of training for general practitioners. These peers participate as experts in recovery and sit as equals with the doctors, sharing aspects of their stories appropriately. In a randomized study, Flanagan et al. (2016) found that GPs who participated in one-hour sessions where peers presented photos and narratives of their recovery stories (from mental health problems) significantly reduced stigmatizing attitudes. In our experience, those parts of the training, where peers openly share their experiences, regularly get the highest feedback ratings. Narratives and personal evidence of recovery, in the form of a real person present in the room, bring hope and living evidence to bear.

It's also possible that this effect may impact on wider communities. Best (2016) presents evidence in favor of the positive impact of "a highly visible recovery community" in changing community attitudes and perceptions. He details how one such UK community, "challenged the assumption of the intractability of substance misuse and involvement in crime."

Potential Harms

But if such initiatives make a difference is it always positive? Does my anxiety relating to addressing second-year students in Edinburgh Medical School have a rational basis? William White, Bill Stauffer, and Danielle Tarino (White et al., 2020) warn against our stories "standing as superficial window dressings while discrimination remains pervasive". Instead, "our stories must support calls for institutional change." There are risks of unexpected outcomes to self and family of sharing one's story publicly that may end up not only having little effect on stigma but causing further harm. For instance, problems arise when the media have their own agendas that can be different from those who would share their experiences publicly. I am reminded of the impact of the stigmatizing newspaper coverage ("Junkie Doc") on my wider family.

Robert Ashford and colleagues (2019) found that harms for those engaging in peer advocacy included further experience of stigma (e.g., if an employer discovered their recovery status there was a risk of dismissal) and spending less time on self-care – "activities being time consuming and emotionally draining, leaving little time for personal relationships, loved ones, friends and self-help affiliations." A further risk is of harm to the wider recovery community/movement through co-opting the larger community with "personal agendas and seeking of celebrity through advocacy." Policy efforts can also be negatively impacted: "Policy makers are being educated by people who don't even necessarily agree with each other and are getting mixed messages" (p. 474).

As I write this chapter, I find myself thinking of the benefit to harm ratio of sharing my own experience as a loose framework for exploring the themes around the place of lived experience in tackling stigma. Is my motivation sound? I suspect it's almost certainly mixed. Could this cause more harm than good? I hope not, but I don't know.

Peer Support and Mutual Aid in Practice

When we established the therapeutic community residential rehabilitation service I currently work in, we knew we wanted to incorporate the support of peers with lived experience of SUDs and recovery (McCartney, 2011). In the early days this was informal, but eventually we were able to access resources to employ a lived experience peer coordinator and to firm up a training and supervision program for our volunteers. The issue of protecting the peer volunteers was foremost, although some of the risks were mitigated by the environment and closed nature of a therapeutic community. The program evaluated well – patients rated the peer support highly – but the impact of peer involvement appeared to be much more profound than simply that of improving patient satisfaction. In the year after the program was established, the completion rates for our three-month therapeutic community program increased from just over 60% to over 70%.

Now, I can't link this intervention causally to the outcome, but it does ring true, and we were certainly very happy to see the improvement.

We were able to test out some of the impact of our peer support program in a modest study (Van Melick et al., 2013). The analyzed interviews of peer supporters found evidence of a positive association between the size of the social network in recovery and positive recovery capital. The peer supporters gave positive evaluations of their experience and offered altruism as a main driver for their volunteering. Peers felt strengthened in their recovery by performing their role and felt quality of life was improved. One interesting finding was that peer supporters were themselves peer-supported, each: "typically linked to at least one high-functioning peer who is usually more experienced in their recovery journey" (p. 196).

Mutual aid groups like the anonymous fellowships and SMART Recovery are ubiquitous and provide peer-to-peer support. A recent Cochrane review of 12-step facilitation and Alcoholics Anonymous involvement (Kelly et al., 2020) found evidence of efficacy for such interventions similar to, or better than, other established professional approaches. The UK's Guidelines on Clinical Management of Drug Misuse and Dependence state: "Service users should be facilitated to link with mutual aid organisations such as Narcotics Anonymous, Cocaine Anonymous, Alcoholics Anonymous and SMART Recovery groups" (Department of Health, 2017). Peer-to-peer support is formalized in the sponsorship arrangement promoted in 12-step groups, where someone with longer recovery experience offers interpersonal support to another. Having a sponsor is associated with abstinence and better outcomes (Wendt et al., 2017), while being a sponsor increases social skills, competence, and self-awareness as well as improving well-being and positive social approval (McGovern et al., 2021). Assertive referral to mutual aid groups is likely to help maintain recovery and could very well help tackle self-sigma. Simple techniques to increase uptake of mutual aid are easy to establish and can be monitored and evaluated as quality measures for services.

Lived Experience Stigma

There is evidence of antipathy toward peer-to-peer support, certainly in the context of mutual aid groups – particularly 12-step groups – although criticism is often directed at the context rather than the individuals. In the edited book, *The Stigma of Addiction: An Essential Guide* (Avery & Avery,

2019) there is a section about mutual aid groups. The authors argue that 12-step mutual aid groups "perpetuate the stigma associated with" addiction (Richter et al., 2019, p. 99). They argue that they do this by having features that "run counter to a science-based understanding of the disease of addiction." Oddly, they do not mention the existing evidence base for the efficacy of mutual aid at the time of writing, since consolidated by the Cochrane Review (Kelly et al., 2020). They go on to say that the best practice for addiction care calls for treatment to be delivered by a qualified health care professional and that mutual aid groups stigmatize people through anonymity.

This perception of people with lived experience not helping things (or making them worse) was picked up by Professor Roy Robertson, a general practitioner and Professor of Addiction Medicine at Edinburgh University, in *Holyrood Magazine* in July 2019 (Robertson, 2019). Professor Robertson writes, "Scotland's policy for the last decade was an expansive and inclusive set of non-medical based recovery initiatives aimed at reducing the stigma in institutions and communities, encouraging peer support and lived experience input at all levels." He goes on,

> Creating an illusionary landscape of alternative treatments, inclusion, aspiration, opportunity and a stigma-free approach driven by graduates from adversity, who have had experience of drug dependency, rather than the graduates from specialist training with the experience of an evidenced-based guidelines driven and governance controlled, such as specialist trained doctors, nurses and pharmacists, is in the realms of fake news and alternative facts.

Views like this may be well intentioned in terms of urging us to stick with the scientific evidence base of what works, but the truth is that from a research perspective we do not yet know the impact of peer interventions in the reduction of stigma, and we need to better understand how peers may help achieve better treatment outcomes for those with SUDs. Perspectives like this also put people like me in a peculiar position: as graduates of both schools – lived experience and professional – where does that leave us? Although Byrne and Wykes (2020) warn against "muddying the waters" by mixing lived experience with professional roles, I like to think that those of us who are in this category have a depth of understanding that might elude some others. Ironically for a medic, my experience of the medical model was that it could not meet my needs on its own. As it turned out, I needed a much more comprehensive approach where peer connections, narratives, experience, and support were major factors. Without these, I am not sure if I would have recovered.

What is it like for peers with lived experience in treatment environments? Byrne et al. (2019) interviewed 13 lived experience practitioners in mental health settings and found that stigma and discrimination were accepted as a "normal" part of working life. Emergent themes from those with lived experience included being asked inappropriate questions by colleagues, lack of differentiation from current service users, being undervalued, and experiencing professional isolation. Byrne and Wykes (2020) report, "the established medical paradigm largely continues to resist the involvement of lived experience, with considerable push back and unwillingness to engage still occurring" (p. 243). In order to counter views where the value of peers with lived experience is diminished to the level of "fake news," and where strong arguments and practices are made to keep to a "professional knows best" mentality, the framing of stigma and discrimination as social injustice is likely to help. Unfortunately, as it can be the institutional norms within medical SUD treatment that risk harming peers with lived experience, the concept of structural stigma seems particularly suited to explain their stigma experiences.

The Scottish Government's drug and alcohol strategy, "Rights, Respect and Recovery" (The Scottish Government, 2018) takes a human rights–based approach, stating: "Everyone has the right to health and to live free from the harms of alcohol and drugs. Everyone has the right to be treated with respect and dignity and for their individual recovery journey to be fully supported." Recognizing stigma as a significant issue, the strategy suggests that "through an increasing visibility of recovery, we can begin to tackle some of the issues of stigma and discrimination that affect so many individuals and family members." As stigma negatively impacts on treatment access and retention, it is crucial that recovering individuals and their families are both visible and heard. Discrimination and social justice are not compatible.

Moving Forward

We need to be gathering evidence more robustly and examine the role of hope in recovery. Having experienced years of substance dependence and then embarking on a process of recovery that was both personal and shared with others, my views on what is possible for my patients have changed. It's fair to say as a GP in inner city practice, while I think I was compassionate, I had fairly low aspirations for my patients with SUDs. Finding recovery and in the process meeting hundreds of other recovering people – "visible recovery" – raised the bar in terms of my expectation, and of what is possible when we hold higher hopes for our patients.

Currently practice is underdeveloped in SUD treatment and support settings, but this is changing. Parliamentarians here in Scotland are clear that they want to listen to those with lived experience as part of policy making. Indeed, there is evidence of this in operation. In the action plan (The Scottish Government, 2019) for the Scottish Government's drug and alcohol policy, "Rights, Respect and Recovery," there is a commitment to tackle stigma – "We will establish an expert group to develop a programme of work to address the stigma experienced by all people affected by problem alcohol and drug use including family members." The same paper is clear on how this can be actioned as the government commits to: "Work with key experts, including those with lived and living experience to address stigma as a way to prevent and reduce related harm." We are in a changing and developing landscape. In Scotland, as elsewhere, many people are calling for SUDs to be treated as a public health issue rather than a criminal justice one. Advocacy voices are being heard on social media, TV, and radio. There is a social rights, perhaps even civil rights, movement abroad. A significant proportion of those fighting for better outcomes are people with current and past experience of problem and nonproblem substance use and those identifying as in recovery.

We need more research in this area. Corrigan and colleagues (2017) suggest the relatively small and mostly descriptive literature on SUD stigma contrasts with research on mental health stigma. They lay out recommendations to tackle both public and self-stigma. In their systematic review of peer support "at the intersection of homelessness and substance use services," Miler and colleagues (2020, p. 1) note the growing acceptance of the unique place of peers in such services, including their capacity to create effective support and trust, based on "shared experience and lack of judgement" (p. 13). This capacity is increasingly valued, though is not without challenges as we have seen (Byrne et al., 2019). The planned integration of peer-to-peer support services and mutual aid interventions should be part of recovery-oriented systems of care (Kaplan, 2008). Such elements are likely to lead to amelioration of stigmatization in systems, though we must not lose sight of the importance of evaluating this as we go. Miler et al. (2020) lay out some guidelines both for research and also to help avoid problems when integrating peers formally into services.

The Fruits of Recovery

There is an irony about the fruits of recovery that I have experienced profoundly. In recovery, with help from others, I founded a residential rehabilitation service and, as I write, I am chairing a group set up by the Scottish Government to help improve access, capacity, and outcomes from residential rehabilitation. I would not have done either of these things had it not been for my experience of addiction and recovery. Even my personal experiences of feeling stigmatized have been worked through and learning has helped me move on. Again ironically, as I write, I have been quoted in the press in a positive light in relation to work done for the Scottish Government. Crucially, I could not have done this work without the peer-to-peer support that has underpinned my recovery. Perhaps my own guilt around my behaviors in active addiction pushed me into action as a form of redemption or amends, but I believe there is a stronger force at play. It comes from gratitude of finding a way out of a severe SUD, it comes from peers who have recovered ahead of me who gave me hope, and it comes from understanding more about what helps in the transformational process of recovery.

Summary

Stigmatization, whether it comes from self, society, or institutions, is damaging. The very act of recalling my own examples has felt traumatic and emotional at times, though I am also grateful for the learning that comes from such experiences. There are various strategies to tackle stigma, but evidence suggests that the most effective is through contact. While evidence on the role and impact on stigma of peers with lived experience of SUDs and recovery is emergent, there are grounds for hope that peer involvement can make positive impacts across all of the domains of stigmatization. This may be done through advocacy and campaigning, the sharing of narratives, integration of peers into treatment and support settings, and assertive referral to mutual aid of those seeking help. Further research in this area will help to identify impact and inform practice.

References

Ashford, R. D., Brown, A. M., Canode, B., McDaniel J., & Curtis B. (2019). A mixed-methods exploration of the role and impact of stigma and advocacy on substance use disorder recovery. *Alcoholism Treatment Quarterly, 37*(4), 462–480. https://doi.org/10.1080/07347324.2019.1585216

Avery, J. D., & Avery, J. J. (2019). *The stigma of addiction: An essential guide.* Springer.

Balasanova, A. A., MacArthur, K. R., & DeLizza, A. A. (2020). "From all walks of life": Attending an Alcoholics Anonymous meeting to reduce addiction stigma among medical students. *Academic Psychiatry, 44*(6), 714–720. https://doi.org/10.1007/s40596-020-01302-0

Best, D. (2016). An unlikely hero? Challenging stigma through community engagement. *Drugs and Alcohol Today*, *16*(1), 106–116. http://dx.doi.org/10.1108/DAT-09-2015-0054

Birtel, M. D., Wood, L., & Kempa, N. J. (2017). Stigma and social support in substance abuse: Implications for mental health and well-being. *Psychiatry Research*, *252*, 1–8. https://doi.org/10.1016/j.psychres.2017.01.097

Byrne, L., Roper, C., Happell, B., & Reid-Searl, K. (2019). The stigma of identifying as having a lived experience runs before me: Challenges for lived experience roles. *Journal of Mental Health*, *28*(3), 260–266. https://doi.org/10.1080/09638237.2016.1244715

Byrne, L., & Wykes, T. (2020). A role for lived experience mental health leadership in the age of Covid-19. *Journal of Mental Health*, *29*(3), 243–246. https://doi.org/10.1080/09638237.2020.1766002

Corrigan, P. W., Kerr, A., & Knudsen, L. (2005). The stigma of mental illness: Explanatory models and methods for change. *Applied and Preventive Psychology*, *11*(3), 179–190. https://doi.org/10.1016/j.appsy.2005.07.001

Corrigan, P. W., Larson, J. E., & Rüsch, N. (2009). Self-stigma and the "why try" effect: Impact on life goals and evidence-based practices. *World Psychiatry: Official journal of the World Psychiatric Association (WPA)*, *8*(2), 75–81. https://doi.org/10.1002/j.2051-5545.2009.tb00218.x

Corrigan, P. W., & Penn, D. L. (1999). Lessons from social psychology on discrediting psychiatric stigma. *The American Psychologist*, *54*(9), 765–776. https://doi.org/10.1037//0003-066x.54.9.765

Corrigan, P. W., Schomerus, G., Shuman, V., et al. (2017). Developing a research agenda for reducing the stigma of addictions, part II: Lessons from the mental health stigma literature. *The American Journal on Addictions*, *26*(1), 67–74. https://doi.org/10.1111/ajad.12436

Department of Health. (2017). *Clinical guidelines on drug misuse and dependence: UK guidelines on clinical management*. Independent Expert Working Group. https://assets.publishing.service.gov.uk/government/uploads/system/uploads/attachment_data/file/673978/clinical_guidelines_2017.pdf

Earnshaw, V. A., Bergman, B. G., & Kelly, J. F. (2019). Whether, when, and to whom?: An investigation of comfort with disclosing alcohol and other drug histories in a nationally representative sample of recovering persons. *Journal of Substance Abuse Treatment*, *101*, 29–37. https://doi.org/10.1016/j.jsat.2019.03.005

Flanagan, E. H., Buck, T., Gamble, A., Hunter, C., Sewell, I., & Davidson, L. (2016). "Recovery speaks": A photovoice intervention to reduce stigma among primary care providers. *Psychiatric Services (Washington, D.C.)*, *67*(5), 566–569. https://doi.org/10.1176/appi.ps.201500049

Goffman, E. (1963). *Stigma: Notes on the management of spoiled identity*. Penguin.

Kaplan, L. (2008). *The role of recovery support services in recovery-oriented systems of care* [White paper]. Center for Substance Abuse Services, Substance Abuse and Mental Health Services Administration.

Kelly, J. F., Humphreys, K., & Ferri, M. (2020). Alcoholics Anonymous and other 12-step programs for alcohol use disorder. *The Cochrane database of*

Systematic Reviews, 3(3), Article CD012880. https://doi.org/10.1002/14651858.CD012880.pub2

Longabaugh, R., Wirtz, P. W., Zywiak, W. H., & O'Malley, S. S. (2010). Network support as a prognostic indicator of drinking outcomes: The COMBINE Study. *Journal of Studies on Alcohol and Drugs, 71*(6), 837–846. https://doi.org/10.15288/jsad.2010.71.837

Maunder, R. D., & White, F. A. (2019). Intergroup contact and mental health stigma: A comparative effectiveness meta-analysis. *Clinical Psychology Review, 72*, Article 101749. https://doi.org/10.1016/j.cpr.2019.101749

McCartney, D. (2011). LEAP and the recovery community in Edinburgh. *Journal of Groups in Addiction & Recovery, 6*(1–2), 60–75. https://doi.org/10.1080/1556035X.2011.570554

McGovern, W., Addison, M., & McGovern, R. (2021). An exploration of the psycho-social benefits of providing sponsorship and supporting others in traditional 12 step, self-help groups. *International Journal of Environmental Research and Public Health, 18*(5), Article 2208. https://doi.org/10.3390/ijerph18052208

Mead, S., Hilton, D., & Curtis, L. (2001). Peer support: A theoretical perspective. *Psychiatric Rehabilitation Journal, 25*(2), 134–141. https://doi.org/10.1037/h0095032

Mead, S., & MacNeil, C. (2006). Peer support: What makes it unique? *International Journal of Psychosocial Rehabilitation, 10*(2), 29–37.

Miler, J. A., Carver, H., Foster, R., & Parkes, T. (2020). Provision of peer support at the intersection of homelessness and problem substance use services: A systematic "state of the art" review. *BMC Public Health, 20*(1), 641–618. http://doi.org/10.1186/s12889-020-8407-4

PADS. (2018). *Recovering Connections: Changing stigma to respect.* Partnership for Action on Drugs in Scotland, Communities subgroup. www.sfad.org.uk/content/uploads/2018/05/PADS-S2R-final.pdf

Reif, S., Braude, L., Lyman, D. R., et al. (2014). Peer recovery support for individuals with substance use disorders: Assessing the evidence. *Psychiatric Services (Washington, D.C.), 65*(7), 853–861. https://doi.org/10.1176/appi.ps.201400047

Richter, L., Vuolo, L., & Salmassi, M. S. (2019). Stigma and addiction treatment. In J. D. Avery & J. J. Avery (Eds.), *The stigma of addiction: An essential guide* (pp. 93–130). Springer.

Robertson, R. (2019, July 19). *Who owns the drug problem, and who is to be bold?* www.holyrood.com/comment/view,who-owns-the-drug-problem-and-who-is-to-be-bold_10596.htm

Sawer, F., Davis, P., & Gleeson, K. (2019). Is shame a barrier to sobriety? A narrative analysis of those in recovery. *Drugs Education, Prevention and Policy, 27*(1), 79–85. http://doi.org/10.1080/09687637.2019.1572071

Singleton, N. (2011). *Getting serious about stigma in Scotland: The problem with stigmatising drug users.* UK Drug Policy Commission. www.ukdpc.org.uk/wp-content/uploads/Policy%20report%20-%20Getting%20serious%20about

%20stigma%20in%20Scotland_%20the%20problem%20with%20stigma tising%20drug%20users.pdf

The Scottish Government. (2018). *Rights, Respect and Recovery: Scotland's strategy to improve health by preventing and reducing alcohol and drug use, harm and related deaths.* www.gov.scot/publications/rights-respect-recovery/

(2019). *Rights, Respect and Recovery: Action plan.* www.gov.scot/publications/rights-respect-and-recovery-action-plan/

UK Drug Policy Commission. (2010). *Representations of drug use and drug users in the British press.* www.ukdpc.org.uk/wp-content/uploads/Evidence%20review%20-%20Representations%20of%20drug%20use%20and%20drug%20users%20in%20the%20British%20press.pdf

Van Melick, M., McCartney, D., & Best, D. (2013). Ongoing recovery support and peer networks: A preliminary investigation of recovery peer supporters and their peers. *Journal of Groups in Addiction & Recovery, 8*(3), 185–199. https://doi.org/10.1080/1556035X.2013.785211

Wendt, D. C., Hallgren, K. A., Daley, D. C., & Donovan, D. M. (2017). Predictors and outcomes of twelve-step sponsorship of stimulant users: Secondary analyses of a multisite randomized clinical trial. *Journal of Studies on Alcohol and Drugs, 78*(2), 287–295. https://doi.org/10.15288/jsad.2017.78.287

White, W. L. (2007). The new recovery advocacy movement in America. *Addiction, 102*(5), 696–703. https://doi.org/10.1111/j.1360-0443.2007.01808.x

(2009). *Peer-based addiction recovery support: History, theory, practice, and scientific evaluation.* Chicago, Great Lakes Addiction Technology Transfer Center, and Philadelphia, Philadelphia Department of Behavioral Health and Intellectual Disability Services.

White, W., Stauffer, B., & Tarino, D. (2020). *Personal privacy and public recovery advocacy.* www.williamwhitepapers.com/blog/2020/11/personal-privacy-and-public-recovery-advocacy-bill-white-bill-stauffer-and-danielle-tarino.html

CHAPTER 12

The Role of Media Reporting for Substance Use Stigma

Eva Baumann, Philip Horsfield, Anna Freytag, and Georg Schomerus

The Mass Media's Role in Shaping Public Opinion toward Mental Disorders and Substance Use Disorders

What people know and how they think about mental health-related issues, how they try to make sense of drug use, addiction, consumption practices, and risk behaviors, is considerably influenced by the way the topic is talked about and framed in their social environment. Besides interpersonal conversations, the media serve as an important source for health information in general (Johnson & Case, 2013) and mental health issues as well as substance use in particular (Borinstein, 1992; Nelson et al., 2015).

In mental health-related information-seeking, the Internet plays an important role as a source for information, especially among those who already use online devices (Eichenberg et al., 2013). Particularly those with mental health challenges, former or current mental health problems, or people with psychological distress turn to the Internet for seeking information and getting support regarding their mental health (Gowen, 2013; Powell & Clarke, 2006). But even if the topic is outside people's immediate lives, media reports on social reality, behaviors, problems, and experiences of distant others allow for vicarious experiences and the witnessing of events (Frosh & Pinchevski, 2009). As a cultural resource, the media can also act as a resource in individuals' attempts to legitimize their own behavior (Lundahl, 2020).

Moreover, media coverage of mental health-related issues and substance use disorders (SUDs) not only influences the public's and policy makers' attitudes and beliefs but also reflects what people think about these issues (Seale, 2002). Thus, the relationship between media portrayals, public opinion, and policymaking appears not to be one-directional but rather reciprocal (Chapman & Lupton, 1994).

Concerning mental illness in general, and SUDs in particular, the media's role appears crucial. If certain health-related issues, such as

SUDs, receive more news media coverage than others, the media agenda influences the public's perception that this issue appears as a particularly pressing societal problem (Fan, 1996). This agenda-setting and priming effect (Scheufele & Tewksbury, 2007) may shape the public's opinion and the people's perceptions and expectations of social reality (McGinty, Kennedy-Hendricks, & Barry, 2019).

Research has revealed that inaccurate, sensationalist, or negatively connotated media representations of SUDs and the people who suffer from them, as well as the language and terminology used therein, play an important role in shaping a distorted view on the problem and in directing stigmatizing public attitudes (Botticelli & Koh, 2016; Goodyear et al., 2018; Kelly et al., 2016; Richter & Foster, 2014; Seidel et al., 2017; Wakeman, 2013, 2017). Thus, if people with an addiction (especially to illicit drugs) are portrayed in the context of crime, immorality, uncontrollability of behavior, and personal weakness, the media may influence individuals' cognitive patterns, attitudes, and behavioral intentions. They thus form public perceptions and attitudes that generate and reinforce the stigma of addiction and thereby possibly promote stigmatizing, discriminating behaviors (Ayers & Myers, 2012; Hughes et al., 2010, 2011; Lancaster et al., 2012; Nunez-Smith et al., 2010).

These false perceptions and stereotypes not only create an additional psychological burden for those affected and their relatives, but they also increase self-stigmatization and may have a negative impact on help-seeking behaviors (Avery & Avery, 2019; Fraser et al., 2017). Hence, media coverage can exacerbate the harm that SUDs cause to those affected and the communities in which they live. This emphasizes the importance of focusing on the way the media cover the issue – how they frame the illness itself and the people suffering from SUDs.

Journalistic News Selection, Media Frames, and Framing of Mental Health Issues

As outlined in the section above, mass media provide a particularly important source for information about mental health to the public (Borinstein, 1992). But due to limited space and time in the media, and also due to limited cognitive capacities and awareness of their audiences, journalists have to select topics for publication based on certain news values (Galtung & Ruge, 1965). Illicit drugs are known to be newsworthy (Hughes et al., 2010), and "the availability of a case study, problems to expose, areas of unmet need to highlight, involvement of high-profile people, tragedy, controversy and new research" (Holland, 2018, p. 1774) have been identified as key factors that make mental health issues interesting for journalists. In the context of SUDs, negativism, conflicts, and crime appear as obvious additional factors that journalists use as selection criteria of news reporting (Kay-Lambkin et al., 2019).

The way journalists report on health issues does not reflect reality one-to-one. As media coverage can never present events or phenomena of reality in their whole complexity, the media always reduce the issue to a certain perspective, select and define relevant aspects of perceived reality, and make them more salient than others (Entman, 1993). This process of selecting and emphasizing specific aspects of an issue always leads to a specific perspective on the topic and on the people involved. By focusing on "a particular problem definition, causal interpretation, moral evaluation, and/or treatment recommendation" (Entman, 1993, p. 52), journalists create frames as patterns of interpretation, thereby constructing reality and adding coherence to the issue. A frame can be defined as a "central organizing idea or storyline that provides meaning to an unfolding strip of events, weaving a connection among them. The frame suggests what the controversy is about, the essence of the issue" (Gamson & Modigliani, 1987, p. 143).

The public, meanwhile, recognizes those frames, makes sense of them through their own preexisting models and personal experiences, and uses them to understand the world they live in (Entman et al., 2009). Thus, the media can play a significant role in the way people perceive mental disorders and persons affected and on what they think and know about mental health (Dorfman et al., 2005). This framing effect particularly occurs if people neither have their own direct experiences with mental health issues nor are in touch with people suffering from a mental disorder.

Regarding mental health, it must be assumed that the way the mass media frame mental health and disorders is predominantly negative while protective factors – positive, salutogenic (health- and prevention-oriented) aspects – are a less important issue in the media. Instead, the mass media mostly cover the issue from a pathogenetic, risk- and problem-oriented perspective, emphasizing the dangerousness and peculiarities of people affected and often report in the context of violence and crime (Aragonès et al., 2014; Coverdale et al., 2002; Klin & Lemish, 2008; McGinty et al., 2014; Slopen et al., 2007). This suggests social distance from the out-group, that is, people with mental disorders who are often being held individually responsible for being affected while neglecting social and structural factors (Aragonès et al., 2014; Zhang et al., 2016). Further, media coverage of mental disorders is estimated to predominantly convey a perspective that rather perpetuates misinformation, misconceptions, and stigma instead of emphasizing the importance of social coherence and increasing resilience- and prevention-oriented beliefs (Aragonès et al., 2014; Coverdale et al., 2002; Henson et al., 2009; Klin & Lemish, 2008).

Media Coverage of Illicit Drugs and Other SUDs

Overall, there is evidence that illicit drug use, SUDs, and people with addiction are covered in a rather unfavorable way in the news media by "emphasizing negative traits, such as weak moral character or propensity for violence" (McGinty, Kennedy-Hendricks, & Barry, 2019, p. 205). Content analyses of newspaper coverage of illicit drugs and drug addiction have shown that media reporting is distorted toward a criminal and deviance framing and that drug addiction is portrayed in a negative light emphasizing individuals' dangerousness, responsibility, and culpability (Hughes et al., 2011; Taylor, 2008). News coverage on the opioid epidemic "polarizes individuals as good or bad with little attention paid to underlying institutional interests both in the creation of the problem or in the solutions that are proposed" (Webster et al., 2020, p. 1). Taylor (2008) suggests that news media coverage and governmental beliefs mirror each other, both focusing on drug use as a serious problem that is dangerous and causes further criminality. McGinty et al. (2016) revealed that media often frame opioid abuse as a criminal justice issue with claims for law enforcement solutions to arrest and prosecute responsible individuals, while prevention-oriented approaches are scarce.

A systematic review by Kay-Lambkin et al. (2019) of 30 Australian and international research studies on media portrayals and framings of drug use, drug users, and SUDs revealed a pronounced focus on sensationalist and alarmist framings with links to crime, violence, moral weakness, legal issues/consequences, drug seizures, and an inevitability of negative outcomes when people use drugs, at the expense of reporting on education, prevention, and early intervention and treatment. The review also concluded a strong degree of media exaggeration, in that "the reported rise of [alcohol or drug] use was often disproportionate to the actual size of the problem and was frequently inconsistent with the evidence, and shaped public perceptions and anxiety about the drug of concern" (Kay-Lambkin et al., 2019, p. 16).

A frame analysis of US television news reports about heroin and cocaine use by Orsini (2017) revealed that narratives on drug-related danger and violence were common and predominantly appeared in contexts of crime, deviance, and tragedy. By contrast, narratives focusing on public health and harm reduction, decriminalization, or legalization of illicit substances were lacking (Orsini, 2017). The predominant frames focused on drug busts and ongoing physical violence, on dangerous use, and violent traffickers or were narratives about "fallen stars." The author concluded that "media framing has not evolved substantially from the stigmatizing representations prevalent in the 1980s and 1990s US media reports" (Orsini, 2017, p. 189). Also, media framing in Iranian national television has turned out not to accurately present the social reality of addiction due to censorship and framing of addiction in line with governmental and political beliefs (Afzali et al., 2020).

Some studies show that illicit drugs and substances are evaluated more negatively and framed more narrowly than others. While heroin, for example, is often reported in the context of legal problems, ecstasy and cocaine are more likely to be reflected as health and social problems (Hughes et al., 2011). Netherland and Hansen (2016) found a consistent contrast in popular press articles with criminalized urban black and Hispanic heroin injectors on the one hand and sympathetic portrayals of suburban white prescription opioid users on the other hand.

Another important facet of media framing of SUDs refers to the way the stories are told. Research has shown that drug stories are framed episodically rather than thematically (Jernigan & Dorfman, 1996). That means journalists depict events through the perspective of individuals, often using personal exemplars and individual narratives (McGinty, Kennedy-Hendricks, & Barry, 2019). They emphasize the individuals' responsibility for the problem and put less attention on structural as well as societal facilitators and triggers that can facilitate the audiences to neglect structural and systemic factors in their perceptions of the social problem (Iyengar, 1996).

Another key issue is that language contributes to the development, perpetuation, and reinforcement of public stigma toward people with SUDs (Seidel et al., 2017). McGinty et al. (2018) have shown that the proportion of news stories mentioning stigmatizing terms is high overall and increased from 37% in 2008 to 45% in 2018. Referring to someone as a "substance abuser" is suggestive of willful misconduct, while the term "person with a substance abuse disorder" places the behavior beyond their control (Kelly et al., 2015, 2016). It has also been confirmed that persons with SUDs prefer person-first language (Pivovarova & Stein, 2019). Vignette studies have further revealed that, beyond general public attitudes

(Goodyear et al., 2018), attitudes among clinicians and policy makers were significantly more negative when the vignette described the person as an "addict" or an "abuser" rather than a "person with a substance use disorder" (Kelly et al., 2015; Kelly & Westerhoff, 2010). This impact of language on the attitudes of medical professionals and policy makers ties into the notion of structural discrimination, a matter that still receives little attention. Thus, it is important to use accurate and nonstigmatizing terminology and person-first language (Kelly et al., 2015, 2016; Richter & Foster, 2014).

The stigma surrounding SUDs not only refers to media portrayal in the news but also in fictional and nonfictional entertainment media that can also have an impact on how people view themselves and how they are viewed by others. For example, in a content analysis of the reality TV show "The Osbournes," most messages referring to alcohol and tobacco consumption implied approval for using these substances, while drug use messages rather implied rejection (Blair et al., 2005).

Even though media ecology and news media consumption have rapidly changed in the past decades with social network sites becoming more and more essential to how people select and experience news (Bergström & Jervelycke Belfrage, 2018), there is only little evidence on content and impact of social media and online media portrayals of alcohol consumption and other drug use (Kay-Lambkin et al., 2019; McGinty, Stone, et al., 2019). Russell and colleagues (2020) recently conducted a study on news posts and comments on the Facebook pages of US newspapers and showed that the majority of commenters addressed opioid addiction as a legitimate social problem that warrants intervention and support. But there was also a substantial amount of dismissive comments expressing anger and contempt for people using opioids (Russell et al., 2020).

Overall, there is some ambiguity in research findings on media coverage of illicit drug addiction and SUDs that should also be mentioned here: at least in terms of quantity, it should be noted that some content analyses conclude that most reports are written neutrally and are less sensationalizing and biased than often suggested (Hughes et al., 2010, 2011). Against this backdrop, and in light of the many predictors and risk factors at play in the development and perpetuation of SUD stigma, efforts to promote nonstigmatizing media reporting practices need to be situated within a broader, more holistic destigmatization strategy. This is all the more important as research has already revealed that media depictions "emphasizing positive traits, such as perseverance and determination in the face of adversity and/or successful recovery" have the power to reduce stigma if the issue is framed appropriately (McGinty, Kennedy-Hendricks, & Barry, 2019, p. 205) and if adequate language and terminology is used (Atayde et al., 2021). For example, it has been shown that media exposure can lead to more positive drug-related dispositions, such as regarding the attitude that too little money is spent to address addiction (Nielsen & Bonn, 2008).

McGinty et al. (2015) examined the impact of portraying addiction as "treatable" on stigmatizing attitudes. Their results suggest that vignettes featuring persons with successfully treated addictions were associated with a "lower desire for social distance, greater belief in the effectiveness of treatment and less willingness to discriminate against persons with [those] conditions" (McGinty et al., 2015, p. 73). Thus, the importance and stigma-reducing potential of adequate media portrayals are obvious, and research underlines the need for significant efforts to reframe the portrayal of SUDs in the media. Communication efforts should take into account that parasocial contact and vicarious experience via media narratives can contribute to a decrease in stereotypes as well as stigmatizing attitudes and behaviors (McKeever, 2015; Schiappa et al., 2005; Wong et al., 2017).

Content and Objectives of Selected Media Guidelines

As described above, research on the media's role in the stigmatization of SUDs and people affected with these disorders emphasizes that the media bear a responsibility toward society and public health. Hence, there is a clear need for sensitizing journalists and their way of covering mental illnesses in general and SUDs in particular. However, journalists need to be supported and motivated in reporting on drug use, drug users, and SUDs in an accurate, balanced, and responsible manner (Kay-Lambkin et al., 2019).

Media guidelines can provide recommendations on adequate expressions and on how to report in a nonstigmatizing, evidence-led manner. They can provide journalists with (sometimes extensive) scientific evidence and credible resources for reference as journalists should more closely align the framing of their stories with the scientific and statistical evidence (Kay-Lambkin et al., 2019).

Over the past decades, in anglophone countries, several guidelines and resources directed at journalists, editors, and other opinion leaders have been published to counter stigmatizing media reporting practices in the fields of suicide and mental illnesses in general by providing evidence-based guidance. Only very few such instruments have focused specifically

Table 6. *Overview of selected media guidelines on mental health/SUD*

Guideline Name and/or Editor	Year	Country of Origin	URL
Press Association Guidelines			
Advisory Guidelines on Drugs and Drug Addiction by the Australian Press Council	2001	Australia	www.presscouncil.org.au/document-search/guideline-drugs-and-drug-addiction
Associated Press stylebook	2020	USA	www.apstylebook.com/
Quick Reference Pamphlets			
AOD Mediawatch	2017	Australia	www.aodmediawatch.com.au/guidelines-for-journalists/
Everymind/Mindframe	2019	Australia	mindframe.org.au/alcohol-other-drugs/communicating-about-alcohol-other-drugs
Carter Center	2015	USA	www.cartercenter.org/resources/pdfs/health/mental_health/2015-journalism-resource-guide-on-behavioral-health.pdf
Resource Manuals			
US National Institute on Drug Abuse	2018	USA	www.drugabuse.gov/publications/media-guide/dear-journalist
Drugscope UK	2011	UK	www.onlinelibraryaddictions.stir.ac.uk/files/2017/07/DrugScopeMediaGuideSpreads.pdf
Drug Policy Commission	2012	UK	www.ukdpc.org.uk/publication/dealing-with-the-stigma-of-drugs/

on addiction and other SUDs. While one could argue that the existing guidelines on mental health reporting already encompass SUDs by definition, the stigma, prejudice, and discrimination that people with SUDs experience differs from that attached to other mental disorders that claim specific guidelines (Schomerus et al., 2011). Eight currently available guidelines that focus specifically on SUDs are described as examples in more detail below. Their general characteristics are presented in Table 6.

The earliest resource, the Advisory Guidelines on Drugs and Drug Addiction by the Australian Press Council (APC), was published in

2001. The remainder were unveiled over the past decade, five within the last five years. Except for the US National Institute on Drug Abuse (NIDA), a governmental institution, the authoring bodies and organizations are independent research institutions, not-for-profit organizations, networks operating in the field of drug use and addiction, or press associations. They explicitly emphasize the important role of the media in shaping public opinion by highlighting the interconnections between media portrayals, public attitudes, stigma, and help-seeking.

In terms of the substances covered, the guidelines of the Associated Press (AP), AOD Mediawatch, Everymind, the Carter Center (CC), and NIDA are focused on the notions of and mechanisms behind substance addiction and other SUDs, rather than pinpointing specific classes of substances. Drugscope UK (now defunct), the Drug Policy Commission (UKDPC, now defunct), and the APC advisory guidelines consider illicit drugs specifically from a harm reduction perspective, but also address addiction and substance misuse within that scope.

The self-stated aims of the documents use a variety of different adjectives to describe or measure journalistic quality, including "responsible," "objective," "fair," "balanced," "sensitive," "respectful," "nonjudgmental," and "accurate" reporting. The documents differ somewhat in terms of how they support their readership and convey their message and can be broadly allocated to three categories: 1) press association guidelines, 2) quick-reference pamphlets, and 3) resource manuals.

(1) Press-association guidelines (AP, APC) list succinct and practicable recommendations and principles for reporting on SUD-related matters. The APC provides eight advisory guidelines on how to report responsibly on drugs and drug addiction to reduce harm. The AP stylebook entries for "alcoholic" and "addiction" are short glossary entries comprising express word-choice recommendations and key facts to consider when reporting on addiction.

(2) The documents in the "quick-reference pamphlets" category (Everymind, AOD, CC) provide research-informed contextual and scientific information on a range of stigma and SUD-related issues with corresponding imperative recommendations on how journalists should adapt their reporting practices so that the presented context and scientific facts are given proper and balanced consideration. The pamphlets here range from 2 to 27 pages in length.

(3) The remaining documents (NIDA, DrugScope UK, UKDPC) can be termed "resource manuals." While the manuals do make some

practice recommendations, they rely less on the formulation of express journalistic "do's and don'ts." Instead, they provide comprehensive contextual, statistical, and scientific information across multiple chapters devoted to specific stigma and SUD-related issues to which journalists should refer when writing a story. They also provide extensive glossaries of addictive substances and SUD-related terminology, links to credible data, information and support resources, and case studies of individuals who (used to) use alcohol or other drugs. Accordingly, the resource manuals are the longest documents considered here, ranging from 30 to 140 pages in length.

Key Issues of Selected Media Guidelines

Across the eight guidelines introduced here, there are frequently recurring issues and perspectives that become apparent and that can be regarded as a form of consensus on what journalists should consider when covering drugs, addiction, and other SUD-related matters. Most documents confront journalists with the impact that their reporting has on public opinion and how unbalanced, inaccurate, and irresponsible portrayals and framing can perpetuate negative public misconceptions, impede help-seeking, and contribute to the harm that the stigmatized experience and the economic and public health burden suffered by society. They particularly address sensationalist or alarmist depictions (CC, DrugScope UK, Everymind, AOD Mediawatch, UKDPC), associations with crime, violence, and delinquency (Everymind, DrugScope UK, UKDPC), and moral failing/weakness (Everymind, DrugScope UK, UKDCP) as dysfunctional ways of portrayal. Journalists are essentially made aware of their responsibility and opportunity to report responsibly, fairly, and accurately against the backdrop of the negative consequences that can result from failing to fulfill that responsibility. Some sources also highlight the impact of media coverage on public debate and policymaking.

Reflecting the Role of Stigma

Stigma is addressed by all but one document (the APC advisory guidelines). The concept of stigma constitutes the central focus of the AOD pamphlet, the UKDPC manual, Everymind, and the CC pamphlet (reducing stigma and discrimination features in the mission statement of the Mental Health Program of the CC). NIDA, with its primary focus on providing journalists with fast and user-friendly access to the latest scientific information, contains a definition and concise outline of the causes and effects of stigma and discrimination in its glossary of SUD-related terminology. The AP stylebook addresses stigmatization as a consequence of using punitive or judgmental language.

Overall, the documents present stigma as a consequence of prevailing public misconceptions (NIDA, Everymind, UKDPC), myths (NIDA, DrugScope UK), stereotypes (Everymind, CC, UKDPC, DrugScope UK), ignorance (DrugScope UK, UKDPC), negative attitudes (NIDA, Everymind, CC, UKDPC), and misinformation (Everymind, CC, DrugScope UK, AP) that manifests itself in the form of prejudice (CC, UKDCP, DrugScope UK, AP), discrimination (NIDA, AOD Mediawatch, CC, UKDCP), bias (CC, UKDPC), fear (DrugScope UK), social exclusion (CC, UKDPC), and ultimately harm (Everymind, AOD Mediawatch) to individuals and society. The key consequence of stigma that is addressed is its impact on help-seeking behavior (Everymind, UKDPC, CC, AP, AOD, DrugScope UK, NIDA). The causes and consequences of stigma are in most instances presented to journalists from the public's perception and experience of stigmatization.

Four guidelines (Everymind, CC, AP, Drugscope UK) expressly distinguish between perceived/public stigma and self-stigma. In the other sources, the possibility of self-stigmatization is not ruled out and rather is present only by the association in that alcohol and drug users are members of that public.

Recommendations on Responsible, Balanced, and Accurate Reporting

The quick reference pamphlets (CC, AOD Mediawatch, Mindframe), as well as the APC advisory guideline, make several recommendations on how to report on issues related to addiction, drugs, and other SUD-related matters that largely pertain to promoting balance, accuracy, and responsible reporting. They focus primarily on the objective of reducing or minimizing the harms associated with drugs and drug use and advise journalists to refrain from providing detailed accounts of consumption methods, from reporting in a manner that encourages experimentation (e.g., avoid glamorization) or can assist in manufacture, and from quoting the legal dose of any particular substance.

Responsibility is also addressed in a wider sense, in that reporting is deemed responsible when it is conducted in a contextually balanced and scientifically accurate manner. The quick-reference pamphlets all provide practical advice for how journalists can report in a fair, objective, and balanced fashion to better align media depictions with social and scientific reality. Some guidelines discourage journalists from focusing on issues like violence, crime, short-term statistical trends, and celebrity stories. Instead, they motivate journalists to seek expert advice, especially to ensure that exaggeration does not occur. Most documents encourage journalists to improve the quality of their reporting by providing facts on the (neuro) science behind drugs and their effects on the brain and behavior, especially addiction. Key recurring matters in this regard include information on causes and risk factors associated with drug use. They present addiction as a complex disorder with biological mechanisms affecting the brain and its capacity to control behavior that is also determined by genetic, psychological, social, cultural, and environmental factors that are at play in the causation and persistence of addiction and other SUDs.

Several guidelines (CC pamphlet, DrugScope UK, UKDPC, and NIDA) provide indexes or glossaries of commonly misused substances along with their health effects, origins, appearances, consumption methods, prevalence of use, costs, dosages, risks, and mortality and/or offer links to credible sources for further information pertaining to SUDs and alcohol or drug use. Most documents at hand seek to improve contextual balance and accuracy by providing journalists with statistical data or credible sources for such data that provide an appropriate picture of the prevalence and epidemiology of substance use and SUDs as public health issues.

AOD Mediawatch, CC, UKDPC, DrugScope UK, and NIDA emphasize the need for action in public health promotion including public communication by providing data and figures on the economic burden (in terms of economic costs, health, and crime) of drug use for society, on drug-related mortality in contrast to mortality and harms associated with alcohol and/or tobacco; some also provide links to institutions and other bodies that can offer reliable statistics for SUD-related matters. Raising awareness for the significant health, social, and economic harms associated with the use of drugs may help to reduce a critical questioning of funding of addiction prevention measures and contribute to a decrease of stigma in the public.

The Role of Contextualizing Symptomatic Descriptions in the Course of Disease

Treatment and recovery are addressed to some degree by most guidelines covered in this review. They provide scientific information and credible data pertaining to a number of treatment- and recovery-related issues, most prominently, that treatment can be successful and recovery is possible. They refer to use and effectiveness of methadone, substitution, or medication-assisted treatment and mention that treatment and recovery are highly individualized, complex, and difficult. Journalists are recommended to highlight the availability, effectiveness, and accessibility of treatment in their reports. Five sources list treatment and support service providers (DrugScope UK, UKDPC, NIDA, CC, Everymind) and journalists are encouraged to add contact details of relevant services at the end of any report on SUDs.

Besides treatment and recovery, prevention and early intervention are addressed in several documents (Everymind, AOD Mediawatch, CC, Drugscope UK, APC) that highlights the role of the media in shaping public opinion and as a source of information. The guidelines invite journalists to reinforce the notion that SUDs are serious, but often preventable diseases and to raise awareness about SUDs and opportunities for prevention and early intervention by describing the signs and symptoms that, when they persist over time, can be indicative of SUDs. Some of the guidelines also refer to the role of the education system that alone cannot offer appropriate drug education without the support from families, youth and community groups, and other stakeholders.

The Role of Language

Another central issue is the role and importance of words journalists choose and which can have an impact on the development and perpetuation of stigma. The AP stylebook, CC, and Everymind highlight that stigmatizing or punitive-sounding language can be inaccurate by emphasizing the person rather than the disease and can impede help-seeking. The consensus (AOD, AP, CC, Everymind, UKDPC, DrugScope UK) is that journalists should avoid derogatory words and instead use person-first language. The most common specific recommendations in this regard are to use the phrasing "person who uses or used to use XY" rather than (former) "drug user," "abuser," "alcoholic," "addict," "drunk" as well as more derogatory terms like "junkie" or "crackhead." Beyond person-first language, some guidelines stress the need to avoid judgmental language or language that casts a veil of negativity on SUDs and the people affected by them ("dirty/clean" vs. "person who (no longer) uses drugs"). Four documents (Everymind, CC, UKDPC, AP) recommend using language that accurately reflects the scientific facts behind substance use and addiction as diseases of the brain rather than a matter of controllable personal choice.

For instance, a person's substance use should be described as "problematic" rather than as a "drug habit," and rather than speaking of "drug abuse," the term "use" should be applied with the appropriate modifier (such as "risky," "unhealthy," "excessive," "heavy").

Discussion

The review of literature in this chapter emphasizes the crucial role mass media plays in regard to the stigmatization of illicit drug use and other SUDs. The selection of news stories on addiction and SUDs, the way the issues are framed, and the language used play an important role in shaping the public and policy makers' agenda and public opinion. This holds both dysfunctional – that is, problematic and stigmatizing – but also functional – that is, sensitizing, disabusing and balancing – consequences. To meet their responsibility, journalists are challenged to comprehensively address these relevant social problems while reporting in a nonstigmatizing, evidence-led way.

Media guidelines aim to help journalists successfully meet these challenges. The guidelines described here promote accurate, responsible, and balanced reporting as means of minimizing harm and stigma, and thus dismantling barriers to help-seeking. Drawing awareness to accurate, balanced, and credible knowledge and information on drug, alcohol, and SUD-related issues can help to prevent or postpone initiation. It can encourage individuals in need of treatment to seek it sooner and is capable of contributing to prevention and early intervention.

In light of the many predictors and risk factors at play in the development and perpetuation of SUD-related stigma, efforts to promote non-stigmatizing media reporting practices need to be situated within a broader, more holistic destigmatization strategy. For this, considering the specific characteristics and stigma-related facets of SUDs is just as important as the national contexts. Developing and disseminating influential media guidelines claims for a participatory approach involving experts and other stakeholders, journalists and editors, people with lived experiences, but also their relatives and peers. Further, a comprehensive formative, processual, and summative evaluation of the suitability and usability of such guidelines and their impact on reporting is required.

References

Afzali, R., Dero, Q. Y., & Nosrati, R. (2020). Representation of addiction and drugs victims through TV media. *Journal of Ethnicity in Substance Abuse*, 1–36. https://doi.org/10.1080/15332640.2020.1793863

Aragonès, E., López-Muntaner, J., Ceruelo, S., & Basora, J. (2014). Reinforcing stigmatization: Coverage of mental illness in Spanish newspapers. *Journal of Health Communication*, *19*(11), 1248–1258. https://doi.org/10.1080/10810730.2013.872726

Atayde, A. M. P., Hauc, S. C., Bessette, L. G., Danckers, H., & Saitz, R. (2021). Changing the narrative: A call to end stigmatizing terminology related to substance use disorders. *Addiction Research & Theory*, *29*(5), 1–4. https://doi.org/10.1080/16066359.2021.1875215

Avery, J. D., & Avery, J. J. (Eds.). (2019). *The stigma of addiction: An essential guide*. Springer International Publishing. https://doi.org/10.1007/978-3-030-02580-9

Ayers, B., & Myers, L. B. (2012). Do media messages change people's risk perceptions for binge drinking? *Alcohol and Alcoholism (Oxford, Oxfordshire)*, *47*(1), 52–56. https://doi.org/10.1093/alcalc/agr052

Bergström, A., & Jervelycke Belfrage, M. (2018). News in social media. *Digital Journalism*, *6*(5), 583–598. https://doi.org/10.1080/21670811.2018.1423625

Blair, N. A., Yue, S. K., Singh, R., & Bernhardt, J. M. (2005). Depictions of substance use in reality television: A content analysis of The Osbournes. *BMJ (Clinical Research Ed.)*, *331*(7531), 1517–1519. https://doi.org/10.1136/bmj.331.7531.1517

Borinstein, A. B. (1992). Public attitudes toward persons with mental illness. *Health Affairs*, *11*(3), 186–196. https://doi.org/10.1377/hlthaff.11.3.186

Botticelli, M. P., & Koh, H. K. (2016). Changing the language of addiction. *JAMA*, *316*(13), 1361–1362. https://doi.org/10.1001/jama.2016.11874

Chapman, S., & Lupton, D. (1994). *The fight for public health: Principles and practice of media advocacy*. BMJ Books.

Coverdale, J., Nairn, R., & Claasen, D. (2002). Depictions of mental illness in print media: A prospective national sample. *The Australian and New Zealand Journal of Psychiatry*, *36*(5), 697–700. https://doi.org/10.1046/j.1440-1614.2002.00998.x

Dorfman, L., Wallack, L., & Woodruff, K. (2005). More than a message: Framing public health advocacy to change corporate practices. *Health Education & Behavior: The Official Publication of the Society for Public Health Education*, *32*(3), 320–336; discussion 355–362. https://doi.org/10.1177/1090198105275046

Eichenberg, C., Wolters, C., & Brähler, E. (2013). The internet as a mental health advisor in Germany: Results of a national survey. *PLoS ONE*, *8*(11), e79206. https://doi.org/10.1371/journal.pone.0079206

Entman, R. M. (1993). Framing: Towards clarification of a fractured paradigm. *Journal of Communication*, *43*(4), 51–58.

Entman, R. M., Matthes, J., & Pellicano, L. (2009). Nature, sources, and effects of news framing. In K. Wahl-Jorgensen & T. Hanitzsch (Eds.), *The handbook of journalism studies* (pp. 175–190). Routledge. https://doi.org/10.4324/9780203877685.ch13

Fan, D. P. (1996). News media framing sets public opinion that drugs is the country's most important problem. *Substance Use & Misuse*, *31*(10), 1413–1421. https://doi.org/10.3109/10826089609063984

Fraser, S., Pienaar, K., Dilkes-Frayne, E., et al. (2017). Addiction stigma and the biopolitics of liberal modernity: A qualitative analysis. *The International Journal on Drug Policy*, *44*, 192–201. https://doi.org/10.1016/j.drugpo.2017.02.005

Frosh, P., & Pinchevski, A. (Eds.). (2009). *Media witnessing: Testimony in the age of mass communication*. Palgrave Macmillan.

Galtung, J., & Ruge, M. H. (1965). The structure of foreign news. *Journal of Peace Research*, *2*(1), 64–90. https://doi.org/10.1177/002234336500200104

Gamson, W. A., & Modigliani, A. (1987). The changing culture of affirmative action. In R. G. Braungart & M. M. Braungart (Eds.), *Research in political sociology* (pp. 137–177). JAI Press.

Goodyear, K., Haass-Koffler, C. L., & Chavanne, D. (2018). Opioid use and stigma: The role of gender, language and precipitating events. *Drug and Alcohol Dependence*, *185*, 339–346. https://doi.org/10.1016/j.drugalcdep.2017.12.037

Gowen, L. K. (2013). Online mental health information seeking in young adults with mental health challenges. *Journal of Technology in Human Services*, *31*(2), 97–111. https://doi.org/10.1080/15228835.2013.765533

Henson, C., Chapman, S., McLeod, L., Johnson, N., McGeechan, K., & Hickie, I. (2009). More us than them: Positive depictions of mental illness on Australian television news. *Australian and New Zealand Journal of Psychiatry*, *43*, 554–560. https://doi.org/10.1080/00048670902873623

Holland, K. (2018). Making mental health news. *Journalism Studies*, *19*(12), 1767–1785. https://doi.org/10.1080/1461670X.2017.1304826

Hughes, C. E., Lancaster, K., & Spicer, B. (2011). How do Australian news media depict illicit drug issues? An analysis of print media reporting across and between illicit drugs, 2003–2008. *The International Journal on Drug Policy*, *22*(4), 285–291. https://doi.org/10.1016/j.drugpo.2011.05.008

Hughes, C. E., Spicer, B., Lancaster, K., Matthew-Simons, F., & Dillon, P. (2010). *Monograph No. 19: Media reporting on illicit drugs in Australia: Trends and impacts on youth attitudes to illicit drug use. DPMP Monograph Series*. National Drug and Alcohol Research Centre.

Iyengar, S. (1996). Framing responsibility for political issues. *The ANNALS of the American Academy of Political and Social Science*, *546*(1), 59–70. https://doi.org/10.1177/0002716296546001006

Jernigan, D., & Dorfman, L. (1996). Visualizing America's drug problems: An ethnographic content analysis of illegal drug stories on the nightly news. *Contemporary Drug Problems*, *23*(2), 169–196.

Johnson, J. D., & Case, D. O. (2013). *Health information seeking*. Peter Lang.

Kay-Lambkin, F., Hunt, S., Geddes, J. M. M., & Gilbert, J. (2019). *Evidence check: Media reporting of alcohol and other drug use*. https://mindframemedia

.imgix.net/assets/src/uploads/Evidence-Check-Media-Reporting-of-Alcohol-and-other-Drug-Use-7.3.19_Final.pdf

Kelly, J. F., Saitz, R., & Wakeman, S. (2016). Language, substance use disorders, and policy: The need to reach consensus on an "addiction-ary." *Alcoholism Treatment Quarterly*, *34*(1), 116–123. https://doi.org/10.1080/07347324.2016.1113103

Kelly, J. F., Wakeman, S. E., & Saitz, R. (2015). Stop talking 'dirty': Clinicians, language, and quality of care for the leading cause of preventable death in the United States. *The American Journal of Medicine*, *128*(1), 8–9. https://doi.org/10.1016/j.amjmed.2014.07.043

Kelly, J. F., & Westerhoff, C. M. (2010). Does it matter how we refer to individuals with substance-related conditions? A randomized study of two commonly used terms. *The International Journal on Drug Policy*, *21*(3), 202–207. https://doi.org/10.1016/j.drugpo.2009.10.010

Klin, A., & Lemish, D. (2008). Mental disorders stigma in the media: Review of studies on production, content, and influences. *Journal of Health Communication*, *13*(5), 434–449. https://doi.org/10.1080/10810730802198813

Lancaster, K., Hughes, C. E., & Spicer, B. (2012). News media consumption among young Australians: Patterns of use and attitudes towards media reporting. *Media International Australia*, *143*(1), 16–27. https://doi.org/10.1177/1329878X1214300104

Lundahl, O. (2020). Media framing of social media addiction in the UK and the US. *International Journal of Consumer Studies*, *45*(5), 1103–1116. https://doi.org/10.1111/ijcs.12636

McGinty, E. E., Goldman, H. H., Pescosolido, B., & Barry, C. L. (2015). Portraying mental illness and drug addiction as treatable health conditions: Effects of a randomized experiment on stigma and discrimination. *Social Science & Medicine*, *126*, 73–85. https://doi.org/10.1016/j.socscimed.2014.12.010

McGinty, E. E., Kennedy-Hendricks, A., Baller, J., Niederdeppe, J., Gollust, S., & Barry, C. L. (2016). Criminal activity or treatable health condition? News media framing of opioid analgesic abuse in the United States, 1998–2012. *Psychiatric Services*, *67*(4), 405–411. https://doi.org/10.1176/appi.ps.201500065

McGinty, E. E., Kennedy-Hendricks, A., & Barry, C. L. (2019). Stigma of addiction in the media. In J. D. Avery & J. J. Avery (Eds.), *The stigma of addiction: An essential guide* (pp. 201–214). Springer International Publishing. https://doi.org/10.1007/978-3-030-02580-9_11

McGinty, E. E., Pescosolido, B., Kennedy-Hendricks, A., & Barry, C. L. (2018). Communication strategies to counter stigma and improve mental illness and substance use disorder policy. *Psychiatric Services (Washington, D.C.)*, *69*(2), 136–146. https://doi.org/10.1176/appi.ps.201700076

McGinty, E. E., Stone, E. M., Kennedy-Hendricks, A., & Barry, C. L. (2019). Stigmatizing language in news media coverage of the opioid epidemic:

Implications for public health. *Preventive Medicine, 124,* 110–114. https://doi.org/10.1016/j.ypmed.2019.03.018

McGinty, E. E., Webster, D. W., Jarlenski, M., & Barry, C. L. (2014). News media framing of serious mental illness and gun violence in the United States 1997–2012. *American Journal of Public Health, 104*(3), 406–413. https://doi.org/10.2105/AJPH.2013.301557.

McKeever, R. (2015). Vicarious experience: Experimentally testing the effects of empathy for media characters with severe depression and the intervening role of perceived similarity. *Health Communication, 30*(11), 1122–1134. https://doi.org/10.1080/10410236.2014.921969

Nelson, D. E., Pederson, L. L., Mowery, P., et al. (2015). Trends in US newspaper and television coverage of tobacco. *Tobacco Control, 24*(1), 94–99. https://doi.org/10.1136/tobaccocontrol-2013-050963

Netherland, J., & Hansen, H. B. (2016). The war on drugs that wasn't: Wasted whiteness, "dirty doctors," and race in media coverage of prescription opioid misuse. *Culture, Medicine, and Psychiatry, 40*(4), 664–686. https://doi.org/10.1007/s11013-016-9496-5

Nielsen, A. L., & Bonn, S. (2008). Media exposure and attitudes toward drug addiction spending, 1975–2004. *Deviant Behavior, 29*(8), 726–752. https://doi.org/10.1080/01639620701839492

Nunez-Smith, M., Wolf, E., Huang, H. M., et al. (2010). Media exposure and tobacco, illicit drugs, and alcohol use among children and adolescents: A systematic review. *Substance Abuse, 31*(3), 174–192. https://doi.org/10.1080/08897077.2010.495648

Orsini, M. M. (2017). Frame analysis of drug narratives in network news coverage. *Contemporary Drug Problems, 44*(3), 189–211. https://doi.org/10.1177/0091450917722817

Pivovarova, E., & Stein, M. D. (2019). In their own words: Language preferences of individuals who use heroin. *Addiction (Abingdon, England), 114*(10), 1785–1790. https://doi.org/10.1111/add.14699

Powell, J., & Clarke, A. (2006). Internet information-seeking in mental health: Population survey. *British Journal of Psychiatry, 189*(3), 273–277. https://doi.org/10.1192/bjp.bp.105.017319

Richter, L., & Foster, S. E. (2014). Effectively addressing addiction requires changing the language of addiction. *Journal of Public Health Policy, 35*(1), 60–64. https://doi.org/10.1057/jphp.2013.44

Russell, D., Thames, K. M., Spence, N. J., & Koeval, C. M. (2020). Where the fault lies: Representations of addiction in audience reactions to media coverage of the opioid epidemic. *Contemporary Drug Problems, 47*(2), 83–102. https://doi.org/10.1177/0091450920929102

Scheufele, D. A., & Tewksbury, D. (2007). Framing, agenda setting, and priming: The evolution of three media effects models. *Journal of Communication, 57*(1), 9–20. https://doi.org/10.1111/j.1460-2466.2006.00326.x

Schiappa, E., Gregg, P. B., & Hewes, D. E. (2005). The parasocial contact hypothesis. *Communication Monographs, 72*(1), 92–115. https://doi.org/10.1080/0363775052000342544

Schomerus, G., Lucht, M., Holzinger, A., Matschinger, H., Carta, M. G., & Angermeyer, M. C. (2011). The stigma of alcohol dependence compared with other mental disorders: A review of population studies. *Alcohol and Alcoholism (Oxford, Oxfordshire), 46*(2), 105–112. https://doi.org/10.1093/alcalc/agq089

Seale, C. (2002). *Media and health*. Sage.

Seidel, M., Cashaw-Davis, L., Connolly-Leach, V., et al. (2017). *Using person-first language across the continuum of care for substance use disorders & other addictions: Words matter to reduce stigma*. https://preventionactionalliance.org/wp-content/uploads/2018/02/Language-across-the-Continuum-for-People-with-Addictive-Disorders-1-18.pdf

Slopen, N. B., Watson, A. C., Gracia, G., & Corrigan, P. W. (2007). Age analysis of newspaper coverage of mental illness. *Journal of Health Communication, 12*(1), 3–15. https://doi.org/10.1080/10810730601091292

Taylor, S. (2008). Outside the outsiders: Media representations of drug use. *Probation Journal, 55*(4), 369–387. https://doi.org/10.1177/0264550508096493

Wakeman, S. E. (2013). Language and addiction: Choosing words wisely. *American Journal of Public Health, 103*(4), e1–e2. https://doi.org/10.2105/AJPH.2012.301191

(2017). Medications for addiction treatment: Changing language to improve care. *Journal of Addiction Medicine, 11*(1), 1–2. https://doi.org/10.1097/ADM.0000000000000275

Webster, F., Rice, K., & Sud, A. (2020). A critical content analysis of media reporting on opioids: The social construction of an epidemic. *Social Science & Medicine, 244*, 112642. https://doi.org/10.1016/j.socscimed.2019.112642

Wong, N. C. H., Lookadoo, K. L., & Nisbett, G. S. (2017). "I'm Demi and I have bipolar disorder": Effect of parasocial contact on reducing stigma toward people with bipolar disorder. *Communication Studies, 68*(3), 314–333. https://doi.org/10.1080/10510974.2017.1331928

Zhang, Y., Jin, Y., Stewart, S., & Porter, J. (2016). Framing responsibility for depression: How U.S. news media attribute causal and problem-solving responsibilities when covering a major public health problem. *Journal of Applied Communication Research, 44*(2), 118–135. https://doi.org/10.1080/00909882.2016.1155728

CHAPTER 13

Reducing Substance Use Stigma in Health Care

Sven Speerforck and Georg Schomerus

Introduction

As the chapters of this book have outlined from several perspectives, the stigma surrounding substance use disorders (SUDs) has detrimental effects on people who use substances, their recovery process, and their social network. Besides family, friends and work, a central and sensitive context for experiences of stigmatization is the health care setting itself, for people with mental disorders in general (Henderson et al., 2014) and for people with SUD in particular. Although this setting is generally designed to help people experiencing serious health problems, it has the potential to effectively impede recovery for people with diagnosed SUD by obvious and rather subtle discrimination as a consequence of stigma.

Substance Use Stigma in the Health Care Context

To understand stigma in health care contexts for people with SUD, it appears reasonable to differentiate between *access* and *quality* of care. Regarding access, a literature review for the Mental Health Commission of Canada found that policies and practices produce inequitable access for people with mental health and substance use issues by inequitable distribution of resources, undertreatment of physical and mental health problems, withholding of services, and fragmented care (Livingston, 2020). Quality of care is affected by a combination of individual stigmatizing attitudes by people working in health care, and the structural realities of the health care system itself, including many traditional discriminatory therapeutic principles. Professionals engaging in stigmatizing practices can thus be considered as "agents of structural stigma" (Livingston, 2020). Here, we focus on the harmful effects of substance use stigma on the *quality* of care in everyday clinical practice and provide recommendations to address stigma and improve quality of care in clinical settings.

A systematic review by van Boekel et al. summarized studies investigating stigmatizing attitudes toward people who use substances among health professionals and their potentially harmful consequences for health care delivery (van Boekel et al., 2013). The authors conclude that professionals often perceive violence, manipulation, and poor motivation as impeding factors in the health care delivery and that many professionals lack adequate education, training, and support structures. Inequalities in health care provision for people with SUD are not only experienced, but regularly expected, by general practitioners, mental health professionals, and by their clients (Biancarelli et al., 2019; van Boekel et al., 2016b). A Dutch survey found that about one-fifth of participants with SUDs reported to have been treated unfairly in the health care context by a primary care physician, other health care professionals, and mental health specialists (van Boekel et al., 2016a). Qualitative research indicates that stigmatizing, devaluing, and infantilizing health service experiences appear to be common for people living with substance use issues, especially when using opioids (Biancarelli et al., 2019; Earnshaw et al., 2013; Paquette et al., 2018). Although, according to van Boekel et al. (2016a), the odds are much higher of experiencing unfair treatment in more personal social situations (e.g., family, friends, work), the consequences of substance use stigma within the health care setting are likely to be particularly severe. For example, by analyzing trajectories of perceived discrimination and stigma among more than 400 people experiencing homelessness using longitudinal data from the Canadian Housing First trial, Mejia-Lancheros et al. found that experiences of discrimination in health care settings were especially predictive of higher perceived mental illness stigma and discrimination trajectories in general over 2 years (Mejia-Lancheros et al., 2020).

People working in health care have a particularly high responsibility to act without stigma. The power gradient that drives stigma (Link & Phelan, 2014) is particularly palpable in the health care setting; representatives of the health care system have a societal normative and tangible power. In health care, where helpful and benevolent structures and professionals are assumed, both obvious and rather subtle enactments of harmful stereotypes are legitimizing stigma and discriminatory behavior. For example, perpetuating negative stereotypes like assigning guilt to someone with SUD with the structural authority of a health care worker will have particularly grave consequences.

The potential harm done by stigmatizing health care environments is manifold, and aligns with pervasive problems in treating SUDs; avoidance or delay of treatment to avoid stigma is particularly harmful for a group of disorders where delay and failure to initiate treatment are ubiquitous (Probst et al., 2015; Wang et al., 2007). Inferior care due to stigmatizing attitudes is particularly harmful for disorders with high comorbidity and severe acute and long-term health consequences like SUDs (Rehm et al., 2009). Increasing self-stigma in a context with particular normative power adds to the already severe impediment to recovery through self-stigma (Corrigan et al., 2006; Schomerus et al., 2011).

Understanding Stigma for Better Interventions

Besides structural and policy changes, the detrimental effects of substance use stigma in the health care context can be reduced by either targeting the potential perpetrators of stigma (e.g., health care workers) or by empowering clients to overcome stigma and discrimination (Nyblade et al., 2019). Despite substance use stigma being increasingly addressed in research and by policy makers, the evidence of interventions to reduce SUD stigma within the health care context is still scarce (Earnshaw, 2020; Livingston et al., 2012; Nyblade et al., 2019). In a systematic review of interventions Nyblade et al. identified several promising strategies to reduce stigma in health care settings; besides the "provision of information," "skills-building activities," and "structural or policy changes" interventions including "participatory learning," "contact with the stigmatized group," and "empowerment" seemed to be effective (Nyblade et al., 2019). However, contrasting 29 interventions focusing on mental illness stigma only 4 included SUDs:

(1) Investigating a recovery teaching program in a randomized control design Feeney et al. (2013) reported an increase in knowledge about recovery as well as more positive attitudes toward mental illness including alcohol dependence in a group of medical students.

(2) The effects of multimedia in person "recovery speaks" by people living with a mental illness and/or SUD were examined in 27 primary care providers in a randomized controlled study (Flanagan et al., 2016). The intervention yielded fewer negative stereotypes, reduced attributions of dangerousness, and less desire for avoidance, as well as more desire to help and more hope for recovery.

(3) In a community sample including health care providers and educators, mental health first aid training was associated with less stigmatizing attitudes (Morawska et al., 2013). However, no control group was included, and SUDs were only considered within the training not as vignette conditions.

(4) Sarah Wakeman and colleagues (2017) evaluated an institutional SUD intervention (quasi-experimental / no control group) comprising an inpatient addiction consult team, a postdischarge addiction clinic, recovery coaches, and SUD treatment within a general hospital. They found beneficial effects on general internists' attitudes, preparedness, and clinical practice related to SUDs.

More recently, Khenti and coworkers (2019) evaluated a multicomponent pilot intervention including site-based teams, contact-based training, anti-stigma awareness campaigns, recovery-based art workshops, and a review of internal policies and procedures in primary care providers, and found it to be effective in changing attitudes toward mental illness and substance use problems.

Overall, to reduce the harmful effects of substance use stigma in the health care context and increase quality of care, it seems necessary to develop, refine and implement curricula for health care workers that address substance use stigma, inform on current concepts of harm reduction and adequate use of medication, and focus on empowerment and recovery (Renner, 2019; Wakeman et al., 2015). For example, the Boston University School of Medicine in 2019 implemented a model curriculum for SUDs emphasizing the need to encounter people who use substances with respect and dignity, the efficacy of SUD treatment and harm reduction, the detrimental effects of substance use stigma, and recurrences of use as part of recovery (Renner, 2019). Since contact-based and participatory approaches are particularly promising to reduce stigmatizing attitudes among health care workers (Nyblade et al., 2019), it seems reasonable to complement curricula accordingly. Stigma-reducing interventions in the health care context should emphasize standardized measures, rigorous evaluation, and the local context. Nyblade et al. (2019) found that interventions were considered most effective when tackling multiple stigmas, while remaining attentive to the need of individuals, focusing on empowerment, targeting all levels of health facility staff, leveraging technology, and concentrating on simultaneously targeting multiple ecological levels such as individual practices and health facility policies. Future and more rigorous studies are needed to build a more solid evidence base for reducing substance use stigma in professional settings. Particularly, studies should address the effects of real-world interventions, not only on changing professionals' attitudes and behavior, but also on improving patients' health outcomes.

In the following, we will look in more detail at some particularly consequential situations where people with SUD meet the health care

Table 7. *Recommendations for changes in clinical practice to change substance use stigma*

General
- Use language sensitively and stimulate open discussions within the treatment team
- Lead by example and attention to establish a transparent and self-reflective environment
- Refine curricula considering substance use stigma, medication, recovery, harm reduction, empowerment, and active participation of people with lived experience
- Transform high threshold / low tolerance setting to low threshold / high tolerance

Emergency Medicine
- Avoid premature conclusions to prevent overlooking symptoms of diseases and physical health
- Sensitize team that enacted substance use stigma is medical malpractice
- Actively avoid "giving a look," extra waiting, and pedagogic behavior
- Establish transparency regarding consultations and procedures

Primary Care
- Embrace long and individually determined recovery processes
- Include substance use as natural part of a general health-risk-behavior assessment
- Be transparent regarding your available time
- Educate yourself on pharmacological treatment of SUDs and local services
- Get familiar with patient-centered care and motivational interviewing

Psychiatric Ward
- Avoid separation of patients (with SUD and between SUDs) and special admission processes
- Abolish traditional standard rules (e.g., token/card system, periodical substance testing, bag controls, concealed withdrawal treatment)
- Review and rethink "well-known" clients who use substances
- Bring people with lived experience to your team
- Educate team about substance use stigma and empowering treatment modules (e.g., patient-centered care, motivational interviewing, acceptance and commitment therapy, community reinforcement approach)

system. Although occurrences and implications of substance use stigma naturally overlap between different medical situations, it seems useful to highlight characteristics and potential recommendations for different medical contexts to make considerations of specific changes to professional practice more tangible. We thus focus on three typical situations, where professional medical health care for people with SUD is expected: emergency medicine, primary care, and the psychiatric ward. A summary of our recommendations for daily clinical practice can be found in Table 7. Given the limited evidence base, many of our recommendations must be considered as best clinical-ethical practice, based on the available literature, discussions with clinicians (both authors work as clinical psychiatrists), and with people with lived experience.

Stigma and Different Situations in Health Care

Emergency Medicine

Assumingly, every mental health professional with experience in liaison psychiatry can recall someone with an SUD who has been treated unfairly and in a stigmatizing way by colleagues in the health system. A British survey among emergency service staff reported greater mental health stigma compared to the general population, which was largely predicted by fear and less sympathy (Hazell et al., 2021). Given the overrepresentation of SUD-related intoxication and acute crisis in emergency medicine departments, it is likely that here, stigmatizing attitudes regarding SUDs are even higher than in other medical contexts. Mendiola et al. (2018) found that emergency physicians had generally lower regard for people who use substances than other medical conditions with behavioral components and about 54% of them indicated that they at least "somewhat agree" that they "prefer not to work with patients with substance use who have pain." The following case report is a typical example illustrating potentially harmful consequences of neglect, stigmatizing assumptions, and insufficient education around SUDs in emergency medicine.

Case Report

On a late Saturday evening, the attending gynecologist in a general hospital requested help from a consultant psychiatrist with an "agitated" 37-year-old female, who had given birth to a boy 3 weeks earlier. She had been admitted to the emergency department at 5 am in the morning with severe abdominal cramps and intermittent pain most severe around the navel. The patient was a mother of seven, all other children living in foster families. She was currently unemployed and living in a mother–child facility with her 3-week-old son. According to her medical file, she had used methamphetamine for 2 days during her pregnancy. The gynecological treatment team conducted a urinary drug test, which tested positive for methamphetamine. Other laboratory tests ordered were a basic blood count showing discreet signs of inflammation. A gynecological ultrasound scan revealed no irregularities. The preliminary diagnosis was "amphetamine withdrawal" and no further diagnostics were organized throughout the day. The responsible treatment team called the psychiatrist in to "help with the worsening withdrawal" and to transfer the patient to a psychiatric ward.

When assessing her, it became clear quickly that she was "agitated" due to worsening recurrent pain around her navel (8/10 visual analogue scale) and had never experienced similar symptoms before. She was reluctant to admit

> her current use of methamphetamine because she was afraid of having the baby taken from her. During the interview she was increasingly irritated about having to see a psychiatrist, because she was in pain and nobody had talked to her regarding her substance use or other mental health issues or announced the visit of a psychiatrist. She denied any mental health problems or symptoms of withdrawal, wanted pain relief, and wanted to know what caused her pain. The attending gynecologist was informed by the psychiatrist that localized abdominal pain is not typical of a methamphetamine withdrawal and that the "agitation" was most likely a product of serious pain. Further laboratory diagnostics, medical imaging, and consultation by an urologist and a surgeon to rule out other diagnoses like urolithiasis, mesenteric ischemia, or hernias, were recommended. Additionally, pain medication, which so far had been withheld from her due to concerns about her SUD, was advised. The gynecology team, still suspecting withdrawal to be the probable cause, consulted a surgeon who conducted another ultrasound scan. The surgeon diagnosed a medium-large umbilical hernia containing greater omentum without clear signs of incarceration. He also concluded that a withdrawal of methamphetamine as a cause of the pain and abdominal spasms could not be ruled out. In the morning, she left the hospital against medical advice because she wanted to take care of her son and feared that otherwise he might be taken from her.

In the presented case, the responsible physician read about methamphetamine use during pregnancy in the medical records. Since that substance use during pregnancy is highly stigmatized among health care professionals (R. Stone, 2015), that probably stimulated prejudices of guilt and moral failure that preceded and indirectly justified diagnostic nihilism apart from a gynecological ultrasound scan and a urinary drug test. When combining lack of proper diagnostics, failure to communicate with the patient, and reluctance to prescribe sufficient analgesic medication, (un)conscious motives around disciplining are probably explaining large parts of this discriminatory behavior. Untreated pain and discrimination by hospital staff are frequently mentioned by people who use substances when explaining their reasons to leave the hospital against medical advice (Simon et al., 2020). As in this case, stigmatizing behavior by professionals is often disguised and promoted by a rather poor medical education about substances and their related disorders (Deans & Soar, 2005; Peckover & Chidlaw, 2007), facilitating wrong attributions of physical symptoms to substance use. The false attribution of pain around the navel to methamphetamine withdrawal, which usually provokes symptoms like lethargy, sleepiness, and increased appetite and is not associated with pain, proved remarkably resistant, persisting in the surgeon's conclusion even after the psychiatrist had explicitly evaluated this causal explanation as highly unlikely. The nondisclosure of the recent drug use, which in this case was motivated by fear of losing child custody, is a common strategy by people using substances to avoid stigma in health care settings (Biancarelli et al., 2019) thereby reproducing stereotypes of moral failure, distrust, and manipulative behavior.

More subtle behaviors like making people who use substances wait extra time, withholding treatment or services, or giving them "looks" have detrimental effects on people who use substances as well (Fogler, 2020). In emergency departments, time is a particularly meaningful and limited resource – that is why being as transparent as possible regarding the upcoming procedures and the estimated waiting time is so important to people who use substances who are most likely already shaming themselves for being there. Transforming emergency departments from high threshold/low tolerance settings to settings with low threshold/high tolerance seems necessary to reduce barriers and shame that hamper subsequent treatment. People in need of the emergency department are often in a personal crisis and exceptional situation – for some it is their first health care contact related to substance use. Reinforcing shame by subtle stigmatizing behaviors increases ambivalence, decreases trust in health care providers, and directly interferes with help-seeking and recovery. This is contrary to what an emergency department is supposed to provide for patients.

Primary Care

In contrast to emergency medicine, primary care physicians typically see people who use substances over a long time and are familiar with their medical history and social backgrounds. Due to the important role of family doctors and general practitioners in every health system their attitudes and willingness to engage in appropriate clinical practice are of particular importance. A recent survey among 361 primary care physicians in the USA found high levels of stigmatizing attitudes toward people with opioid use disorder (E. M. Stone et al., 2021). Less than 30% of those physicians were willing to have a person taking medication for opioid use disorder as a neighbor or marry into their family. Further, higher stigma was associated with a lower likelihood of prescribing opioid use disorder medication and lower support for policies intended to increase access to that medication. In a sample of 149 general internal medicine physicians 31% felt that SUD is different from other chronic diseases because they believed using substances is a choice and only 9% felt prepared to provide a brief intervention or discuss medication treatments (Wakeman et al., 2016). Importantly, the preparedness to engage in appropriate clinical practice was significantly associated with favorable attitudes toward substance use issues. Conversely, people not seeking help for substance use problems mention fear of stigma as a main reason not to seek help in primary care settings (Probst et al., 2015). Further studies also highlighted the probable link between negative attitudes of health professionals and negative consequences for patients' feelings of empowerment and subsequent treatment outcomes. Patients who reported greater perceived discrimination by health professionals and dissatisfaction with the treatment were less likely to complete their treatment (Brener et al., 2010). Foucault's theory of objectification suggests that clinicians may unwittingly impose their beliefs and prejudices on consumers and in fact disempower the very people they want to empower (Curtis & Harrison, 2001). There is a high risk that substance use stigma and its consequences for provision of adequate health care might exacerbate in times of particularly limited resources and need for prioritization like the Covid-19 pandemic (Dannatt et al., 2021; Schomerus et al., 2021). However, the link between negative attitudes of professionals and their translation into poor clinical practice merits further investigation.

Primary care physicians are also a primary resource in addressing substance use stigma. Being accustomed to addressing unhealthy behaviors of their patients, like low physical activity, an unhealthy diet, or smoking, they can counter the taboo surrounding SUDs by addressing the use of substances as one part of such general health-risk-behavior assessments focusing on prevention (Crowley & Kirschner, 2015; Schomerus et al., 2017). Screening and brief interventions for substance use problems by primary care physicians have been shown to be effective (Bertholet et al., 2005) and provide an opportunity to address substance use early and in a stigma-free way.

To reduce the stigma of SUD it seems important to be able to embrace long and individually determined recovery processes of people who use substances. "Longtime patients" often make many positive changes over the years that become more visible to their primary care physician. In contrast, short-term contacts, for example in emergency settings, often result in overemphasizing recurrence of use and unsuccessful attempts, thereby fueling substance use stigma around guilt and moral failure. The patient–doctor relationship may also profit from explicitly acknowledging the long-term character of many treatment courses, and by adopting an attitude of empowerment rather than control. This may include core principles from patient-centered care with a holistic and individualized focus to care, shared decision-making, and enhanced therapeutic alliance (Marchand et al., 2019). Particularly motivational interviewing with its conceptual framework around "expressing empathy," "developing discrepancies," "rolling with resistance," and "supporting self-efficacy" seems useful for primary care physicians to engage in long-term, successful, and empowering treatment courses for people who use substances (Martins & McNeil, 2009).

Psychiatric Ward

Unlike primary care physicians, psychiatric wards are supposed to provide a highly specialized therapy setting for mental disorders including serious courses of SUDs. Among psychiatric patients SUDs are highly prevalent. A nationwide Danish population-based study including 463,000 psychiatric inpatients found that about 30% of inpatients were diagnosed with SUD, being most frequent in patients with personality disorders (46%), schizophrenia (37%), and bipolar disorder (32%) (Toftdahl et al., 2016). Given the high prevalence, effectively addressing the stigma of SUDs is crucial in this context. Substance use should be addressed among all patients as unhealthy behavior potentially requiring special medical counseling and treatment to reduce shame about using substances. The treatment team should be able to provide patient-centered care (Marchand et al., 2019) as well as empowering treatment modules (e.g. motivational interviewing, acceptance and commitment therapy [ACT], or community reinforcement approach). Evidence for the stigma-reducing properties of these psychotherapeutic interventions is scarce. For example, ACT has been shown to reduce stigmatizing attitudes toward people who use substances in a sample of SUD counselors (Hayes et al., 2004) and to reduce shame and internalized stigma in people receiving residential substance use treatment (Luoma et al., 2008). Like other third-wave behavior therapy interventions, ACT focuses on methods such as experiential acceptance, mindfulness, and cognitive defusion to reduce the impact of negative thoughts and feelings. This might as well be true for stigmatizing attitudes. Reflecting the contact-based nature of successful interventions, it seems reasonable to include peer-providers in the treatment team. Working with people with lived experience who are currently in recovery will likely have beneficial effects for both professionals and people who use substances. For the latter, peer-providers can serve as concrete role models and are able to engage more individually and personally, thereby tackling self-stigma and shame. Regarding the treatment team, peer-providers sharing their personal story of struggle and recovery can help to reduce harmful and stigmatizing stereotypes around SUDs (Flanagan et al., 2016; Khenti et al., 2019; Wakeman et al., 2017). This is particularly important, since acute crises and recurrences are overrepresented in psychiatric wards and thus appear to staff as disproportionally likely events (Henderson et al., 2014). Employing people with lived experience in a well-planned, carefully introduced, and sufficiently funded manner enables them to become a fully accepted, rewarding, and stimulating member of the treatment team.

Besides psychotherapeutic and peer-led interventions, addressing two peculiarities of SUD treatment on the psychiatric ward seems particularly important: the separation of patients between SUD treatment and "regular" mental health care, and traditional standard rules that apply exclusively to people who are treated for SUD. Separation of the treatment of people who use substances from those with other psychiatric diagnoses is common practice, not the least because in many countries, SUD services operate separately from other mental health services. This separation impedes the necessary parity for mental health and substance use issues (Livingston, 2020). Within SUD treatment, there is often further differentiation by different SUDs (e.g., "illegal vs. alcohol"). This separation seems problematic, since it perpetuates stereotypes around alienation, facilitates the neglect of other mental health problems (e.g., trauma, affective disorders, anxiety disorders, psychosis), and has the potential to booster self-stigma through harmful group identification processes.

The idea of separation and a necessary "special treatment" also often manifests itself in specific admission processes (e.g., waiting lists) and traditional standard rules for people who use substances. Practices like a token/card system incentivizing treatment compliance, periodical substance testing, bag searches, or concealed withdrawal treatment are persistent on psychiatric wards all around the world. These are stigmatizing, depowering, and self-worth-reducing practices that perpetuate stereotypes of criminality and distrust. There is no evidence regarding the benefit of these measures for recovery processes and less harmful substance use following discharge. Although some of these rules might at times be necessary to protect individuals or to keep therapeutic settings functioning, they should only be applied individually after informed consent. For example, it might be helpful for someone who uses substances to expect a jointly done bag search after admission when they have a history of substance consumption on the ward that has previously led to interruptions of treatment. Or it might reduce ambivalence to consume substances when drug or alcohol tests are provided regularly. But this should be communicated transparently as a potentially helpful and optional diagnostic offer rather than as a standard for all people who use substances, thereby enforcing stigmatizing and depowering stereotypes of low self-control, weakness of will, and crime (Nieweglowski et al., 2018). When suspending these sets of rules, it is important to have the whole team on board on multiple ecological levels such as individual attitudes and practices as well as health facility policies and environment (Nyblade et al., 2019). Team members might often perceive these rules as necessary to structure daily routine, consider them legitimate based on lifelong work experience, and, on a more subconscious level, as justified by stigmatizing stereotypes about SUDs. Getting rid of "unit-wide rules" might often be perceived by staff as a loss of structural safety. These and other challenges during the change process should be addressed kindly, consistently, and repetitively and reflected within regular team meetings (Horner et al., 2019). Accepting and empathically working with recurrence of use can lead to patients being more often readmitted to the psychiatric ward. It is important to acknowledge the resulting structural extra expenses (e.g., admission procedures), to confront feelings of frustration within the treatment team and to carefully reassess people who use substances who are admitted to the ward more regularly. To overcome initial resistance, it seems important to educate all members of the clinical and nonclinical treatment team on the principles of patient-centered care, the stigma of SUD, its harmful consequences for people who use substances, and on current concepts of harm reduction and recovery (Marchand et al., 2019; Renner, 2019; Wakeman et al., 2015).

Language

Since "language shapes the way we think and determines what we can think about" (Benjamin Lee Whorf, 1897–1941, quoted by Hannah Arendt Center for Politics and Humanities, 2015) it is an important aspect to address when discussing professional approaches to SUDs. Professionals in the mental health setting are used to the importance and power of language and to carefully use it to treat and stimulate processes of positive change. Given the outstanding importance of language in the professional mental health setting, the longstanding use of pejorative and characterizing language like "junkie," "dirty," "addict," or "alcoholic" in the context of SUD is grossly harmful. Stigmatizing stereotypes and assumptions materialize in pejorative and dehumanizing descriptions of human conditions around mental health, thereby shaping clinical decisions and a reality in which discrimination appears more justified. This is empirically reflected by numerous qualitative (van Boekel et al., 2013) and at least four quantitative studies of which one investigated attitudes of mental health professionals:

(1) When individuals were referred to as "substance abusers" instead of "having a substance use disorder" participants from the general population were more likely to perceive "substance abusers" as engaging in willful misconduct, having greater social threat, and deserving more punishment (Kelly et al., 2010).

(2) This holds also true regarding mental health clinicians. Compared to those in the "substance use disorder" condition, those in the "substance abuser" condition agreed more with the notion that the character was personally culpable and that punitive measures should be taken (Kelly & Westerhoff, 2010).

(3) In a nationwide online survey among the general population using vignettes on opioid use Goodyear et al. (2018) found higher stigmatizing attitudes towards an individual labeled as being a "drug addict" in comparison to an individual labeled as having an "opioid use disorder."

(4) Building on these results Ashford et al. (2018) applied implicit and explicit stigma measures in an online sample and conclude that terms like "addict," "alcoholic," "opioid addict," and "substance abuser" are potentially stigmatizing and should be omitted. Terms like "recurrence of use" and "pharmacotherapy" might yield less stigma.

The importance of language around SUDs has been poignantly addressed in the last years by several authors. Sarah Wakeman conclusively argued to avoid vocabulary around "abuse" and "abuser" and to not label a patient with a chronic and treatable disorder as the "perpetrator of disease." This can be done by facilitating a moralistic view of the disorder (Wakeman, 2013) and to use simply "treatment" instead of "medication assisted treatment" for SUDs since pharmacotherapy, especially for opioid use disorders, is a highly effective and evidence-based treatment comparable to insulin for diabetes (Wakeman, 2017). John Kelly together with Sarah Wakeman and Richard Saitz strongly cautioned clinicians to "stop talking dirty" in the *American Journal of Medicine* (Kelly et al., 2015) and proposed an "Addiction-ary" to establish an "agreed-upon terminology to aid precise and unambiguous clinical and scientific communication and help reduce stigmatizing and discriminatory public health and social policies" (Kelly et al., 2016, p. 116). Regarding the scientific communication in particular many journals specialized on SUDs strongly encourage authors to use a stigma-free and especially sensitive language in their manuscripts. For example, the Editorial Board of *Substance Abuse* made "an appeal for the use of language that (1) respects the worth and dignity of all persons ('people-first language'); (2) focuses on the medical nature of substance use disorders and treatment; (3) promotes the recovery process; and (4) avoids perpetuating negative stereotypes and biases through the use of slang and idioms" (Broyles et al., 2014, p. 217). In their Editorial the authors noted that the journal's name "substance abuse" itself must now be considered as a diagnostic anachronism and an arguably pejorative term (Broyles et al., 2014, p. 219). Following a debate on the "complex, interrelated conceptual and practical considerations involved in retaining, or changing, the name" the authors consider the question as "by no means resolved" (p. 220). However, the journal's name remains unchanged up to now.

This might well be a result of common challenges and pitfalls when sensitivity and zeitgeist change, and a traditionally used terminology is rightfully identified as pejorative and stigmatizing. Professionals are only one stakeholder group among many others, and they clearly have no sovereignty in interpreting and defining all aspects of language around SUDs on their own. It seems paramount to empower people with lived experience of SUDs to lead inclusive discussions around a preferred terminology and to finally determine an appropriate way of being addressed. As a result, the outcome is most likely complex, depending on the cultural context, and individually determined. For example, it seems problematic to ask Alcoholics Anonymous to change its name or to ask a person with alcohol use disorder to stop referring to themselves as an "alcoholic," when this concept helped them abstain from alcohol use for many years. Changing the language around SUDs is an ongoing and vivid process. Within this process no unrealistic homogeneity in perspectives should be assumed nor should we be content with changing labels, when changing attitudes and behavior is the goal. This does certainly not implicate professional apathy regarding the changes of the language around SUDs. Instead, mental health professionals should actively appreciate and support the process of language change by being reflective and curious to learn from people who use substances and colleagues and accept the uncertainty along the way. Stimulating discussions around professional language of SUDs and its sensitive use on a macro level (e.g., publications, legislation, interviews, and diagnostic manuals) is an important part of this process. On a micro level medical doctors and other mental health professionals also bear responsibility for the therapeutic milieu they are working in. To create a perceptive and sensitive therapeutic environment without stigmatizing language or behavior is a major part of this responsibility. To arrive at a stigma-free therapeutic environment the use of stigmatizing language or stigmatizing stereotypes and behavior should be addressed reliably and repetitively in way that is not shameful for the recipient. Mental health professionals bear a responsibility to kindly, clearly, and constantly engage in conversations with colleagues about obvious and subtle stigmatizing language and behavior toward people who use substances particularly when talking informally and in a trusted environment. This might be done by referring to current research around the stigma of SUD or personal reports from people who use substances who have experienced stigma and discrimination. Serving as an attentive, predictable, and perceptive role model regarding the language around SUDs will most likely help the therapeutical team to avoid stigmatizing language and behavior and strongly influence students and trainees to reflect about the language they use. That way the terminology used by the treatment team can be transparently adapted and discussed. These discussions should happen particularly with direct involvement of the patients within the setting.

In mental health, but also in all other medical contexts, professionals have a responsibility to encounter help-seeking patients without pejorative, stigmatizing, and self-worth-diminishing terminology or behavior. Health care professionals need to avoid inflicting direct and very real harm by increasing shame and reducing self-worth through stigmatizing settings, language, and concepts. Particularly regarding SUDs this must not be mistaken as a question of being nice, but of potential medical malpractice and discrimination perpetuating substance use stigma and hampering recovery (Botticelli & Koh, 2016; Richter & Foster, 2014). Reducing substance use stigma is in fact an integral and profoundly important part of caring for people who use substances and should be considered as such.

References

Ashford, R. D., Brown, A. M., & Curtis, B. (2018). Substance use, recovery, and linguistics: The impact of word choice on explicit and implicit bias. *Drug and Alcohol Dependence, 189*, 131–138. https://doi.org/10.1016/j.drugalcdep.2018.05.005

Bertholet, N., Daeppen, J.-B., Wietlisbach, V., Fleming, M., & Burnand, B. (2005). Reduction of alcohol consumption by brief alcohol intervention in primary care: Systematic review and meta-analysis. *Archives of Internal Medicine, 165*(9), 986–995. https://doi.org/10.1001/archinte.165.9.986

Biancarelli, D. L., Biello, K. B., Childs, E., et al. (2019). Strategies used by people who inject drugs to avoid stigma in healthcare settings. *Drug and Alcohol Dependence, 198*, 80–86. https://doi.org/10.1016/j.drugalcdep.2019.01.037

Botticelli, M. P., & Koh, H. K. (2016). Changing the language of addiction. *JAMA, 316*(13), 1361–1362. https://doi.org/10.1001/jama.2016.11874

Brener, L., von Hippel, W., von Hippel, C., Resnick, I., & Treloar, C. (2010). Perceptions of discriminatory treatment by staff as predictors of drug treatment completion: Utility of a mixed methods approach. *Drug and Alcohol Review, 29*(5), 491–497. https://doi.org/10.1111/j.1465-3362.2010.00173.x

Broyles, L. M., Binswanger, I. A., Jenkins, J. A., et al. (2014). Confronting inadvertent stigma and pejorative language in addiction scholarship: A recognition and response. *Substance Abuse, 35*(3), 217–221. https://doi.org/10.1080/08897077.2014.930372

Corrigan, P. W., Watson, A. C., & Barr, L. (2006). The self-stigma of mental illness: Implications for self-esteem and self-efficacy. *Journal of Social and Clinical Psychology, 25*(8), 875–884. https://doi.org/10.1521/jscp.2006.25.8.875

Crowley, R. A., & Kirschner, N. (2015). The integration of care for mental health, substance abuse, and other behavioral health conditions into primary care: Executive summary of an American College of Physicians position paper. *Annals of Internal Medicine, 163*(4), 298–299. https://doi.org/10.7326/M15-0510

Curtis, J., & Harrison, L. (2001). Beneath the surface: Collaboration in alcohol and other drug treatment. An analysis using Foucault's three modes of objectification. *Journal of Advanced Nursing, 34*(6), 737–744. https://doi.org/10.1046/j.1365-2648.2001.01803.x

Dannatt, L., Ransing, R., Calvey, T., et al. (2021). The impact of stigma on treatment services for people with substance use disorders during the COVID-19 pandemic: Perspectives of NECPAM members. *Frontiers in Psychiatry, 12*, Article 634515. https://doi.org/10.3389/fpsyt.2021.634515

Deans, C., & Soar, R. (2005). Caring for clients with dual diagnosis in rural communities in Australia: The experience of mental health professionals. *Journal of Psychiatric and Mental Health Nursing, 12*(3), 268–274. https://doi.org/10.1111/j.1365-2850.2005.00830.x

Earnshaw, V. A. (2020). Stigma and substance use disorders: A clinical, research, and advocacy agenda. *The American Psychologist, 75*(9), 1300–1311. https://doi.org/10.1037/amp0000744

Earnshaw, V., Smith, L., & Copenhaver, M. (2013). Drug addiction stigma in the context of methadone maintenance therapy: An investigation into understudied sources of stigma. *International Journal of Mental Health and Addiction, 11*(1), 110–122. https://doi.org/10.1007/s11469-012-9402-5

Feeney, L., Jordan, I., & McCarron, P. (2013). Teaching recovery to medical students. *Psychiatric Rehabilitation Journal, 36*(1), 35–41. https://doi.org/10.1037/h0094745

Flanagan, E. H., Buck, T., Gamble, A., Hunter, C., Sewell, I., & Davidson, L. (2016). "Recovery speaks": A photovoice intervention to reduce stigma among primary care providers. *Psychiatric Services (Washington, D.C.), 67*(5), 566–569. https://doi.org/10.1176/appi.ps.201500049

Fogler, S. (2020, December 8). *As a physician and a patient, I've seen the damage caused by the stigma of addiction. It must end*. STAT. www.statnews.com/2020/12/08/stigma-weaponized-helps-fuel-addiction-crisis/

Goodyear, K., Haass-Koffler, C. L., & Chavanne, D. (2018). Opioid use and stigma: The role of gender, language and precipitating events. *Drug and Alcohol Dependence, 185*, 339–346. https://doi.org/10.1016/j.drugalcdep.2017.12.037

Hannah Arendt Center for Politics and Humanities. (2015). *Benjamin Lee Whorf's thoughts on thinking: On language*. https://hac.bard.edu/amor-mundi/benjamin-lee-whorfs-thoughts-on-thinking-on-language-2015-03-25#:~:text=%E2%80%9CLanguage%20shapes%20the%20way%20we,what%20we%20can%20think%20about.%E2%80%9D

Hayes, S. C., Bissett, R., Roget, N., et al. (2004). The impact of acceptance and commitment training and multicultural training on the stigmatizing attitudes and professional burnout of substance abuse counselors. *Behavior Therapy, 35*(4), 821–835. https://doi.org/10.1016/S0005-7894(04)80022-4

Hazell, C. M., Koc, Y., O'Brien, S., Fielding-Smith, S., & Hayward, M. (2021). Enhancing mental health awareness in emergency services (the ENHANcE I project): Cross-sectional survey on mental health stigma among emergency services staff. *BJPsych Open, 7*(3), E77. https://doi.org/10.1192/bjo.2021.37

Henderson, C., Noblett, J., Parke, H., et al. (2014). Mental health-related stigma in health care and mental health-care settings. *The Lancet: Psychiatry, 1*(6), 467–482. https://doi.org/10.1016/S2215-0366(14)00023-6

Horner, G., Daddona, J., Burke, D. J., Cullinane, J., Skeer, M., & Wurcel, A. G. (2019). "You're kind of at war with yourself as a nurse": Perspectives of inpatient nurses on treating people who present with a comorbid opioid use disorder. *PLoS ONE, 14*(10), e0224335. https://doi.org/10.1371/journal.pone.0224335

Kelly, J. F., Dow, S. J., & Westerhoff, C. (2010). Does our choice of substance-related terms influence perceptions of treatment need? An empirical investigation with two commonly used terms. *Journal of Drug Issues, 40*(4), 805–818. https://doi.org/10.1177/002204261004000403

Kelly, J. F., Saitz, R., & Wakeman, S. (2016). Language, substance use disorders, and policy: The need to reach consensus on an "addiction-ary." *Alcoholism Treatment Quarterly, 34*(1), 116–123. https://doi.org/10.1080/07347324.2016.1113103

Kelly, J. F., Wakeman, S. E., & Saitz, R. (2015). Stop talking 'dirty': Clinicians, language, and quality of care for the leading cause of preventable death in the United States. *The American Journal of Medicine, 128*(1), 8–9. https://doi.org/10.1016/j.amjmed.2014.07.043

Kelly, J. F., & Westerhoff, C. M. (2010). Does it matter how we refer to individuals with substance-related conditions? A randomized study of two commonly used terms. *The International Journal on Drug Policy, 21*(3), 202–207. https://doi.org/10.1016/j.drugpo.2009.10.010

Khenti, A., Bobbili, S. J., & Sapag, J. C. (2019). Evaluation of a pilot intervention to reduce mental health and addiction stigma in primary care settings. *Journal of Community Health, 44*(6), 1204–1213. https://doi.org/10.1007/s10900-019-00706-w

Link, B. G., & Phelan, J. (2014). Stigma power. *Social Science & Medicine, 103*, 24–32. https://doi.org/10.1016/j.socscimed.2013.07.035

Livingston, J. D. (2020). *Structural stigma in health-care contexts for people with mental health and substance use issues: A literature review.* www.researchgate.net/profile/james-livingston/publication/341945036_structural_stigma_in_health-care_contexts_for_people_with_mental_health_and_substance_use_issues_a_literature_review/links/5eda7dcc299bf1c67d42177e/structural-stigma-in-health-care-contexts-for-people-with-mental-health-and-substance-use-issues-a-literature-review.pdf

Livingston, J. D., Milne, T., Fang, M. L., & Amari, E. (2012). The effectiveness of interventions for reducing stigma related to substance use disorders: A systematic review. *Addiction (Abingdon, England), 107*(1), 39–50. https://doi.org/10.1111/j.1360-0443.2011.03601.x

Luoma, J. B., Kohlenberg, B. S., Hayes, S. C., Bunting, K., & Rye, A. K. (2008). Reducing self-stigma in substance abuse through acceptance and commitment therapy: Model, manual development, and pilot outcomes. *Addiction Research & Theory, 16*(2), 149–165. https://doi.org/10.1080/16066350701850295

Marchand, K., Beaumont, S., Westfall, J., et al. (2019). Conceptualizing patient-centered care for substance use disorder treatment: Findings from a systematic scoping review. *Substance Abuse Treatment, Prevention, and Policy, 14*(1), 37. https://doi.org/10.1186/s13011-019-0227-0

Martins, R. K., & McNeil, D. W. (2009). Review of motivational interviewing in promoting health behaviors. *Clinical Psychology Review, 29*(4), 283–293. https://doi.org/10.1016/j.cpr.2009.02.001

Mejia-Lancheros, C., Lachaud, J., O'Campo, P., et al. (2020). Trajectories and mental health-related predictors of perceived discrimination and stigma among homeless adults with mental illness. *PLoS ONE, 15*(2), e0229385. https://doi.org/10.1371/journal.pone.0229385

Mendiola, C. K., Galetto, G., & Fingerhood, M. (2018). An exploration of emergency physicians' attitudes toward patients with substance use disorder. *Journal of Addiction Medicine, 12*(2), 132–135. https://doi.org/10.1097/ADM.0000000000000377

Morawska, A., Fletcher, R., Pope, S., Heathwood, E., Anderson, E., & McAuliffe, C. (2013). Evaluation of mental health first aid training in a diverse community setting. *International Journal of Mental Health Nursing, 22*(1), 85–92. https://doi.org/10.1111/j.1447-0349.2012.00844.x

Nieweglowski, K., Corrigan, P. W., Tyas, T., et al. (2018). Exploring the public stigma of substance use disorder through community-based participatory research. *Addiction Research & Theory*, *26*(4), 323–329. https://doi.org/10.1080/16066359.2017.1409890

Nyblade, L., Stockton, M. A., Giger, K., et al. (2019). Stigma in health facilities: Why it matters and how we can change it. *BMC Medicine*, *17*(1), 25. https://doi.org/10.1186/s12916-019-1256-2

Paquette, C. E., Syvertsen, J. L., & Pollini, R. A. (2018). Stigma at every turn: Health services experiences among people who inject drugs. *The International Journal on Drug Policy*, *57*, 104–110. https://doi.org/10.1016/j.drugpo.2018.04.004

Peckover, S., & Chidlaw, R. G. (2007). Too frightened to care? Accounts by district nurses working with clients who misuse substances. *Health & Social Care in the Community*, *15*(3), 238–245. https://doi.org/10.1111/j.1365-2524.2006.00683.x

Probst, C., Manthey, J., Martinez, A., & Rehm, J. (2015). Alcohol use disorder severity and reported reasons not to seek treatment: A cross-sectional study in European primary care practices. *Substance Abuse Treatment, Prevention, and Policy*, *10*(1), 32. https://doi.org/10.1186/s13011-015-0028-z

Rehm, J., Mathers, C., Popova, S., Thavorncharoensap, M., Teerawattananon, Y., & Patra, J. (2009). Global burden of disease and injury and economic cost attributable to alcohol use and alcohol-use disorders. *The Lancet*, *373* (9682), 2223–2233. https://doi.org/10.1016/S0140-6736(09)60746-7

Renner, J. A. (2019). Counteracting the effect of stigma on education for substance use disorders. *Focus (American Psychiatric Publishing)*, *17*(2), 134–140. https://doi.org/10.1176/appi.focus.20180039

Richter, L., & Foster, S. E. (2014). Effectively addressing addiction requires changing the language of addiction. *Journal of Public Health Policy*, *35*(1), 60–64. https://doi.org/10.1057/jphp.2013.44

Schomerus, G., Bauch, A., Elger, B., et al. (2017). Das Stigma von Suchterkrankungen verstehen und überwinden [Understanding and overcoming the stigma of substance use disorders]. *SUCHT*, *63*(5), 253–259. https://doi.org/10.1024/0939-5911/a000501

Schomerus, G., Baumann, E., Sander, C., Speerforck, S., & Angermeyer, M. C. (2021). Some good news for psychiatry: Resource allocation preferences of the public during the COVID-19 pandemic. *World Psychiatry: Official Journal of the World Psychiatric Association (WPA)* [accepted for publication].

Schomerus, G., Corrigan, P. W., Klauer, T., Kuwert, P., Freyberger, H. J., & Lucht, M. (2011). Self-stigma in alcohol dependence: Consequences for drinking-refusal self-efficacy. *Drug and Alcohol Dependence*, *114*(1), 12–17. https://doi.org/10.1016/j.drugalcdep.2010.08.013

Simon, R., Snow, R., & Wakeman, S. (2020). Understanding why patients with substance use disorders leave the hospital against medical advice: A qualitative study. *Substance Abuse*, *41*(4), 519–525. https://doi.org/10.1080/08897077.2019.1671942

Stone, E. M., Kennedy-Hendricks, A., Barry, C. L., Bachhuber, M. A., & McGinty, E. E. (2021). The role of stigma in U.S. primary care physicians' treatment of opioid use disorder. *Drug and Alcohol Dependence, 221*, 108627. https://doi.org/10.1016/j.drugalcdep.2021.108627

Stone, R. (2015). Pregnant women and substance use: Fear, stigma, and barriers to care. *Health & Justice, 3*(1), 1–15. https://doi.org/10.1186/s40352-015-0015-5

Toftdahl, N. G., Nordentoft, M., & Hjorthøj, C. (2016). Prevalence of substance use disorders in psychiatric patients: A nationwide Danish population-based study. *Social Psychiatry and Psychiatric Epidemiology, 51*(1), 129–140. https://doi.org/10.1007/s00127-015-1104-4

van Boekel, L. C., Brouwers, E. P. M., van Weeghel, J., & Garretsen, H. F. L. (2013). Stigma among health professionals towards patients with substance use disorders and its consequences for healthcare delivery: Systematic review. *Drug and Alcohol Dependence, 131*(1–2), 23–35. https://doi.org/10.1016/j.drugalcdep.2013.02.018

(2016a). Experienced and anticipated discrimination reported by individuals in treatment for substance use disorders within the Netherlands. *Health & Social Care in the Community, 24*(5), e23–e33. https://doi.org/10.1111/hsc.12279

(2016b). Inequalities in healthcare provision for individuals with substance use disorders: Perspectives from healthcare professionals and clients. *Journal of Substance Use, 21*(2), 1–8. https://doi.org/10.3109/14659891.2014.980860

Wakeman, S. E. (2013). Language and addiction: Choosing words wisely. *American Journal of Public Health, 103*(4), e1–e2. https://doi.org/10.2105/AJPH.2012.301191

(2017). Medications for addiction treatment: Changing language to improve care. *Journal of Addiction Medicine, 11*(1), 1–2. https://doi.org/10.1097/ADM.0000000000000275

Wakeman, S. E., Kanter, G. P., & Donelan, K. (2017). Institutional substance use disorder intervention improves general internist preparedness, attitudes, and clinical practice. *Journal of Addiction Medicine, 11*(4), 308–314. https://doi.org/10.1097/ADM.0000000000000314

Wakeman, S. E., Pham-Kanter, G., Baggett, M. V., & Campbell, E. G. (2015). Medicine resident preparedness to diagnose and treat substance use disorders: Impact of an enhanced curriculum. *Substance Abuse, 36*(4), 427–433. https://doi.org/10.1080/08897077.2014.962722

Wakeman, S. E., Pham-Kanter, G., & Donelan, K. (2016). Attitudes, practices, and preparedness to care for patients with substance use disorder: Results from a survey of general internists. *Substance Abuse, 37*(4), 635–641. https://doi.org/10.1080/08897077.2016.1187240

Wang, P. S., Angermeyer, M., Borges, G., et al. (2007). Delay and failure in treatment seeking after first onset of mental disorders in the World Health Organization's World Mental Health Survey Initiative. *World Psychiatry: Official Journal of the World Psychiatric Association (WPA), 6*(3), 177–185.

CHAPTER 14

Final Considerations and Future Directions for Erasing the Stigma of Substance Use Disorders

Patrick W. Corrigan and Georg Schomerus

The message is clear. The stigma of substance use disorders (SUDs) may be as harmful to people as the symptoms and disabilities that arise from these disorders. As explained well in several chapters, stigma appears at many levels that vary across the international theater. Our goal in this book was to bring together scholars and advocates to summarize both research and wisdom about SUD stigma and stigma change. In going forward, we believe that research must be driven by the advocate's imperative (Corrigan, 2018). Namely, its value is measured in its enhancing advocates' agendas to erase the stigma. In this final chapter, we consider three themes that emerge from the book to advance the advocate's imperative. First, we broadly consider goals that define the advocate's agenda. Second, we describe who is the best advocate to erase stigma. Third, noting that stigma is essentially a social construct, we review how stigma and stigma change varies around the world. We hope the imperative rings clear throughout the chapter. Even though much of what we know emerges from addiction science and related professional disciplines, SUD stigma is social injustice, not disease process. Like all groups experiencing discrimination, SUD stigma is resolved only when the injustice is erased.

What Is the Goal of Stigma Change?

Repeated authors in the book likened the stigma of SUD to such social injustices as racism, sexism, ageism, and homophobia, defining its components in terms of stereotypes (negative beliefs about a group), prejudice (agreement with the stereotype leading to negative emotions), and discrimination. While we think most readers seek a world devoid of stereotypes and prejudice, eradicating discrimination is the immediate goal. As people with SUD often say, "it would be nice if people didn't hold prejudicial beliefs about me, BUT at the end of the day, don't block my life opportunities because of my drug choices. Don't stop me from getting a job, living in a good place, or getting good health." This is the call to stop discrimination.

Definitions of stigma become more complex when describing specific types. In our introductory chapter, we defined three: (1) public stigma is the negative effects leading to discrimination that result when the public endorses stereotypes about people with SUD; (2) self-stigma is the harm to self-esteem and self-efficacy that occurs when some people internalize stereotype; and (3) structural stigma is the effect of institutional rules, policies, and regulations that disadvantage the stigmatized group, even absent of stigmatizing attitudes of those following the rules. All three forms of stigma have consequences on multiple levels. Enacted stigma directly harms people with SUD, leading to inferior health care, job, and housing discrimination, etc. Anticipated stigma leads to avoidance of situations where stigma is expected to occur, for example health care, or seeking other help. It may also lead to label avoidance. In order to avoid the egregious effects of the SUD label, people will not travel to frequent places where the label is bestowed. For example, they don't seek out treatment in evidence-based clinics in order to avoid the label of being an "addict." Each type leads to a different agenda governing both goals of stigma change and related actions (see Chapter 9 by Kundert and Corrigan). The *services agenda* recognizes barriers of anticipated stigma and label avoidance to treatment engagement. We know that research has identified evidence-based services that can help people address their SUD. Many people will avoid stigma by not engaging in SUD services where the label occurs. "Hey, that's Harry coming out of the SUD clinic. He must be a druggie!" Strategies that generally decrease stigma will increase use of SUD treatments.

The *rights agenda* focuses on public stigma and structural stigma. Namely, the public's endorsement of prejudice leading to discrimination leads to loss of life opportunity, a fundamental civil right. Just as activists fight for similar rights for people of color, women, and the LGBTQ community, so the rights agenda seeks to stop stigma in order to promote rightful aspirations among people with SUD. Finally, the *self-worth* agenda seeks to replace self-stigma and shame with self-esteem and agency. This is frequently accomplished by promoting empowerment and self-determination among people with SUD.

Especially noteworthy about different agendas is finding that agendas often work at cross-purposes. For example, one way to decrease SUD stigma, in order to promote service engagement, may actually challenge the rights and self-worth agendas. Advocates have tried to decrease stigma by framing SUD as a treatable disease (McGinty et al., 2015), often using a medical model to illustrate treatment and disease. However, antistigma efforts that frame a behavioral health condition as a biological disorder, at least in terms of mental health (Kvaale et al., 2013), may decrease sigma related to blame (e.g., "people with SUD have brain disorder and hence are not responsible for their symptoms") thereby promoting treatment engagement. But the brain disorder message also undermines recovery, the idea that the person can get better. A population study in Germany showed biological causal beliefs of alcohol use disorder linked to less blame, but also stronger beliefs that someone with this disorder is different from other people, and more dangerous (Schomerus et al., 2014). Addictions are hardwired in so people can't beat their symptoms. And the threat to recovery markedly increases public stigma (undermining the rights agenda). "I don't want to hire that addict. He looks good now, but his symptoms are hardwired in and will eventually come back." Threats to recovery also undermine hope and aspirations that exacerbate self-stigma and the self-worth agenda.

Targeting Stigma Change

A goal of erasing the stigma of SUD across the worldwide population is worthy but not likely to be achieved. Although great strides have been made against racism, sexism, and homophobia, bigotry endures in several ways. Targeted stigma change is likely the goal in the short term. Benefits will be more poignant when stigma change is noted in people in positions of power vis-à-vis the life opportunities of those stigmatized for SUD:

- employers and educators who are the vehicles for obtaining lifelong vocational goals;
- physical and behavioral health providers who need to engage their patients with SUD in shared decision-making;
- landlords and realtors who are the doorkeepers to personally satisfying housing;
- government officials who write the laws that form the structural barriers to life opportunities;
- members of the criminal justice system – for example, police, the courts, defense and prosecution, parole – who are charged with carrying out the laws related to SUD.

Targeting stigma assumes a strategic approach to goals and actions. Hence, instead of general programs, antistigma interventions need to be crafted for the specific audience. What, for example, do antistigma advocates want to change in employers versus the criminal justice system? What strategies best impact the change goals that drive the overall antistigma effort? For employers, this might include enforcing rules that diminish SUD considerations in terms of hiring and that promote reasonable accommodations to help them remain successful employers. In terms of criminal justice, this might be establishment of drug courts where judge, defense, and prosecutions join with the person with SUD to develop a restorative plan. Target approaches will affect the form of antistigma interventions. Among other things, credible presenters of targeted antistigma programs must come from the targeted population. Employers with antistigma messages are going to have more authority with other employers; doctors when speaking to the health community. These presentations are enhanced when the employer, for example, is accompanied by one of their employees with SUD; the role of the first-person voice is discussed more below. Together, employer and employee with SUD make a compelling story about the value of reasonable accommodations.

Affirming Attitudes

Erasing the stigma of SUD is not enough. Consider what President Lyndon Johnson said about racism in the United States. Speaking about African Americans, he said: "You do not wipe away the scars of centuries by saying: Now you are free to go where you want, and do as you desire, and choose the leaders you please" (The American Presidency Project, 1965).

Johnson used this as a clarion call for affirming beliefs and behaviors. It's not enough to remove the stain of intolerance and bigotry; they need to be replaced by recognizing both cultural and individual strengths of people of color leading to respect and admiration. Society needs to sculpt itself into a place of hope and aspiration for these groups. Social structures need to be crafted that actively promote opportunity for achieving these aspirations.

And so, the stigma of SUD is truly reduced when we surpass the elimination of disrespectful beliefs about people with SUD with views of recovery, hope, self-determination, and goals. Beliefs, however, are never enough. Actions that help people with SUD pursue their goals must follow. These might include reasonable accommodations that not only help people escape the tyranny of the legal system, but support ambitions related to education, work, housing, and health. This requires governmental bodies that fund social programs that support community goals.

Who Makes the Best Advocates?

Typically, doctors come to mind when thinking about diagnosing and treating SUD. They are the experts with years of experience who have mastered the evidence to guide development of effective intervention programs. In a similar light, one might think antistigma programs are most successful when the respected doctor educates the public about SUD and the harm of stigma. They use their position of respect to convince the population of the malice wrought by stigma. However, if there is one recurring message from this book, it is that SUD antistigma programs must be led by people who are harmed by the stigma: people with SUD. Consider Chapter 11 by McCartney on the role of peers. People with lived experience know best the harm wrought by this kind of bigotry and efforts to erase it. They are also most credible in terms of sharing what it means to be the butt of SUD sigma. People with lived experience are the advocates who define the imperatives of antistigma, proaffirmation efforts.

By no means are we saying doctors and other stakeholders have no role in antistigma programs. Consider this: the two editors of this book (GS and PC) are white males who hugely support affirming programs for people of color and women. But we do so as allies. We sit in the proverbial back seat, ready and willing to endorse and otherwise assist in ways to stomp out racism and sexism as defined by people of color and women. In part, this gives a meta-message: that we in the dominating (and oppressive) group – white males – not only recognize the agency of women and people of color but pledge our willingness to follow their direction. Similarly, readers of this book who do not identify as people with SUD are allies, an energized people ready to join imperatives for stigma change.

An additional caveat is worth mentioning here. Given the prominence of addiction science, there may nonetheless be a tendency to medicalize antistigma messages and pull doctors out of the back seat. This is great if the doctor is also a person with SUD. Otherwise, dear SUD professional, please join the ranks of allies. GS and PC are doctors who do not identify as people with SUD and are proudly supporting from the rear.

Who then are these advocates? The simple definition is "people who identify with SUD." We do not mean to imply there are litmus tests that indicate the person with lived experience. There is no bar that people must meet to identify with SUD or present themselves as advocates. What does identity mean in this definition? We suggest some version of the statement, "I view myself as currently or in the past to be a person with life challenges related to substance use." How bad does SUD need to be to identify? Clearly, there is not a severity test. We should never presume that one person's SUD (the person who ended up in detox four times and jailed for possession) is more legitimate than another (the person who is able to control one's alcohol use with prayer). Consider the essence of identity. A person who says that they have been challenged by SUD has, indeed, been challenged. They are "qualified" to step up as an antistigma advocate.

Are all SUDs and their stigma equivalent? This book mostly focused on SUDs related to alcohol or illegal drugs. There are other SUDs, however, such as tobacco products and caffeine. Is the stigma of cigarettes and caffeine worth acting against? One way of answering the question is by considering whether people vote with their feet. If there are enough people with SUDs related to tobacco or caffeine to regularly come together and express concern about corresponding stigma, then it is a social justice cause worth pursuing. Perhaps the more difficult issue here is heterogeneity. Do people who are criminalized by the justice system for SUD share sufficiently similar priorities to organize as a single effort? Will the message – don't stigmatize people who abuse drugs or smoke cigarettes – be clear to the public? Although, ultimately, this is an empirical question, the final goal should not be overlooked. Whether as joined forces or campaigns specific to a substance, the stigma of people with different SUDs must be replaced with affirming attitudes and actions.

There are additional considerations regarding who are advocates. In Chapter 6, Dittrich and Schomerus described the complexity here in terms of intersectionality, that is, people harmed by the stigma of SUD often align with other stigmatized identities. These are also often social determinants of health and health care that include ethnicity, gender, age, and LGBTQ. Stigma's harm and corresponding needs for affirmation of a black person with SUD likely differs significantly from the white person with SUD. Moreover, people with SUD often experience additional stigma due to poverty, homelessness, co-occurring mental health or physical disorders, and involvement in the criminal justice system. Hence, the advocate question must include these other identities.

Peer Advocate and Recovery

Identity statements are often qualified as a person with SUD *in recovery*. Recovery is a complex idea here especially when contrasted with how the concept has evolved in mental health that embraces two definitions (Ralph & Corrigan, 2004):

(1) Recovery as outcome: symptoms and disabilities of even the most severe psychiatric disorders remit such that people are able to pursue the gamut of personally defined life goals. This corresponds with long-term follow-up research that shows more than half of people with schizophrenia either become entirely symptom free or experience significant times of remission (Jobe & Harrow, 2005). This has led to benchmarks of recovery that include sustained remission of symptoms that make up a diagnosis and at least part-time engagement in an instrumental role such as work or school (Liberman, 2008).

(2) Recovery as process: recovery is a dynamic and ongoing experience in which people pursue life goals with hope despite recurring mental health symptoms. In this light, a central goal of psychiatric services is to help people manage symptoms and disabilities, so they are successful in their personally defined pursuits (Andresen et al., 2003).

Does recovery in SUD rest on a similar two-factor distinction: outcome versus process? Abstinence seems to be the commonly endorsed expectation for people with SUD (US Department of Health and Human Services et al., 2012). Outcome is to help people remain free of addictive substances (Scott et al., 2005). Alternatively, harm reduction has emerged in some ways to frame recovery in SUD as more of a process. Harm reduction advocates recognize that abstinence is not the only way to health. For them, recovery is an individualized process focused on decreasing the deleterious impact of, rather than completely extinguishing, substance use behaviors (Hawk et al., 2017). Despite substance use, people can aspire to personally meaningful goals with hope.

We do not offer authoritative evidence that resolves outcome versus process models of SUD recovery or some interaction thereof. The point here is to be transparent about who is the SUD antistigma advocate in recovery. Do we presume this is a person abstinent from substances or might they be successfully pursuing life goals despite living with substance use? This is not a trivial question given strong opinions in the broader SUD community about abstinence being the only indicator of recovery. For example, if a group of advocates in recovery wish to organize against stigma, will those who are abstinent tolerate others in the alliance who are living with continued substance use?

Disclosure as Vehicle to Stigma Change

As Talluri and Corrigan discussed in Chapter 10 on disclosure, the stigma of SUD is largely hidden. Unlike race or gender, the public cannot tell whether an individual with SUD is part of a stigmatized SUD group from external cues. Hence, strategic disclosure is key to being an advocate. This does not mean carte blanche sharing of all one's experiences with SUD. Rather, individual advocates decide to craft a message that both reflects their personal story of self-esteem as well as a statement that challenges the stigma. They should respect their right to keep private any part of their story. Research suggests effective disclosures that challenge public stigma include (1) on-the-way down stories, experiences that represent the life challenges of SUD and (2) on-the-way-up rules, that despite these significant challenges the person did recover, accomplished goals, and lives a personally satisfying life. The disclosure ends with the change goal that corresponds with the target. "And so, don't discriminate against me because of my SUD. Give me opportunities I am due as a citizen in our society related to ... work, education, health, relationships, and involvement in the criminal justice system."

Stigma in the International Theatre

Stigma is a socially created construct and, as such, hugely varies by social context, for example, ethnic, religious, and other cultural forces as embodied in nation states. Manthey and colleagues (Chapter 7) nicely review ways in which SUD and stigma vary across the international sphere. As Baumann and colleagues showed in Chapter 12, media grounded by different national perspectives often embodies stigma in that zeitgeist. The media, in its varied forms, may significantly fan the flames of stigma on one hand or has the potential for disrupting it on the other. It worsens stigma imbalance and inaccurate representations of people with SUD. This often occurs when the media focuses on danger and criminal behavior related to SUD. The media seems to be naturally attracted to the violent – if it bleeds it leads. As a result, advocacy groups have partnered with media organizations to propose language guides for reporters. Consider the advisory guidelines on drugs and drug addiction by the Australian Press Council (2001). Specific use of language is often a focus of the guidelines.

The media can also be a tool for reducing stigma. McGinty and colleagues (2015) showed that media messages featuring people with successfully treated SUDs led to lower social distance and less willingness to discriminate against people with SUD. Media-based efforts to change stigma have significantly blossomed on the mental health side, with Beyond Blue in Australia. Similar nation-based efforts may benefit people struggling with the stigma of SUD.

Stigma Reified by Government into Policy

Nation states and their governments enact laws and policies that often become structural barriers to life opportunities of people with SUD. See Chapter 4 by Livingston et al. Consider, as an example, limitations on SUD disability protections in the United States, especially as they compare to benefits for people with psychiatric disability. Although alcohol and other substance use disorders are clearly disabling, preventing many people from being fully employed and earning a sustainable income, the US Social Security Administration (SSA) does not provide income or medical benefits to these groups of people, though they may qualify if the disorders are associated with other disabilities. People with psychiatric disabilities are fully covered by SSA.

The 1990 Americans with Disabilities Act (ADA) is meant to protect Americans with disabilities in the workplace and public settings, as well as provide them reasonable accommodations. ADA provides full protections to people with psychiatric disabilities, even when they relapse. People with alcohol and other substance use disorders may receive ADA protections, though they lose them if the person relapses. In fact, alcohol and substance use on the job are permissible grounds for dismissal. Limits to SSA and ADA not only demonstrate structural stigma but provide clear directions for policy change that promote opportunity for people with SUD.

The Criminalization of SUD: The criminalization of SUD is the most noticeable manifestation of policy that worsens sigma and discrimination. Richard Nixon's *War on Drugs* (launched in 1971) and Nancy Reagan's *Just Say No!* (1986) are two of the more stunning nation-led campaigns that intensified criminal ideas about SUD. This led to extreme incarceration due to possession and minor sales infractions in the USA and around the world. Among other things, these ideas were seeds for a new Jim Crow era (Alexander & West, 2012) where large groups of men of color were locked away with long, long prison sentences. Despite this history, there seems to be some optimism, with several areas of the USA, as well as Australia and New Zealand, decriminalizing drug use, though mostly focusing on either the medical or recreational use of marijuana. Western Europe seems to be especially progressive in decriminalizing SUD as outlined in a somewhat dated case study of Portugal, Germany, and the Netherlands (Anderson, 2012). Portugal decriminalized all drug use in 2001, meaning no criminal penalties were attached to possession or use, though people trafficking could still be arrested. The Netherlands is known around the world for tolerance of cannabis, though its

1976 Opium Law does specify incarceration for more "hard" drugs such as cocaine and heroin. Germany seems to be a bit more conservative although it has evolved its perception of drug use from criminal to public health. For example, the German Federal Ministry of Health inaugurated its Action Plan on Drugs and Addiction that specifically calls for treatment and therapy as part of the plan for addressing the needs of people with SUD. In this spirit, the United Nations Commission on Narcotic Drugs proposed "Resolution 61/11: Promoting Non-Stigmatizing Attitudes to Ensure the Availability of, Access to and Delivery of Health, Care and Social Services for Drug Users" in 2020 (United Nations Office on Drugs and Crime, 2020). In the spirit of the German experience, this bit of progressive policy is meant to change government's approach toward SUD from criminal to public health, specifically seeking to diminish stigma in order to better engage people in services.

We admit to guardedly using the word "progressive" here; moving forward is in the eye of the beholder. While there are many countries that have embraced efforts to decriminalize SUD, others continue to express moral and criminal concerns about possession and use. And trafficking continues to be anathema across most countries. Consider, for example, that severe sentences including execution exist for possession or trafficking in Iran, Thailand, Malaysia, China, Philippines, Saudi Arabia, and Vietnam as well as lengthy prison sentences in Columbia, Costa Rica, Dubai, Laos, North Korea, and Turkey (American Addiction Centers, 2021). This difference reflects a fundamental tension between progressive notions of decriminalization versus respect for diversity among countries, especially those that hold religious or moral views that are fundamentally at odds with changing criminal laws about SUD. Although we, the authors of this chapter, have strong feeling about SUD and criminal law, our goal here is to stress an essential point. Countries around the world differ on their views of SUD that will likely limit consensuses on policies like these.

Still, we believe that addressing SUD in a stigma-free way will yield better results in terms of harm reduction and outcomes of SUD while not increasing drug use and its negative consequences. These effects are measurable, and as scientists, it is our task to compile the evidence that we do not "need" stigma to effectively address SUD. For example, an evaluation of the Portuguese decriminalization strategy showed slight increases in overall drug use – that was very similar to developments in neighboring countries without policy changes and in the entire European Union – and a meaningful and unique decline in the number of problematic drug users (Hughes & Stevens, 2010). Our hope is that such evidence will inform world policy changes from traditional views on how to deal best with substance use in our societies.

Community-Based Participatory Research

We believe community-based participatory research (CBPR) is essential for science to incorporate diverse international perspectives in understanding and impacting the stigma of SUD. As Sheehan and colleagues outlined in Chapter 8, CBPR defines a partnership between researchers and the community of interest related to SUD stigma. At the base, this means the CBPR team needs to empower people with SUD in its research efforts during the project. But community becomes layered when research examines SUD embedded within specific countries and cultures. Hence, research on European blacks need to have people of African heritage with SUD as central to their enterprise. The story becomes even more complex when we realize the diversity of African heritage – for example, Mediterranean versus Sub-Saharan states or countries that are fundamentally Christian versus Muslim. These levels recapitulate the challenges of intersectionality we discussed earlier.

Final Thoughts

Do we end with optimism? It is encouraging that the stigma of SUD is being recognized as a social injustice that needs to be erased just as other forms of injustice including the stigma of mental illness, but also more fundamentally experiences related to racism, sexism, and homophobia. But bigotry is a stubborn foe; even though the world has more firmly embraced visions of diversity and heritage, intolerance based on skin color, gender, or sexual orientation remains prominent, often violently so. However, we do not mean to end this book with a pall of pessimism. We are a group of readers that embrace dignity for people with SUD and join efforts to erase paralyzing stigma. Chapters herein not only summarize what we know about SUD stigma and stigma change, but also provide direction and agenda for ongoing work. Perhaps the biggest insight for us in this journey is the imperative to give voice to the essential advocate. People with SUD need to define and implement antistigma efforts. The rest of us join them as allies. In the process, we make small (targeted) steps to affirm the life opportunities of those with SUD.

References

Alexander, M., & West, C. (2012). *The new Jim Crow: Mass incarceration in the age of colorblindness*. Revised ed. New Press.

American Addiction Centers. (2021, July 16). *Drug laws around the world: Death penalty for drugs*. DrugAbuse.com. https://drugabuse.com/blog/the-20-countries-with-the-harshest-drug-laws-in-the-world/

Anderson, S. (2012). European drug policy: The cases of Portugal, Germany, and The Netherlands. *The Eastern Illinois University Political Science Review, 1*(1), Article 2. http://thekeep.eiu.edu/eiupsr/vol1/iss1/2

Andresen, R., Oades, L., & Caputi, P. (2003). The experience of recovery from schizophrenia: Towards an empirically validated stage model. *The Australian and New Zealand Journal of Psychiatry, 37*(5), 586–594. https://doi.org/10.1046/j.1440-1614.2003.01234.x

Australian Press Council. (2001). *Guideline: Drugs and drug addiction*. www.presscouncil.org.au/document-search/guideline-drugs-and-drug-addiction/

Corrigan, P. (2018). *The stigma effect: Unintended consequences of mental health campaigns*. Columbia University Press.

Hawk, M., Coulter, R. W. S., Egan, J. E., et al. (2017). Harm reduction principles for healthcare settings. *Harm Reduction Journal, 14*, Article 70. https://doi-org.ezproxy.gl.iit.edu/10.1186/s12954-017-0196-4

Hughes, C. E., & Stevens, A. (2010). What can we learn from the Portuguese decriminalization of illicit drugs? *The British Journal of Criminology, 50*(6), 999–1022.

Jobe, T. H., & Harrow, M. (2005). Long-term outcome of patients with schizophrenia: A review. *The Canadian Journal of Psychiatry, 50*(14), 892–900. https://doi.org/10.1177/070674370505001403

Kvaale, E. P., Haslam, N., & Gottdiener, W. H. (2013). The "side effects" of medicalization: A meta-analytic review of how biogenetic explanations affect stigma. *Clinical Psychology Review, 33*(6), 782–794. https://doi-org.ezproxy.gl.iit.edu/10.1016/j.cpr.2013.06.002

Liberman, R. P. (2008). *Recovery from disability: Manual of psychiatric rehabilitation*. American Psychiatric Publishing, Inc.

McGinty, E. E., Goldman, H. H., Pescosolido, B., & Barry, C. L. (2015). Portraying mental illness and drug addiction as treatable health conditions: Effects of a randomized experiment on stigma and discrimination. *Social Science & Medicine, 126*, 73–85. https://doi.org/10.1016/j.socscimed.2014.12.010

Ralph, R. O., & Corrigan, P. W. (Eds.). (2004). *Recovery in mental illness: Broadening our understanding of wellness*. American Psychological Association. https://doi-org.ezproxy.gl.iit.edu/10.1037/10848-000

Schomerus, G., Matschinger, H., & Angermeyer, M. C. (2014). Causal beliefs of the public and social acceptance of persons with mental illness:

A comparative analysis of schizophrenia, depression and alcohol dependence. *Psychological Medicine, 44*(2), 303–314.
Scott, C. K., Foss, M. A., & Dennis, M. L. (2005). Pathways in the relapse-treatment-recovery cycle over 3 years. *Journal of Substance Abuse Treatment, 28*(2), S63–S72.
The American Presidency Project. (1965, June 4). Commencement address at Howard University: "To fulfill these rights." www.presidency.ucsb.edu/documents/commencement-address-howard-university-fulfill-these-rights
United Nations Office on Drugs and Crime. (2020). *Resolution 61/11: Promoting non-stigmatizing attitudes to ensure the availability of, access to and delivery of health, care and social services for drug users.* www.unodc.org/documents/commissions/CND/CND_Sessions/CND_61/CND_res2018/CND_Resolution_61_11.pdf
US Department of Health and Human Services, SAMHSA, & CBHSQ. (2012). *Results from the 2012 National Survey on Drug Use and Health: Summary of national findings.* www.samhsa.gov/data/sites/default/files/NSDUHnationalfindingresults2012/NSDUHnationalfindingresults2012/NSDUHresults2012.htm

Index

abstinence, 22, 258
Acceptance and Commitment Therapy (ACT), 189
action-based research. *See* participatory action research
activism, as anti-stigma strategy, 10–11, 167–168
ADA. *See* Americans with Disabilities Act
addiction. *See* substance use disorders
addiction identity, 180–182
addiction services. *See* substance use services
advocacy, stigma reduction through, 199–200, 256–259
affirming attitudes, 255
Affordable Care Act, 111
Africa. *See* sub-Saharan Africa
African Americans. *See* Black community
African Canadians, 110–112
agendas, stigma reduction
  rights, 163, 166–169, 172–173, 253–254
  self-worth, 163, 169–170, 172–173, 253–254
  services, 163–166, 172–173, 253–254
AIDS. *See* human immunodeficiency virus
alcohol use
  acceptable, 2
  global, 107–108
  during parole, 59–62
  public policy on, 23–24
  risks associated with, 2
  in South Asia, 126–127
  in sub-Saharan Africa, 117–120
alcohol use disorder (AUD)
  continuum model of, 7–8
  cultural variation in stigma of, 2–3
  European stigma toward, 115–116
  in former Soviet Union, 121–126
  self-stigma of, 5–6
  in South Asia, 127–128
  stigma of other mental disorders compared with stigma of, 1–2
  structural stigma against, 7
Alcoholics Anonymous, 60, 181, 205

Americans with Disabilities Act (ADA), 188, 260
anticipated stigma, 4–6, 26–27, 253–254
anti-stigma interventions. *See* stigma reduction
AP. *See* Associated Press
APC. *See* Australian Press Council
Argentina, 113–115
Associated Press (AP), media advisory guidelines of, 219–221
AUD. *See* alcohol use disorder
Australian Press Council (APC), media advisory guidelines of, 219–221
authenticity, disclosure and, 181–182
autonomy, recovery role of, 73–75
avoidance. *See* label avoidance; social avoidance

ban the box policies, 34–35
behavioral model of SUD, 9
benevolence stigma, 92–93
bioethics, 69
  as individually-focused, 72–77
  limitations of, 73–77
  SUD impacts of, 73–77
biological disorder, SUDs as, 35, 253–254
biopsychosocial model of SUDs, 69–72
Black community
  criminalization of, 48–49, 91–92
  history of intersectionality and, 88–89
  intersectional stigma experienced by, 91–92, 96
  police interactions with, 53–56
  structural discrimination against, 110–112, 260–262
  substance use stigma compounded with racism against, 26–27
  SUD stigma experiences of, 15–22
blame. *See* responsibility
Brazil, 113–115
British Doctors and Dentists Group, 197–199, 201–202
broadcasting one's experience, 185–186
buprenorphine, 24, 26–28, 32, 91–92

265

Canada
  criminal justice involvement in substance use in, 46–49, 62–64
  SUD stigma in, 109–112
cannabis use
  global, 107
  legalization of, 62–64, 109–110, 112, 116–117, 260–262
  public policy on, 23–24
  risks associated with, 2
  in South Asia, 126–127
CBPR. *See* community-based participatory research
CER. *See* community engaged research
Chile, 113–115
cigarette smoking. *See* smoking
class. *See* socioeconomic status
clinical practice, SUD stigma reduction in, 234–236
cocaine use, 91–92, 217
Colombia, 113–115
communication, media. *See* media
communication campaigns
  negative stereotypes in, 170–171
  stigma reduction using, 33–37, 164–165
community engaged research (CER), 144–145. *See also* community-based participatory research
community re-entry, 59–62
community-based participatory research (CBPR), 144, 154, 160, 262
  benefits of, 158
  case study illustrating, 145–149
  compensation and resource access in, 159
  confidentiality and dual roles in, 155–156
  definition of, 144–145
  disclosure and, 187–188
  dissemination and implementation of findings from, 152–154
  inclusion of people with lived experience in, 154–155
  lived experience researcher protection in, 156–157
  models for implementation of, 159–160
  power sharing in, 157–158
  principles of, 147–149
  research participant protection in, 156
  stakeholder engagement in, 152–154
  stakeholder identification and selection in, 151–152
  stigma research gap closure through, 149–151
  study conduction in, 152–153
  study planning and design in, 152–153
compensation, in community-based participatory research, 159

confidentiality, in community-based participatory research, 155–156
consent, disclosure without, 31
consistency, ethical, 82–83
contact, stigma reduction through, 10–11, 168–169, 171–172, 197–199, 202–203
contextually aware engagement, in ethics of SUD stigma, 81–82
continuum model of SUD, 1–11
co-production, 144–145. *See also* community-based participatory research
correctional staff, stigmatizing attitudes in, 56–62
courts. *See* criminal justice system
crime, substance use relationship with, 48–49
criminal justice system, 46–48
  in former Soviet Union, 125–126
  hybridized healthcare interventions with, 52–53, 62–64
  racism in, 48–49
  rate of SUDs among people in, 48–49
  reduction of stigma in, 46–48, 62–64
  stigma influence on policies of, 31–32
  stigma occurrence within, 53
    community re-entry, 59–62
    incarceration, 56–59
    police interactions, 53–56
  stigma promotion of SUD involvement by, 48–49
  criminalization of substances, 50–51, 166–167
  inequitable social conditions, 49–50
  underfunding of substance use services, 51–53
  targeted stigma reduction and, 254–255
criminal justice-oriented policies, 25–26
criminal record, 61–62
criminalization
  of marginalized groups, 48–51, 91–92
  of substances, 46–48, 62–64, 166–167
  disclosure and, 188
  global, 112, 116–117
  racial differences in, 34–35
  stigma promotion of, 50–51
  as structural stigma, 6–7, 50–51, 260–262
  substance use regulation by, 2–3
culture
  disclosure perception and, 188
  stigma variation with, 2–3, 127–128, 260–262

DARE. *See* Drug Abuse Resistance Education
decriminalization of substances, 62–64, 112, 116–117, 167–168, 260–262
denormalization, stigma as resource for, 78–81

Index

depression, SUD stigma compared with stigma of, 1–2
disclosure of substance use, 15–22
  approaches to, 185–186
  without consent, 31
  costs and benefits of, 183–185
  criminalization complication of, 188
  HOP program for, 182–190
  identity role in, 180–182
  incarceration and, 56–59
  in recovery stories, 202–203
  research on, 187
  stigma reduction through, 180, 182–189, 258–259
  story crafting for, 187
  tests of candidates for, 186
discrimination
  eradication of, 252–253
  global, 130–131
  against healthcare professionals with lived experience, 202–203, 205–207
  in healthcare settings, 232–246
  intersectionality in, 88–90
  media promotion of, 213–214
  public stigma and, 4–5
  structural, 110–112, 260–262
  structural stigma and, 6–7, 50–51
  substance use regulation by, 2–3
doctors. *See* physicians
DPA. *See* Drug Policy Alliance
Drug Abuse Resistance Education (DARE), 165
drug enforcement. *See* criminal justice system
Drug Policy Alliance (DPA), 167–168
drug prohibition laws, 50–51, 167–168
drug treatment courts, 52–53
DSM-5, SUD severity grading in, 7–8
dynamic model of responsibility, 9

education
  criminal record as barrier to, 61–62
  as stigma reduction strategy, 10–11, 164–165, 167–168
emergency medicine, stigma reduction in, 237–239
employment
  criminal record as barrier to, 61–62
  individualized placement and support, 172
  stigma as barrier to, 195–197
  targeted stigma reduction and, 254–255
empowerment
  recovery role of, 73–75
  self-worth agenda to promote, 163, 169–170, 172–173, 253–254
enacted stigma, 3–4, 119–120, 253–254
ethical consistency, 82–83

ethical literacy, 81–83
ethics, 68
  bioethics impacts on SUDs, 73–77
  HIV/AIDS pandemic lessons in, 77–78
  individually-focused, 72–77
  literacy, engagement and consistency as ways forward in, 81–83
  medical model and, 69–72
  obstacles impeding, 83
  person-centered care and, 75–77
  policy debate omission of, 70–71
  public health, 78
  responsibility in, 71–72
  social responsibility and, 73–77
  stigma as public health resource and, 78–81
  stigma as values-based concern of, 68–69
Europe, SUD stigma in, 115–117
evidence-based treatment
  services agenda to promote engagement with, 163–166, 172–173, 253–254
  stigma toward, 24–27, 37
  qualitative research exploring, 31–32
  reduction of, 33–37, 163–166, 172–173, 253–254
  survey research examining, 28–30
  underfunding of, 51–53

family, as stigma victims, 4–5, 203–204
family stigma, in South Asia, 128–129
former Soviet Union, 121, 126
  narcological system of
    current state of, 122–124
    different approaches to supersedence of, 124–125
    history of, 121–122
  SUD stigma perspectives and experiences in, 125–126
framing, media, 213–219
funding, for substance use services, 51–53

gay men, deliberate stigmatization of, 77–81
gender
  non-binary, 93–94
  in South Asia stigma experience, 129
  in sub-Saharan Africa stigma experience, 120
  SUD stigma and, 92–93
Germany, 260–262
global perspectives. *See* international perspectives on stigma
goals, of stigma change, 252–255
government. *See* policy
Greece, 116–117

harm reduction, 258
  intersectional stigma identification using, 96–97
  lived experiences of, 22
  self-worth agenda and, 169–170
harm-reduction services
  communication strategies to increase support for, 35–36
  in former Soviet Union, 124–125
  during incarceration, 56–59
  media guidelines for reporting on, 224–225
  peer support and, 172
  police interference with use of, 53–56
  stigma interference with, 4–7, 24, 28–32
  underfunding of, 51–53
HCV. *See* hepatitis C virus
health, stigma consequences for, 4–5
health information, media selection and framing of, 213–219
health insurance, as treatment barrier, 110–112, 260
health messaging. *See* public health campaigns
healthcare. *See also* substance use services
  hybridized criminal justice interventions with, 52–53, 62–64
  incarceration and, 56–59
  individually-focused ethics in, 72–73
  intersectionality in provision of, 97–98
  person-centered care in, 75–77
  stigma as barrier to, 6–7, 50–53
  stigma influence on policy in, 32
  structural discrimination in denial of, 110–112, 260
  SUD stigma in, 29–30, 32, 51–53, 70–71, 119–120, 129, 232–246
  SUD stigma reduction in, 232–246
    better interventions through, 234–236
    clinical practice change recommendations for, 234–236
    emergency medicine, 237–239
    language role in, 243–246
    primary care, 239–241
    psychiatric ward, 241–243
healthcare professionals
  language used by, 243–246
  stigma reduction advocacy by, 256–259
  stigmatizing attitudes in, 29–30, 32, 51–53, 70–71, 119–120, 129, 232–246
  SUD stigma experienced by, 202–203, 205–207
hepatitis C virus (HCV), 108
heroin use, 91–92, 217
high-income countries, SUD stigma in
  Europe, 115–117
  North America, 109–112

HIV. *See* human immunodeficiency virus
homelessness, 96–97
Honest Open Proud (HOP), 182–190
hope, 201–202, 207–208
human immunodeficiency virus (HIV)
  ethics lessons from pandemic of, 77–78
  injection drug use and, 108
  in sub-Saharan Africa, 118
hybridized health-justice interventions, 52–53, 62–64

identity
  disclosure of SUD and, 180–182
  pride in, 181–182
illegal drug use
  European stigma toward, 116–117
  global, 107–109
  stigma as public health resource against, 78–81
illicit drugs
  decriminalization of, 62–64, 112, 116–117, 167–168, 260–262
  media coverage of, 214–219
  public policy on, 23–24
  stigma of licit substances compared with stigma of, 27–28, 34–35
illness model of SUD, 9
incarceration
  rate of SUDs among people in, 48–49
  stigma in, 56–59
India. *See* South Asia and India
Indigenous people
  criminalization of, 48–49
  police interactions with, 53–56
indiscriminant disclosure, 185–186
individual responsibility, 9, 29, 33–34, 73–77
individualized placement and support (IPS), 172
individually-focused ethics
  bioethics as, 72–77
  limitations of, 73–77
  SUD impacts of, 73–77
inequitable social conditions, in criminal justice system involvement in substance use, 49–50
injection drug use, 108
Inspiring Change curriculum, 159–160
institutional policies, stigma and, 23–25, 28–30, 33–37, 195–197
institutional stigma. *See* structural stigma
internalized stigma. *See* self-stigma
international perspectives on stigma, 107–109, 259–262
  Europe, 115–117
  former Soviet Union countries, 121–126
  global implications of SUD stigma and, 130–131

high-income North America, 109–112
India and South Asia, 126–130
Latin America, 113–115
sub-Saharan Africa, 117–121
intersectional stigma, 88, 91, 98–100
  in addition to race, gender, sexual orientation, and class, 96–97
  disclosure and, 188–189
  gender and SUD stigma, 92–93
  history of intersectionality, 88–89
  implications of, 98–100
  in interventions and health care provision, 97–98
  racialized drug stigma, 91–92, 96
  resilience model of, 89–90
  risk model of, 89–90
  sexual orientation and SUD stigma, 93–94
  socioeconomic status and SUD stigma, 94–96
intersectionality
  history of, 88–89
  in practice, 97–98
intervention. *See also* evidence-based treatment; harm-reduction services; substance use services
  healthcare stigma reduction for better, 234–236
  hybridized health-justice, 52–53, 62–64
  intersectionality in, 97–98
  stigma as impediment to, 3–7, 24, 108–109, 115–116
interventional stigma, 24, 37. *See also* policy
involuntary residential treatment, 52–53
IPS. *See* individualized placement and support

jail. *See* incarceration
journalism. *See also* media
  media guidelines for, 219–226
  mental health news selection and framing in, 214–216
Just Say No! campaign, 260–262

label avoidance, 253–254
  language impact on, 165–166
  public stigma and, 4–5
  as recovery impediment, 7–8
  self-stigma and, 5–6
labels
  need for changes in, 7–8
  police officer use of, 53–56
  public stigma and, 4–5
language
  in healthcare settings, 243–246
  media guidelines on use of, 225–226
  neutral, 165–166
Latin America, SUD stigma in, 113–115

law enforcement officers. *See* police officers
legislation
  harms caused by, 50–51
  stigma relationship to, 23–24
  as structural stigma, 195–197, 260–262
  on substance use, 2
LEROs. *See* lived-experience recovery organisations
LGBTQIA+ communities, 93–94
literacy, ethical, 81–83
lived experience
  advocacy by people with, 256–259
  community-based participatory research inclusion of people with, 154–159
  of criminal justice system, 46–48, 62–64
    community re-entry, 59–62
    criminalization of substances, 50–51
    incarceration, 56–59
    inequitable social conditions, 49–50
    police interactions, 53–56
    underfunding of substance use services, 51–53
  healthcare professionals with, 202–203, 205–207
  of institutional stigma, 195–197
  of public stigma, 193–194
  of self-stigma, 15–22, 197–199
  of SUD stigma, 15–22, 194–195
lived experience peer involvement, 193–209
  in policy making, 207–208
  potential harms of, 203–204
  in practice, 204–205
  professional, public and institutional stigma reduction through, 202–203
  recovery with and without, 200–202
  research needed in, 207–208
  self-stigma reduction through, 197–199
  stigma towards, 205–207
lived-experience recovery organisations (LEROs), 201

mandatory minimum sentencing policies, 25–26
marginalized groups. *See also* community-based participatory research; intersectional stigma
  in criminal justice system involvement in substance use, 49–50
  criminalization of, 48–51, 91–92
  deliberate stigmatization of, 77–81
  structural discrimination against, 110–112, 260–262
mass media. *See* media
media, 213
  framing by, 213–219
  illicit drug coverage by, 214–219

media (cont.)
    public opinion shaping by, 213–214
    SUD stigmatization in, 193–194, 213–219, 222–223, 226, 259
media guidelines, 213, 226
    content and objectives of, 219–222
    key issues of, 222–226
medical model of SUDs, 69–72, 253–254
mental disability, 96–97
mental health diseases (MHD)
    disclosure of, 182
    identity relationship to, 180–182
    intersectional stigma in, 98–100
    media framing of, 213–219
    SUD stigma compared with stigma of other, 1–2
mental healthcare
    during incarceration, 56–59
    stigma as barrier to, 6–7
methadone, 24–28, 56–59
Mexico, SUD stigma in, 113–115
MHD. *See* mental health diseases
minority stress, 93–94
moral model, of SUDs, 70–71
multiple jeopardy perspective, 89–90
mutual aid, 197–207

naloxone distribution, stigma against, 24, 30
narcological monitoring, in Russia, 122–124
narcology, Soviet system of, 121–125
Narcotics Anonymous, 60, 181, 205
National Institute on Drug Abuse (NIDA), media advisory guidelines of, 219–222
Netherlands, 116–117, 260–262
news. *See also* media
    journalist selection of, 214–216
nicotine use, 2. *See also* smoking
NIDA. *See* National Institute on Drug Abuse
NIMBY phenomenon, 27–28, 31–32
non-binary gender, 93–94
non-disclosure, 185–186
non-urban areas, SUD stigma in people living in, 96–97
North America, SUD stigma in, 109–112
nurses, stigmatizing attitudes in, 29–30, 32, 51–53, 129, 232–246

online media, SUD stigmatization in, 218
opioid substitution treatment
    in former Soviet Union, 124–125
    during incarceration, 56–59
    in South Asia, 129
    stigma against, 24–28, 32
opioid use
    global, 107
    intersectional stigma and, 91–92
    media coverage of, 216–218
    public policy on, 23–24
    in South Asia, 126–127
opioid use disorder
    in South Asia, 127–128
    stigma against interventions for, 24–32
overdose, police involvement in, 53–56
overdose prevention sites, stigma against, 24, 29

PAR. *See* participatory action research
pardon, of criminal record, 61–62
parole, substance use during, 59–62
parole hearings, substance use disclosure in, 56–59
participatory action research (PAR), 144–145. *See also* community-based participatory research
    in intersectionality, 100
PCC. *See* person-centered care
PDMP. *See* prescription drug monitoring program
peer support, 193–209
    community support through, 60
    potential harms of, 203–204
    in practice, 204–205
    recovery with, 200–202, 257–258
    research needed in, 207–208
    self-worth promotion through, 169–170, 172
    stigma reduction through, 197–200, 202–203, 207–208
    stigma towards, 205–207
    wider impacts of, 202–203
peer support groups. *See also specific groups*
    community support through, 60
peers, disclosure to, 15–22
person-centered care (PCC), 75–77
person-first language, 225–226
Peru, 113–115
pharmacists, stigmatizing attitudes in, 32, 51–53
pharmacy-level policies, stigma influence on, 32
physical disability, 96–97
physical health, poor, 96–97
physicians
    stigma reduction advocacy by, 256–259
    stigmatizing attitudes in, 29–30, 32, 51–53, 129, 232–246
    SUD stigma experienced by, 202–203, 205–207
police officers
    in former Soviet Union, 125–126
    stigmatizing attitudes in, 30, 53–56
police-based diversion programs, 52–53
policy. *See also* punitive policies
    deliberate use of stigma in, 78–81

ethics omission from debates on, 70–71
in HIV/AIDS pandemic, 77–78
lived experience peer involvement in, 207–208
media influence on, 213–214
stigma relationship to, 23–25, 37, 260–262
　influence of policy on stigma, 27–28
　influence of stigma on policy implementation, 26–27
　influence of stigma on policy support and enactment, 25–26, 28–30
　qualitative research exploring, 31–32
　strategies to reduce, 33–37
　survey research examining, 28–30
as structural stigma, 24–25, 50–51, 195–197, 260–262
Portugal, 116–117, 260–262
poverty
　in criminal justice system involvement in substance use, 49–50
　deliberate stigmatization and, 78–81
　SUD stigma and, 94–96
power sharing, in community-based participatory research, 157–158
prescription drug monitoring program (PDMP), 26–27
prescription opioid misuse, 91–92
press. *See* media
press association guidelines, 219–221
prevention of substance use, 165, 170–171, 225
preventive monitoring, 122–124
pride, in identity, 181–182
primary care, stigma reduction in, 239–241
prison. *See* incarceration
professional stigma, 202–203
professionals. *See* healthcare professionals
progressive model of self-stigma, 5–6
prohibition laws, 50–51, 167–168
protest, as anti-stigma strategy, 10–11, 167–168
psychiatric ward, stigma reduction in, 241–243
public health
　development of ethics of, 78
　HIV/AIDS pandemic ethics lessons for, 77–78
　stigma as resource of, 78–81
public health campaigns
　negative stereotypes in, 170–171
　stigma reduction using, 33–37, 164–165
public opinion, media shaping of, 213–214
public policies
　deliberate use of stigma in, 78–81
　in former Soviet Union, 125–126
　stigma relationship to, 23–25
　　influence of policy on stigma, 27–28
　　influence of stigma on policy implementation, 26–27

influence of stigma on policy support and enactment, 25–26, 28–30
qualitative research exploring, 31–32
strategies to reduce, 33–37
survey research examining, 28–30
public stigma, 3–5, 253–254
　disclosure reduction of, 258–259
　harms caused by, 4–5
　lived experiences of, 193–194
　media promotion of, 217–218
　peer support in reduction of, 202–203
　policy relationship with, 25–30
　protest, contact and education roles in elimination of, 10–11
　racialized drug, 91–92
　self-stigma reinforcement by, 197–199
　in South Asia, 128–129
　in sub-Saharan Africa, 119–120
punitive policies. *See also* criminal justice system
　limits of, 46
　social justice aspects of, 34–35
　societal preference for, 51–53
　stigma relationship to, 24–28, 37
　strategies to reduce, 33–37

quick-reference pamphlets, media advisory guidelines in, 219–221

racialized drug stigma, 91–92, 96
racism
　affirming attitudes replacement of, 255
　in criminal justice system, 48–49
　criminalization of drug use and, 34–35
　stigma of substance use compared with, 17
　substance use stigma compounded with, 26–27
recovery
　autonomy role in, 73–75
　disclosure of, 202–203
　empowerment role in, 73–75
　label-avoidance as impediment to, 7–8
　lived experiences of, 15–22
　media guidelines for reporting on, 224–225
　outcome *versus* process of, 257–258
　peer support in, 197–202, 204–205, 208–209, 257–258
　person-centered care in, 75–77
　self-determination role in, 73–75
　social and individual responsibility role in, 9
　stigma as impediment to, 3–7, 24, 108–109, 115–116, 232
　visible, 207–208
recovery identity, 180–182
re-entry, community, 59–62

regulations
  stigma relationship to, 23–24
  stigma role in, 2–3
relapse, 15–22
relational autonomy, 73–75
research. *See also* community-based participatory research
  in intersectionality, 100
  stigma interference with, 144
residential treatment, involuntary, 52–53
resilience model, of intersectional stigma, 89–90
resource manuals, media advisory guidelines, 219–222
responsibility
  media, 219, 222–224
  medical model and, 71–72
  for substance use, 2–3, 9, 29, 33–34, 73–77
Rights, Respect and Recovery, 194–195, 205–208
rights agenda, of stigma reduction, 163, 166–169, 172–173, 253–254
risk model, of intersectional stigma, 89–90
Russia, 121–126

schizophrenia, SUD stigma compared with stigma of, 1–2
Scotland
  drug death rate in, 194–195
  lived experience peer support in, 199–200, 205–207
  media SUD stigmatization in, 193–194
  policy making in, 207–208
selective disclosure, 185–186
self-determination
  recovery role of, 73–75
  self-worth agenda to promote, 163, 169–170, 172–173, 253–254
self-disclosure, 19
self-stigma, 3–6, 253–254
  ACT as intervention for, 189
  criminalization promotion of, 50–51
  disclosure as intervention for, 180, 182–189
  harms caused by, 5–6
  lived experiences of, 15–22, 197–199
  media promotion of, 213–214
  peer support in reduction of, 197–199
  progressive model of, 5–6
  reduction of, 257
  in South Asia, 127–128
  in sub-Saharan Africa, 118
self-worth, 169–170, 172
self-worth agenda of stigma reduction, 163, 169–170, 172–173, 253–254

service user research, 144–145. *See also* community-based participatory research
services agenda of stigma reduction, 163–166, 172–173, 253–254
SES. *See* socioeconomic status
7th Step Society, 46–47, 60
sexual orientation, SUD stigma and, 93–94
shame
  peer support impact on, 201–202
  self-stigma and, 197–199
  stigma reduction to minimize, 169–170
Sick Doctors Trust, 201
SMART Recovery, 205
smoking
  risks associated with, 2
  stigma role in denormalization of, 78–81
  in sub-Saharan Africa, 119–120
social activism, as stigma reduction strategy, 10–11, 167–168
social avoidance, 185
social cleansing, 114
social constructions, policy targeting of, 25–26
social function, of SUD stigma, 1–11
social injustice
  in criminal justice system involvement in substance use, 49–50
  rights agenda targeting of, 163, 166–169, 172–173, 253–254
  SUD stigma as, 262
social intolerance, 125–126
social media
  disclosure on, 189
  SUD stigmatization in, 218
social responsibility, 9, 29, 33–34, 73–77
social stigma. *See* public stigma
socioeconomic status (SES)
  in criminal justice system involvement in substance use, 49–50
  deliberate stigmatization and, 78–81
  SUD stigma and, 94–96
South Asia and India, 126, 129–130
  gender and SUD stigma in, 129
  public and structural stigma in, 128–129
  self-stigma in, 127–128
  substance use patterns in, 126–127
Soviet Union. *See* former Soviet Union
sponsorship, 205
status degradation ceremony, 56–59
statutes, stigma relationship to, 23–24
stereotypes
  education to challenge, 10–11
  eradication of, 252–253
  language impact on, 165–166
  media promotion of, 213–214
  in public health campaigns, 170–171

public stigma and, 4–5
self-stigma and, 5–6
substance use regulation by, 2–3
stigma. *See also specific forms of stigma; specific topics*
  anticipation of, 3–6, 26–27, 253–254
  conceptual changes needed in, 1–11
  cultural variation in, 2–3, 127–128, 260–262
  definitions of, 15, 253–254
  as ethical concern, 68–69
  gender and, 92–93
  global implications of, 130–131
  harms caused by, 1–11, 232, 252–254
  in HIV/AIDS pandemic, 77–78
  intervention and recovery impediment by, 3–7, 24, 108–109, 115–116, 232
  labeling role in, 4–5, 7–8
  towards lived experience peer involvement, 205–207
  media promotion of, 193–194, 213–219, 222–223, 226, 259
  process of, 88
  as public health resource, 78–81
  race and, 91–92, 96
  racism compared with, 17
  regulation of substance use by, 2–3
  research interference by, 144
  responsibility role in, 2–3, 9, 29, 33–34, 73–77
  sexual orientation and, 93–94
  social function of, 1–11
  socioeconomic status and, 78–81, 94–96
  of SUDs compared with other mental disorders, 1–2
  as treatment barrier, 3–7, 24, 108–109, 115–116, 163–164
stigma reduction, 252–254
  ACT as intervention for, 189
  through advocacy, 199–200, 256–259
  affirming attitudes in, 255
  conflict among agendas of, 170–171
  contact as strategy for, 10–11, 168–169, 171–172, 197–199, 202–203
  in criminal justice system, 46–48, 62–64
  disclosure as intervention for, 180, 182–189, 258–259
  education as strategy for, 10–11, 164–165, 167–168
  goals of, 252–255
  in healthcare, 232–246
    better interventions through, 234–236
    clinical practice change recommendations for, 234–236
    emergency medicine, 237–239
    language role in, 243–246
  primary care, 239–241
  psychiatric ward, 241–243
  international theatre of, 259–262
  intersectionality in, 257
  optimism for, 262
  overlap and coordination of agendas of, 171–172
  peer support in, 193–209
  protest as strategy for, 10–11
  public communication campaigns for, 33–37, 164–165
  rights agenda of, 163, 166–169, 172–173, 253–254
  self-worth agenda of, 163, 169–170, 172–173, 253–254
  services agenda of, 163–166, 172–173, 253–254
  of structural stigma, 46–48, 62–64
  targeted, 254–255
story crafting, for substance use disclosure, 187
structural stigma, 3–4, 6–7, 253–254
  criminalization as, 6–7, 50–51, 260–262
  harms caused by, 6–7, 50–53
  lived experiences of, 195–197
  media promotion of, 217–218
  peer support in reduction of, 202–203
  in police interactions, 53–56
  policy as, 24–25, 50–51, 195–197, 260–262
  reduction of, 46–48, 62–64
  self-stigma reinforcement by, 197–199
  in South Asia, 128–129
  substance use service underfunding as, 51–53
  in United States, 110–112, 260–262
sub-Saharan Africa, 121
  alcohol use in, 117–120
  enacted stigma in, 119–120
  gender and SUD stigma in, 120
  HIV in, 118
  internalized stigma in, 118
  smoking in, 119–120
substance use. *See also specific topics*
  acceptable, 2
  crime relationship with, 48–49
  criminalization of, 46–48, 62–64, 166–167
  disclosure and, 188
  global, 112, 116–117
  racial differences in, 34–35
  stigma promotion of, 50–51
  as structural stigma, 6–7, 50–51, 260–262
  substance use regulation by, 2–3
  ethical responses to, 68–69
  legislature changes regarding, 2
  policy on, 23–24
  prevention of, 165, 170–171, 225
  responsibility for, 2–3, 9, 29, 33–34, 73–77

substance use. (cont.)
  risks associated with, 2
  South Asian patterns of, 126–127
  stigma as means to regulate, 2–3
substance use disorders (SUD). *See also specific topics*
  bioethics impacts on, 73–77
  biological causal explanations of, 35, 253–254
  biopsychosocial model of, 69–72
  continuum model of, 1–11
  global prevalence of, 107–109
  identity relationship to, 180–182
  illness compared with behavioral model of, 9
  labeling of people with, 4–5, 7–8
  lived experiences of, 15–22
  media stigmatization of, 193–194, 213–219, 222–223, 226, 259
  medical model of, 69–72, 253–254
  moral model of, 70–71
  social function of stigma against, 1–11
  stigma as impediment to treatment and recovery from, 3–7, 24, 108–109, 115–116, 232
  stigma of other mental disorders compared with stigma of, 1–2
substance use services
  global barriers to, 108–109
  hybridized criminal justice interventions with, 52–53, 62–64
  during incarceration, 56–59
  intersectionality in, 97–98
  media guidelines for reporting on, 224–225
  person-centered care in, 75–77
  police interference with use of, 53–56
  services agenda to promote engagement with, 163–166, 172–173, 253–254
  sexual minority access to, 93–94
  stigma as barrier to, 3–7, 24, 108–109, 115–116, 163–164
  stigma toward, 23–25, 37
    influence of policy on stigma, 27–28
    influence of stigma on policy implementation, 26–27
    influence of stigma on policy support and enactment, 25–26, 28–30
    qualitative research exploring, 31–32
    strategies to reduce, 33–37, 163–166
    survey research examining, 28–30
  structural discrimination in denial of, 110–112, 260
  underfunding of, 51–53
substance use stigma. *See* stigma
SUD. *See* substance use disorders
support groups. *See* peer support groups
synthetic opioids, 23–24
syringe services programs, 24, 29, 32

targeted stigma reduction, 254–255
tobacco use, 107, 126–127. *See also* smoking
treatment-seeking, services agenda to promote, 163–166, 172–173, 253–254
tuberculosis, alcohol use and, 118–120
12-step groups, 15–22, 60, 181, 205–207

underfunding, of substance use services, 51–53
United Kingdom, media SUD stigmatization in, 193–194
United Kingdom's Equality Act 2010, 195–197
United States
  stigma relationship with policy in, 28–30
  structural discrimination in, 110–112, 260–262
  substance decriminalization in, 167–168
  substance use policies in, 23–24
  SUD stigma in, 109–112
Uruguay, 113–115
user-controlled research, 144–145. *See also* community-based participatory research

victim-blaming, 78–81
visible recovery, 207–208

war on drugs, 6–7, 50–51, 78–81, 260–262
why try effect, 197
withdrawal, in criminal justice system, 53–59
women
  intersectional stigma experienced by, 88–89, 92–93
  in South Asia, 129
  in sub-Saharan Africa, 120
  SUD stigma experiences of, 15–22
work camps, Soviet Union, 121–122, 124
world. *See also* international perspectives on stigma
  substance use and SUDs around, 107–109

Printed in the United States
by Baker & Taylor Publisher Services